DISCOVER THE ANGELS
DO YOU KNOW

- Which angel is the special protector of po... ...cers?
- What is the symbolic meaning of the color blue and its angel?
- Which angel offers particular guidance and protection in October?
- Which religion believes all angels are male?
- What famous Hollywood actor played angels in two different movies?
- Which culture believes genies are a form of guardian angels?

The answers and so much more are in . . .

The Encyclopedia of Angels

CONSTANCE VICTORIA BRIGGS grew up in Alexandria, Virginia, and began her writing career in journalism in 1989. She has worked for Time-Life Books and written for newsletters and magazines. Having studied Judaism, Christianity, Islam, and various Eastern beliefs, Briggs has an extensive background in religion and spirituality. Inspired by her personal angelic experiences, she has become deeply involved in the study of angels. *The Encyclopedia of Angels* is the result of her years of research. In her spare time, Briggs writes fiction and runs a spiritual group focusing on angels. She continues to study ancient religious history and mythology, as well as metaphysical and New Age topics. Constance and her husband make their home in Schaumburg, Illinois.

The Encyclopedia of Angels

CONSTANCE VICTORIA BRIGGS

A PLUME BOOK

PLUME
Published by the Penguin Group
Penguin Putnam Inc., 375 Hudson Street,
New York, New York 10014, U.S.A.
Penguin Books Ltd, 27 Wrights Lane,
London W8 5TZ, England
Penguin Books Australia Ltd, Ringwood,
Victoria, Australia
Penguin Books Canada Ltd, 10 Alcorn Avenue,
Toronto, Ontario, Canada M4V 3B2
Penguin Books (N.Z.) Ltd, 182–190 Wairau Road,
Auckland 10, New Zealand

Penguin Books Ltd, Registered Offices:
Harmondsworth, Middlesex, England

First published by Plume, an imprint of Dutton Signet,
a member of Penguin Putnam Inc.

First Printing, November, 1997
10 9 8 7 6 5 4 3 2 1

 REGISTERED TRADEMARK—MARCA REGISTRADA

LIBRARY OF CONGRESS CATALOGING-IN-PUBLICATION DATA:
Briggs, Constance Victoria.
    The encyclopedia of angels / Constance Victoria Briggs.
        p.   cm.
    Includes bibliographical references.
    ISBN 0-452-27921-6
    1. Angels—Dictionaries.   I. Title.
BL477.B75   1997
291.2'15'03—dc21   97-17193
                                             CIP

Printed in the United States of America
Set in Galliard
Designed by Leonard Telesca

BOOKS ARE AVAILABLE AT QUANTITY DISCOUNTS WHEN USED TO PROMOTE PRODUCTS OR SERVICES.
FOR INFORMATION PLEASE WRITE TO PREMIUM MARKETING DIVISION, PENGUIN PUTNAM INC.,
375 HUDSON STREET, NEW YORK, NEW YORK 10014.

With love and gratitude, I dedicate this book to God and the angels who are my inspiration. To my husband, Ghobad, whose endless love and encouragement helped make this book possible, and to my mother, Arnita, for her love and support.

INTRODUCTION

*T*he *Encyclopedia of Angels* was born from an idea that came to me years ago, when I was on a spiritual journey, trying to get answers to some of the age-old questions: "Why are we here?" "Who is God?" "Is there life after death?" etc. In my search for answers, I studied the Bible, philosophy, and world religions. I talked to people from all walks of life, with different social, economic, and religious backgrounds. And although I received a lot of information, much of it led to even more questions.

However, there was always one constant—angels. I learned that angels exist in almost every culture and religion. Not only do people of various social, cultural, and economic backgrounds believe in angels, many of them have had angelic experiences. The different cultures may not always categorize them as angels, but they do believe in real spirits that guard and aid people in times of need.

Drawing from my knowledge of world religions acquired during six years of special missionary work, I soon began documenting what I learned. I began organizing my research in a database with the hopes of one day writing an angelic reference book—*The Encyclopedia of Angels*.

It was my intention to make *The Encyclopedia of Angels* a user-friendly book. I wanted to create a resource to which people could refer for answers to specific questions on angels. Questions such as "Who is the angel of the Annunciation?" "What are the names of the four archangels in Islam?" "Which angel is frequently portrayed in armor?" "How many throne angels are there?" "What angels are called by names in the Bible?" "What gods in classical mythology had angelic functions?" "Why did the angels fall?" These questions and more are answered in *The Encyclopedia of Angels*, in a concise, easy-to-read format. Without such a reference book, people would have to purchase and leaf through a large collection of angelic, religious, and philosophical books to answer their questions.

The Encyclopedia of Angels lists the names and orders of the angels and their functions. Various angelic hierarchies that have been created throughout the centuries are also included. For the sake of completeness and additional information, most of the entries of this book contain boldface cross-references. The book is further complemented by appendixes.

Another unique feature of *The Encyclopedia of Angels* is that it contains more than just the names of angels. It also lists painters who used angels in their art; poets and literary writers who wrote about angels; prophets, saints, and great philosophers who talked about angels; and even movies and television shows with angelic themes. Moreover, the book gives information on the world's ancient and modern religious beliefs regarding angels.

It is my desire that this book bring everyone who reads it unlimited joy and pleasure, and bring them closer to the angels.

NOTE

Please note that the **boldface** words found throughout the book are cross-references. In addition, the hierarchy of angels mentioned throughout the book refers to the angelic hierarchy created by Dionysius the Pseudo-Areopagite.

The Encyclopedia of Angels

I am well aware that many will say that no one can possibly speak with spirits and angels so long as he is living in the body. Many say it is all fancy, others that I recount such things to win credence, while others will make other kinds of objection. But I am deterred by none of these: for I have seen, I have heard, I have felt.

—EMANUEL SWEDENBORG

✤**AARON:** The first high priest of the Jews. He was the older brother of the prophet **Moses** and acted as his spokesman. Because of his faithfulness and service on earth, God made him a great angel in Heaven. He is said to reside in Maon, the **Fifth Heaven.**

✤**ABABALOI:** An angel that is invoked in magic practices.

✤**AB'ABYAH:** One of the seventy-eight names of **Metatron.**

✤**ABADDON (GOD'S DESTROYER):** The angel of the bottomless pit, the chief of the demonic locusts. Abaddon is the Hebrew name for the Greek god **Apollyon.** The book of Revelation 9:11 refers to him as a king. Abaddon is also in charge of the locusts that God sets loose to destroy the wicked people of earth in the last days. Revelation 9:1–4 states, "I saw a star [angel] that had fallen from heaven to earth, and he was given the key to the shaft of the bottomless pit; he opened the shaft of the bottomless pit, and from the shaft rose smoke like the smoke of a great furnace, and the sun and the air were darkened with the smoke from the shaft. Then from the smoke came locusts on the earth, and they were given authority like the authority of scorpions of the earth. They were told not to damage the grass of the earth or any green growth or any tree, but only those people who do not have the seal of God on their foreheads." These locusts are sometimes referred to as "demonic locusts." See **Abyss.**

✳**ABADDONA (THE REPENTANT ONE):** A fallen Seraph. He was once a magnificent angel in Heaven, until he sinned against God. He later repented of his transgressions.

✳**ABAGTHA:** One of the **angels of confusion.**

✳**ABALIM (GREAT ANGELS):** The Hebrew name for the order of angels called **Thrones.**

✳**ABAN:** An angel in Persian mythology who governs the month of the same name. In Persia the month of Aban runs between the middle of October through the middle of November, with the dates falling around October 23–November 21.

✳**ABATHUR MUZANIA:** See **Abyatur.**

✳**ABBATON (DEATH):** An angel of death, and a guardian of the underworld.

✳**ABDALS:** An elite class of angels found in Islam. They preside over the operation of the universe. Selected personally by God, the identities of the seventy Abdals are kept secret from the other angels. When one dies, God selects another angel to replace him.

✳**ABDIEL (GOD'S SERVANT):** A high-ranking angel in Heaven, and a faithful servant of God. His name can be found in the **Book of Raziel,** and in John Milton's epic poem *Paradise Lost.* In *Paradise Lost,* he is portrayed as a powerful Seraph who battles with and overthrows the rebellious angels who turned against God to serve Satan. A variation of Abdiel is Adabiel.

✳**ABDIZUEL:** An angel who oversees one of the twenty-eight **lunar mansions,** as mentioned in the **Cabala.**

✳**ABEDNEGO:** One of three Hebrew men in the Book of Daniel (3:1–30) who were rescued from a fiery **furnace** by an angel.

✳**ABEKO:** An alias used by the she-demon **Lilith** when working evil schemes against mortals.

✳**ABEL:** An angel who judges the souls of mortal men once they reach Heaven. He determines if they will enter Paradise or be thrown into Hell.

✳**ABEZETHIBOU:** An angel who rules **Tartarus** (the underworld).

✳**ABEZI:** A **fallen angel.** According to legend, Abezi was once a mighty and glorious angel. He fell from grace when he developed a strong hatred for the Hebrews. He fought against Moses in Egypt and aided **Pharaoh** in his attempts to keep the Hebrews in bondage. He worked with Pharaoh's magicians **Jannes and Jambres** in order to accomplish this. However, his methods were thwarted when God had him drowned in the Red Sea. From that day forward he has been considered a demon of the Red Sea.

✤ABEZI-THIBOD: A variation of the name **Abezi.**

✤ABHEIEL: An angel who oversees one of the twenty-eight **lunar mansions,** as mentioned in the **Cabala.**

✤ABITO: An alias used by the she-demon **Lilith** when working evil against the daughters of **Eve.**

✤ABOEZRA: An angel of God who is called upon in the consecration of salt.

✤ABORTION(S), ANGEL OF: **Kasadya,** an angel from the **Grigori** class. Kasadya taught women of earth how to perform abortions.

✤ABRACADABRA (I BLESS THE DEAD): An ancient magical word. It is believed by some to be of Balkan origin. It is also thought to be derived from the name **Abraxis** (an angel of **gnosticism**). Others contend that it was derived from the Hebrew term *ha brachah dabarah*, which means "speak the blessing." During ancient times it was used for protection and could be found inscribed on amulets and talismans, to guard against ailments and attacks from demons. In spells it was used for summoning angels for protection against evil spirits.

✤ABRAHAM: Israel's first great patriarch, and the founder of Judaism. In the Book of Genesis 18:1–2, Abraham was visited by three angels as he sat at the entrance of his tent. The account states, "The Lord appeared to Abraham by the oaks of **Mamre,** as he sat at the entrance of his tent in the heat of the day. He looked up and saw three men standing near him." The angels had come to tell Abraham that his wife, **Sarah** (who was elderly and barren), would give birth to a son. The angels also informed him of the impending destruction of two nearby cities, **Sodom and Gomorrah.** In a later account, God tests the faith of Abraham by instructing him to offer his beloved son, **Isaac,** as a sacrifice. However, an angel of the Lord prevents Abraham from carrying out this act (Genesis 22:12). According to Judaic lore, when it was time for Abraham to die, God sent the archangel **Michael** to tell him that he should prepare for death. The soul of Abraham was escorted to Heaven by angels. See **Sacrifice.**

✤ABRASAX: A variation of the name **Abraxis.**

✤ABRAVENEL, DON ISAAC: A renowned Jewish scholar, and deep religious thinker. Abravenel lived during the period when the Jews were driven out of Spain. He drew on his faith in God and his belief in angels to see him through the terrible ordeal. Years later in an exposition, he wrote that the angels of **Jacob**'s ladder were with the Jews during their suffering, and that the Jews would ascend to Heaven with their guardian angels. He believed that this ascension would take place during his lifetime.

✦ABRAXAS: A variation of the name **Abraxis.**

✦ABRAXIS: A superior angel in **gnosticism.** The name Abraxis originally referred to the Almighty. In addition, he is the nucleus of 365 emanations from which the universe was believed to have been created. According to gnostic beliefs, he is a great prince of the superior order of angels called **Aeons.** He is also invoked in the magical arts. His name is sometimes found inscribed on talismans and amulets and is used in spells. The famous magic word **abracadabra** is believed to have originated from the name Abraxis. He can also be found in the **Book of Raziel,** and in Persian mythology. A variation of Abraxis is Abrasax.

✦ABRID: In mysticism Abrid is the angel of the summer equinox. His name can also be found inscribed upon charms to ward off **Malochia** (the evil eye).

✦ABRIGRIEL: A "**transformation** angel," featured in the book *Ask Your Angels* (by Alma Daniel, Timothy Wyllie, and Andrew Ramer). In *Ask Your Angels*, Abrigriel explains the roles of angels working with earth in the modern age, and how angels are working with humankind to bring about positive changes for the future.

✦ABRIMAS: An angel of the Sabbath.

✦ABRINAEL: One of the presiding angels over the twenty-eight **lunar mansions.**

✦ABRUEL: The Arabic name for the archangel **Gabriel.**

✦ABRUNAEL: An angel that presides over one of the twenty-eight **lunar mansions.**

✦ABSANNIS: One of the seventy-eight names of the mighty angel **Metatron.**

✦ABULIEL: An angel that conveys the prayers of the Jews to God.

✦ABUNDANCE: A popular devi (angel) in Hinduism. She is believed to bring good fortune to those who call on her. She is also called **Lakshmi.**

✦ABUZOHAR: An angel who represents the power of the moon.

✦ABYATUR: The angel of the North Star. In Heaven he watches over the scales that are used to weigh the deeds of mortal men after they die. He is also called Abathur Muzania. He was originally an angel from Mandaean lore.

✦ABYSS, ANGEL OF THE: **Abaddon** (in Greek he is called Apollyon). The word *abyss* is derived from the Greek word *abyssos*, which means "the bottomless pit." In the Book of **Revelation** the abyss is where the archangel **Michael** will lock Satan away for a thousand years. Revelation 20:1–3 tells us, "Then I saw an angel coming down from heaven, holding in his hand the key of the abyss and a heavy chain. He seized the dragon, that ancient serpent—that is, the Devil, or Satan—and chained him up for a thousand years. The angel threw him into the abyss, locked it, and sealed it, so that he could not deceive the nations anymore." The abyss is also where the demonic locusts dwell. These are locusts that God lets loose upon wicked mankind in the last days. In Babylonian lore there is a female angel of the abyss named Apsu. In Judaic lore the angel **Azaz'el** was thrown into an abyss. God blamed him for the angels coming to earth and teaching humankind the secrets of Heaven. Because of this, God had **Raphael** bind him and throw him into an abyss located in the desert in Duda'el.

✦**ACCUSATIONS, ANGEL OF:** An angel who accuses sinners in front of God. Satan is officially the Angel of Accusations. Daily he writes down the misdeeds of Israel so that he can accuse them in front of God. It is his hope that God will eventually destroy them. Other accusing angels include **Sammael** and **Dubbiel.** They also record the misconduct of Israel. They, like Satan, would like to see Israel wiped off the face of the earth. They write down the sins of Israel on tablets and give these tablets to the Seraphim, to give to God. The Seraphim, knowing that God is not interested in their accusations, burn the tablets.

✦**ACHAIAH:** The angel of patience. According to legend, Achaiah enjoys uncovering the knowledge of the secrets of the universe.

✦**ACHAMOTH:** The daughter of the **Pistis-Sophia.** The Pistis-Sophia is the mother of the mighty angels called the **Aeons.**

✦**ACHATHRIEL:** An angel whose name has power. It can be found on amulets in an effort to frighten away evil spirits.

✦**ACHSAH:** One of three angels of **charity.** The other two are Hasdiel and **Zadkiel.**

✦**ACHTARIEL:** A variation of the name **Aktriel.**

✦**ACLAHAYE:** The angel of gambling.

✦**ADABIEL:** A variation of **Abdiel.**

✦**ADAM (BRIGHT ANGEL):** The first created human. In the beginning Adam and his wife, **Eve,** lived happily and peacefully in the beautiful Paradise garden that God had created for them. They walked with God and were in constant company of the angels; that is, until they sinned by eating the fruit from the forbidden **Tree of Life.** Because of this act of disobedience, they were cast out of Paradise, thrown into a harsh barren world. A world their descendants inherited. After they were expelled from Paradise, God placed two Cherubim and a turning flaming sword at the entrance of the garden to prevent the couple from reentering. According to Judaic lore, when Adam and Eve were first created, they were assigned two guardian angels. These angels, from the class of angels called the **Virtues,** were to protect the couple from demons. In addition, three attending angels, named **Aebel, Anush,** and Shetel, ministered to and took care of the needs of Adam and Eve. Legend has it that upon his death, Adam was buried by four archangels: Uriel, Raphael, Michael, and Gabriel.

✤**ADDICTIONS, ANGEL OF:** The archangel **Raphael.** He can be called upon for assistance in breaking addictive habits.

✤**ADERNAHAEL:** A variation of the name **Adnachiel** (the angel of **November**).

✤**ADIRAEL:** A fallen angel who once reflected God's splendor. He later became a dark angel and a servant of Hell. He now reports to **Beelzebub, Prince of Devils.**

✤**ADITYAS:** An elite group of radiant angels in Vedic beliefs. They are seven angels who reflect God's brilliant light and glory. There is Varma, the ruler of the Adityas and also the most splendid one; the others include Bhaga, Daksha, **Indra, Mithra,** Savitar, and Surya.

✤**ADLER, MORTIMER J.:** Celebrated twentieth-century American thinker, and author of such noted works as *Ten Philosophical Mistakes, Aristotle for Everybody, How to Think About God, The Great Ideas,* and *The Angels and Us.* In his book *The Great Ideas,* Adler speculates on the existence of angels. He also examines the reasons why the Jews, Christians, and Muslims believe in angels. In addition, he looks at the numerous ways in which angels are viewed as objects of religious beliefs and philosophical thought. In his book *The Angels and Us,* Adler looks at angels in art and religion. He also explores the many theological and philosophical ideas on angels. *The Angels and Us* was a forerunner for later books published on the subject of angels.

✤**ADMAEL:** An angel who stands guard over the earth.

✤**ADNACHIEL:** The angel of **November,** the ruler of **Sagittarius,** and prince of the order of **Angels.** God gave Adnachiel a cure for **stomach ailments** for humans, through an Ethiopian talisman. Variations of the name Adnachiel are Adernahael and Advachiel.

✤**ADOIL:** A spirit made up of great energy and power. According to lore, Adoil burst into existence, like a flash of lightning, at God's command. It was through Adoil that God created all the visible things in the world.

✤**ADONAEL:** A great angel who is capable of overthrowing the demons of disease. In the Testament of **Solomon** he is the angel who overpowers **Metathiax,** the demon who causes kidney pain.

✤**ADONAETH:** In the Testament of **Solomon** he is listed as an angel who can overpower **Ichthion,** the demon who causes paralysis in humans.

✤**ADONAI:** See **Adonay.**

✤**ADONAI YIREH:** The name of the mountain where an angel of the Lord called to **Abraham** from Heaven to prevent him from sacrificing his son, **Isaac.** Abraham named the mountain Adonai Yireh after a ram was found in the bushes. It had been put there by God to be used as a sacrifice instead of Isaac. It means "the Lord provides." See **Sacrifice.**

✤**ADONAIOS:** One of the seven **Archons** (angels) of **gnosticism.**

✤**ADONAY:** In Phoenician lore Adonay is an angel of the **presence.** In Hebrew, Adonay (also Adonai) means "God."

✤**ADRAMALEC:** A fallen angel who is analogous with **Beelzebub.** He is called the ruler of fire because of his association with fire sacrifices (in Samaria he was a god to whom children were sacrificed by fire). He is described as having the wings of an eagle and the body of a lion. However, when invoked, he manifests as a donkey. In John Milton's poem *Paradise Lost*, he is an Assyrian god who is overpowered by **Raphael** and **Uriel** in battle. A variation of the name Adramalec is Adrameleck.

✤**ADRAMELECK:** A variation of Adramalec.

✤**ADRIEL:** One of the angels of the twenty-eight **lunar mansions.** In rabbinical lore he is an angel of death.

✤**ADRIGON:** One of the seventy-eight names of **Metatron.**

✤**ADRIL:** An angel who oversees one of the twenty-eight **lunar mansions,** as mentioned in the **Cabala.**

✤**ADRIRION:** An angel who stands guard over the palace of Wilon, the **First Heaven.**

✤**ADVACHIEL:** A variation of **Adnachiel.**

✤**ADVERSARY:** See **God's Adversary.**

✤**ADVERSITY, ANGEL OF:** Satan the Devil, who is also called the "spirit of adversity." Satan was given the title of the angel of adversity, because it was he who first created adverse conditions on the earth. Adversity was unknown in the world until he deceived Adam and Eve into sinning. Because of their sin they were cast out of Paradise and into a harsh, barren world, which all of their descendants inherited. From that time forward the descendants of Adam and Eve have been living in a hostile world.

✤**AEBEL:** An angel assigned by God to serve Adam and Eve while they were in Paradise. He and two other angels named **Anush** and Shetel were given the responsibility of taking care of the needs of Adam and Eve. The three angels returned to Heaven after the couple sinned and were cast out of the Garden of Eden.

✤**AEONS (CYCLES OF CREATION):** Superior angels of **gnosticism,** said to be the first beings created by God. They are believed to number somewhere around 365. Ruling princes of the Aeons include **Dynamis, Pistis-Sophia,** and **Abraxis.** According to lore, some of the Aeons turned away from God when they became fascinated with human sexuality. Aeons can also be found in **Manichaeism.**

✤**AESHMA:** A short version of **Aeshma Daeva.**

✤**AESHMA DAEVA:** A high-ranking demon in Zend lore. In Persian mythology he was called **Asmodeus.** He was eventually incorporated into Judaic beliefs as a demon of judgment. He is sometimes referred to as Aeshma. A variation of Aeshma Daeva is Ashma Daeva.

✤**AF:** A daunting angel who represents the wrath of God. He issues punishment to those who displease God by destroying them. He is ranked among the angels of destruction. His brother is **Hemah,** a fearsome angel of ancient Judaic beliefs.

✤**AFAROF:** An angel who can stop **Obizuth,** a she-demon who is sworn to destroy the world's children.

✤**AFTIEL:** The angel who presides over the time of day referred to as dusk.

✤**AGNES OF MONTEPULCIANO:** See **Saint Agnes of Montepulciano.**

✤**AGNI:** In Vedic beliefs Agni was an angel who ruled over fire. He was also a messenger between God and mankind.

✤**AGNIEL:** Originally an angel from the **Grigori** class. He turned away from God when he came to earth to pursue women. Once on earth he taught humans the forbidden knowledge of using roots in magic. His teachings have been with mankind for thousands of years and are still in practice in many parts of the world today.

✤**AGRAT-BAT-MAHLAHT:** A she-demon who is a consort of Sammael, the angel of poison. She is also one of four angels of **prostitution** (the others are Eisheth Zenunim, **Lilith,** and **Naamah**).

✤**AGREAS:** A fallen angel from the order of angels called the **Virtues.** He later became a high-ranking demon of Hell. He is said to enjoy bringing earthquakes upon humankind. He is so powerful that when needed, he can call on thirty-one armies of demons to carry out this destructive task.

✤**AGRICULTURE, ANGEL OF:** Risnuch.

✤**AHAITIN:** Another name for **Angra Mainyu,** the spirit of darkness in **Zoroastrianism.**

✤**AHANIEL:** See **Childbirth.**

✤**AHIEL:** See **Childbirth.**

✤**AHJMAEL:** An angel from ancient Islamic lore. He was called upon in ancient ceremonies to frighten away evil spirits.

✤**AHMAD, MIRZA GHULAM:** A Moslem scholar who taught that God established two structures for the operation of the universe: the visible and the invisible worlds. He held that no part of the visible world could operate without the guidance of the angels in the invisible world. He believed that God made angels administrators of the universe, and that it is because of them that there is change and progress.

✤**AHRIMAN:** Another name for **Angra Mainyu,** the spirit of darkness in **Zoroastrianism.**

✤**AHURA MAZDA (WISE LORD):** The Supreme Being in **Zoroastrianism.** Zoroastrians believed him to be the creator of all things. He was the possessor of knowledge and immortal powers. He was the source of all that is light, joyful, beautiful, and good. His adversary was named **Angra Mainyu,** the spirit of darkness in Zoroastrianism. Six archangels called **Amesha Spentas** assist Ahura Mazda. Another name for Ahura Mazda is Ohrmazd.

✤**AHURAS:** Angels in Aryan lore. They are also referred to as the gods of hidden knowledge. In Hinduism Ahuras are considered dark spirits. Variations of the word Ahuras are **Asuras** and **Azuras.**

✤**AILOAIOS:** One of the seven **Archons** (angels) of **gnosticism.**

✤**AIR, ANGEL OF:** An angel found in Essene beliefs. To the **Essenes,** the angel **Haniel** personified the angel of air. The **Sylphs** are the elemental spirits who rule the air.

✤**AIR AND WINDS, ANGEL OF:** In Persian mythology the mighty angel named **Vayu** is the angel of air and winds. He was believed to bring life in the rain, and death in the storm. He was the producer of lightning and made the dawn appear. In adverse weather conditions, people prayed to Vayu.

✤**AISHIM:** A variation of **Izachim.**

✤**AKASHIC RECORDS:** A spiritual library that contains the recorded history of the universe from creation to the present day. The angels are believed to use the Akashic Records to provide humans with needed information to help with difficult problems, and to answer questions on God, the Heavens, and the future.

✤**AKATRIEL:** A variation of the name **Aktriel.**

✤**AKKAD(IAN):** In Akkadian lore angels are called **Anunna.** Demons are referred to as Maskim.

✤**AKRASIEL:** Another name for the angel **Raguil.** Raguil was one of the angels who escorted **Enoch** on his tour of earth and **Sheol.**

✤**AKRIEL:** The angel of barrenness. He is appealed to for assistance in cases of infertility. He is also called upon for curing imbecility.

✤**AKTRIEL:** An angelic prince in Heaven who ranks higher than most of the other angels. He is considered by some to be the Angel of the Lord. Elisha ben Abuya, an ancient mystic who visited Heaven, wrote of seeing

Aktriel at Heaven's entrance with myriads of angels attending him. Variations of the name **Aktriel** are Achtariel and Akatriel.

✤**Akzariel:** An angel who is called upon to ward off evil spirits.

✤**Al Ussa:** A female angel from Arabic lore.

✤**Al-Zabamiyah:** A variation of **Al-Zabaniya.**

✤**Al-Zabaniya:** In Islam the Al-Zabaniya are nineteen guardians of Hell. They are also called **Violent-Thrusters.** A variation of Al-Zabaniya is Al-Zabamiyah.

✤**Al'alyah:** One of the seventy-eight names of the mighty angel **Metatron.**

✤**Alat:** An angel who stands guard over the palace of **Arabot**, the **Seventh Heaven.**

✤**Albion, Angel of:** A fictional angel created by **William Blake** for his work *Visions of the Daughters of Albion.*

✤**Alchemy, Angel of:** The angel of alchemy is **Och,** who brought the knowledge of alchemy to the earth.

✤**Alcin:** An angel who stands guard over the west wind.

✤**Alimon:** An angel of ancient Judaic lore. He was called upon to protect individuals against harm from weapons in war. He worked closely with two other angels: Tafthi and Reivtip.

✤**Alkanosts:** Female angels of Russian folklore. The Alkanosts were winged, birdlike female figures who offered irresistible pleasures to men. They had the faces of beautiful young women, and the bodies of birds. They symbolized temptation, misery, and death. The cost to experience the pleasures of the Alkanosts was the loss of one's life.

✤**Allah:** God the Almighty in Islam. Surah 35 of the Koran states, "Praise be to Allah, Who created [out of nothing] the heavens and the earth, Who made the angels, messengers with wings—two or three or four [pairs]: He adds to Creation as He pleases: for Allah has power over all things." In the Koran, angels are seated around the great throne of Allah. The angels ask Allah to pardon sinners and act as mediators between Him and mankind. The archangel **Israfel** praises Allah continuously in many different languages. Angels are said to be created from the breath of Allah to glorify and praise him.

✤**Almiras:** The angel of invisibility.

✤**Almon:** An angel who stands guard over the palace of Zebul, the **Fourth Heaven.**

✤**Almond Tree, Angel of the:** The archangel **Michael.** It was Michael who planted the almond tree in the Garden of Eden, at the beginning of creation.

✤**Alphun:** The guardian angel of doves.

✤**Altar(s):** A table or stand where prayers and offerings are made to God. The Bible speaks of a magnificent golden altar that stands before the throne of God. Around it angels gather listening to the prayers of the saints that are being offered up to God. "An angel with a golden censer came and stood at the altar; he was given a great quantity of incense to offer with the prayers of all the saints on the golden altar that is before the throne." (Revelation 8:3) Today, many people have altars in their homes, where they pray, meditate, and call on the angels for assistance and guidance.

✤**Amabael:** One of several angels who preside over **winter.**

✤**Amael:** A ruling prince over the order of angels called **Principalities.**

✤**Amaliel:** The angel of weakness. He is also the angel of scolding and chastisement.

✤**Amamael:** An angel who stands guard over the palace of Sehaqim, the **Third Heaven.**

✤**Amasras:** Originally an angel from the **Grigori** class. He rebelled against God's laws when he came to earth to have sexual relations with women. He also taught mankind how to use spells and incantations. This was forbidden knowledge to men. His teachings have been with mankind for thousands of years and are still in practice in many parts of the world today. He along with the angel **Agniel** also instructed humans on how to use roots in magic and medicine.

✤**Ambassadors:** The name of a group of angels who promote peace.

✤**Ambriel:** An angel of many titles. He is the angel of **May,** the prince of **Thrones,** and the ruler of Gemini. A variation of the name Ambriel is Amriel.

✤**Ambrose, Saint:** See **Saint Ambrose.**

✤**Ameretat:** One of the archangels in **Zoroastrianism.** She is the angel of immortality and protector of vegetation. She is represented by Haoma, plants, and flowers.

✤**America(ns):** At the nation's birth, **George Washington** was visited by a female angel. In a vision, the angel showed him the history of America. Americans. A 1991 Gallup Poll reveals that sixty-nine percent of Americans believe in angels. Thirty-two percent feel that they have had contact with an angel.

✤**American Indians:** See **Native Americans.**

✤**Amesha Spenta(s):** Archangels in **Zoroastrianism.** Six archangels assist **Ahura Mazda** (God). Together with Ahura Mazda, they represent seven fundamental moral ideas: Ahura Mazda (Holy Spirit); **Vohu Manah** (wisdom); **Asha** (truth); **Armaiti** (devotion); **Khshathra Vairya** (desirable dominion); **Haurvatat** (wholeness);

and **Ameretat** (immortality). Each Amesha Spenta is a protector of an aspect of creation: Ahura Mazda—mankind; Vohu Manah—cattle; Asha—fire; Armaiti—earth; Khshathra Vairya—sky; Haurvatat—water; Ameretat—plants. They are also referred to as Amshashpands and Amshaspendas.

✦**AMIZO:** An alias used by **Lilith,** a notorious she-demon.

✦**AMNEDIEL:** One of the angels of the twenty-eight **lunar mansions.**

✦**AMNIXIEL:** One of the angels of the twenty-eight **lunar mansions.**

✦**AMOR:** Another name for **Cupid,** ancient Rome's winged god of love.

✦**AMPHAROOL:** The angel who presides over the advancement of flying, transport, and instant travel.

✦**AMQAQYAH:** One of the seventy-eight names of **Metatron.**

✦**AMRAEL:** An angel whose name has power. It can be found on amulets in an effort to chase away evil spirits.

✦**AMRIEL:** A variation of the name **Ambriel.** Ambriel is prince of the order of angels called **Thrones.**

✦**AMSHASHPANDS:** Another name for the **Amesha Spentas** (archangels in **Zoroastrianism**).

✦**AMSHASPENDAS:** Another name for the **Amesha Spentas** (archangels in **Zoroastrianism**).

✦**AMURDAD:** Another name for **Ameretat,** an archangel of Zoroastrianism. She presides over the immortality of souls and of vegetation on earth.

✦**AMUTIEL:** An angel who rules one of the twenty-eight **lunar mansions**.

✦**AMWAKEL:** An angel whose name has power. It can be found on amulets in an effort to frighten away evil spirits.

✦**AMY:** In Heaven he was of the class of angels called the **Authorities.** He eventually fell from his position in Heaven (the reasons are not clear) and later worked his way up to becoming a high-ranking official in Hell. According to lore, he is hopeful of someday returning to his heavenly status.

✦**ANABIEL:** An angel who is called upon for help in curing stupidity.

✦**ANAEL:** A variation of the name **Haniel.**

✦**ANAFIEL:** A variation of the name **Anapiel YHWH,** a great prince in Heaven, who is the keeper of the keys to the palaces of Heaven.

✦**ANAHITA:** See **Ardvi Sura Anahita.**

✦**ANAITIS:** Another name for **Ardvi Sura Anahita,** the angel of fertility in Persian mythology.

✦**ANAKIM:** The offspring of the **Watchers** and mortal women. The Watchers are angels who left their positions in Heaven to come to the earth to marry women and produce children. Their children, the

Anakim, became giant mutants on earth. In the writings of **Enoch,** God referred to these children as "evil spirits." They are also called **Nephillim.**

✤**ANANCHEL:** The angel of sanctity.

✤**ANAN'EL:** A fallen angel, from the group of angels known as the **Grigori.** He fell from grace when he along with several other angels came to the earth to marry women and produce children.

✤**ANAPHIEL:** A variation of the name **Anapiel YHWH.**

✤**ANAPIEL YHWH:** A majestic prince of Heaven. His glory is said to overshadow the most beautiful chambers of Arabot (the **Seventh Heaven**). He is the **Prince of Water** and keeper of the keys to the palaces of Arabot. He is also the guardian of the keys to the heavenly passageways. It was Anapiel YHWH who carried the prophet **Enoch** to Heaven. According to legend, he once flogged the great angel **Metatron** with sixty lashes of fire as punishment for wrongdoing. Variations of the name Anapiel YHWH are Anafiel, Anaphiel, and Anpiel.

✤**ANAUEL:** The angel who oversees trade and commerce on earth. He also presides over the workings of financiers.

✤**ANCIENT CIVILIZATIONS:** Ancient civilizations that believed in angels and angel-type deities included the Egyptians, Greeks, Romans, Persians, Maoris, Japanese, Babylonians, Mesopotamians, Norsemen, Aryans, and the Russians.

✤**ANCIENT OF DAYS:** A name found in the **Cabala** used for **Kether,** one of the angels of the **Holy Sefiroth.** Also, in the Book of Daniel 7:9–10 God is referred to as the Ancient of Days. There he is described in great detail from a vision of **Daniel.** Daniel also wrote of the great number of ministering angels that surrounded him. "I kept on beholding until there were thrones placed and the Ancient of Days sat down. His clothing was white just like snow, and the hair of his head was like clean wool. His throne was flames of fire, its wheels were a burning fire. There was a stream of fire flowing and going out from before him. There were a thousand thousands [angels] that kept ministering to him, and ten thousand times ten thousand that kept standing right before him." (Note: In some translations the term Ancient of Days is replaced with Ancient One.)

✤**ANDERSON, JOAN WESTER:** Best-selling author of angel books including the popular *Where Angels Walk, True Stories of Heavenly Visitors.* Anderson's first experience with angels occurred on Christmas Eve, 1983. That night her son Tim and a college friend became stranded in a severe snowstorm when their car broke down. They had been driving home to Illinois from Connecticut for Christmas. As they sat helpless in freezing temperatures afraid they were going to die, a tow truck suddenly pulled in behind them. They were towed safely to a friend's home. The driver and the truck later mysteriously disappeared. Anderson considered the driver of the tow truck to be an angel who had responded to her prayers for Tim's safety. Awed by this experience, Anderson was inspired to write *Where Angels Walk, True Stories of Heavenly Visitors.* It was on the national religion best-seller list for two years straight. She later wrote two other angel books entitled *Where Miracles Happen, True Stories of Heavenly Encounters* and *An Angel to Watch over Me, True Stories of Children's Encounters with Angels.*

✤**ANDIBEHIST:** A variation of **Ordibehesht.** The angel of the month of April in Persian mythology.

✤**ANDROGYNY:** In Christianity, angels are portrayed as genderless, sexless beings. Some angelologists believe that angels carry the male and female polarities within them and have the ability to assume the appearance of either gender.

✤**ANFIAL:** An angel who stands guard over the palace of Zebul, the **Fourth Heaven.**

✤**ANGAROS:** The ancient Persian word for "courier." It is one of the words that the word *angel* was originally derived from.

✤*ANGE PASSE:* A French expression. When a sudden hush occurs in a conversation, the French say, *"Ange passe,"* which means, an angel has passed above.

✤**ANGEL CIRCLES:** A term used for groups of people who come together to call upon the angels for assistance in their daily lives.

✤**ANGEL COLLECTORS CLUB OF AMERICA:** A club for angel lovers and collectors. The club has local chapters, a biannual convention, and a newsletter. Dues are $12. Interested persons can write to Angel Collectors Club of America, 16342 W. 54th Street, Golden, CO 80403.

✤**ANGEL CONFERENCES AND CONVENTIONS:** The following organizations hold angel conferences and conventions: Angel Collectors Club of America; Angels of the World; and Tapestry. See **Angel Organizations.**

✤**ANGEL CROWNED WITH A RAINBOW:** In the Book of Revelation 10:1, the apostle **John** sees in his vision an angel who wears a rainbow on his head. "And I saw another strong angel descending from heaven, arrayed with a cloud, and a rainbow was upon his head, and his face was as the sun, and his feet were as fiery pillars."

✤**ANGEL HIERARCHIES:** In an effort to create order in the angel world, theologians created angel hierarchies. These hierarchies ranked the orders of angels from the highest to the lowest. The most recognized hierarchy is that of **Dionysius the Pseudo-Areopagite,** in which he ranked the angels in three choirs in the following order: first, **Seraphim, Cherubim,** and **Thrones;** second, **Dominations, Virtues,** and **Powers;** third, **Principalities, Archangels,** and **Angels. Saint Thomas Aquinas,** Saint Hildegarde, and **Dante** all adopted this hierarchy and incorporated it into their writings. Dante helped contribute to its popularity by including it in his classic poem *The Divine Comedy.* In addition, the Roman Catholic Church embraced it, improving its credibility. Today it is the most popular hierarchy of angels in the world. Through the centuries many other great thinkers also created angel hierarchies. Among those are **Saint Ambrose, Saint Jerome, Saint Gregory the Great, Rudolph Steiner,** and **Billy Graham.** Some great works of literature that include angel hierarchies include *Apologia Prophet David* by Saint Ambrose, *Homilia* by Saint Gregory the Great, *The Celestial Hierarchy* by Saint Thomas Aquinas, *Summa Theologica* by Dionysius the Pseudo-Areopagite, *Etymologiarum* by Isidore of Seville, *Mishne Torah* by **Moses Maimonides,** *De Fide Orthodoxa* by **Saint John of Damascus,** and *The Magus* by Francis Barrett.

✦Angel Monks: Early Eastern authors frequently compared the lives of monks with the lives of angels. They held that monks who led angelic lives would eventually metamorphose into angels.

✦ANGEL MUSICIANS: See **Music.**

✦ANGEL NEWS: See **Angel Publications.**

✦*ANGEL ON MY SHOULDER:* A 1946 film in which a murdered gangster makes a pact with Satan. The gangster would like to return to earth as a human. His wish is granted and he comes back to earth as a man. While on earth he acts as a judge while trying to outwit Satan. The movie stars Anne Baxter, George Cleveland, Paul Muni, and Onslow Stevens. It was directed by Archie Mayo.

✦ANGEL ORACLE: The angel oracle is a divination tool introduced in the book *Ask Your Angels* by authors Alma Daniel, Timothy Wyllie, and Andrew Ramer. The oracle is a means of accessing spiritual information from the angels. It is used in much the same way as other divining tools such as **tarot cards** and rune stones. It is based on C. G. Jung's idea of synchronicity.

✦ANGEL ORDERS: See **Orders of Angels.**

✦ANGEL ORGANIZATIONS: The following is a listing of angel organizations within the United States. For more membership information, please write to the following addresses: Angel Collectors Club of America (16342 W. 54th Street, Golden, CO 80403); Angelic Alliance (P.O. Box 95, Upperco, MD 21155); Angels of the World (2232 McKinley Avenue, St. Albans, WV 25177); AngelWatch Foundation, Inc. (P.O. Box 1397,

Mountainside, NJ 07092); Questhaven (P.O. Box 20560, Escondido, CA 92029); Tapestry (P.O. Box 3032, Waquoit, MA 02536). (Note: When writing for information, please enclose a business-size, self-addressed stamped envelope.)

✤ANGEL PUBLICATIONS: Popular publications on angels include: *Angel News* (519 W. Plantation Boulevard, Lake Mary, FL 32746); *Angel Times* (4360 Chamblee-Dunwoody Road, Atlanta, GA 30341); *Angelic Thoughts* (42 Pearwood Road, Rochester, NY 14624); and the *Angels Worldwide Newsletter* (Box 54112, Longsdale West PO, North Vancouver, BC V7M 3L5, Canada).

✤*ANGEL TIMES:* See **Angel Publications.**

✤ANGEL WALK: See **Religious Groups.**

✤ANGEL WRAPPED IN A CLOUD: In the Book of Revelation 10:1–3, the apostle **John** is given an apocalyptic vision from an angel who is wrapped in a cloud: "And I saw another mighty angel coming down from Heaven, wrapped in a cloud, with a rainbow over his head; his face was like the sun, and his legs like pillars of fire. He held a little scroll open in his hand. Setting his right foot on the sea and his left foot on the land, he gave a great shout, like a lion roaring. And when he shouted, the seven thunders sounded."

✤ANGEL YEAR: According to occultists, an angel year is 365 earth years.

✤ANGELA OF FOLIGNO: See **Saint Angela of Foligno.**

✤ANGELIC: According to *Webster's New World Dictionary*, the word *angelic* means to be "of an angel, or the angels." It is also defined as being "like an angel in goodness, beauty, and innocence." *Angelic* is also the name of a form of writing created in England by **John Dee** and Edward Kelly during the 1500s. It was named Angelic because Dee used it in his work with the angels. He also used it in magic. Today it is considered to be the most powerful alphabet to be used in magic. Ceremonial magicians use it to record rituals and also to send messages to the angels. It is believed that the writing can open doors to other realms and open up communications with the angels and other spiritual entities. It is also called Enochian, and in some magical workings it is called Celestial.

✤ANGELIC ALLIANCE: See **Angel Organizations.**

✤ANGELIC COURT: See **Court of Heaven.**

✤ANGELIC DOCTOR: A title held by **Saint Thomas Aquinas.** He was given this title because of his studies in and discourses on angels. Aquinas believed that angels were necessary to fill the gap between God and mankind. He held that countless numbers of angels exist, and that they are all immortal.

✦**ANGELIC PRINCES:** A term used when referring to the **Sarim,** a high order of angels.

✦**ANGELIC SCHOOL:** The angelic school is a place where the angels gain knowledge and insights on the mysteries of the universe. When **Enoch** visited the **Sixth Heaven,** he saw angels being schooled in a number of sciences including astronomy, ecology, and oceanography. In addition to the sciences they also studied vegetation on earth and in Heaven. There were also angels who studied the behavior of mankind. In the angelic classroom all of the angels were dressed alike and looked alike and were being taught by the archangels. The **Akashic Records** are thought to be located there. **Asroilu YHWH** is said to be the head of the angelic school.

✦*ANGELIC THOUGHTS:* See **Angel Publications.**

✦**ANGELIC WRITING:** See **Angelic.**

✦**ANGELICO, FRA:** A Florentine painter (also known as Giovanni da Fiesole, 1400–1455) who specialized in painting religious subjects. Many of his paintings include beautiful portrayals of angels, which he depicted as feminine, ethereal, celestial beings. Such paintings of his include *The Angel of the Annunciation*, *The Last Judgment*, *Coronation of the Virgin*, and *St. Dominic.*

✦**ANGELOI:** The last class of angels found within the angel hierarchy created by German philosophic genius and clairvoyant **Rudolph Steiner.** The Angeloi stand one stage higher than mankind. They work more with humans than any other class of angels. The guardian angels are also from the Angeloi class. In most other hierarchies the Angeloi are referred to as **Angels.**

✦**ANGELOLATRY:** The adoration and worship of angels. Throughout history many have speculated on whether it is appropriate to pay homage to angels. Many have held that revering angels is entirely inappropriate, citing the account in the Bible found in Revelation 22:8–9. After the apostle **John** had been shown a vision by an angel, he fell down at the angel's feet and was about to worship him. The angel stopped him, saying, "You must not do that! I am a fellow servant with you and your comrades the prophets, and with those who keep the words of this book. Worship God!" An account found in the *Apocalypse of Zephaniah* seems to support this idea. In this account, while visiting Heaven **Zephaniah** prostrated himself before a great angel named **Eremiel.** Eremiel told him, "Take heed. Don't worship me. I am not the Lord Almighty." *(Apocalypse of Zephaniah 6:15).*

✦**ANGELOLOGY:** The branch of theology that studies the roles, characteristics, and history of angels. Primary sources for studying the angels include the **Avesta** of Zoroastrianism, the Hebrew and Christian Greek scriptures of the Bible, Islam's Koran, and the Apocryphal and Pseudepigraphical books of Judaism.

✤**ANGELOPHANY:** A term used in angelology meaning a visitation by an angel.

✤**ANGELOS:** An ancient Greek word for "angel." It was derived from the Hebrew word *malakh*, which means "messenger."

✤**ANGELS:** The word *angel* is a generic term that is generally used for all spiritual creatures that dwell in the heavenly realm. The word *angel* means "messenger." It was derived over time from several languages, including the Hebrew word *malakh*, meaning "messenger"; the Persian word *angaros*, meaning "courier"; and the Greek word *angelos*, which also means "messenger." Angels are spiritual beings who perform various services for people on God's behalf. They act as intercessors between God and humankind. This is because God is too overwhelming a force for man to come face-to-face with. According to the Bible no man can see God's face and live (Exodus 33:20). Therefore, angels are thought to be a necessary link between God and humans. ORDERS OF ANGELS. In the angelic hierarchy, Angels are the last order of angels and are only one stage higher than man. These angels work more closely with humans than any other class of angels. The **guardian angels** are from this order. Ruling princes of the order of Angels include Phaleg, **Adnachiel, Gabriel,** and Chayyliel. KNOWLEDGE OF THE ANGELS. The angels are credited with teaching mankind the knowledge of agriculture, meteorology, psychiatry, astronomy, pharmacy, language, writing, medicine, herbal remedies, alchemy, gemology, diagnosing and curing diseases, how to perform abortions, magic, and astrology. (Note: Some of this knowledge was forbidden to humans and the angels who brought it to earth were severely reprimanded.)

✤*ANGELS IN THE OUTFIELD:* A 1951 movie about angels who come to the assistance of the Pittsburgh Pirates baseball team. The angels help the team to rise to the top of their profession after an angel makes a deal with the team's manager. The angel promises to help the team if the manager will change his wicked ways. The film stars Paul Douglas. A remake of the movie was released in 1994, starring Danny Glover.

✤**ANGELS OF FIRE:** A title held by the **Watchers,** who are said to be made of fire.

✤**ANGELS OF THE SEA:** A term used when referring to dolphins.

✤**ANGELS OF THE WORLD:** See **Angel Organizations.**

✤*ANGELS, THE MYSTERIOUS MESSENGERS:* A 1994 television documentary that examines the purpose of angels, and the roles of angels throughout history. It also gives real-life accounts of people who have had angel experiences. The film is narrated by Patty Duke. It features authors of popular angel books such as **Sophy Burnham, Terry Lynn Taylor, Eileen Freeman,** and Malcolm Godwin.

✣**ANGELUCCI, ORFEO:** In 1952 businessman Orfeo Angelucci was contacted by aliens who informed him that he had a special mission to accomplish while on earth. The beings spoke to him about earth's future and the dangers to the planet. Some have likened his experience to that of the prophet **Ezekiel** in the Bible. His experience has led some to wonder if the angels of the Bible were actually superior extraterrestrials, whose visits to earth could have only been interpreted in ancient times as beings sent from God.

✣**ANGELUS:** A devotional prayer in Catholicism. The prayer is said at morning, noon, and night to commemorate the **Annunciation.** In the Annunciation, the archangel **Gabriel** appeared to the Virgin Mary to announce that she would give birth to the savior.

✣*ANGELUS NOVUS:* A famous painting by **Paul Klee** of an angel. It hangs in the Israel Museum.

✣**ANGELUS OCCIDENTALIS:** A general term used for the various classes of angels found in Judaism, Christianity, Islam, and Zoroastrianism. All four religions believe that the angels emanate from God and are sent forth to administer to the universe and aid mankind.

✣*ANGELWATCH:* A bimonthly newsletter about angels. It was created by **Eileen Freeman,** author of the best-selling angel book entitled *Touched by an Angel.* The newsletter includes angel stories, angel experiences, and is a resource guide. For subscription information write to *AngelWatch,* P.O. Box 1362, Mountainside, NJ 07092. Please enclose a self-addressed stamped envelope.

✣**ANGELWATCH FOUNDATION, INC.:** See **Angel Organizations;** *AngelWatch.*

✣**ANGER, ANGEL OF: Af.** Af represents God's anger toward the sinful state of the world.

✣**ANGERES:** In Sanskrit the word *angeres* means "divine spirit." It is one of the words that the word *angel* was originally derived from.

✣**ANGIRAS:** A variation of *angeres.*

✣**ANGRA MAINYU:** The spirit of darkness (Satan) in Zoroastrianism. He is **Ahura Mazda's** (the Supreme Being's) adversary. He is also called the Lie, the destructive spirit, Leader of the Demonic Hordes, and demon of demons. His followers were given the name **daevas** by Zoroaster. From *daevas* comes the word *devil.* Zoroastrians believe that Angra Mainyu resides in a dark abyss in the North. When he manifests, he takes on one of three forms: a lizard, a snake, or a male youth. He is the creator of death, disease, and evil. Zoroastrians hold him responsible for all of mankind's sorrows. Some Zoroastrians believe that he was created by Ahura Mazda himself and that he eventually turned against him and became his chief opponent. He is also called Ahaitin and Ahriman.

✦**ANIEL:** The angel of the sun. He is said to reflect the sun's beauty. Aniel is also a variation of the name **Haniel.**

✦**ANIMALS, ANGELS AS:** According to many accounts of personal angelic experiences published in recent years, angels sometimes take on the forms of animals when manifesting to humans to give assistance. The most common animals they appear as are dogs and birds. They sometimes appear in the form of a dog when protection is needed, or a bird to relay divine messages, or to give encouragement. In addition, certain angels and groups of angels are identified and even represented by animals. In Assyrian art the **Cherubim** were portrayed in many different forms. These included lions, bulls, and sphinxes. The she-demon named **Leviathan** is said to manifest as a large crocodile. The angel **Camael** is said to appear as a leopard when invoked. **Angra Mainyu** takes on the form of either a lizard or a snake. **Adramalec** manifests as a donkey.

✦**ANIMALS, ANGELS OF:** Behemiel and Hariel are guardian angels of domestic animals. The angel who presides over the death of domestic animals is **Hemah.** The angel Jehiel guards and protects animals in the wild.

✦**ANIMASTIC:** The name of the guardian angel of Moses.

✦**ANIMASTICS:** An order of angels who are great princes in Heaven.

✦**ANIQUEL:** A variation of the name **Anituel.**

✦**ANIQUIEL:** A variation of the name **Anituel.**

✦**ANITUEL:** An angel who turned away from God's divine laws. He later became a prince of the dark spirits and a high-ranking demon of Hell. Variations of the name Anituel are Aniquel and Aniquiel.

✦**ANIXIEL:** See **Childbirth.**

✦**ANIYEL:** A variation of the name **Haniel.**

✦**ANMAEL:** A fallen angel. According to Judaic legend, Anmael fell from grace when he agreed to reveal the secret name of God to a woman if she would have sexual relations with him.

✦**ANNIHILATION, ANGEL OF: Harbonah.** He is one of the angels of destruction who is sent forward by God to annihilate the evildoers in the world.

✦**ANNOUNCEMENTS, ANGEL OF:** In Judeo-Christian lore the archangel **Gabriel** is the angel of announcements. In the Bible, Gabriel delivered the important announcements of the births of John the Baptist and Jesus

Christ. In Persian mythology **Surush** is the angel who delivers divine announcements.

✦**ANNOUNCER:** The meaning of the name **Nabu.** Nabu is one of the angels who keeps records for God in Heaven.

✦**ANNUNCIATION, THE:** The title given to the archangel **Gabriel**'s announcement to **Mary** that she was to give birth to the savior. In the Annunciation Gabriel was sent by God to Nazareth to visit a virgin named Mary. The Bible tells us, "In the sixth month of Elizabeth's pregnancy God sent the angel Gabriel to a town in Galilee named Nazareth. He had a message for a girl promised in marriage to a man named Joseph. The girl's name was Mary. The angel came to her and said, 'Peace be with you! The Lord is with you and has greatly blessed you!' Mary was deeply troubled by the angel's message, and she wondered what his words meant. The angel said to her, 'Don't be afraid, Mary; God has been gracious to you. You will become pregnant and give birth to a son, and you will name him Jesus. He will be great and will be called the Son of the Most High God. The Lord God will make him a king, as his ancestor David was, and he will be the king of the descendants of Jacob forever; his kingdom will never end!' " (Luke 1:26–33) The Annunciation has been a favorite subject of artists for centuries. THE ANNUNCIATION IN ART. One of the most popular paintings is **Fra Angelico**'s *Angel of the Annunciation*. Other artists who have portrayed the Annunciation include **Leonardo da Vinci** (*The Annunciation,* ca. 1472, Uffizi Gallery, Florence); Gaudenzio Ferrari (*The Annunciation,* ca. 1512–13, Gemäldegalerie, Berlin); Carlo Crivelli (*Annunciation with Saint Emidius,* 1486, National Gallery, London); Petrus Christus (*Annunciation,* 1452, Gemäldegalerie, Berlin); Orazio Gentileschi (*Annunciation,* ca. 1623, Galleria Sabauda, Turin).

✦**ANNUNCIATION, ANGEL OF THE:** The archangel **Gabriel.**

✦**ANOINTED CHERUB:** According to Judeo-Christian lore, Satan was once the most beautiful angel in Heaven. He was also the Anointed Cherub. He turned away from this favored position because of his desire to be worshiped as a god.

✦**ANPIEL:** A variation of the name **Anapiel YHWH,** a great prince in Heaven.

✦**ANSHE SHEM:** A phrase in which demons are called in some magical practices.

✦**ANTHRIEL:** An angel named by New Age angelologists as one of twelve archangels.

✦**ANUNNA:** An elite group of angels in Akkadian beliefs.

✦**ANUSH:** An attending angel to **Adam** before Adam's great sin. Anush and the two other attending angels (**Aebel** and Shetel) returned to Heaven after Adam and Eve were cast out of Paradise.

✤**APAOSHA:** The demon who caused drought, in ancient Persian lore. His antithesis is **Tishtrya** the angel of rain.

✤**APAP'EL:** One of the seventy-eight names of **Metatron.**

✤**APHREDON:** In **gnosticism** he is the angel who governs the indivisible.

✤**APOCALYPSE, ANGEL OF THE:** The angel who heralds the news of the end of the world. Several angels hold the title of the angel of the Apocalypse. They include **Gabriel, Haniel, Raphael, Michael, Oriphiel, Sammael,** and **Zachariel.**

✤**APOCALYPSE OF ZEPHANIAH:** See **Zephaniah.**

✤**APOCRYPHA:** Fourteen books of the Septuagint (Greek version of the Old Testament) that were left out of the Holy Canon because of doubtful authorship. The majority of the scriptures of the Apocrypha were composed during the Jewish exile in Babylonia (586 to 538 B.C.). During the second century B.C., they were translated from Hebrew to Greek. The books consist of the first and second books of Esdras, Tobit, Judith, Esther, The Wisdom of Solomon, Ecclesiasticus, Baruch, Letter to Jeremiah, Prayer of Azariah, The Song of the Three Young Men, Susanna, Bel and the Dragon, The Prayer of Manasses, and the first, second, third, and fourth books of Maccabees. It is believed that the rabbi of the period left the books out of the Holy Canon not only because of doubtful authorship, but also because of the many listings of angels. The presence of so many angels threatened the Judaic belief in monotheism. The rabbi of the period felt that the books bordered on paganism because angels were named for almost every function of the universe, just as the pagan gods and goddesses of the day were. See **Pseudepigrapha.**

✤**APOLLION:** A variation of the name **Apollyon.**

✤**APOLLYON:** Chief of the Demonic Locusts. The name Apollyon is also the Greek name for **Abaddon,** the angel of the abyss. Variations of the name Apollyon are Apollion, Appollyon, and Appolyon.

✤**APOSTATE ANGEL(S):** Angels who have turned against God's laws. They are also called fallen angels and demons. The first apostate angel was Satan. He became an apostate angel when he told the first lie to Eve in the Garden of Eden. The angels who followed him also became apostates. Others include the **Watchers,** who left their positions in Heaven to come to earth to have sexual relations with women (Genesis 6:2). Since this was a forbidden act, they, too, became apostate angels. In regard to these angels, the Bible states, "Remember the angels who did not stay within the limits of their proper authority, but abandoned their own dwelling place: they are bound with eternal chains in the darkness below, where God is keeping them for that great Day on which they will be condemned" (Jude 6).

✦APOSTLE(S), ANGEL OF THE: Helped Jesus' twelve disciples. After the death of Jesus, the apostles went forward in the ministry following in his footsteps. They performed many miracles, such as healing the sick and casting out demons. Out of jealousy of the apostles' successful ministry, the Sadducees (a Jewish sect of the time) had the apostles thrown into prison. During the night an angel of the Lord came and released them. Acts 5:19–20 tells us: "But that night an angel of the Lord opened the prison gates, and led the apostles out, and said to them, 'Go and stand in the Temple, and tell the people all about this new life.' "

✦APPARITIONS: The name of a high order of angels.

✦APPEARANCE OF ANGELS: In the Bible, the first angels appeared as ordinary men who ate and drank with the prophets. The Book of Genesis 18:1–2 tells us, "As Abraham was sitting at the entrance of his tent during the hottest part of the day, he looked up and saw three men standing there. As soon as he saw them, he ran out to meet them." However, as the centuries unfolded, the appearance of angels changed. IN ART. Throughout history the angels have appeared in art in various ways. They have been portrayed as genderless, winged beings, dressed in long white robes; as chubby, little babies called **putti;** as musicians playing instruments; and as soldiers dressed in armor. They are often described in scripture as fear-inspiring creatures. For example, in Revelation the Cherubim are described as having "many eyes"; and in the chronicles of **Enoch,** the **Kalkydra** are described as having heads of crocodiles and bodies of lions. EARTHLY VISITATIONS. When visiting mortals, angels take on a variety of appearances. How they appear depends on a person's beliefs, cultural or religious. For example, an angel would probably not appear to a Buddhist believer in a halo, white robe, and wings. That is the image of a traditional Judeo-Christian angel. Angels generally appear in a form that is acceptable to the particular individual they are visiting. Joan of Arc saw angels with auras, long robes, and wings. During World War I, when appearing to soldiers in battle, angels took on the forms of spectral riders with bows and arrows. According to modern reports, the angels often come disguised as mortals. This can be a man, woman, or child of any race or culture. Once they have given the assistance needed, they simply vanish. Many times, not until the encounter is over does a person realize he or she has met an angel. There have also been reports of angels appearing as animals, such as birds to bring messages, and dogs for protection. In their natural state they are beings of light and energy. On rare occasions, the angels will appear as closely as possible to their natural state, either as a brilliant light or spirals of light.

✤**APPLE TREE, ANGEL OF THE:** It was the archangel **Gabriel** who first planted the apple tree in the Garden of Eden.

✤**APPOLLYON:** A variation of **Apollyon.**

✤**APPOLYON:** A variation of **Apollyon.**

✤**APRIL, ANGEL OF:** In Judaic Christian lore the angel of April was Asmodel. In Persian mythology it was **Ordibehasht.**

✤**APSARAS:** Beautiful fairies of Hindu lore. They specialize in giving sensual pleasure to the gods. They were sometimes sent from Heaven to prevent wicked men from doing harm, by distracting them with their beauty and sexual expertise.

✤**APSU:** In Babylonian mythology, Apsu is the female angel of the abyss.

✤**AQUARIEL:** An angel named by New Age angelologists as one of twelve **archangels.**

✤**AQUARIUS, ANGEL OF:** The archangel **Gabriel.**

✤**AQUINAS, THOMAS:** See **Saint Thomas Aquinas.**

✤**ARABI, IBN:** A famous Sufi poet who held that his famous book of poetry, *The Meccan Revelations,* was given to him by the angel of inspiration.

✤**ARABIA:** Arabic beliefs in angels stem from their belief in Islam. Islam's Holy Koran speaks of four archangels who are charged with safeguarding mankind and keeping track of the good and bad deeds of men. They are **Mikhail,** who provides men with food and knowledge; **Jibril,** the faithful servant, who brought a revelation to **Muhammad; Azrael,** the angel of death; and **Israfel** the angel of **music.** In rites of exorcism, the Arabs call on guardian angels. These angels include Ahjmael, Amrael, Amwakel, Atail, Azarail, Dardail, Durbail, Hamwakil, Itrail, Kharurail, Lumail, Mahkail, Ruyail, Sarakikail, Sarhmail, and Tankfil.

✤**ARABOT, ANGELS OF:** Arabot is the name of the **Seventh Heaven.** God and the highest orders of angels dwell here, including the Seraphim, Cherubim, and the throne angels. In addition, there are 496,000 camps of ministering angels. Each camp is said to have 496,000 angels. Each angel of these camps is brilliant in appearance and as large as a great sea. Arabot is where the court of Heaven convenes. It is also where God will judge the souls of men on judgment day. When the angels stand before God's throne, they are in four rows. At the head of each row stands a great prince of Heaven. In the Third Book of Enoch, **Metatron** explains to **Enoch** how it is that so many angels are able to stand before God: "Just as a bridge is laid across a river and everyone crosses over it, so a bridge is laid from the beginning of the entrance to its end, and the ministering angels go over it and recite the song before God." The archangel **Michael** is the ruling prince of Arabot.

✦**ARACIEL:** A variation of the name **Araqiel,** the angel of geography.

✦**ARAEL:** The angel of birds. The Testament of **Solomon** lists him as one of the archangels. He is also an angel who can thwart the powers of Sphandor (a demon who paralyzes limbs). The name Arael is also a variation of the name **Ariael,** who is known as the Lion of God.

✦**ARAKEB:** One of the leaders from the group of **Watchers** who came to earth to pursue women.

✦**ARAKIBA:** An angel from the class of angels called **Watchers.**

✦**ARAKIEL:** A variation of the name **Araqiel.**

✦**ARALIM:** Another name for the order of angels called **Thrones.** The Thrones inspire confidence in the power of God. Variations of the name Aralim are Arelim and **Erelim.**

✦**ARAMAEANS:** The Aramaeans worshiped the angel **Rimmon** as a god. Rimmon was the angel of storms.

✦**ARAMAIC:** Another name for the angel **Gader'el.** Gader'el taught mankind how to construct and manufacture arms.

✦**ARAMYAH:** One of the seventy-eight names of **Metatron.**

✦**ARAPIEL YHWH:** A great angelic prince in Heaven.

✦**ARAQIEL:** The angel who taught earth's geography to humankind. He is also one of the five angels who lead the souls of men to the judgment of God after they reach Heaven. Variations of the name Araqiel are Araciel, Arakiel, Arkiel, Arqael, and Araquiel.

✦**ARAQUIEL:** A variation of the name **Araqiel.**

✦**ARARA:** An angel from the Testament of **Solomon.**

✦**ARARIEL:** A variation of the name **Ariael.**

✦**AR'ARYAH:** One of the seventy-eight names of the mighty angel **Metatron.**

✦**ARAZIEL:** A variation of the name **Arazyal.**

✦**ARAZYAEL:** A variation of the name **Arazyal.**

✦**ARAZYAL:** A leader of the **Watchers.** Arazyal instigated the idea of the Watchers coming to earth to have sexual relations with women. The angels who listened to him were severely punished for their transgression. A variation of the name Arazyal is Arazyael.

✦**ARCH FIEND:** A title held by **Satan** the Devil.

✦**ARCHAI:** An order of angels found in various angelologies. They are also called the Original Forces. They govern the realm from Venus to Earth. According to German clairvoyant **Rudolph Steiner,** the Archai come to earth in the form of saints, prophets, and other spiritual leaders. They come to guide and lead humankind to a higher level of spirituality.

✤ARCHANGEL GABRIEL: See **Gabriel.**

✤ARCHANGEL MICHAEL: See **Michael.**

✤ARCHANGEL RAPHAEL: See **Raphael.**

✤ARCHANGEL URIEL: See **Uriel.**

✤ARCHANGELOI: Another name for the archangels.

✤ARCHANGELS: High-ranking angels who act as messengers to God. They are thought to be the most important mediators between God and mankind. The word *archangel* is often misapplied, as it is used as a generic term referring to all angels above the order of **Angels.** In the angelic hierarchy they are one step above the Angels. ARCHANGELS IN RELIGION. Islam recognizes four archangels. They are **Jibril, Mikhail, Azrael,** and **Israfel.** Judaism and Christianity recognize seven archangels. The four most well known are **Raphael, Gabriel, Michael,** and **Uriel.** The names of the other three are uncertain and have been a source of debate by theologians for centuries. They are thought to be three of the following angels: **Raziel, Remiel, Sariel, Metatron, Anael, Raguil, Barakiel, Chamael, Jophiel, Zadkiel,** Jeduhiel, **Simael, Zaphiel,** and **Aniel. Enoch** names the seven archangels as Uriel, Raguil, Michael, Saraqael, Gabriel, **Haniel,** and Raphael. Some New Age angelologists believe there to be twelve archangels instead of the traditional seven. They include Anthriel, Aquariel, **Chamuel,** Gabriel, Jophiel, Michael, Omniel, Perpetiel, Raphael, Uriel, Valeoel, and Zadkiel. The ruling princes of the order include Metatron, Raphael, Michael, Gabriel, **Barbiel,** Jehudiel, and Barakiel. In addition, the archangels command the heavenly army in an ongoing war with Satan and his legions of angels. In some hierarchies they are referred to as the Archangeloi.

✤ARCHANGELS OF PUNISHMENT: See **Punishment.**

✤ARCHAS: One of the angels who watches over the earth.

✤ARCHETYPAL ANGEL(S): The gods and goddesses of the polytheistic religions, such as those of ancient Greece, Rome, Egypt, and India, were the archetypal angels of Judaism, Christianity, and Islam. Some of the primary gods and goddesses that the angels were patterned after include the Greek god **Eros,** the Greek god **Hermes,** the Roman god **Cupid,** the Greek goddess **Iris,** the Roman god **Mercury,** the Egyptian goddess **Isis,** and the Greek muses **Calliope, Clio, Erato, Euterpe, Melpomene, Polyhymnia, Terpsichore,** and **Thaleia.**

✤ARCHIVES, ANGEL OF THE: The angel responsible for maintaining the heavenly archives is **Radweri'el YHWH.** A passage in 3 Enoch talks about Radweri'el YHWH's role as the heavenly archivist: "He takes out the scroll box in which the book of records is kept, and brings it into the presence of the Holy One [God]. He breaks the seals of the scroll box, opens it, takes out the scrolls and puts them in the hand of the Holy One. The Holy One receives them from his hand and places them before the scribes, so that they might read them out to the Great Law Court which is the height of the Heaven of Arabot, in the presence of the Heavenly household" (3 Enoch 27:1–2). (Note: The Book of Records is the record of mankind's deeds. It is the basis from which God's judgment is formed.)

✤**ARCHON(S):** A high-ranking order of angels. The Archons are guardians of entire nations. The archangels **Gabriel, Michael, Raphael,** and **Uriel** are among some of the many angels who make up the Archons. In gnosticism, the Archons are named Jaldabaoth, Jao, Sabaoth, Adonaios, Astanphaios, Ailoaios, and Oraios. They are equated in some writings with the **Aeons.** DEMON ARCHONS. In gnosticism, seven Archons represent the seven deadly sins. The names of these **Archons** are **Pride,** Envy, Wrath, Lust, **Sloth, Greed,** and **Falsehood.** They are equated with seven planetary bodies: Pride—Jupiter; Envy—Moon; Wrath—Mars; Lust—Venus; Sloth—Saturn; Greed—Sun; Falsehood—Mercury. The antitheses of these demon Archons are Pride—**Zadkiel;** Envy—Gabriel; Wrath—**Sammael;** Lust—**Aniel;** Sloth—**Kafziel;** Greed—Raphael; Falsehood—Michael.

✤**ARCICIAH:** One of the angels who watches over the earth.

✤**ARDARCEL:** The angel of fall.

✤**ARDAREL:** An angel who presides over the element of **fire.**

✤**ARDIFIEL:** One of the twenty-eight angels who presides over the **lunar mansions.**

✤**ARDORS:** A variation of the name **Ardours.**

✤**ARDOS:** The name of the top of **Mount Hermon.** Here two hundred angels descended after deciding to come to the earth to have sexual relations with mortal women. These angels were of the **Grigori** class.

✤**ARDOURS:** An order of angels found in various angelologies. They are also featured in John Milton's poem *Paradise Lost.* A variation of the name Ardours is Ardors.

✤**ARDVAHISHT:** Another name for **Asha,** an angel found in Zoroastrianism.

✤**ARDVI SURA ANAHITA:** The angel of fertility in Zoroastrianism. She presides over water and fruitfulness on the earth. According to Zoroastrian lore, she sanctifies the seeds of men, purifies the wombs of women, and cleanses their breast milk. She is beautiful and strong. Born from nobility, she wears a golden tiara that holds a hundred stars. She drives a chariot that is pulled by four strong horses named rain, sleet, cloud, and wind. She also fertilizes crops and nurtures livestock. Variations of the name Ardvi Sura Anahita include Anahita and Anaitis.

✦**AREAROS:** A variation of the name **Armaros.** Armaros was one of the angels from the group of **Watchers** who came to the earth to pursue women.

✦**ARELIM:** Another name for the order of angels called **Thrones.**

✦**ARFIEL:** An angel who stands guard over the palace of Raquia, the **Second Heaven.**

✦**ARIAEL:** An angel who belongs to the order of angels called **Thrones.** He is known as the Lion of God. He is the Lord of the Earth and Prince of Waters. In *Paradise Lost,* John Milton portrayed him as a fallen angel who was defeated by **Abdiel** during the war in Heaven. Variations of the name Ariael are Arariel, Ariel, and **Arael.**

✦**ARIEL:** A variation of the name **Ariael.**

✦**ARIES, ANGEL OF:** **Machidiel.**

✦**ARIOCH:** An angel who fell from grace.

✦**ARIOKH:** A variation of **Ariukh.**

✦**ARISTAQIS:** One of several angels who brought the secret knowledge of Heaven to earth.

✦**ARIUKH:** God assigned Ariukh along with another angel named Pariukh to be a guardian over the writings of **Enoch.**

✦**ARK:** See **Ark of the Covenant.**

✦**ARK OF THE COVENANT, ANGELS OF THE:** The Ark of the Covenant was a gold-covered wooden chest that held the two stone tablets on which the Ten Commandments were written. At each end of the Ark was a golden sculptured Cherub with its wings spread holding up the Ark. The instructions for the making of the Ark are given in the Book of Exodus 25:17–20: "And you must make a cover of pure gold, two and a half cubits its length and a cubit and a half its width. And you must make two cherubs of gold. Of hammered work you are to make them on both ends of the cover. And make one cherub on this end and one cherub on that end. On the cover you are to make the cherubs at its two ends. And the cherubs must be spreading out their two wings upward, screening over the cover with their wings, with their faces one toward the other. Toward the cover the faces of the cherubs should be." (Note: *Cherub* is the singular of *Cherubim.*) The **Cherubim** symbolized God's protective spirit over the Hebrews, and God's sacred knowledge written on the tablets. According to Judaic lore, the names of the angels depicted on the Ark were Zarall and Joel.

✦**ARKIEL:** A variation of the name **Araqiel,** the angel of geography.

✤**ARMAGEDDON:** The final war between the forces of good and evil. In the war the archangel **Michael** will lead the heavenly army against Satan and his demons. It is prophesied in the Book of **Revelation** that the angels will win in the war and will lock Satan and his followers away for a thousand years in the **abyss.** There are five angels of judgment who, once the war is finished, will lead the souls of man to stand before the judgment of God. They are **Araqiel,** Rumael, Samiel, **Uriel, Aziel.**

✤**ARMAITI (FIT MINDEDNESS):** The angel of devotion in Zoroastrianism. She is also one of the **Amesha Spentas** (archangels), and the protector of the earth. She embodies religious unity, worship, and devout obedience. Because of Zoroaster's deep devotion and obedience to God, she is said to have appeared to him personally. She is troubled when the wicked are not justly punished, and joyful when the righteous care for the land and cattle. Those in opposition to her include Taromaiti, also called Presumption, and Pairimaiti, whose name means "crooked-mindedness."

✤**ARMAROS:** One of the angels who came to the earth to have sexual relations with women. He is also one of the angels who brought the secrets of Heaven to humans on earth. Variations of the name Armaros are Armers, Arearos and **Pharmoros.**

✤**ARMEN:** One of several angels who brought the secret knowledge of Heaven to earth.

✤**ARMERS:** A variation of **Armaros.**

✤**ARMIES:** The Book of Job 25:3 asks, "Is there any number to his armies?" The name *armies* is another name for the Celestial Army, which is God's army of angels in Heaven. These angels, at the command of the archangel **Michael,** cast Satan and his demons out of Heaven.

✤**ARMISAEL:** The guardian angel of the womb and unborn. He is summoned during the time of childbirth for a successful delivery.

✤**ARMOR:** Angels are sometimes depicted in art suited in armor. This symbolizes their role in the ongoing battle of good versus evil, and also the war in Heaven. The archangel **Michael** is usually depicted in armor, carrying a shield and unsheathed sword. This represents his roles as God's Warrior, and commander in chief of the Celestial Army.

✤**ARQAEL:** A variation of the name **Araqiel.**

✤**ARROW:** A symbol of the archangel **Raphael.** He is sometimes portrayed in art as carrying a sharp arrow.

✤**ARSABRSBIAL:** An angel who stands guard over the palace of Makon, the **Sixth Heaven.**

✤**ARSIEL:** A fallen angel who is referred to as the Dark Prince of Gehenna.

✤ARSON: An angel who safeguards the east wind.

✤ART: The subject of angels has been the inspiration for many great artists. Throughout art history, angels can be found in paintings, drawings, illustrations, and sculpture. Some of the world's greatest masterpieces reflect the beauty and majesty of the angels. In the ancient world, angels could be found in the artwork of Mesopotamia, Egypt, Greece, Rome, Asia Minor, and India. As time passed, the images of angels changed. They have been depicted as babies, youths, adults, and birds. During the Byzantine period angels were portrayed as male. Gothic angels looked like adolescents. Thirteenth-century angels were masculine and strong in appearance. Angels of the fourteenth, fifteenth, and sixteenth centuries were portrayed with an air of youth, innocence, and vitality. Later they took on a more androgynous appearance. During the seventeenth century artists portrayed angels in the ways they personally viewed them. In addition, the way angels are depicted in art often reflects the individual characteristics of the angel. For example, the archangel **Michael,** leader of the Heavenly Army, is often portrayed in armor or carrying an unsheathed sword. **Gabriel,** the angel of revelation, is sometimes shown carrying a torch. The depiction of angels with wings became popular during the Renaissance. In the later part of that era, they were often portrayed as chubby little babies known as Cherubs. **Aureoles** became popular during the Renaissance as well. Many paintings show angels, saints, and holy people as having an aureole surrounding either the head or body. Famous artists who have portrayed angels in their work include: **Fra Angelico, William Blake, Sandro Botticelli, Marc Chagall, Eugène Delacroix, Gustave Doré, Piero della Francesca, Paul Gauguin,** Vincent van Gogh, El Greco, Edouard Manet, **Michelangelo Buonarroti, Lorenzo Monaco, Raphael Santi, Rembrandt Harmenszoon van Rijn,** Peter Paul Rubens, Titian, Sir Anthony Van Dyck, Jose Maria Velasquez, and **Leonardo da Vinci.** See **Appendix 4.**

✤ARTOSAEL: A demon who causes problems with the eyes. He can be thwarted by the angel **Uriel.**

✤ARTS, ANGEL OF: See **Arts and Music.**

✤ARTS AND MUSIC, ANGELS OF: The archangel **Uriel** is the angel of arts and music. In Greek mythology **Melpomene, Thaleia, Euterpe,** and **Polyhymnia** were the muses of the arts.

✤ARYAN(S): Aryan beliefs in angels and angelic-type deities date back to 2500 B.C., when the Aryans settled in Iran. They believed in spiritual beings called **Ahuras,** also known as the gods of hidden knowledge. The Ahuras later became angels in Persian lore. In addition, the Aryans believed in devas and nature spirits. One Aryan angelic-type deity was Dyeus, god of the sky. Dyeus was believed to bring rain. He was also guardian of the Aryan people. According to lore, he destroyed their adversaries with storms and bolts of lightning. His mate was the earth goddess, who caused the vegetation to grow. Other angelic deities included the sun god, the moon god, the god of dawn, and the god of the flame. These gods and goddesses were transformed into angels in later history.

✤**ASAEL (MADE BY GOD):** One of the **Watchers** who fell from God's favor when he came to the earth to cohabitate with women and produce offspring. Asael is also a variation of the name **Asel.**

✤**ASAPH:** An angel credited with writing Psalm 50 and Psalms 73–83 of the Bible. In Heaven he commands the angels who continuously sing praises to God.

✤**ASASYAH:** One of the seventy-eight names of **Metatron.**

✤**ASBEEL (GOD'S DESERTER):** A fallen angel from the class of angels known as the **Watchers.** In the chronicles of **Enoch** he is listed as having led the angels into disobedience by encouraging them to pursue mortal women. Asb'el is a variation of Asbeel.

✤**ASB'EL:** See **Asbeel.**

✤**ASCENSION:** In religious and spiritual beliefs, the word *ascension* is associated with souls rising to Heaven after death. Many believe that angels escort the soul as it ascends to Heaven. In the modern era the word *ascension* is defined in a new way. There is the belief that some people ascend to a higher state of being and later return to earth to become teachers and healers as Jesus was. It is believed that the earth will evolve from the third dimension to the fifth dimension. During this evolution, the earth's atmosphere will greatly shift, causing climatic disturbances such as storms, great earthquakes, and other adverse conditions. Those who come back to teach after their ascension will prepare the people of the earth for the move into the fifth dimension. The angels are said to be working with the ascended masters who are overseeing this change. One of the leaders is the archangel **Michael** (Note: Eric Klein's book *The Crystal Stair* features channeled information from higher beings regarding the ascension. It also includes messages from the archangel Michael.)

✤**ASCENSION OF CHRIST:** During his ascension, Jesus was escorted to Heaven by two angels. The Bible describes them as "two men in white garments" (Acts 1:10–11). As the apostles watched Jesus ascend, the angels informed them that Jesus would return in the same manner. According to lore, these angels were from the class of angels called

Virtues. It is said that it took Jesus and the angels three days to ascend to the **Seventh Heaven** (also known as Arabot).

✤**ASDER'EL:** An angel from the order of angels called the **Watchers.** Asder'el brought the knowledge of the phases of the moon to earth. This knowledge continues to be used throughout the world to this day.

✤**AS'EL:** A variation of **Asel.**

✤**ASEL:** One of the leaders of the **Watchers.** Asel along with many other Watchers sinned against God's laws when they came to earth to pursue women. Variations of the name Asel are As'el and Asael.

✤**ASHA:** The male counterpart of **Ashi,** an angel in Zoroastrianism. Asha is the angel of truth and the protector of fire. Considered the most beautiful of all the **Amesha Spentas,** Asha represents divine law, order, and morality. Those who follow him are called Ashavan. Those who do not follow him cannot enter Heaven. Godly people pray to see Asha so that they may follow him to Paradise where they will live forever in peace and righteousness. He fights death, the wicked, sickness, and all that is in opposition to the goodness of **Ahura Mazda** (God). In Hell he makes certain that the good are not disciplined beyond what their transgression merits. **Indra,** the spirit of apostasy, is his opponent. This is because apostasy lures men away from God. He is also called Asha Vahishta.

✤**ASHA VAHISHTA:** Another name for **Asha.**

✤**ASHAVAN:** The name of the followers of **Asha,** the angel of truth, in Zoroastrianism.

✤**ASHI:** The angel of blessings in Zoroastrianism. The female form of **Asha.**

✤**ASHMA DAEVA:** A variation of the name of **Aeshma Daeva,** a high-ranking demon.

✤**ASHMEDAI:** A messenger of God in Judaism. In some writings he is considered evil. According to lore, Ashmedai was the serpent who deceived Eve in the Garden of Eden.

✤**ASHRULYAI:** An angel who stands guard over the palace of Wilon, the **First Heaven.**

✤**ASMADAI:** A variation of the name **Asmodeus.**

✤**ASMODAI:** A variation of the name **Asmodeus.**

✤**ASMODEL:** The angel who governs the month of April.

✤**ASMODEUS:** The angel of judgment. Asmodeus was first found in Persian lore (originally his name was **Ashma Daeva**). Gradually he was adopted into Judaism where he became a high-ranking demon. Banished to Egypt by the archangel **Raphael,** Asmodeus ended up in Hell where he became controller of the gaming houses. He is said to be the child of Tubal-Cain and **Naamah.** King **Solomon** once had him captured and brought to him for interrogation. Asmodeus told Solomon that he was the offspring of a human and an angel. His demonic activity includes plotting against newlyweds and marring the beauty of virgins. According to the Testament of Solomon, Asmodeus can be rendered powerless by the archangel Raphael, as well as a liver and smoking gall of a fish. Variations of the name Asmodeus are Asmadai and Asmodai.

✤**ASPIRATIONS, ANGEL OF:** The archangel **Gabriel.**

✤**ASROILU YHWH:** A great angelic prince in Heaven. He is head of the angelic school. The angelic school is a place where the angels gain knowledge and insights on the mysteries of the universe.

✤**ASSUMED BODIES:** A term referring to the bodies that angels take on to perform their earthly missions. Angels are thought by many theologians and scholars to be incorporeal beings lacking in substance, taking on assumed bodies when they come to earth. Some have contended that these bodies are not real bodies at all, but visions of bodies that are incapable of performing the natural functions of an earthly body. However, the Bible contradicts this thinking. In their assumed bodies, the first biblical angels ate and drank with the prophet **Abraham** (Genesis 18:1–8). In addition, there were angels who came to earth and had sexual relations with women, with whom they also fathered children (Genesis 6:2). See **Nature of Angels.**

✤**ASSYRIA(NS):** The Assyrian cosmology included several angelic-type deities. There was Barku, the god of storms. Barku was another name for **Rimmon,** an angel of storms. For the exorcism of demons, Assyrians called on Lamassu, a deity who thwarted evil spirits. There were also the Lumazi, spirits who the Assyrians believed created the universe.

✤**ASTANPHAEUS:** An angel of the **presence.**

✤**ASTANPHAIOS:** One of the seven **Archons** (angels) of gnosticism.

✤**ASTAROTH:** A high-ranking demon in Hell. He is the masculine form of **Astarte.**

✤**ASTARTE:** The female equivalent of the demon **Astaroth.** To some she is the she-demon who rules the souls of the dead. To others she is the **Queen of Heaven.** The Egyptians and the Indo-Europeans worshiped her as a goddess. In Aramaic she was known as the Morning Star of Heaven. Other names by which Astarte has been called include Astroarche, **Athtar, Isis,** Nut, Hathor, Stella Maris, and Venus in the Morning.

✤**ASTAS:** One of the seventy-eight names of **Metatron.**

✤**ASTERAOTH:** An angel who has the ability to thwart the demon named **Power.**

✤**ASTROARCHE:** Another name for **Astarte.**

✤**ASTROLOGY, ANGEL OF: Baraqiyal.** Baraqiyal brought the knowledge of astrology to the earth. This knowledge has been widely used for centuries and is still being used around the world today. Astrology was considered one of the mysteries of Heaven. Baraqiyal fell from grace when he revealed this knowledge to mankind.

✤**Astronomy, Angel of: Kokabi'el.** Kokabi'el brought to the earth the knowledge of the stars and the constellations.

✤**Asuras:** Another name for the Persian angels called **Ahuras.**

✤**Asuryal:** An angel from the chronicles of **Enoch.** God sent Asuryal to warn **Noah** of the impending flood.

✤**Atail:** An angel summoned in Arabic ceremonies to ward off evil spirits.

✤**Atar:** The angel who presides over fire in Zoroastrianism.

✤**Atarculph:** A fallen angel.

✤**Atatyah:** One of the seventy-eight names of **Metatron.**

✤**Athanasius, Saint:** See **Saint Athanasius.**

✤**Athena:** The goddess of war and peace in Greek mythology. In the first book of the *Iliad* (a Greek epic poem), Athena acts as a guardian spirit toward Achilles. Only he can see her and hear her. She comes to give him advice on how to perform in combat against Agamemnon. In the *Odyssey,* **Ulysses** is several times rescued by **Zeus** through the intervention of Athena, again posing as a guardian spirit.

✤**Atheniel:** One of twenty-eight angels who preside over the **lunar mansions.**

✤**Athtar:** The Egyptian name for **Astarte,** a she-demon. The Egyptians referred to her as Venus in the Morning.

✤**Atliel:** One of twenty-eight angels who preside over the **lunar mansions.**

✤**Atonement Day:** See **Day of Atonement.**

✤**Atrugiel YHWH:** A great angelic prince in Heaven.

✤**Attaris:** An angel who presides over the winter season.

✤**Attaryah:** One of the seventy-eight names of the mighty angel **Metatron.**

✤**Atuniel:** The angel of fire in rabbinic lore.

✤**Aufiel:** A variation of the name **Haniel.** Haniel is the angel of Venus and the angel of love.

✤**August, Angel of: Hamaliel.** He is also the angel of Virgo.

✤**Augustine, Saint:** See **Saint Augustine.**

✤**Auphanim:** A variation of the name **Ophanim.** Ophanim is another name for the order of angels called the **Thrones.**

✤**Aureola:** See **Aureole.**

✤**Aureole(s):** Père Lamy once wrote, "Their garments are white, but with an unearthly whiteness. I cannot describe it, because it cannot be compared to earthly whiteness; it is much softer to the eye. These bright Angels are enveloped in a light so different from ours that by comparison everything seems dark." In his *Divine Comedy*, **Dante** wrote, "They had their faces all of living flame, And wings of gold and all the rest so white that never snow has known such purity." Angels are often described in scripture and literature with phrases such as "white as snow," "like lightning," and "shining ones." These terms all refer to the brilliant light that the angels radiate. This light is called the aureole. It is a radiant light that encircles the head or body of an angel. This light is said to be different from what humans perceive on earth. It is a brilliant light, but not blinding. It symbolizes God's divine light, the purity of the angels, and their holy position in Heaven. The higher their position in the angelic hierarchy, the more radiant the light becomes. The Seraphim and Cherubim are the highest angels in Heaven. According to scripture, they are so radiant that the other angels cannot look upon them. A variation of *aureole* is *aureola*. See **Halo.**

✤**AURIEL:** The angel of night. The name Auriel is a variation of **Uriel.**

✤**AUSIEL:** The angel of **Aquarius.** A variation of the name Ausiel is Ausiul.

✤**AUSIUL:** A variation of the name **Ausiel.**

✤**AUTHORITIES:** Another name for the class of angels called **Powers.** The Powers are the angels who bring balance to the earth.

✤**AUTUMN, ANGEL OF:** The archangel **Michael.** The angels **Guabarel,** Tarquam, and **Gabriel** have also been listed as angels of autumn.

✤**AVARTIEL:** An angel who, when summoned, protects individuals from wicked spirits.

✤**AVATAR(S):** Ten semi-angelic beings in Hinduism who were incarnations of **Vishnu.** When manifested, they came in human and animal form. The names of the avatars are Buddha, Kalki, Krishna, Kurma, Matsga, Narasimha, Parasurana, Rama, Vamana, and Varaha.

✤**AVENGING ANGELS:** Angels who punish the wicked in Hell.

✤**AVESTA, THE:** The holy book of **Zoroastrianism.** The Avesta includes the Gathas, which are twenty-one hymns of Zoroaster; and the Yasna, a collection of prayers and invocations. In the Avesta, Zoroaster wrote down his experiences with numerous angels. Included are **Ahura Mazda,** the Supreme Being; **Angra Mainyu,** the spirit of darkness; the **Amesha Spentas,** archangels; and ministering angels.

✤**AVIAL:** An angel who stands guard over the palace of Zebul, the **Fourth Heaven.**

✤**AVICENNA:** Persian philosopher and physician (A.D. 980–1037). He was the most renowned philosopher in Medieval Islam. Avicenna believed that the angels are responsible for the movement, balance, and order of the universe.

✦**Ayil:** The angel of **Sagittarius.**

✦**Azael (Whom God Strengthens):** In the chronicles of **Enoch** he was a ministering angel in Heaven. He later became a fallen angel when he came to the earth along with **Uzzah** and **Azzah** and taught sorcery to humans. He also had sexual relations with a mortal woman named **Naamah.** She later gave birth to a son and named him Azza, which means "strong one."

✦**Azarail:** An angel summoned in Arabic beliefs for help in chasing away evil spirits.

✦**Azarias:** An alias used by the archangel **Raphael** in the *Book of Tobit*, where he is a companion to the young **Tobias.**

✦**Azariel:** An angel that is called upon to thwart evil spirits. He is also one of twenty-eight angels who preside over the **lunar mansions.**

✦**Azaril:** A variation of the name **Azrael,** the angel of death in Islam.

✦**Azaz'el:** Chief of the **Watchers.** God blamed Azaz'el for the Watchers coming to earth and teaching humankind the secrets of Heaven. Azaz'el taught humans the art of making knives, swords, shields, and breastplates. He taught women to use jewelry and cosmetics. Because of this God had **Raphael** bind him and throw him into an abyss in the desert in Duda'el. Boulders were thrown on top of him. His face was covered so that he could not see the light. In the occult Azaz'el is a demon. In Judaic lore, it was Azaz'el who refused to bow down to Adam, whom God had placed above the angels. See **Day of Atonement.**

✦**Azbogah YHWH:** A great angelic prince in Heaven. He clothes the new arrivals in Heaven in garments of righteousness.

✦**Azeruel:** One of the angels of the twenty-eight **lunar mansions.**

✦**Aziel (He Whom God Gives Strength):** The angel of hidden treasures. He is one of the five angels of judgment who lead the souls of man to stand before the judgment of God. He is also listed as one of the angels of the twenty-eight **lunar mansions.**

✦**Azrael:** The angel of death in both Islam and Judaism. In Judeo-Christian beliefs he is the archangel **Raphael.** According to Islamic beliefs, Azrael is seated on a throne in Makon, the **Sixth Heaven.** Variations of Azrael are Azaril and Izrail.

✦**Azriel:** One of the leaders of the angels of destruction. He is also an angel who watches over the earth.

✦**Azur:** The angel who ruled the month of November in ancient Persia.

✤**AZURAS:** A variation of the name **Ahuras,** which are angels in Persian mythology.

✤**AZZA:** A variation of the name **Shemyaza.** It is also the name of a son of **Azael** and a mortal woman named **Naamah.**

✤**AZZAH:** In 3 Enoch, Azzah is a ministering angel who questions God about his making **Enoch** a lofty angel and giving him a high position in Heaven. Says 3 Enoch 4:7, "Lord of the Universe, what right has this one to ascend to the height of heights? Is he not descended from those who perished in the waters of the Flood? What right has he to be in heaven?" Because of this he was cast out of Heaven forever. According to legend, he was punished by being hung upside down between Heaven and earth. He is later portrayed in the writings of Enoch as a fallen angel who brought the knowledge of sorcery to the earth.

B

It is not because angels are holier than men or devils that makes them angels, but because they do not expect holiness from one another, but from God alone.

—WILLIAM BLAKE

✦**BAAL-BERYTH:** A fallen angel. He was once a member of the **Cherubim** class. After his fall from grace he became the "master of ceremonies" in Hades.

✦**BAAL-PEOR:** A fallen angel who was once a lord of the order of **Principalities.** He later became a duke of Hell, taking on such titles as Demonic Ambassador to France and Guardian Demon of Paris. Variations of the name Baal-Peor are Belphegor and Belfagor.

✦**BAALZEBUB:** A variation of **Beelzebub.**

✦**BABIES, ANGEL OF: Temeluchus.**

✦**BABY ANGELS: Putti.**

✦**BABYLON, ANGELS OF:** An ancient city of Mesopotamia famous for its richness and luxury. The people of Babylon believed in a number of angelic beings. Among them were the winged bull-men, and the spirit messengers called Sukalli. Babylonians believed that each individual had a guardian spirit protecting him. These spirits mediated between them and the gods. If an individual performed an unrighteous act, the spirit would leave him. If the individual repented, the spirit would forgive him and return. When **Zoroastrianism** was introduced into Babylon's culture, many Babylonian gods were turned into angels. These angels later became a part of Judaism and Christianity. The Babylonians considered the seven planets to be gods, and these are thought to be the archetypal seven archangels. One notorious deity of Babylonian lore was **Rimmon,** the god of thunder and lightning. When adopted into Christianity, he became a demon of Hell. See **Babylon the Great.**

✤**BABYLON THE GREAT, ANGEL OF:** In some Christian beliefs, the term Babylon the Great is symbolic of all of the false religions on earth. In **Revelation** 14:8 an angel flies through the air saying, "She has fallen! Babylon the Great has fallen, she who made all the nations drink of the wine of the anger of her fornication." The fall of Babylon the Great is one of the many events that some Christians believe will occur before the end of the world, also known as **Armageddon.**

✤**BACHLIEL:** An angel who safeguards the south wind.

✤**BAD ANGELS:** See **Corrupt Angels, Demons, Fallen Angels.**

✤**BAHALIEL:** An angel who safeguards the east wind.

✤**BALAAM:** In the Bible, Balaam was a diviner who was famous for the curses he put on people. In Numbers chapter twenty-two, it tells the story of Balaam and the angel. Balaam was sent by the king of Moab to put a curse on the Hebrews. Balaam hesitated at first, because he feared the Hebrew God. However, he decided to go after God gave authorization for his trip, on the condition that he would speak only what God himself told him to say. However, God was angered when, during the trip, Balaam started thinking about the rewards that Balak the King had promised him if he would put a curse on the Hebrews. God then sent an angel with a drawn sword to prevent him from continuing on the journey. Unbeknownst to Balaam, the donkey he was riding saw the angel standing in the middle of the road. The donkey, frightened, turned off the road to avoid the angel. Balaam, unable to see the angel, beat the donkey to make her turn back onto the road. The angel spoke through the donkey to Balaam and finally opened Balaam's eyes so that he could see him. When Balaam saw the angel standing before him, he prostrated himself on his face and confessed his sin. He offered to return home. However, the angel instructed him to continue on the journey, but told him not to say anything except what God told him.

✤**BALAM:** A fallen angel who once belonged to the order of angels called the **Dominations.** He later became a powerful demon in Hell.

✤**BALANCE, ANGEL OF:** The archangel **Michael** is sometimes referred to as the Master of Balance.

✤**BALL, LUCILLE:** In *Forever Darling*, a popular 1956 film, Lucille Ball plays Susan Bewell, a wacky socialite who is visited by her guardian angel, played by veteran screen actor James Mason.

✤BALM: The archangel **Raphael** is said to carry a golden vial of balm. This symbolizes his position as the angel of healing.

✤BALTHIOUL: An angel found in the Testament of **Solomon.** Balthioul has the power to thwart the demon named **Distress.**

✤BAND OF ANGELS: The phrase *band of angels* usually applies to a "group" or a "gathering" of angels. It also means a troupe of angel musicians.

✤BANKERS, ANGEL OF: **Anauel.**

✤BAPTISMAL WATER, ANGEL OF: The archangel **Raphael.**

✤BARACHIEL: A variation of the name **Barakiel,** a ruler of the **Seraphim.**

✤BARADI'EL: The ruling prince of the **Third Heaven,** also known as Sehaqim.

✤BARAKIEL (GOD'S LIGHTNING): One of the magnificent angelic princes of Heaven. He is ministered to by 496,000 angels. He holds the titles of Angel of February, Ruler of Lightning, Ruler of Raquia (the **Second Heaven**), Angel of Pisces, and Leader of the Confessors. He is also an archangel in both Judaism and **Gnosticism.** In addition, he is called upon for luck at winning games of chance. Variations of the name Barakiel are Baraqiel, Baraquiel, Barchiel, and Barkiel.

✤BARAQIEL: A variation of the name **Barakiel.**

✤BARAQIJAL: An angel from the class of angels called **Watchers.** A variation of the name Baraqijal is Bariqijael.

✤BARAQIYAL: A leader of the group of angels who came to the earth to have sexual relations with women. These angels were from the **Grigori** class.

✤BARAQUIEL: A variation of the name **Barakiel.** Barakiel is the ruling angel of Raquia, the **Second Heaven.**

✤BARATTI'EL: A great prince in Heaven. According to lore Baratti'el is holding up the **Seventh Heaven.**

✤BARBATOS: A fallen angel.

✤BARBELO: A fallen angel, and one of the daughters of **Pistis-Sophia** (mother of the **Aeons**). Outside of Satan she was considered the most beautiful angel in Heaven. It has been said that she was even more glorious than God himself. The reason for her fall is unknown.

✤BARBIEL: The angel of October, and the angel of Scorpio. He is also a prince of the **archangels,** and a prince of the **Virtues.** In addition, he is one of the angels who preside over the twenty-eight **lunar mansions.** Variations of the name Barbiel are Barbuel and Baruel.

✤BARBONAH: A variation of the name **Harbonah,** the angel of annihilation.

✤**BARBUEL:** A variation of the name **Barbiel,** the angel of October.

✤**BARCELONI, AL:** An author of mystical writings during the post-Talmudic period. His writings were the first to name all of the archangels in Islam. Although Islam recognizes four archangels, the Koran lists only two, **Jibril** and **Mikhail.** The two unnamed angels according to Barceloni are **Azrael** and **Israfel.**

✤**BARCHIEL:** A variation of the name **Barakiel.**

✤**BARDAS:** One of the seventy-eight names of the mighty angel **Metatron.**

✤**BARDIEL:** The angel of hailstorms.

✤**BARESCHAS:** A fallen angel. He is called on by men to help them acquire the affections of a desired woman. A variation of the name Bareschas is Baresches.

✤**BARESCHES:** A variation of the name **Bareschas.**

✤**BARIQIJAEL:** A variation of **Baraqijal.**

✤**BARKIEL:** A variation of the name **Barakiel.**

✤**BARKU:** Another name for **Rimmon,** the angel of storms.

✤**BARRENNESS, ANGELS OF:** The angels **Akriel** and **Zidkiel** are both angels of barrenness. When called upon, they are believed to help women to conceive. There are two accounts in the Bible involving women who were barren. Abraham's wife, **Sarah,** was unable to conceive children, as was Elizabeth, the wife of **Zechariah.** Both women were aided in becoming pregnant by angels (Genesis 18:1–15; Luke 1:5–19).

✤**BARSAFAEL:** A demon who causes headaches. In the Testament of Solomon, King **Solomon** captures and imprisons Barsafael through the use of a **magic ring.**

✤**BARTH, KARL:** A Swiss Protestant theologian (1886–1968). Barth was one of the leading thinkers of Protestantism in the twentieth century. He expounded on his beliefs in many writings. One such writing was his *Church Dogmatics,* in which he wrote that angels had been misrepresented in art. He felt that Christian art was entirely inappropriate in its depiction of angels. He deplored paintings that portrayed angels as babies and believed that the angels should have been pictured as mighty and powerful beings. He felt that the angels were so magnificent, the human imagination could never capture their real beauty and splendor.

✤**BARUCH (GOD BLESSES):** The name Baruch has two meanings. First, Baruch is a guardian of the **Tree of Life.** He is one of three angels sent by God to assist humankind. In the occult he is considered a demon. Baruch is also a writer of four Apocryphal books filled with information and tales of angels. The books are named the Book of Baruch, the Apocalypse of Baruch, the Greek Apocalypse of Baruch, and the Rest of the

Words of Baruch. The books were written at different periods between the first century and the second century A.D.

✦**Baruchiel:** An angel given in the Testament of **Solomon** as being able to thwart the powerful demon named **Strife.** He is also thought to be one of the three unnamed archangels of Judeo-Christian beliefs.

✦**Baruel:** A variation of the name **Barbiel.** He is also one of the angels who preside over the twenty-eight **lunar mansions.**

✦**Basas'el:** One of the angels who brought the secret knowledge of Heaven to earth.

✦**Bashmallin:** A high order of angels that are equated with the **Dominations.** They are also called Hashmallim.

✦**Batanel:** A fallen angel from the **Grigori** class.

✦**Batar'el:** One of the leaders of the group of **Watchers** who came to earth to pursue women.

✦**Batarjal:** A fallen angel.

✦**Batna:** An alias used by the she-demon **Lilith** when working evil against humans.

✦**Battle in Heaven:** See **War in Heaven.**

✦**Bazazath:** An angel found in the Testament of **Solomon.** Bazazath has the ability to thwart a powerful demon called the **Winged Dragon.**

✦**Be an Angel Day:** A day set aside for people to dispense goodwill to one another and do special favors for each other. It is observed on August 22.

✦**Bear Deity:** The angel **Dubbiel,** who was the guardian angel of Persia, was also known as the bear deity.

✦**Bearer of Light:** A title held by **Lucifer,** denoting the brilliance he radiates.

✦**Beart, Emmanuelle:** Star of the movie *Date With an Angel.* Beart plays an angel whose mission is to come to earth and escort the soul of a dying young man back to Heaven.

✦**Beatrice Portenari:** An angel in **Dante**'s poem *The Divine Comedy.* She was a woman whom Dante loved his entire life (from the tender age of nine until his death). He vowed to write about her as no man had ever written about a woman. He ultimately chose to portray her as a splendid, beautiful angel. Beatrice can also be found in Dante's poem *La Vita Nuova.*

✦**Beatty, Warren:** Film actor Warren Beatty directed and starred in one of the most popular movies featuring angels, the 1978 film *Heaven Can Wait.* In the film Beatty plays Joe Pendleton, a quarterback who has an accident and meets with an early death. This leads Joe and the angels on a comedic search for a suitable earthly replacement for Joe's spirit.

✤**BEAUTY:** The name of one of the ten **Holy Sefiroth.** The Holy Sefiroth are angels of the **Cabala.**

✤**BEAUTY OF GOD:** The meaning of the name **Iophiel,** a high-ranking angel of Heaven.

✤**BEDALIEL:** An angel called upon in exorcisms to ward off demons.

✤**BEDRIMULAEL:** An angel invoked in magic.

✤**BEELZEBOUB:** A variation of **Beelzebub.**

✤**BEELZEBOUL:** A variation of **Beelzebub.**

✤**BEELZEBUB:** In the Testament of **Solomon,** Beelzebub calls himself the **ruler of the demons.** He was once the highest-ranking angel in Heaven. In John Milton's *Paradise Lost,* Satan addresses Beelzebub as a fallen **Cherub.** In the New Testament, the Pharisees accused Jesus of casting out devils by means of Beelzebub, the Prince of Devils (Matthew 12:24–29). Beelzebub is also known as Lord of the Flies and The Lord of Chaos. In some writings he is Satan. Other accounts suggest that the two are separate entities. In the Old Testament he was the god of Ekron, whom Ahaziah wanted to confer with but was stopped by the prophet **Elijah**'s interruption (2 Kings 1:1–6, 16). The name Beelzebub is said to be the Hebrew name for the Canaanite god, Baalzebul. He is also found in **Dante**'s *Divine Comedy,* Gurdjieff's *All and Everything, Beelzebub's Tales,* and *Beelzebub's Tales to His Grandson.* Variations of the name Beelzebub are Beelzeboub, Baalzebub, and Beelzeboul.

✤**BEERLAHAIROI, ANGEL OF:** In the Bible, Beerlahairoi is the well in which the pregnant **Hagar** (the handmaid to Abraham's wife, **Sarah**) was visited by an angel of the Lord. After fleeing into the wilderness to escape the wrath of Sarah, Hagar came upon a well. There an angel of the Lord appeared to her and told her that she would give birth to a son, and that she should call him Ishmael. He informed her that God would multiply her seed by many. Awed by this experience, Hagar called the well Beerlahairoi, which means "the well of him who lives and sees me" (Genesis 16:1–14).

✤**BEERSHEBA, ANGEL OF:** At his wife Sarah's request, the prophet **Abraham** sent the handmaid **Hagar** and their son Ishmael away. Eventually, Hagar wandered into the wilderness of Beersheba. Exhausted and dehydrated, she put her son Ishmael under a bush and walked away, asking God not to let her see it when he died. God, who heard the boy's crying from Heaven, sent an angel to speak with her. The angel called out to her saying, "What are you troubled about, Hagar? Don't be afraid. God has heard the boy crying. Get up, go and pick him up, and comfort him. God will make a great nation out of his descendants." Then God opened her eyes, and she saw a well. (Genesis 21:17–19)

✤**BEHEMIEL:** An angel who watches over domestic animals.

✤**BEHEMOTH:** A demon listed in the chronicles of **Enoch.**

✤**BEINGS OF LIGHT:** A phrase often used when referring to the angels. It refers to the light and energy that the angels radiate when they appear to humans on earth. This light is said to be different from the light that humans perceive on earth. The light of the angels is brilliant yet not blinding. It is said to have a soft, gentle glow.

✤**BELBEL:** A demon.

✤**BELETH:** A fallen angel from the class of angels called the **Powers.** He is also a chief demon of Hell who commands eighty-five troops of devils. Variations of his name include Byleth, Bilet, Bileth.

✤**BELFAGOR:** A variation of the name **Baal-Peor.** Baal-Peor is a fallen angel who was once a great lord of the order of **Principalities.** He later became a duke of Hell.

✤**BELIAEL:** An angel who safeguards the north wind.

✤**BELIAL:** A variation of **Beliar.**

✤**BELIAR (WORTHLESS):** The **Prince of Darkness.** He is said to be the first angel created and the first to fall. He is formerly of the class of angels called **Virtues.** His titles also include Angel of Darkness and Destruction and Ruler of Sheol. In 2 Corinthians 6:14–15, Paul uses the name Beliar (in some translations it is Belial) as a synonym for the Devil. Paul states, "What sharing does light have with darkness? Further, what harmony is there between Christ and Beliar?" The **Essenes** believed that the world was controlled by Beliar. In the scroll *The War of the Sons of Light Against the Sons of Darkness,* Beliar is referred to as the Prince of Darkness. The army serving under Beliar is referred to as the Dark Legions. In many writings Beliar and Satan are the same.

✤**BELPHEGOR:** A variation of the name **Baal-Peor.** A fallen angel who was once a lord of the order of **Principalities.** He later became a great duke of Hell.

✤**BENAD HASCHE:** Female angels of Arabic lore.

✤**BENAIAH:** In Judaic lore, Benaiah was an emissary of King **Solomon.** He helped Solomon to capture the powerful demon **Asmodeus.**

✤**BENE ELOHIM:** A variation of **Bene ha-Elohim.**

✤**BENE HA-ELOHIM (GOD'S CHILDREN):** Angels who sing praises of God both night and day. In some writings they are equated with the **Grigori.** Other writings refer to them as "sons of God." A variation of Bene ha-Elohim is Bene Elohim.

✤**BENEVOLENCE, ANGELS OF:** There are three angels of benevolence: Achsah, Hasdiel, and **Zadkiel.**

✤**BEQA (VIRTUOUS PERSON):** A fallen angel. He rebelled against God the day he was created. After his fall, he took the name **Kasbel,** which means "deceiver of God." A variation of the name Beqa is Biqa.

✤**BERNADETTE OF LOURDES:** See **Soubirous, Bernadette.**

✤**BESHTER:** An angel in charge of providing nourishment to mankind. In Persian lore Beshter was equated with the archangel **Michael.**

✤**BESIHI:** One of the seventy-eight names of **Metatron.**

✤**BETHNAEL:** One of twenty-eight angels who rule the **lunar mansions.**

✤**BETHUEL:** An angel who wards off evil spirits.

✤**BETRYAL:** One of the angels who brought the secret knowledge of Heaven to earth.

✤**BEWELL, SUSAN:** The name of a character from the popular 1956 movie entitled *Forever Darling.* In the film Lucille Ball plays young socialite Susan Bewell, who is visited by her guardian angel. The angel is played by veteran screen actor James Mason.

✤**BEZALIEL:** An angel who watches over the north wind.

✤**BEZRIAL:** An angel who stands guard over the palace of Sehaqim, the **Third Heaven.**

✤**BHAGA:** One of the **Adityas** (angels) of Vedic beliefs.

✤**BIBLE, ANGELS OF THE:** The Bible is the holy book of Christianity. It contains the Hebrew scriptures, also called the Old Testament, and the Christian Greek scriptures, which make up the New Testament. In the Bible, angels are mentioned nearly three hundred times. They are portrayed as spiritual beings who generally come as messengers of God. According to the Book of **Job,** they existed before humankind and witnessed the creation of the earth (Job 38:7). They are pure and uncorrupted beings; however, the scriptures reveal that they are not immune to temptation, sin, and falling away from God's laws (Genesis 6:1–2, Job 4:18, Matthew 25:41, 2 Peter 2:4, Revelation 12:9). **Gabriel, Michael,** and **Abaddon** are the only angels listed by name in the Bible. Satan is the only fallen angel to be called by name. ANGEL OF THE LORD. Found in the Old Testament, the Angel of the Lord (also Angel of God) is God's personal spokesman. He has no individual characteristics except that he is a mediator for God. In the New Testament he is personalized as the **Holy Spirit** and also the archangel Gabriel. In addition to acting as a spokesman for God, he gives guidance and instructions, judges and destroys disobedient people, protects and delivers the good, and brings announcements about important births such as those of **Isaac, Samson, John the Baptist,** and **Jesus.** When he appears to men, he is sometimes mistakenly addressed as "God." He appears to **Hagar** in the wilderness (Genesis 16:7–13, 21:17–20), **Abraham** at **Mount Moriah** (Genesis 22:11–18), **Moses** in the **burning bush** (Exodus 3:2), and to **Gideon** at Ophrah (Judges 6:11). ANGELIC FUNCTIONS. In addition to acting as messengers, the angels performed other functions in the Bible. They appeared to men to bring orders from God. They sometimes gave aid to servants of God including military assistance. They stood in for God in showing God's wrath toward the Hebrews. They even destroyed entire cities of evildoers, such as **Sodom and Gomorrah.** OLD TESTAMENT. In the Bible's Old Testament the angels have very humanlike qualities. They appear as ordinary men and eat and drink as humans do. The first mention of angels in the Old Testament are the two **Cherubim** whom God places outside of the **Garden of Eden** (Genesis 3:23, 24). People from the Old Testament who had encounters with the angels include Abraham, **Balaam, Daniel, Shadrach, Meshach, Abednego, Ezekiel, Elijah, Manoah,** Gideon, Hagar, **Jacob, Joshua, Isaiah, Lot,** and Moses. Hagar was visited by an angel twice while in the wilderness (Genesis 16:1–14 and 21:17–19). Abraham was visited by three angels who announced to him that his wife, Sarah, would conceive and give birth to a son (Genesis 18). Abraham was later prevented by an angel from sacrificing his son Isaac (Genesis 22:1–12). Lot was visited by two angels who came to warn him of the destruction of **Sodom** (Genesis 19: 1–22). Jacob dreamed of a heavenly ladder with angels coming and going between Heaven and earth (Genesis 28:12). Jacob also wrestled with an angel (Genesis 32:25). An angel of the Lord spoke to Moses in the midst of a burning bush (Exodus 3:2). Balaam is prevented from continuing on a journey by an angel who confronts him with a drawn sword (Numbers 22:22–35). An angel visited Joshua to inspire confidence in him (Joshua 5:13–15). An angel visited Gideon to assure him that God was with him (Judges 6:11–14). An angel announced the birth of Samson to Manoah and his wife (Judges 13: 2–5). An angel comforted Elijah (1 Kings 19:4–8). Isaiah had a vision of angels (Isaiah 6:1–7). Shadrach, Meshach, and Abednego were saved from a fiery furnace by an angel (Daniel 3:24–28). An angel rescued Daniel from a lion's den (Daniel 6:22). The archangel Gabriel interprets a prophecy for Daniel (Daniel 8:15–17). The archangel Michael interprets a vision for Daniel (Daniel 10:12–14). Ezekiel also saw angels in a vision (Ezekiel 1:4–9). NEW TESTAMENT. The angels of Christianity act as messengers and ministers of God. They announce the **Last Judgment,** separate the good from the wicked, carry the prayers of the devoted to God, give strength to the meek, and comfort the discouraged. There are two **archangels** listed by name in the New Testament, Michael (Revelation 12:7) and Gabriel (Luke 1:19, 1:26). Another angel listed by name is Abaddon, the angel of the abyss (Revelation 9:11). People in the New Testament who received visitations from angels include **Zechariah,** who was visited by Gabriel to inform him that he was to become a father (Luke 1:11, 18–20). The **Virgin Mary** was also visited by Gabriel, who told her that she would give birth to the Messiah (Luke 1:26–33). An angel appeared to **Joseph** in a dream informing him that Mary was pregnant by the Holy Spirit (Matthew 1:20–21). An angel appeared to **shepherds** in a field and informed them that their savior had been born (Luke 2:9–15). Jesus was ministered to, strengthened, and escorted to Heaven by angels (Matthew 4:11, Luke 22:43, Acts 1:10–11). An angel appeared to two women, both named Mary, as they visited the **tomb of Jesus** (Matthew 28:2–6). **Peter** was rescued from prison by an angel (Acts 5:19). While sailing in a violent storm, **Paul** was comforted by an angel (Acts 27:23–24). **Philip** the evangelist was guided by an angel to an Ethiopian eunuch to baptize him (Acts 8:26). King **Herod** was struck to death by an angel (Acts 12:23). **John** was given a revelation of the last days by an angel (Revelation 1:1).

✦**BIGTHA:** One of the angels of **confusion.**

✦**BILET:** A variation of the name **Beleth,** a chief demon of Hell.

✦**BILETH:** A variation of the name **Beleth,** a chief demon of Hell.

✦**BINAH:** One of the ten **Holy Sefiroth.** He is also called Understanding.

✦**BIQA:** A variation of the name **Beqa.**

✦**BIRDS(s):** Throughout history birds have been a symbol for angels. **Birds of God** is a term sometimes used when referring to the angels. In addition, various birdlike beings can be found in religious beliefs around the world. In Russian folklore the **Alkanosts** are known as Birds of Paradise. The Alkanosts are winged, birdlike female figures. Native North Americans worshiped a god they referred to as **Thunderbird.** He is symbolized by the eagle and the hawk. In Etrurian beliefs there was **Charon,** the god of the dead. He had huge wings and a large crooked nose resembling the beak of a bird. He carried the souls of the dead to Hades. In Judaic lore there is the **Phoenix,** a bird who resides in Heaven. He is charged with protecting the earth from the rays of the sun.

✦**BIRDS, ANGEL OF:** Ariael.

✦**BIRDS OF GOD:** A term used in **Dante's** *Divine Comedy* when referring to angels.

✦**BIRDS OF PARADISE:** The **Alkanosts** are also called Birds of Paradise. These beautiful winged beings give pleasure to the men who inhabit Paradise.

✤BIRTH(S), ANGELS OF: The angel of birth is named **Lailah.** In addition, the archangel **Gabriel** is responsible for the foretelling of important births.

✤*BISHOP'S WIFE, THE:* A 1947 movie about a jaunty angel named **Dudley** who is sent to earth on a mission to help a bishop in need of a new church. The movie stars Cary Grant, James Gleason, David Niven, and Loretta Young. It is directed by Henry Koster.

✤BIZTHA: One of the angels of **confusion.**

✤BLACK, ANGEL OF: The color black represents the angel **Auriel,** who is the angel of the night. Black also represents **Casziel,** the angel of **tears.**

✤BLACK ANGELS: A term used in Islam in referring to demons.

✤BLACK ONE: **Kali,** who is one of the **Shakti** of Hinduism, is often referred to as the Black One. She is said to be the absolute energy in which colors fuse into formless darkness.

✤BLAKE, WILLIAM: English poet, artist, visionary, and mystic (1757–1827). As a child Blake saw a tree filled with angels. Later in life, he believed that his work was guided by angels and credited his creative genius to them. During his lifetime he created a large number of memorable drawings and paintings featuring angels. Some of the most famous include *Elohim Creating Adam, Satan Smiting Job with Sore Boils, The Good and Evil Angels, The Simoniac Pope, A Father's Memoirs of His Child, The Meeting of a Family in Heaven*, and *What Gleams for Joy*. He also illustrated poets such as **Dante, Milton,** and Bunyan. About angels Blake once wrote, "It is not because angels are holier than men or devils that makes them angels, but because they do not expect holiness from one another, but from God alone."

✤BLESSED MOTHER: In Catholicism the **Virgin Mary** is sometimes referred to as the Blessed Mother. She is one of the highest angels in Heaven. She is also referred to as the **Queen of Angels,** the **Queen of Peace,** and the Blessed Virgin. Through the **visionaries** of Medjugorje the Blessed Mother is calling mankind to God.

✤BLESSED VIRGIN: See **Blessed Mother.**

✤BLESSINGS, ANGEL OF: In Zoroastrianism the angel of blessings is Ashi. Ashi is the female form of **Asha.**

✤BLIZZARDS, ANGEL OF: **Shalgiel.**

✤BLUE, ANGEL OF: The color blue represents the **Cherubim.** It symbolizes the wisdom that they emanate. Light blue represents the archangel **Raphael,** the angel of healing. For Raphael it symbolizes the healing powers of God. Blue is also the traditional color of the Virgin Mary.

✤BLUEPRINT ANGELS: Angels that carry the blueprints of creation.

✤BOBEL: An angel of **disease.**

✤BODHISATTVA(S): Spiritual beings in Buddhism, sometimes referred to as Buddhas-to-be. Once mortal beings on earth, the Bodhisattvas have reached Nirvana, but have put off their own salvation to become emissaries of God. In their enlightened state, they return to earth to help humans. They act as healers, spiritual guides, and teachers. In addition, they act as guides for the souls of those who are near death. In Heaven, they are privileged beings who receive all the rewards of those who have reached salvation.

✤BODIES OF ANGELS: See **Assumed Bodies, Nature of Angels.**

✤BONAVENTURE, SAINT: See **Saint Bonaventure.**

✤BOOK OF DANIEL: See **Daniel.**

✤BOOK OF JOB: See **Job.**

✤BOOK OF JUBILEES: A book of the **Pseudepigrapha** in which **Gabriel** relates to **Moses** the circumstances surrounding the creation, and the events that happened shortly thereafter. These events make up the book of **Genesis.** The Book of Jubilees tells of the angels giving **Noah** information about herbal remedies. It states that the angels taught men to make laws and to be fair and just to one another. It shows how good and evil began, with the Ruler of Evil Spirits, **Mastema,** standing in opposition to God. (Note: Mastema is equated with Satan.)

✤BOOK OF MORMON: The Holy Book of the Mormons. In 1823, an angel named Moroni appeared to Joseph Smith and led Smith to a place where golden tablets, hidden away for centuries, were buried. The tablets included inscribed text that was foreign to Smith. With the help of Moroni, the text was translated and eventually became known as the Book of Mormon. The Book of Mormon reveals the story of a Hebrew family who in 600 B.C. fled from the desolation of Jerusalem. The family boarded a ship that later ended up in North America. The offspring of this family are thought to be the forefathers of Native Americans. Family records from an elder named Mormon reported that Jesus appeared to them after his crucifixion. Mormon's son Moroni buried the records of his father around A.D. 400. Those were the tablets that the angel Moroni later led Joseph Smith to. After his death Moroni was transformed into an angel and became the revealer of the Book of Mormon. Smith later founded the Church of Jesus Christ of the Latter-Day Saints. Today, a statue of the angel Moroni stands on a hill in Palmyra, New York, where Moroni first led Smith to the tablets.

✤BOOK OF RAZIEL: According to lore, the Book of Raziel (also called the Book of the Angel Raziel) was written by the angel **Raziel.** It is said to have contained information on celestial and earthly mysteries. It also had over a thousand keys to unlock those mysteries. Raziel first gave the book to **Adam.** Adam passed it on to **Enoch.** Enoch gave it to **Noah,** who later patterned the ark from the instructions laid out in it. The book is also said to have contained medical information to aid humankind. It was later given to King **Solomon,** who kept it for a short time. The book turned up during medieval times under the ownership of Eleazer of Worms, a writer who was given credit for authoring the book.

✤**BOOK OF THE PIOUS:** In Hebrew it is called Sefer Hasidim. One of the most noteworthy documents written during the Jewish Middle Ages, it was put together during the twelfth century in Germany. It taught self-discipline and godly conduct. Demons are found throughout the text as well as ways to exorcise them.

✤**BOOK OF TOBIT:** See **Tobias.**

✤**BOOKS OF ENOCH:** Composed during the second century B.C., the Books of Enoch relay the prophet Enoch's experiences with God, the angels, and his travels through the seven heavens. The books contain more information on angels than can be found in any other source. It includes the names of angels, their responsibilities, qualities, and per-sonalities. It lists the angels of hailstorms, wind, lightning, storms, comets, windstorms, hurricanes, thunder, earthquakes, snow, rain, day-light, night, the sun, moon, and other heavenly bodies. The books also give information on the fallen angels, their sexual relationships with women, their corruption of humankind, Enoch's unsuccessful attempt to act as mediator for them, and the foretelling of their demise. The writ-ings of **Enoch** were not included in the Holy Canon because the rabbis of the period doubted their authorship. The books were at one time well read by the Jews and were considered inspired canonical scripture by ear-lier rabbis. The angels Ariukh and Pariukh were named as the guardian angels of the writings of Enoch.

✤**BOOKS ON ANGELS:** In the recent past there have been many books written on the subject of angels. Every year several new titles go into print. Many of today's angel books tell of true stories of people who have had encounters with angels. Other books tell of the history surrounding the angels. Still others concentrate on communicating with the angels. Some of the most popular angel books in recent history include books by **Mortimer J. Adler, Joan Wester Anderson, Sophy Burnham, Eileen Freeman, Billy Graham, Terry Lynn Taylor,** Malcolm Godwin, and authors Alma Daniel, Timothy Wyllie, and Andrew Ramer. In his book *The Angels and Us*, Mortimer J. Adler looks at angels in art and religion. He also explores the many theological and philosophical ideas on angels. Published in 1982, *The Angels and Us* was a forerunner for later books published on angels. From a personal experience, Joan Wester

Anderson was inspired to write her first book, *Where Angels Walk, True Stories of Heavenly Visitors.* It is a collection of true angel experiences. In 1990, Sophy Burnham's *A Book of Angels* leaped onto the scene and into the hearts of angel lovers of all ages. It helped to increase the interest in and awareness of angels. It examines the history and beliefs in angels from various cultures around the world. It also includes a collection of personal angel experiences. Eileen Freeman's popular book *Touched by an Angel* gives experiences of people whose lives were changed by angels. Terry Lynn Taylor's *Messengers of Light: The Angels' Guide to Spiritual Growth* shows people how to recognize angels, how to communicate with them, and how to bring them into one's life daily. Billy Graham's book *Angels: God's Secret Agents* chronicles his experiences with angels, as well as those of others who believe that angels came to their aid in moments of need. Malcolm Godwin's spectacular angel book, *Angels, an Endangered Species,* is one of the most interesting angel books to date. It takes the reader on a journey through the history and lore of angels, past and present. It offers interpretations and explanations for the worldwide beliefs in angels. Another intriguing book of a different nature is *Ask Your Angels,* written by Alma Daniel, Timothy Wyllie, and Andrew Ramer. *Ask Your Angels* is a guide to working with the angels. It tells how the angels are working with **mankind** and explains how to ask the angels for help and guidance. It also gives simple instructions on how individuals can communicate more effectively with the angels. See **Appendix 2.**

✤**BOSCH, HIERONYMUS:** Dutch artist (1450–1516) who painted religious subjects featuring angels. Two of the most famous paintings of his including angels are *The Entrance to Heaven* and *The Last Judgment.*

✤**BOTTICELLI, SANDRO:** Florentine Renaissance painter (1444–1510). He was famous for his mythological and religious scenes. One of his most famous paintings featuring angels is the *Mystic Nativity,* painted in 1500.

✤**BOTTOMLESS PIT, ANGEL OF THE: Abaddon.** See **Abyss; Apsu.**

✤**BOUNTEOUS IMMORTALS:** Another name for the **Amesha Spentas,** archangels in Zoroastrianism.

✤**BOWLS OF THE WRATH OF GOD:** See **Vials of the Wrath of God.**

✤**BREUGHEL, PIETER:** Flemish painter (1525–1569) who specialized in painting religious histories, many of which featured angels. One of his most famous is *The Fall of the Rebel* Angels.

✤**BRIATHOS:** An angel who possesses the ability to thwart the powerful demon named **Scepter.**

✤**BRIDE OF CHRIST:** The **Pistis-Sophia,** who is the mother of the superior order of angels called **Aeons,** is said to be the Bride of Christ mentioned in the Book of Revelation 21:9 where it states, "One of the seven angels who had the seven bowls full of the seven last plagues came to me and said, 'Come and I will show you the Bride, the wife of the Lamb.' " The Bride of Christ is said to represent the righteous people, and the lamb represents Christ.

✦Bridge of Heaven: See Arabot.

✦Briel: An angel who is called upon during the birth of babies. It is hoped that by calling on Briel, mother and child will have a safe delivery.

✦Bright and Poisonous One: Sammael, who is the angel of poison, is also called the Bright and Poisonous One. The title originated with the Sumerians. The name Sam means "poison," the word el stands for "angel," thus the name is a combination of the two, and the title Bright and Poisonous One was derived from it.

✦Bright Angel: Adam. In the book The Life of Adam and Eve, Adam is referred to as the bright angel.

✦Bright Star: In Persian mythology the angel Tishtrya was called the bright star. Tishtrya brought rain to the earth.

✦Brilliant One Who Heals: The meaning of the name Raphael. Raphael is the angel of healing.

✦Brilliant Ones: Another name for the class of angels called Virtues. The title is inspired partly because of the luminosity that all angels share, and because of their brilliant ideas involving heroes. The Virtues are said to have the ability to inspire strength and courage when they are needed most, without the hero or heroine ever realizing it.

✦Bringer of Good News: A title held by the archangel Gabriel, who is the angel of revelation. Gabriel brought the good news to Zechariah that he was to become a father (Luke 1:11–14, 19); he brought the good news to the Virgin Mary that she was going to give birth to the Messiah (Luke 1:26); and he brought the good news of Islam to Muhammad.

✦Bringer of Light: A title held by Lucifer, whose name means "he who gives light." This is a surprising title for Lucifer since he is equated with Satan, the spirit of darkness. However, the term refers to the glorious light that apparently radiates all around him. Because of this he is also called the Star Which Heralds the Rising Sun and the Morning Star.

✦Broom Tree, Angel of the: At the beginning of creation, when God first made the Garden of Eden, the archangel Raphael planted the first broom tree.

✦Brotherhood, Angel of: In Persian mythology, the angel of brotherhood was named Mihr. Mihr inspired love and harmony in humans toward their fellowman.

✤**Brown, Angel of:** The color brown represents the archangels **Gabriel** and **Uriel.**

✤**Brownies:** Helpful spirits from the **fairy** class. According to lore, Brownies seek out people who are deserving and perform helpful tasks for them. They are small beings, with pointed ears. They are called Brownies because of their brown complexion, and the brown clothing they wear.

✤**Brunnhilde:** Queen of the Northern Angels of Death, also called the **Valkyries.** In German mythology, the Valkyries, under Brunnhilde's direction, oversaw wars and chose who would live and who would die. They also carried the souls of the heroes to the hall of heroes, known as Valhalla.

✤**Buchuel:** An angel who drives away evil spirits.

✤**Buddhas-to-be:** See **Buddhism.**

✤**Buddhism:** The angels of Buddhism are called **Bodhisattvas,** also known as Buddhas-to-be. The Bodhisattvas are emissaries of God who act as spiritual guides to humankind. Mara is the spirit of darkness in Buddhism. He keeps Buddhists imprisoned in the cycle of reincarnation, a cycle from which all Buddhists struggle to become free. To the Buddhists this is the equivalent of Hell.

✤**Budh Avatar:** One of the **Avatars** (angels) in Vedic beliefs. *Buddha* is a variation of Budh Avatar.

✤**Bull(s):** An animal associated with **Cherubim.** In Assyrian art, the Cherubim were sometimes depicted as having human faces and the bodies of bulls.

✤**Burma:** In Burma people believed in the existence of **Nats,** which are guardian spirits who dwell next to people and sometimes within them. When the Nats come, they offer help and assistance. They can be called upon through propitiatory rites. There are both good and evil Nats.

✤**Burnham, Sophy:** Author of the best-selling angel books *A Book of Angels* and its sequel, *Angel Letters. A Book of Angels* traces angels in history, throughout various cultures and religious systems around the world. It includes Burnham's own personal experiences with angels, as well as experiences of people from around the country. *Angel Letters* is a follow-up to *A Book of Angels* and discloses extraordinary real-life angel stories. She has also written two novels, *Revelations* and *The President's Angel.*

✤**Burning Bush, Angel of the:** While tending his flock one day, **Moses** drove the herd into the wilderness and came upon **Mount Horeb.** Nearby, he noticed a bush that was on fire; however, the bush was not burning. The Book of Exodus 3:2 tells the story: "And the angel of the Lord appeared unto him in a flame of fire out of the midst of a bush: and he looked, and, behold, the bush burned with fire, and the bush was not consumed." Moses wondered aloud why the bush didn't burn. Then a voice spoke to him from the bush asking him not to come any closer, telling him to remove his sandals because he was standing on holy ground. This was the Angel of the Lord speaking to him as a mediator for God. The angel informed Moses that God had heard the cries of the Hebrews, and that he was sending Moses to speak with **Pharaoh,** in order to lead the Hebrews out of bondage (Exodus 3:1–10). The archangel **Michael** is thought to have been the angel in the burning bush.

✤BUSASEJAL: A **fallen angel.**

✤BUSTHARIEL: An angel who protects individuals from evil spirits.

✤BUTATAR: The angel of **computations.** He is also summoned in magical ceremonies. A variation of the name Butatar is Butator.

✤BUTATOR: A variation of the name **Butatar.**

✤BUTTERFLY MAIDEN: A female **kachina** (nature spirit) who presides over spring.

✤BYLETH: A variation of the name **Beleth,** a chief demon of Hell who commands eighty-five troops of devils.

Angels and ministers of grace, defend us!
—HAMLET TO HORATIO IN *Hamlet* BY SHAKESPEARE

✤**CABALA, ANGELS OF THE:** The Cabala is a mystical Jewish system of interpretation of the scriptures. It is based on the idea that every word, character, and number of the scriptures contains mysteries. The writings and symbols of the Cabala are used on charms and in magic practices. The Cabala is made up of two books: the Sefer Yezira (Book of Creation) and the **Zohar** (Book of Splendor). In the Cabala, angels are referred to as "shining ones." These shining ones take humankind on a path through the Cabala to God. Ten **Holy Sefiroth** (angels) are listed within the Cabala. They issue from the right side of God. They are **Kether, Chokmah, Binah, Chesed, Geburah, Tiphereth, Netzach, Hod, Jesod,** and **Malkuth.** The **Unholy Sefiroth,** which issue from the left side of God, are Chaigidiel, Gamaliel, Gamchicoth, Golab, Harab Serap, **Lilith, Sammael,** Sathariel, Thaumiel, and Togarini.

✤**CADUCEUS:** A wing-topped staff wound about by two snakes. It is a symbol of healing. It represents the **Seraphim** and the archangel **Raphael.** Both are angels who represent the healing powers. The caduceus is also carried by the winged Greek god **Hermes.**

✤**CAHOR:** The angel of **deception.**

✤**CALLIOPE:** In Greek mythology Calliope was a muse of the arts. She inspired men to write epic poetry. To some, the muses were considered angels.

✤CALVIN, JOHN: French Protestant theologian of the Reformation (1509–1564). From his teachings grew one of the predominate Christian religious systems, called Calvinism. John Calvin did not have much to say on the subject of angels. This is because he did not believe in hypothesizing beyond the information that was given in the Bible. Therefore, his opinions on the angels are not as comprehensive as those of other theologians. He rejected the famous angelic hierarchy by **Dionysius the Pseudo-Areopagite.** He did not believe that each and every individual has a **guardian angel.** He did believe, however, that the angels collectively watched over all of mankind. He once wrote, "Angels are the dispensers and administrators of the Divine beneficence toward us . . . they regard our safety, undertake our defense, direct our ways, and exercise a constant solicitude that no evil befall us."

✤CALVINISM: See **Calvin, John.**

✤CAMAEL (THE ONE WHO SEES GOD): A great celestial prince in Heaven. He is said to be one of God's favorite angels and is given the privilege of standing in the presence of God. He has been given the divine duty of arbitrating between the prayers of Israel and God. It is believed that Camael is the unnamed angel who wrestled with **Jacob** at **Peniel.** Camael is believed to be the angel that appeared to Jesus in the **Garden of Gethsemane** to impart strength to him. He is a leader over twelve thousand angels of destruction. In some writings he is a duke of Hell, who, when invoked, appears in the form of a leopard. According to Judaic legend, he was destroyed by **Moses** when attempting to prevent him from receiving the Torah. He holds the titles Ruler of Tuesday, Prince of the Seraphim, Ruler of Mars, Chief of Powers, the Angel of Relationships, and God of War (to the Druids). In some writings he is named as one of the ten **Holy Sefiroth** (angels of the **Cabala**). Variations of the name are **Chamuel,** Kamael, Khamael, Kemuel, Camiel, Camiul, Cammael, Qemuel, and Quemel.

✤CAMIEL: A variation of **Camael.**

✤CAMIUL: A variation of **Camael.**

✤CAMMAEL: A variation of **Camael.**

✤CANAANITE PRIESTESSES: The Canaanite priestesses were taught the power of the moon and how to utilize its phases from the archangel **Sariel.** This power gave them an edge over the Hebrews, who were at war with the Canaanites over the promised land. Legend has it that, for this, Sariel was cast out of Heaven.

✤CANCER, ANGEL OF: **Muriel** is the angel of the zodiac sign Cancer.

✤**CAPRICORN, ANGEL OF: Haniel** is the angel of Capricorn.

✤**CAPTAIN OF THE HEAVENLY HOST:** A title held by the archangel **Michael** because of his role as commander in chief of the **Celestial Army.**

✤**CAPTAINS OF FEAR:** Angels who work with the Lords of Dread in singing praises to God.

✤**CARCAS:** One of the angels of **confusion.**

✤**CARETAKER ANGELS:** Angels who care for premature infants and children of adultery.

✤**CAREY, KENNETH X.:** Author of the *Starseed Transmissions, The Return of the Bird Tribes,* and *Starseed 2000.* The information in these books was communicated to Carey from the archangel **Raphael.**

✤**CARNIVEAN:** A variation of **Carniveau.**

✤**CARNIVEAU:** A fallen angel formerly from the class of angels called **Powers.** He later became a powerful demon of Hell. Variations of the name Carniveau are Carnivean and Carreau.

✤**CARREAU:** A variation of **Carniveau.**

✤**CASIEL:** A variation of the name **Casziel,** the angel of **Saturday.**

✤**CASMARAN:** The angel who rules over **summer.**

✤**CASSIAN, JOHN:** A monk from the fifth century. Cassian once wrote, "For though we maintain that some spiritual natures exist, such as angels, archangels and other powers . . . yet we ought certainly not to consider them incorporeal. For they have in their own fashion a body in which they exist."

✤**CASSIEL:** A variation of the name **Casziel,** the angel of tears.

✤**CASTIEL:** An angel who presides over **Thursday.**

✤**CASZIEL:** A great prince in Heaven. Casziel holds the titles of the Angel of Saturday, the Angel of Tears, the Ruler of Saturn, and the Angel of Temperance. In **Essene** beliefs, Casziel personifies the angel referred to as Earthly Mother. Variations of the name **Casziel** are Cassiel, Casiel, **Kafziel,** and Kaziel.

✤**CATHERINE OF SIENA:** See **Saint Catherine of Siena.**

✤**CATHOLICISM:** The views on angels in Catholicism stem mainly from the information in the Bible, and the thoughts and ideas of the Saints, and theologians of the Roman Catholic Church. Catholics believe that the angels were created before mankind and were made in the image of God. *The New Catholic Encyclopedia* states, "The Church has defined as dogma that besides the visible world, God also created a kingdom of invisible spirits, called angels, and that He created them before the creation of the world." GUARDIAN ANGELS. In Catholicism it is taught that every person has a **guardian angel.** Some Catholics believe that there are two angels, one on each shoulder. The angel on the left is bad, the angel on the right is good. The two angels are believed to force people to choose between good and bad, between God and Satan. Catholic children are taught the Guardian Angel Prayer: "Angel of God who are my guardian, enlighten, watch over, support and rule men, who were entrusted to you by the heavenly piety. Amen."

✤CATTLE, ANGEL OF: In Zoroastrianism, **Vohu Manah** is the protector of cattle.

✤CAYM: A fallen angel.

✤CAYYIEL: One of the **chief angels** of Heaven.

✤CELESTIAL ARMY: God's army of angels who do battle against the demons. Their commander in chief is the archangel **Michael.** It is also called the Heavenly Army.

✤CELESTIAL BODIES: A phrase used by the apostle **Paul** in the Bible when referring to the bodies of angels. At 1 Corinthians 15:40 Paul says, "There are also celestial bodies, and bodies terrestrial: but the glory of the celestial is one, and the glory of the terrestrial is another." (Note: In some translations the "celestial bodies" are referred to as "heavenly bodies.")

✤CELESTIAL CHOIR: A term sometimes used when referring to the angels.

✤CELESTIAL ENTITIES: A term sometimes used when referring to the angels.

✤CELESTIAL ESCORT: Another name for the **Psychopomp.** They are angels that escort the souls of the dead to Heaven.

✤CELESTIAL MOTHER: A title held by the **Virgin Mary.** On earth she was the mother of the son of God. In Heaven she is the **Queen of Angels** and the Celestial Mother.

✤CELESTIAL ORDERS: A term sometimes used when referring to the different classes of angels. In the angelic hierarchy, nine celestial orders are grouped in three triads that revolve around the **throne of God.** See **Angel Hierarchies.**

✤CELESTIAL SERVANTS: A term applied to angels for their services rendered to humankind. As celestial servants the angels assist in guiding, protecting, teaching, comforting, strengthening, and healing the people of earth.

✤CELESTIAL SPIRIT(S): A term sometimes used when referring to the angels.

✤CELESTIAL THRONE: The heavenly **throne of God.** Seven angels, called throne angels, stand at the throne of God. They are **Gabriel, Phanuel, Michael, Uriel, Raphael,** Israel, and **Uzziel.**

✤**CENSER:** See **Golden Censer.**

✤**CEREMONIAL ANGELS:** Another name for the **ritual angels.**

✤**CERVIEL:** A variation of **Cervihel.**

✤**CERVIHEL:** The angel of strength, and the guardian angel of King David. He is from the group of angels called **Principalities.** Cervihel assisted David in killing the giant Philistine named **Goliath.** Variations of the name Cervihel are Cerviel and Zeruel.

✤**CETARARI:** An angel who presides over **winter.**

✤**CHACHMAL:** An angel whose name can be found on charms worn by pregnant women. It is believed that the charm will aid them in having a safe and successful delivery.

✤**CHACHMIEL:** An angel whose name can be found on charms worn by pregnant women.

✤**CHAFRIEL:** An angel whose name can be found on charms worn by pregnant women.

✤**CHAGALL, MARC:** A noted Russian painter (1887–1985). Chagall took many of his subjects from Jewish life and folklore. Angels were featured in several of his paintings including his famous *Struggle of Jacob and the Angel* and *The Parting of the Red Sea.*

✤**CHAIGIDIEL:** One of the **Unholy Sefiroth.**

✤**CHAIOTH HA-QADESH:** Another name for the order of angels called the **Hayyoth.**

✤**CHALDEA(NS):** There were several angels in Chaldean religious beliefs. The Jewish angel **Labbiel** was a popular deity in Chaldea (God later changed Labbiel's name to **Raphael**). Ishtar, another angel of Judaism, was worshiped as a deity in Chaldea (Ishtar was later named as the angel who transported the prophet **Enoch** to Heaven). The Chaldeans also had the **Jinn** (guardian angels), who were believed to watch over and protect all Chaldeans. There were also the Rectores Mundorum, divine spirits who were administrators of the earth.

✤**CHALKYDRI:** A variation of the name **Kalkydra.** The Kalkydra sing praises to God when the sun rises.

✤**CHAMAEL:** An angel who is thought to be one of the three unnamed of the seven **archangels.** He is also a leader of the **Principalities.**

✤**CHAMUEL (HE WHO SEARCHES FOR GOD):** One of the seven **archangels.** He is also the ruler of the **Dominations,** and one of the rulers of the **Powers.** He is thought by some to have been the angel who strengthened Jesus in the **Garden of Gethsemane.** Chamuel is listed by some modern angelologists as one of the twelve archangels (twelve is a new figure; traditionally there were seven). Variations of the name Chamuel are **Camael,** Kamuel, Simiel, and **Semibel.**

✤**CHANCE, ANGELS OF: Barakiel.** In addition, the winged god **Kairos** holds the scales of chance.

✤**CHANCELLOR OF HEAVEN:** A title held by the powerful angel **Metatron,** representing his exalted position in Heaven. He is also called Angel of the Covenant, **King of Angels,** Prince of the Divine Face, and the Lesser Yahweh.

✤**CHANIEL:** An angel whose name can be found on charms worn by pregnant women. It is believed that the charm will aid them in having a safe and successful delivery.

✤**CHAOS, ANGELS OF:** The equivalent of the angels of **confusion.**

✤**CHARAVAH (DRYNESS):** The angel that God designated to dry up the waters after the great **flood.**

✤**CHARIOTS OF GOD:** In the Book of Psalms 68:17 angels are referred to as "chariots of God": "The chariots of God are twenty thousand, even thousands of angels: the Lord is among them, as in Sinai, in the holy place." The class of angels known as **Thrones** (also called **Ophanim**) are equated with the chariots of God.

✤**CHARITY, ANGELS OF:** The angels of charity are Achsah, Hasdiel, and **Zadkiel.** In the Talmud, the angel of charity is one of four angels that God consults regarding his decision to create mankind.

✤**CHARLES VII OF FRANCE:** When **Joan of Arc** was sixteen she began hearing voices of angels admonishing her to go and help the Dauphin. Obeying the angels, she dressed as a young man and traveled to meet the Dauphin. She successfully convinced him of her divine mission. With the help of Joan of Arc and the angels, the French won their freedom from Britain, and the Dauphin was crowned king at Rheims in the year 1429. He later became known as Charles VII of France.

✤**CHARON:** The **Etruscan** god of the dead. He was the son of Erebus, the god of darkness, and Nyx, goddess of the night. He had huge wings and a large crooked nose resembling the beak of a bird. He carried the souls of the dead to Hades and was the overseer of the cities of the underworld.

✤**CHASKIEL:** An angel whose name can be found on charms worn by pregnant women.

✤**CHASMAL:** The chief of the order of angels called **Hashmallim.** He is also known as the fire-speaking angel. A variation of the name Chasmal is Hashmal.

✤**CHASTISEMENT, ANGEL OF: Amaliel.**

✤**CHAYYLIEL:** A ruling prince of the order of **Angels.**

✤**CHEBAR RIVER:** Located in Babylonia, it is the site where the prophet

Ezekiel saw visions of the **Cherubim** and **Wheels** (Ezekiel 1:1, 3; 3:15, 23; 10:14, 15).

✤**CHEF OF HELL:** According to lore, **Nisroch,** the eagle-headed deity, is chef to the royalty of Hell. He flavors their food with fruit from the **Tree of Life,** over which he once stood guard.

✤**CHERUB(S):** Cherubs are baby angels sometimes referred to as **Putti.** Cherubs are often portrayed in art hovering near a beautiful woman or goddess. The name Cherub originated with the great and powerful angels called Cherubim. They are said to accompany the Virgin Mary during her earthly visitations.

✤**CHERUBIEL:** One of the ruling angels of the **Cherubim.**

✤**CHERUBIM (FULLNESS OF GOD'S KNOWLEDGE):** In the **Zohar** we read, "Come and see. When the sun sets the cherubim . . . beat their wings above and stretch them out, and the melodious sound of their wings is heard in the realms above." The Cherubim are brilliant and mighty angels who dwell close to God in the **Seventh Heaven.** They are the second-highest order of angels in Heaven. They are sometimes referred to as **Cherubs,** but are not to be mistaken for the baby angels, also called Cherubs. According to the Book of **Enoch,** they are majestic and beautiful. The name Cherubim originated in Assyria and is derived from the word *karibu*, which means "one who prays." They emanate a subtle vibration of knowledge and wisdom that they receive from God. They are also the keepers of the celestial records and are said to praise God night and day continuously. In Islam they are called *el-karubiyan*, which means those "brought close to Allah." Originally they were portrayed as mighty guardian figures that appeared in the Near and Middle East. In Assyrian art, Cherubim were depicted as winged creatures with faces of either a lion or a human, on bodies of sphinxes, eagles, and bulls. In the Book of Psalms 18:10, God rides upon a Cherub. The Cherubim are sometimes referred to as **living creatures, winged creatures,** and Holy Beasts. Ruling princes of the Cherubim include **Gabriel, Kerubiel,** Ophaniel, **Raphael, Uriel,** and Zophiel. Satan was also a ruling prince before his fall from grace.

✤**CHESED:** One of the ten **Holy Sefiroth** (angels) of the **Cabala.** He is also called Mercy.

✤**CHIEF AMBASSADOR OF GOD:** The archangel **Gabriel.**

✤**CHIEF AMBASSADOR TO HUMANITY:** A title sometimes used when referring to the archangel **Gabriel.** He obtained this title because of his direct communications with mankind in revealing important events.

✤**CHIEF ANGELS:** The chief angels in Heaven are **Aktriel, Anapiel YHWH, Azbogah YHWH, Barakiel, Camael,** Cayyiel, **Dina, Gabriel,**

Galgalliel, Haniel, Iophiel, Jahoel, Metatron, Michael, Phanuel, Rad-weri'el YHWH, Raziel, Rikbiel YHWH, Sandolphon, Shemuil, Soperi'el YHWH, Soperi'el YWHW, Soqedhozi YHWH, Suriel, Tzadkiel, Uriel, and Zagzagel.

✣CHIEF DEMONS: The chief demons of hell are Anituel, Asmodeus, Astarte, Balam, Beelzebub, Beleth, Beliar, Belphegor, Camael, Dumah, Forneus, Furcalor, Gazarniel, Haroth, Kokabi'el, Lahash, Raym, Salmael, Sammael, and Satan.

✣CHIEF OF DEMONS: Satan the Devil. Sammael and Beelzebub also hold the title of the Chief of Demons.

✣CHIEF OF THE DEMON PRINCES: Dumah.

✣CHIEF OF THE DEMONIC LOCUSTS: Apollyon. See Abaddon.

✣CHIEF OF THE GRIGORI: Azaz'el.

✣CHIEF OF THE GUARDIAN ANGELS: The archangel Raphael.

✣CHIEF OF THE SECRET POLICE OF THE UNDERWORLD: Nergal.

✣CHILDBIRTH, ANGELS OF: Armisael is the guardian angel of the womb and the unborn. He is summoned during childbirth for a safe delivery. The archangel Gabriel is also an angel of childbirth, because of his announcements of special births. In ancient African beliefs, Yemaya was the spirit who presided over childbirth. The Book of Raziel lists sixty-eight angels whose names can be found on charms worn by pregnant women, for a safe delivery. They include Ahaniel, Ahiel, Aniel, Azriel, Briel, Chachmal, Chachmiel, Chafriel, Chaniel, Chaskiel, Diniel, Gabriel, Gazriel, Gediel, Grial, Kadal, Kadmiel, Kaniel, Karkiel, Katchiel, Katzhiel, Kenunit, Kidumiel, Lahal, Lahariel, Machnia, Malchiel, Malkiel, Michael, Neriah, Nuriel, Ofiel, Oriel, Padiel, Psisya, Rachmiah, Rachmiel, Rachsiel, Ramal, Ramiel, Ramucl, Raphael, Rigal, Rsassiel, Rumiel, Samchia, Samchiel, Schachniel, Sensenya, Shebniel, Sniel, Sturiel, Tahariel, Tatrusia, Tsirya, Tsuria, Tzadkiel, Tzartak, Udrgazyi, Udriel, Variel, Yeruel, Yezriel, Ygal, Yofiel, Zechriel, Zumiel, Zuriel.

✣CHILDREN: Children are believed to be visited by angels more often than are adults. This is thought to be due to their innocence and also their openness. This relationship with the angels is believed by some to begin in the womb. According to Judaic lore, as a baby is growing inside the mother's womb, an angel instructs it on the wisdom of the Torah. Just before the child is born, an angel touches the mouth of the baby, so that it will forget what it learned. However, the impression of the wisdom is said to remain with the child during his earthly life. GUARDIAN ANGELS. Children are also thought to be more protected by angels because they are so young and careless. As they grow and are better able to look after themselves, they require less angelic protection. However, when they are very little, it is believed that they have many guardian angels. In Catholicism children are taught that they have two angels, sitting on either shoulder: a good angel and a bad angel. Legend has it that guardian angels of children dwell in a privileged place in Heaven, close to God. This belief stems from the scripture in the Book of Matthew 18:10, where it says, "See to it that you men do not despise one of these little ones; for I tell you that their angels in heaven always behold the face of my Father who is in heaven." The angel Temeluchus is the guardian angel over all children. Premature babies and children of adultery are protected by caretaker angels. The angel Mashith looks after children at their death. Two spiritual beings named in lore wish to harm children. These are **Lilith,** a she-demon who is an enemy of **Eve** and her offspring, and another she-demon named **Obyzouth.**

*CHILDREN OF ANGELS: See **Nephillim, Anakim.**

*CHILDREN OF HEAVEN: A term sometimes used when referring to the angels. It is also a term applied to the **Nephillim,** the children of mortal women and fallen angels.

*CHILDREN OF ISRAEL: See **Israel.**

*CHILDREN OF PRIDE: A phrase sometimes used when referring to the fallen angels, who forsook their places in Heaven because of their pride.

*CHINA: See **Chinese.**

*CHINESE: Chinese angels are called **Shen,** which are immortal spirits in Chinese lore. They are referred to by the Chinese as gods. The Shen perform all of the duties of the angels of Judaism, Christianity, and Islam. They manifest in human or animal form to bring messages, heal, teach, or offer strength and encouragement.

*CHITRIEL (ROD OF GOD): One of the angels of **punishment.**

*CHOIRS, ANGEL OF: See **Heavenly Choirs.**

*CHOKMAH: One of the ten **Holy Sefiroth** of the **Cabala.** His abstract name is Wisdom.

*CHORISTERS: A term used when referring to singing angels. Depictions of choristers are usually found during the **Christmas** season on Christmas cards and decorations. In addition, there have been reports of people who, in need of comforting, have heard beautiful-sounding choral singing. Some believe this phenomenon to be angels of Heaven singing to bring comfort. Choristers also sing praises to God in Heaven.

*CHRISTIAN GNOSTICS: Christian Gnostics believed the seven **archangels** to be **Michael, Gabriel, Raphael, Uriel, Barakiel,** Sealtiel, and **Jehudiel.**

*CHRISTIANITY: The doctrines and religious groups that are based on the teachings of **Jesus** Christ. The angels of Christianity are based on the angels found in the Christian Greek scriptures (New Testament) of the **Bible.** In the Bible they act as messengers and ministers of God. They announce the **Last Judgment,** separate the good from the wicked, give strength to the meek, and comfort the discouraged. Christianity also recognizes seven **archangels.** Only four are known by name: **Michael, Gabriel, Raphael,** and **Uriel.** Angels in Christian beliefs are traditionally viewed as wearing long flowing robes and having huge wings. They are usually depicted as being surrounded by an **aureole** or a **halo** above the head. They are viewed as being pure and virtuous beings, who usually appear androgynous.

✤**CHRISTMAS:** The angels found during the Christmas season represent the angels in the Bible that announced the birth of **Jesus.** These angels include the archangel **Gabriel,** who announced to the **Virgin Mary** that she was going to give birth to the Messiah; the Angel of the Lord, who appeared to the **shepherds** tending flock; and the multitude of angels that appeared with the Angel of the Lord when he spoke to the shepherds (Luke 2:8–15). See **Annunciation.**

✤**CHRISTMAS MOVIES:** Popular movies featuring angels at Christmas include *It Came Upon the Midnight Clear* (1984), about a New York police officer who has died who receives a miracle from Heaven in order to keep a Christmas promise to his grandson. The film starred Mickey Rooney, Scott Grimes, Lloyd Nolan, Barrie Youngfellow, and Annie Potts. It was directed by Peter Hunt. *It Happened One Christmas* (1977) is a remake of *It's a Wonderful Life*. The film stars Marlo Thomas as the main character and Cloris Leachman as the angel. *It's a Wonderful Life* (1946) is a classic movie that has become a favorite during the Christmas holidays. It is the story of George Bailey, a man who craves a life of adventure. However, instead of following his dreams, he gets married, takes over the family business, and takes on the troubles of his hometown (Bedford Falls). Eventually, George faces financial ruin when an opponent attempts to drive him out of business. He takes a look at his life and begins to feel that life has passed him by. Feeling sorry for himself, he decides to commit suicide. However, his guardian angel, **Clarence,** intercedes. Clarence shows George what Bedford Falls and the people he loves would be like if he had never been born. In the end, Clarence convinces George that he has a wonderful life. The film stars James Stewart, Donna Reed, Lionel Barrymore, Thomas Mitchell, Ward Bond, and Henry Travers. It was directed by Frank Capra. *One Magic Christmas* (1985) is a feel-good movie about a young woman who has lost her faith in Christmas. With the help of her young daughter, and a guardian angel, the mother regains her faith in time for the holidays. The movie starred Mary Steenburgen, Harry Dean Stanton, Gary Basaraba, Arthur Hill, Elizabeth Harnois, Robbie Magwood, and Ken Pogue. It was directed by Phillip Borsos.

✤CHUR: In Persian mythology Chur is the angel of the sun's disk.

✤CHURCH OF JESUS CHRIST OF LATTER-DAY SAINTS, ANGEL OF: Moroni.

✤CHUSHIEL: An angel who safeguards the south wind.

✤CITIES, ANGELS OF: Angels have been placed over the great cities of the earth to preserve and protect them. The protectors of these cities come from the order of angels called the **Principalities.**

✤CIVILIZATIONS: See **Ancient Civilizations.**

✤CLAIRE OF MONTEFALCO: See **Saint Claire of Montefalco.**

✤CLARENCE: The lovable angel from the film *It's a Wonderful Life*. When the main character, George Bailey, becomes convinced that he has wasted his life by not pursuing his dreams, and that all his hard work has been for nothing, he regrets ever having been born and plans to commit suicide. That's when Clarence (his full name is Clarence Oddbody), his guardian angel, steps in to stop him. Clarence takes George on a tour of his hometown (Bedford Falls) and shows him what life would be like if he had never been born. In the end he convinces George that he has a wonderful life.

✤CLEMENS, TITUS FLAVIUS: Greek theologian, Christian scholar, and gnostic. Clemens believed that the angels are responsible for the movement, balance, and order of the universe.

✤CLIO: In Greek mythology, Clio was the **muse** of education and knowledge. She inspired men to write down the history of the world.

✤CLOTHING OF ANGELS: Traditionally angels have been portrayed as wearing long white or light-colored robes. In her book *Embraced by the Light*, in which she relays her near-death experience and her trip to Heaven, author Betty J. Eadie wrote of seeing large, "ancient-looking looms," on which material was spun to clothe the new arrivals coming in from the earth. Eadie says, "Its appearance was like a mixture of spun sugar. As I moved the cloth back and forth, it shimmered and sparkled, almost as though it were alive. The material was opaque on one side, but when I turned it over, I was able to see through it." When appearing on earth, angels sometimes dress in the cultural clothing of the person they are visiting.

✤CLOUD(S): In art, angels are often portrayed standing in the clouds. The clouds represent the heavenly sphere.

✤CLOUD OF SILENT WITNESSES: A term used when referring to angels that stand around God's throne. They include the **Seraphim, Cherubim,** and **Thrones.**

✤**CODEX:** A scroll of the scriptures. In art, angels are sometimes depicted carrying a codex. It symbolizes the holy scriptures, and also the angel's role in recording mankind's deeds.

✤**COHABITATION WITH HUMANS:** According to the Book of **Genesis,** and the Book of **Enoch,** it is strictly forbidden for the angels to cohabit with humans. The Book of 1 Enoch tells us that when the angels saw the beautiful **daughters of men,** they decided to come to earth to take wives for themselves and produce children. They were severely punished for this sin. See **Sexual Temptation, Fallen Angels.**

✤**COHORTS OF WRATH:** A term used when referring to the angels of **wrath.**

✤**COINCIDENCE(S):** To remain anonymous, yet assist individuals, angels sometimes manipulate circumstances so that they will appear as a coincidence. They may arrange the meeting of two strangers: one who is in need of help, and the other who is able to give assistance. Or they may even use a situation as simple as a book's falling open to the exact page that gives a much needed answer to a problem. On occasion the angels themselves come to the earth to give aid, taking on the **appearance** of a Good Samaritan who happens along at just the right moment. In a number of reports in recent angel books, Good Samaritans have come to the aid of people, then mysteriously disappeared.

✤**COINCIDENCE, ANGEL OF: Kairos.**

✤**COLEMAN, GARY:** Star of the movie *The Kid with the Broken Halo* (1982). In the film Coleman plays a young angel who has come to earth with an elder angel (Robert Guillaume) to help three ethnic families.

✤**COLIC:** A stomach ailment that causes severe pain. Legend has it that God gave the angel **Adnachiel** a cure for colic through an Ethiopian talisman.

✤**COLLECTING ANGELS:** The name of a group of angels found in the popular angel book *Ask Your Angels,* by Alma Daniel, Timothy Wyllie, and Andrew Ramer. Collecting angels work to help groups of people to stay together. They are also called connecting angels, coordinating angels, and guardian companions of groups.

✤**COLOR(S):** Colors representing the four **archangels** are **Michael**—gold, yellow, and rose red; **Gabriel**—brown, silver, and white; **Raphael**—orange and light blue; **Uriel**—brown. Other colors representing angels include **Ariael**—green; **Auriel** and **Casziel**—black and gray; **Sachiel**—purple and royal blue; **Sammael**—red.

✤**COMEDY, MUSE OF:** In Greek mythology, **Thaleia** inspired men to write comedy.

✤**COMETS, ANGEL OF: Ziquiel.**

✤**COMFORTER(S):** The role of comforter is one of the many functions of angels. The Bible testifies to their roles as comforters through its many tales. An angel comforted **Elijah** by bringing him food and water when he ran away into the wilderness, fleeing from the anger of Jezebel. In the desert, an angel comforted an exhausted **Hagar** after **Abraham** sent her and their son, **Ishmael,** away. The angel assured her of their future and showed her a well of water. While at sea during a frightening storm, the apostle **Paul** was comforted by an angel, who assured him that no one would be injured. The angels are still performing their role of comforters today. Many modern accounts of angels coming in times of need have been relayed in such books as **Sophy Burnham**'s *Angel Letters* and **Joan Wester Anderson**'s *Where Angels Walk, True Stories of Heavenly Visitors.* See **Books on Angels.**

✤**COMMANDER IN CHIEF OF THE CELESTIAL ARMY:** The archangel **Michael.**

✤**COMMANDER OF DEMONS:** See **Chief of Demons.**

✤**COMMERCE, ANGEL OF: Anauel.**

✤**COMMOTION, ANGEL OF: Zi'iel.**

✤**COMMUNICATION:** For centuries people have claimed to be in direct communication with the angels. Many of the saints talked to angels. **Joan of Arc** was encouraged to go and help the Dauphin by angels. In addition, many famous mystics such as **Emanuel Swedenborg** and **Rudolph Steiner** also communicated with angels. Emanuel Swedenborg once said, "I am well aware that many will say that no one can possibly speak with angels. Many say that I recount such things to win credence. But I am deterred by none of these: for I have seen, I have heard, I have felt." Angels communicate with humans in many ways. They may appear directly to the individual to bring a specific message. An example of this would be the archangel **Gabriel** bringing the announcement of the birth of Jesus to the **Virgin Mary.** The angels also communicate through dreams. **Joseph,** the husband of Mary, was visited by an angel in a dream who informed him that Mary was pregnant by the **Holy Spirit.** In biblical times the angels communicated with the prophets through visions. The apostle **John** received a **revelation** from an angel, which is now known as the Revelation of John. One of the most important ways that angels communicate is through **intuition.** Warnings of danger often come from what is referred to as "an inner voice." Many associate this voice with that of their guardian angel. Angels also superimpose themselves on individuals in order to bring a message. A much craftier means that the angels use to reach people is through "coincidence." To keep anonymous, angels will manipulate circumstances to give help to an individual. These circumstances appear to be coincidences, such as the meeting of two strangers. One stranger may be in need of assistance, the other is able to give the needed aid. They may even use a situation as simple as a book's falling open to the exact page that gives a much needed answer to a problem. Whatever the message, whatever the need, the angels communicate help in a variety of ways.

✣COMPANION ANGEL(S): Another name for **guardian angels.**

✣COMPASS POINTS, ANGELS OF THE: See **Directions.**

✣COMPASSION, ANGEL OF: The archangel **Raphael.**

✣COMPLETENESS, ANGEL OF: **Kepharel.**

✣COMPUTATIONS, ANGEL OF: **Butatar.**

✣CONCEPTION, ANGEL OF: **Lailah.**

✣CONDUCTOR OF SOULS: During the Middle Ages, the archangel **Michael** was considered the conductor of souls into the spiritual realm. The conductors of souls are also called **Psychopomp.**

✣CONFESSION, ANGEL OF: **Phanuel.**

✣CONFESSORS: An order of angels led by **Barakiel.**

✣CONFUSION, ANGELS OF: A group of angels sent to earth by God to cause chaotic conditions. In one account God sent the angels of confusion to earth to mix up the **languages** of humans as they attempted to build a tower to Heaven. At Genesis 11:7 God states, "Come now! Let us go down and confuse their language so that they may not listen to one another." According to Judaic lore, there are seven angels of confusion: Abagtha, Bigtha, Biztha, Carcas, **Harbonah,** Mehuman, and **Zethar.**

✣CONNECTING ANGELS(S): See **Collecting Angels.**

✣CONSECRATED SALT, ANGEL OF: Consecrated salt is used in religious and magic ceremonies. The angel Aboezra is a holy angel called upon to bless the consecrated salt.

✣CONSTELLATIONS, ANGELS OF: Angels of the constellations include Rahatiel, the angel who rules the constellations, and **Kokabi'el,** who brought the knowledge of the constellations to earth.

✣CONTEMPLATION, ANGEL OF: **Zaphkiel.**

✣CONVERSING WITH ANGELS: In recent years a variety of books have explained how to converse with angels. Two of the most popular are *Messengers of Light* by **Terry Lynn Taylor** and *Ask Your Angels* by Alma Daniel, Timothy Wyllie, and Andrew Ramer. See **Books on Angels.**

✣COORDINATING ANGELS: See **Collecting Angels.**

✤COPPER ESKIMOS: The Copper Eskimos of the central Canadian Arctic believe that children have individual guardian spirits.

✤CORNELIUS: A captain in the Roman army who received a visit from an angel. The account is found in the Bible's New Testament in the Book of Acts 10:3–4. Cornelius found favor in God's eyes because of his prayers and the help that he gave the Jews. One afternoon an angel appeared to him and said, "Cornelius! God is pleased with your prayers and works of charity."

✤CORPORATIONS, ANGELS OF: The order of angels called **Principalities** keep watch over all large corporations on earth.

✤CORRUPT ANGELS: Another name for the **fallen angels.** They are also called **demons** and devils.

✤COSMETICS: **Azaz'el,** the chief of the **Grigori,** taught women to beautify themselves through the use of cosmetics. He also taught them the art of eye shadow and eyeliner.

✤COSMIC LAW AND ORDER, ANGEL OF: In Zoroastrianism, **Asha** is the angel who kept law and order in the universe.

✤COURT OF HEAVEN: The court of Heaven convenes in **Arabot,** the Seventh Heaven. It includes God, Jesus, Metatron (King of Angels), the great princes of Heaven, the throne angels, the saints and the prophets, the ministering angels, and the angels of destruction. The Bible speaks of the court of Heaven. There God is seated on his throne, and angels are gathered in front of him. Daniel 7:9 10 tells us, "As I watched thrones were set in place, and an Ancient One took his throne, his clothing was white as snow, and the hair of his head like pure wool. A thousand thousands served him, and ten thousand times ten thousand stood attending him. The court sat in judgment, and the books were opened." Those books that are being opened and read by the court have been interpreted as being the books where the good and evil deeds of mankind are recorded. While the court is in session, only the great princes of Heaven that carry the name **YHWH** are allowed to speak. However, it is the seventy-two princes of the kingdoms of the world who read from the books the deeds of mankind. After the books are read, the angels of **punishment** go forth to execute judgment against the wicked. See **Archives.**

✤COURTIERS OF HEAVEN: A phrase sometimes used in referring to the angels.

✤COVENANT, ANGEL OF: The mighty angel **Metatron.** Others who have been named as the angel of the covenant include **Michael,** Phadiel, **Elijah,** and God himself.

✦COVERING CHERUB: A term sometimes used when referring to **Satan.** He is also called the Anointed Cherub.

✦CREATION, ANGELS OF THE: Seven angels reportedly were set in charge of seven **planets** during the creation. They include **Oriphiel, Haniel, Zachariel, Sammael, Raphael, Gabriel,** and **Michael.** They are said to reside in Zebul, the **Fourth Heaven.** In addition, when God created the **Garden of Eden,** he instructed the archangel Michael to assemble two hundred thousand and three angels to plant the garden. The olive tree was planted by Michael, **Uriel** planted the nut tree, Gabriel the apple tree, Raphael the melon bush, and **Satanael** the **vine.**

✦CREATION OF ANGELS, THE: **Saint Augustine** wrote, "Where Scripture speaks of the world's creation, it is not plainly said whether or when the angels were created." Exactly when the angels were created is unknown. The topic has been a source of speculation among theologians and religious scholars for centuries and was hotly debated during the Middle Ages. Some believed that the angels were created before the earth and mankind. Others believe that it was on the first day of creation. Still others contend that it was the second and even the fifth day. The Jewish writing entitled *Midrash ha-Ne'elam* states that the angels were the first created beings. Regarding the position of the Roman Catholic Church, the *New Catholic Encyclopedia* states, "The Church has defined as dogma that besides the visible world, God also created a kingdom of invisible spirits, called angels, and that He created them before the creation of the world." The Bible's Book of Job attests to this fact. Here God reveals that the angels were witnesses of the earth's creation: "Were you there when I made the world? If you know so much tell me about it. Who decided how large it would be? Who stretched the measuring line over it? Do you know all the answers? What holds up the pillars that support the earth? Who laid the cornerstone of the world? In the dawn of that day the stars sang together, and the heavenly beings shouted for joy" (Job 38:4–7).

✦CREATIVITY, ANGEL OF: The archangel **Gabriel.** In Greek mythology, **Thaleia** was the muse of arts and creativity.

✦CROCELL: A high-ranking demon in the underworld. He has forty-eight legions of demons at his command.

✦CROCODILE(s): When invoked, the female demon **Leviathan** is said to manifest as a large crocodile. According to lore, the **Kalkydras,** which are powerful angels in Heaven, have heads like crocodiles'.

✦CROOKED MINDEDNESS: An angel found in Zoroastrianism, also called Pairimaiti. Her opponent is the angel of presumption, also called Taromaiti.

✤**CROWN:** One of the ten **Holy Sefiroth** (angels) in the **Cabala.**

✤**CRYSTAL GAZING, ANGEL OF: Eistibus.**

✤**CUPID:** Rome's winged god of love, who was a companion to **Venus.** He was also called Amor. Cupid was one of the archetypal angels of Judeo-Christian lore. He is usually portrayed as a young angel carrying a bow and arrow.

✤**CUPRA:** An Etruscan angel who belonged to the group of angels called the **Novensiles.** The Novensiles ruled over thunderbolts.

✤**CURSON:** A fallen angel.

✤**CYCLES OF CREATION:** A title held by the **Aeons.**

D *Good night, sweet prince: and flights of angels sing thee to thy rest.*

—HORATIO TO A DYING HAMLET
IN SHAKESPEARE'S *HAMLET*

✤**DAEMON:** A variation of **Daimon.**

✤**DAEVA(S):** The Sanskrit word *daeva* means "being of light." Daevas are found both in **Hinduism** and **Zoroastrianism.** In Hinduism, a daeva is a good spirit that serves God. In Zoroastrianism they are viewed as demons, followers of **Angra Mainyu** (or Ahaitin), the spirit of darkness. It was believed that a daeva would become an enemy of those who performed good deeds. For those who performed evil deeds, a daeva would befriend them. Zoroastrians believed that Angra Mainyu and the daevas reside in a dark abyss in the north. A variation of *daeva* is *div.*

✤**DAGON:** A fallen angel.

✤**DAHARIEL:** An angel who stands guard over the palace of Wilon, the **First Heaven.**

✤**DAIMON(S):** In Greek lore, a daimon (also *daemon*) is a supernatural being who intercedes between God and mankind. The word *angel* was originally derived from this Greek word. The people of Greece believed that each person had his own daimon, which acted as a spiritual guide, offering encouragement, advice, and protection when needed. The belief in guardian angels was adopted from the belief in daimons.

✤**DAIMONION:** A variation of the word **daimon.**

✤**DAKINI:** In **Buddhism,** God's energy is manifested in the form of a dakini. A dakini resides within each **Bodhisattva,** who in turn carries out angelic functions.

✦**DAKSHA:** One of the **Adityas** of Vedic beliefs. (Adityas are seven angels who reflect God's brilliant light and glory.)

✦**DAMSEL OF HERRERA:** During the Inquisition, the Marranos (Spanish Jews) were burned at the stake. Eager to escape their torment, they prayed for "savior angels" to come and rescue them. During that period, a woman named Ines (also referred to as the Damsel of Herrera) was often visited by angels. On several occasions, she was escorted to Heaven where she heard music playing. The angels informed her that the people who had been burned at the stake were now in Heaven and were making beautiful music. When Ines told the Marranos of this, they became hopeful that they would be delivered.

✦**DANCE, MUSE OF:** A muse from Greek mythology. **Terpsichore** inspired people in the art of dance.

✦**DAN'EL:** One of the leaders of the **Watchers** who came to the earth to have sexual relations with women.

✦**DANIEL (GOD HAS JUDGED):** A biblical Hebrew prophet. He authored the apocalyptic Book of Daniel, composed in 164 B.C.E. Until the Book of Daniel, angels in the Bible remained nameless. The archangels **Michael** and **Gabriel** are first introduced in the Book of Daniel. Gabriel interprets a prophecy for Daniel (Daniel 8:15–17), and Michael interprets a vision (Daniel 10:12–14). Other angelic encounters are related also. Daniel was rescued from a den of lions by an angel; and three Hebrew men were rescued from a fiery **furnace** by an angel (Daniel 6:22, 3:26–29). See **Lions' Den.**

✦**DANJAL:** A fallen angel.

✦**DANTE ALIGHIERI:** Noted Italian poet (1265–1321). He authored the classic poem *The Divine Comedy*, a vernacular poem in one hundred cantos (more than 14,000 lines). It is considered one of the greatest masterpieces ever written. In the *Divine Comedy*, Dante goes on a journey through Heaven, Purgatory, and Hell. Along the way he encounters many angels. In the poem he shows the order of both the good and bad angels using the hierarchy of angels from **Dionysius the Pseudo-Areopagite**'s ranking from the first century A.D. Because of the popularity of the *Divine Comedy*, Dionysius' hierarchy of angels became more widely accepted. As a result, it was eventually adopted by the Catholic Church and became the most popular ranking of the angels in history. Dante believed that angels are immortal, ethereal beings, created directly by God. To Dante the sole purpose of the angels was to contemplate and worship God. In the *Divine Comedy*, Dante wrote, "All [the angels], as they circle in their orders, look / Aloft; and downward, with such sway prevail, / That all with mutual impulse tend to God."

✤**DANYAL:** One of the angels who brought the secret knowledge of Heaven to humans on earth.

✤**DARA:** The angel of rivers and rain in Persian mythology.

✤**DARDAIL:** An angel summoned in Arabic ceremonies involving exorcism.

✤**DARK ANGEL(S):** Satan the Devil is often referred to as the Dark Angel. In addition, *dark angels* is a phrase used when referring to Satan's followers, the demons, who were once angels of light. Dark Angel is also a term used when referring to the angel that **Jacob** wrestled for a blessing at **Peniel** (Genesis 32:30). According to lore, Jacob and the Dark Angel merged as they wrestled. The Dark Angel is thought to be either **Michael, Camael, Sammael, Uriel,** or **Metatron.**

✤**DARK ANGELIC RULER:** A title held by **Sammael.**

✤**DARK LEGIONS:** The dark legions are commonly known as Satan's army of angels. In the **Dead Sea Scroll** *War of the Sons of Light Against the Sons of Darkness,* it is the army serving under **Beliar** (Prince of Darkness).

✤**DARK PRINCE OF GEHENNA:** A title held by the fallen angel named **Arsiel.**

✤**DARK SPIRITS:** A phrase referring to **demons.**

✤**DARKIEL:** An angel who safeguards the south wind.

✤**DARKNESS, ANGEL OF:** The angel of **darkness** can be found in religious beliefs around the world. The Jews and the Christians call him **Satan.** The Zoroastrians called him **Angra Mainyu.** In Islam he is called **Iblis. Beliar** and **Beelzebub** are two other commonly used names for the angel of darkness. The **Essenes** referred to him as the spirit of perversity, who encouraged people to participate in wrongdoing.

✤**DARKNESS AND DESTRUCTION, ANGEL OF:** **Beliar.**

✤*DATE WITH AN ANGEL:* A lighthearted 1987 comedy starring Michael E. Knight, Phoebe Cates, and Emmanuelle Beart. It's about an angel who comes to earth to escort the soul of a dying man to Heaven. However, on the way down, the angel breaks her wing and falls unconscious to earth. Stranded on earth, she learns about life and love. She is nursed back to health and also protected by the young man she has come to take to Heaven. The two fall in love. The angel decides to remain on earth, and the young man is given a second chance at life. The film also stars David Dukes and Bibi Besch. It was directed by Tom McLoughlin.

✤**DAUGHTERS OF MEN:** An expression used in the Bible when referring to the women on earth whom the angels lusted after. At Genesis 6:2 it states, "Then the sons of the true God began to notice the daughters of men, that they were good-looking; and they went taking wives for themselves, namely, all whom they chose." The women are also referred to as the daughters of Eve.

✤DAUPHIN: See **Charles VII of France.**

✤DAVID, ANGEL OF: **Cervihel,** who is the angel of strength, was also the guardian angel of King David. Cervihel assisted a young David in the slaying of the Philistine giant **Goliath.**

✤DAWN, ANGEL OF: According to lore, the archangel **Raphael** presides over the dawn.

✤DAY, ANGEL OF THE: **Shamshiel.**

✤DAY OF ATONEMENT: In Judaism, the Day of Atonement is a day of fasting and praying for forgiveness for the past year's sins. According to Jewish lore, on the Day of Atonement a scapegoat was thrown off the cliff at Haradan, plummeting to its death below. It is believed that the goat transferred the sins of the Jews to the fallen angel **Azaz'el,** who was believed to be trapped beneath a huge pile of boulders at the bottom of the cliff.

✤DAY OF JUDGMENT: See **Judgment Day.**

✤DAYLIGHT, ANGEL OF: **Shamshiel.**

✤DAYS OF THE WEEK, ANGELS OF THE: See **Seven Days of the Week.**

✤DEAD SEA SCROLL(S): See **Essenes.**

✤DEATH, ANGEL OF: An angel assigned by God to slay his enemies. According to several religious traditions, he is also the angel that escorts the souls of the dead to the spiritual realm. This can be either Heaven or the underworld. **Azrael** is the angel of death in Islam. In Judeo-Christian lore, **Gabriel, Sammael,** and **Sariel** have all been called the angel of **death.** In Zoroastrianism the angel of death is Mairya. In Babylon it was Mot. In rabbinical lore there are fourteen angels of death: Yetzer-hara, Adriel, **Yehudiam, Abaddon, Sammael, Azrael, Metatron, Gabriel, Mashhit, Hemah,** Malach ha-Mavet, **Kafziel, Kesef,** and **Leviathan.** The angel of death destroyed ninety thousand people during the time of **David.** It slaughtered 185,000 people in the camp of the Assyrians who were fighting against the Jews. The angel of death killed the firstborn of Egypt, the last and final plague of the Egyptians before Israel was set free. The Vikings' **Valkyries** were known as angels of death. The Greeks had **Thanatos,** the god of death, who performed all of the functions of an angel of death. Thanatos came to humans when their life spans were completed and carried them off to Hades. The angel of death is some-times referred to as the grim reaper.

✤DEATH OF DOMESTIC ANIMALS, ANGEL OF: **Hemah.**

✤DECEITFUL DESTROYER: A title held by **Mephistopheles.** Once a magnificent angel in Heaven, he later became a high-ranking demon of hell.

✤**Deceiver of God:** A title held by the fallen angel **Kasbel** (the original name of Kasbel was Beqa). He carries this title because of his attempt to deceive the archangel **Michael** into revealing the secret name of God.

✤**December, Angel of: Haniel.**

✤**Deception:** In the *Testament of Solomon*, Deception is a demon that **Solomon** summoned and interrogated. Deception revealed to Solomon that he was a ruler in the world of darkness. His demonic activities include devising evil schemes to be used against humans. He can be thwarted by the angel Lamechiel.

✤**Deception, Angel of: Satan** and Cahor are both considered angels of deception.

✤**Declarations, Angel of:** The archangel **Gabriel.**

✤**Dee, John:** An English astrologer and occultist. During the 1500s in England, Dr. Dee along with Edward Kelly created a form of writing entitled Angelic. Dr. Dee used the writing in his magical practices. He named the writing Angelic because he frequently consulted the angels in his work and used the writing to send messages to the angels. It is still used today in ceremonial magic to record rituals, and also to send messages to the angels.

✤**Deep, Angel of the: Tam'el.**

✤**Deep Waters:** The angel of deep waters is **Rampel.**

✤**Degalim:** An order of angels.

✤**Deheboryn:** An angel who stands guard over the palace of Wilon, the **First Heaven.**

✤**Deities:** A term sometimes used for angels referring to their lofty position in the Heavens.

✤**Delacroix, Eugène:** Noted French painter (1798–1863). He painted dramatic interpretations of scenes from mythology and religion that often featured angels. One popular illustration depicts the famous account of **Jacob** wrestling with an angel.

✤**Delight in Beauty:** Another name for **Ameretat,** one of the archangels of Zoroastrianism.

✤**Demiurge:** According to Judaic lore, the Demiurge is the creator of the universe. In his works, **Plato** named the Demiurge as the deity who fashions the material world. The gnostics believed him to be **Satan,** Prince of Darkness. The mighty angel **Metatron** is also thought to be the Demiurge. Metatron is a more likely candidate for the Demiurge since he is referred to as the **Lesser Yahweh** (also Lesser YHWH). Yahweh is the original pronunciation of God's name in Hebrew.

✤DEMON(S): The word *demon* originated from the Greek word *daimon*, a supernatural being who intercedes between God and mankind. When the Septuagint was translated, the daimons and demons were merged, and the daimons became the "evil demons." Demons are **fallen angels** that dwell in the lower realms near the vicinity of the earth. Some of them fell from grace when they chose to come to the earth and have sexual relations with women. The Book of 1 **Enoch** and the Book of **Genesis** both tell stories of the angels who forsook their places in Heaven to come to the earth to take wives for themselves from among the **daughters of men.** Other angels fell when they rebelled against God and followed **Satan.** Satan and one-third of the angels were thrown out of Heaven down to the earth. In Islam, Satan and his demons were thrown out of Heaven when they refused to bow down and worship **Adam** after God instructed them to do so. In Islam, demons are called **Shaitans** and are sometimes referred to as black angels. Besides the demons that were thrown out of Heaven, there are others of a different category. These are the angels who left their positions in Heaven to come to earth to have sexual relations with women. In addition, the offspring of these fallen angels are also referred to as demons. According to Judeo-Christian beliefs, demons wreak havoc on the lives of humans. They are also believed responsible for influencing the world in immorality, crime, natural disasters, wars, hunger, disease, and all maladies that cause human suffering on earth. In the Testament of Solomon, the demons go up to the Heavens and fly among the **stars,** listening to the decisions that God makes regarding the lives of men. They are also known for taking control of an individual's body and possessing it. This is dangerous for the individual involved. Demons are sometimes referred to as the **sons of darkness** and **unclean spirits** (Acts 5:16). In ancient times it was believed that each angel had one or more demons that he could render powerless. For humans to thwart the demons, they would have to know the names of these angels. King **Solomon** communicated with many of the most powerful demons when they were interfering with the building of his temple. He accomplished this through a **magic ring** that God had given him to render the demons powerless. As he interrogated them, he was able to extract important information from them, such as their names, their evil deeds, and most important, the angels who could render them powerless. The angels and the demons listed in the Testament of Solomon are as follows: **Uriel** thwarts the demons **Artosael, Error, Kairoxanondalon,** and **Ornias. Gabriel** thwarts **Barsafael. Emmanouel** thwarts the **Lion-Shaped Demon** and **Beelzebub.** Karael thwarts Belbel. Lamechiel thwarts **Deception.** Balthioul thwarts **Distress.** Rathanael thwarts **Enepsigos.** Marmaroth thwarts **Fate** and **Rhyx Anoster. Iaoth** thwarts Kourtael. Iameth thwarts **Kunopegos. Azael** thwarts **Lix Tetrax. Adonael** thwarts **Methathiax. Raphael** thwarts **Asmodeus, Obyzouth,** and **Oropel.** Asteraoth thwarts **Power. Michael** thwarts **Ruax.** Briathos thwarts **Scepter. Arael** thwarts **Sphandor. Sabael** thwarts Sphendonael. Rizoel thwarts **Soubelti.** Baruchiel thwarts **Strife.** Bazazath thwarts the **Winged Dragon.** See **Female Demons, Thirty-six Heavenly Bodies, Fallen Angels, Hell.**

✤**DEMON ARCHONS:** See **Archons.**

✤**DEMON OF DEMONS:** In Zoroastrianism **Angra Mainyu** is known as the demon of demons.

✤**DEMONIC LOCUSTS:** See **Apollyon.**

✤**DEMONOLOGY:** The study of **demons.**

✤**DEPUTY ANGELS:** Angels found in Jewish magical practices. They appear to individuals when summoned to give aid.

✤**DESIRABLE DOMINION:** The name of one of the **Amesha Spentas** archangels in Zoroastrianism. He is also called Khshathra.

✤**DESTINY, ANGEL OF: Manu.**

✤**DESTROYER, THE:** A title given to **Mephistopheles. Abaddon** is also called the Destroyer.

✤**DESTRUCTION, ANGELS OF:** Angels that issue **punishment**s to transgressors of God's laws (also called the angels of punishment) both on earth and in Hell. Jewish legend says that there are ninety thousand angels of destruction. Each carries a sword symbolizing punishment, destruction, and their service to God. Their commander is the archangel **Uriel.** Other leaders include **Af, Azriel, Camael** (leader of a troop of twelve thousand angels of destruction), **Harbonah,** Haron-Peor, **Hemah, Kemuel, Kesef,** Kolazanta, Mashhit, Simbiel, **Gazarniel,** and Za'aphiel. In **Ezekiel** 9:1–6 the angels of destruction are sent to the city of Jerusalem. The account says, "Then I heard God shout, 'Come here, you men who are going to punish the city. Bring your weapons with you.' At once six men came from the outer north gate of the Temple, each one carrying a weapon. With them was a man dressed in linen, carrying something to write with. They all came and stood by the bronze altar. The Lord called to the man in linen, 'Go through the city of Jerusalem and put a mark on the forehead of everyone who is distressed because of all the disgusting things being done in the city.' And I heard God say to the other men, 'Follow him through the city and spare no one; have mercy on no one. Kill the old men, young men, young women, mothers, and children. But don't touch anyone who has the mark on his forehead.' "

✤**DESTRUCTIVE SPIRIT:** In Zoroastrianism **Angra Mainyu** is referred to as the destructive spirit.

✤**DEVA(S):** A type of **nature spirit.** The devas are the architects of the physical realm. They hold the blueprints to all earthly **creation.** Everything that is manifested in the physical realm is watched over by a deva. See **Devic Kingdom.**

✤**DEVI:** The manifestation of God in the female form in Hinduism.

✤**DEVIC KINGDOM:** The devic kingdom consists of the **devas** and the **nature spirits.** The devas are the architects of the physical realm. They hold the blueprints to all earthly **creation.** The nature spirits are responsible for the physical requirements of nature. In the devic kingdom dwell the **fairies, nymphs, sylphs, undines, salamanders,** and **gnomes,** who are all helpers of nature. The gnomes work with the earth, sylphs with air, salamanders with fire, and undines with water.

✤**DEVIL (SLANDERER): God's adversary,** also known as **Satan.** The word *devil* comes from the Greek word *diabolos*, which means "slanderer." Some believe that the word *devil* is derived from the Indo-European *devi* (goddess). It is also said to come from the Persian *daeva*, which means **evil spirit.** It is believed that the Devil is behind all of the wickedness in the world. He is the **Chief of Demons.**

✤**DEVILS:** Another word for **demons.**

✤**DEVOTION:** One of the **Amesha Spentas** (archangels) of Zoroastrianism. She is also called **Armaiti.**

✤**DEVOUTNESS, ANGEL OF:** Ananchel.

✤**DIADEM(S):** A crown sometimes worn by angels in art, to symbolize their heavenly sovereignty and authority.

✤**DIAGNOSIS, ANGEL OF: Pharmoros.** He taught mankind how to diagnose illnesses. He also taught humans pharmacy and the use of herbs for medicinal purposes.

✤**DINA:** A great angelic prince in Heaven. He is responsible for revealing the laws of the Torah.

✤**DINIEL:** See **Childbirth.**

✤**DIONYSIUS THE PSEUDO-AREOPAGITE:** A noted Syrian writer who conceived the most widely accepted hierarchy of angels ever written. During the first century, he wrote four books on mysticism, *Celestial Hierarchies, On the Ecclesiastical Hierarchy, The Divine Names,* and *Ten Letters.* These writings earned him the respect of several popes. His book *Celestial Hierarchies* was about the makeup and characteristics of angels. Although he is believed to have been an Armenian monk, in this writing he pretended to be Dionysius the Areopagite. (Dionysius the Areopagite was a judge of the court of the Areopagus. He was also a convert of the

Apostle Paul. He later became the first bishop of Athens.) In 1450 it was discovered that he was a sham, which is why he later became known as the Pseudo-Areopagite (or the Pseudo-Dionysius). Although others wrote and published angelic hierarchies, his was later adopted by the Catholic Church. Today it is the most widely recognized ranking of angels. In conceiving the hierarchy, Dionysius took the names of the **orders of angels** from the Bible. From the Old Testament he listed the **Seraphim, Cherubim,** and **Thrones** as the three highest orders of angels. He took the other orders from the New Testament, from the Apostle Paul's letters to the Colossians and the Ephesians (Colossians 1:16, Ephesians 1:21). He ranked the angels in the following order: The first choir consisted of the **Seraphim, Cherubim,** and **Thrones.** The second choir included the **Dominations, Virtues,** and **Powers.** The third choir held the **Principalities, Archangels,** and **Angels.** The seven archangels according to Dionysius are **Michael, Gabriel, Raphael, Uriel, Chamuel, Jophiel,** and **Zadkiel.**

✤**DIRACHIEL:** One of twenty-eight angels who preside over the **lunar mansions.**

✤**DIRECTIONS, ANGELS OF THE:** The angels of the four directions are **Michael,** Ruler of the East; **Raphael,** Ruler of the West; **Gabriel,** Ruler of the North; **Uriel,** Ruler of the South.

✤**DISEASE(S), ANGEL OF:** According to 1 **Enoch** 40:9, the archangel **Raphael** presides over cures for illness and disease: "The one who is set over all disease and every wound of the children of the people is Raphael." Other angels of disease include Bobel and **Metathiax.** The demons of disease are mentioned in the Testament of **Solomon.** These demons cause humankind to be stricken with illnesses and afflictions. **Adonael** is the angel who is capable of overpowering the demons of disease. In addition, the angel **Kashdejan** taught men how to cure various diseases, and the angel **Pharmoros** taught men how to diagnosis disease.

✤**DISK OF THE MOON, ANGEL OF THE: Opanni'el YHWH.**

✤**DISK OF THE SUN, ANGEL OF THE: Chur.**

✤**DISRAELI, BENJAMIN:** A British author and statesman of Jewish descent. He became a Christian in 1817. While giving a dissertation on Charles Darwin's *Origin of Species,* Disraeli once stated, "The question is this: Is man an ape or an angel? I am on the side of the angels."

✤**DISSENSION, ANGEL OF: Satan.**

✤**DISTRESS:** In the Testament of Solomon, Distress is a demon that **Solomon** summoned and interrogated. He reveals to Solomon that he was a ruler in the world of darkness. He causes men to lack moderation and sets men against each other. Only the great angel Balthioul can over-power him.

✤DIV: A shortened form of **daeva.**

✤DIVINATION, ANGEL OF: Eistibus.

✤DIVINE BEASTS: Another name for the **Hayyoth.** They are angels of fire who reside in the **Seventh Heaven** with God, supporting God's throne.

✤*DIVINE COMEDY, THE:* See **Dante Alighieri.**

✤DIVINE CORE: The place in the universe where God is said to reside. It is where the **Seraphim, Cherubim,** and **Thrones** encircle him, and where the seven **Throne Angels** stand beside him.

✤DIVINE DECREES: A term used when referring to messages from God that are delivered to humans by angels. **Abraham, Hagar, Manoah, Moses, Zechariah,** and the **Virgin Mary** all received divine decrees. (Genesis 18:10, 16:11, 21:17–18; Judges 13:1–5; Exodus 3:1–10; Luke 1: 11–22, 1:26–38).

✤DIVINE FACE, ANGEL OF THE: Phanuel.

✤DIVINE HEALER: A title held by the archangel **Raphael,** who is the angel of healing.

✤DIVINE HERALD: A title held by the Greek god **Hermes.** Hermes, who wore wings on his cap and feet, was the divine herald for **Zeus.** In Judaism and Christianity, **Gabriel** is the divine herald.

✤DIVINE HUSBAND: A title held by the archangel **Gabriel.**

✤DIVINE INTUITION, ANGEL OF: In Zoroastrianism, **Sraosha** is the angel of divine intuition. He is the brother of **Armaiti,** the angel of devotion.

✤DIVINE LAW: In Zoroastrianism, **Asha** represents divine law, order, and morality in the world.

✤DIVINE LIGHT: The divine light is the light of God, which emanates from the angels when they appear to humans on earth. It is also called the **aureole.**

✤DIVINE PHYSICIAN: A title held by the archangel **Raphael,** who is the angel of healing.

✤DIVINE PRESENCE, ANGELS OF: A term used when referring to the presence of God. When the angels go in before the Divine Presence, they are going to stand before God. Seven **archangels** stand in the Divine Presence: **Uriel, Raguel, Michael,** Seraqael, **Gabriel, Haniel,** and **Raphael.** The angels of the Divine Presence are also called **Elohim.**

✤DIVINE PROTECTOR: A title held by the archangel **Michael,** who is God's warrior and the commander in chief of the Celestial Army.

✤**DIVINE SPIRIT:** The word *angel* is derived from the Sanskrit word *Angiras*, which means "divine spirit."

✤**DJIBRIL:** A variation of the name **Jibril,** an archangel of Islam. Jibril is the Islamic name for the Judeo-Christian archangel **Gabriel.** Jibril dictated the **Koran** to the prophet **Muhammad.**

✤**DJINN:** Another name for **deva.**

✤**DOBIEL:** A variation of the name **Dubbiel,** once the guardian angel of **Persia.**

✤**DOCUMENTARIES:** Noted documentaries on angels include *Angels, the Mysterious Messengers* (1994), narrated by actress Patty Duke, and *In Search of Angels* (1994), narrated by actress Debra Winger.

✤**DOHEL:** The angel who holds the keys to the four corners of the earth. He is also keeper of the keys to the **Garden of Eden.**

✤**DOLPHINS:** Dolphins are called angels of the sea. Some believe that dolphins have a connection to the angels and a message for humankind.

✤**DOMESTIC ANIMALS, ANGELS OF: Behemiel** and **Hariel** are both angels who watch over and care for domestic animals. **Hemah** is the angel of death of domestic animals.

✤**DOMIEL:** A variation of the name **Dommiel.**

✤**DOMINATIONS:** The Dominations are the fourth order of angels in the angelic hierarchy. Known as the channels of mercy, they dwell in the **Second Heaven.** They are responsible for governing angelic duties in all angelic orders lower than themselves. They are also in charge of merging the spiritual and physical worlds. They receive their assignments from God directly and rarely communicate with humans personally. They are variously called Dominions, Lords, Lordships, Kuriotetes, and **Hashmallim.** Their leaders are **Zadkiel, Hashmal,** Yahriel, and **Muriel.**

✤**DOMINION:** Another name for **Khshathra,** one of the **Amesha Spentas** (archangels) in Zoroastrianism.

✤**DOMINIONS:** Another name for the order of angels called **Dominations.**

✤**DOMMARTIN:** An angel from the movie *Wings of Desire.*

✤**DOMMIEL:** A fallen angel, Dommiel is the Prince of Terror and Trembling. He is said to be able to come and go in Hell as he wishes and without the need of keys. Variations of the name Dommiel are Domiel and Dumiel.

✤**DON ISAAC ABRAVENEL:** See **Abravenel, Don Isaac.**

✤**DONEL:** An angel who safeguards the south wind.

✤**DONQUEL:** An angel of love. In magic he is called upon to help men in acquiring the love and affections of a woman.

✤**DORÉ, GUSTAVE:** Noted French engraver, illustrator, painter, and sculptor (1832–1883). Doré is famous for his engraved illustrations (many featuring angels) for approximately 120 books, including John **Milton**'s *Paradise Lost* and **Dante**'s *Divine Comedy*. Two of his most popular illustrations are *Circles of Angels* and *Crystalline Heaven*. Other illustrations of angels include portrayals of **Jacob** wrestling with an angel; Ithuriel and Zephon hunting for **Satan** in the **Garden of Eden;** Satan in the **abyss;** the war in Heaven; Satan contemplating the fall; Satan tempting Jesus; Satan enthroned in Hell; and Satan lost in the abyss.

✤**DORMIEL:** An angel who safeguards the east wind.

✤**DOUMA:** A variation of the name **Dumah.** Dumah is the angel of the stillness of death.

✤**DOVE(S):** Doves represent peace on earth, and God's **Holy Spirit.** The Holy Spirit appeared as a dove over the head of Jesus at his baptism. The angel of doves is Alphun.

✤**DOWNEY, ROMA:** The star of the 1995 television show *Touched by an Angel*. In the show Downey plays an angel who has come to earth to help humans learn important lessons, such as love and compassion. Actress Della Reese played the heavenly messenger who brought Downey messages from above.

✤**DRAGON(S):** Dragons can be found in mythology from around the world. They are generally portrayed as large serpents who spout fire. In some beliefs they are mystical beings thought to have supernatural powers. In angelology the most notorious dragon is that which is depicted in the Bible's Book of **Revelation.** There the dragon is an apocalyptic monster and is used figuratively when referring to **Satan.** Satan is referred to as the "fiery-colored dragon" and the "great dragon." Revelation 12:3, 7–9 tells us that the archangel **Michael** battled with the dragon and cast him out of Heaven: "And war broke out in heaven: Michael and his angels battled with the dragon, and the dragon and its angels battled but it did not prevail, neither was a place found for them any longer in heaven. So down the great dragon was hurled, the original serpent, the one called Devil and Satan, who is misleading the entire inhabited earth; he was hurled down to the earth, and his angels were hurled down with him." The she-demon **Leviathan** is the female equivalent of the dragon that resides in the **bottomless pit.** In addition, dragons are a symbol of healing and are often associated with the **Seraphim,** whose name means "healer." See **She-Dragon.**

✤**DRAGON OF DAWN:** A title held by **Satan.**

✤**DRAGON SLAYER:** A title held by the archangel **Michael (God's Warrior)** for his feat of casting the dragon **(Satan)** out of Heaven (Revelation 12:7–9).

✤**DRAPERIES:** A term used when referring to the robes of angels.

✤**DREAM ANGELS:** Angels that help and guide people through the dream state. For specific needs and or questions, these angels can be called upon before falling asleep, so that answers can be provided during dreaming. The archangel **Gabriel** is the angel in charge of dreams.

✤**DRIAL:** An angel who stands guard over the palace of Maon, the **Fifth Heaven.**

✤**DROUGHT, DEMON OF:** In ancient Persian lore, the demon of drought was named Apaosha. Tishtrya, the angel of rain, has power over him.

✤**DUBBIEL:** A fallen tutelary angel who was once the guardian angel of Persia. Legend has it that before his fall, Dubbiel once substituted for the archangel **Gabriel** in Heaven. Gabriel had been temporarily removed from grace for twenty-one days. Daily Dubbiel records the sins of **Israel** so they can be accused before God. He does this with the hopes that God will remove all the children of Israel from the earth. Variations of the name Dubbiel are Dobiel and Dubiel.

✤**DUBIEL:** A variation of the name **Dubbiel.**

✤**DUDLEY:** An angel from the movie *The Bishop's Wife.* Cary Grant played the angel in the popular 1947 film about a jaunty angel named Dudley who is sent to earth to help a bishop in need of a new church.

✤*DUINO ELEGIES:* A poem written by German poet **Rainer Maria Rilke** in 1923. The poem contains Rilke's highest praise of human existence. In it Rilke uses the angels to exemplify self-fulfillment, surpassing the need for a physical existence. In the poem he writes, "Every angel is terrifying."

✤**DUMAH:** Once the guardian angel of Egypt. He later became the angel of the stillness of death, a ruler of demons, and the angel of silence. In **Gehenna** he is Chief of the Demon Princes. Some sources list him as an angel of punishment. A variation of the name Dumah is Douma.

✤**DUMIEL:** A variation of the name **Dommiel.**

✤**DUNAMIS:** Another name for the class of angels called the **Powers.** The Powers guard the passageways leading to Heaven.

✤**DURBAIL:** An angel summoned in Arabic ceremonies involving exorcism.

✤**DÜRER, ALBRECHT:** Noted German painter and engraver (1471–1528) who often featured angels in his art. Five of his most popular illustrations including angels are *Melancholia*, *Nemesis*, *The Expulsion from Paradise*, *Four Avenging Angels*, and *Winged Man Playing a Lute.* Popular woodcuts include *St. Francis Receiving the Stigmata from the Seraphim*, the *Annunciation*, *Saint Michael and the Dragon*, and the *Pillared Angel from Revelation.*

✤**DURGA:** The greatest of the **Shakti** in Hinduism.

✤**DUSK, ANGEL OF:** Aftiel.

✦**DYEUS:** In **Aryan** beliefs Dyeus was a god who performed angelic functions. He later became an **archetypal angel** in Judeo-Christian beliefs. Dyeus was the god of the sky, who sent the rains, and the Aryan protector, who destroyed their adversaries with storms and bolts of lightning. His mate was the Earth goddess, who caused the vegetation to grow.

✦**DYNAMIS:** In gnostic lore, he is one of the rulers of the **Archons** and the personification of God's divine power. In addition, Dynamis is another name for the class of angels called **Powers.**

Are they not all ministering servants sent forth to serve?

—HEBREWS 1:14

✦**EAGLE-HEADED DEITY: Nisroch** is known as the eagle-headed deity. He is a fallen angel from the order of angels called **Principalities.** After his fall he became the eagle-headed deity worshiped by Sennacherib, king of the Assyrians. In some traditions he is a lord of Hell.

✦**EARTH, ANGELS OF:** In Persian mythology the angel of earth is Isphan Darmaz. To the **Essenes,** the angel of earth was personified in the archangel **Michael.** In Zoroastrianism, the guardian angel of earth is **Armaiti.** The angel **Ariael** is called Lord of the Earth. **Araqiel** taught the secrets of earth's geography to humankind. Other angels who watch over the earth include Admael, Archas, Arciciah, **Azriel,** Harabael, Saragael, and Yabbashael.

✦**EARTHQUAKES, ANGEL OF:** The angel who causes earthquakes, **Ra'asiel.** Another angel of earthquakes is **Agreas.**

✦**EAST, ANGEL OF THE:** The archangel **Michael** is the angel of the east.

✦**EAST OF EDEN:** God placed two angels from the **Cherubim** and a turning, **flaming sword** east of Eden to guard the **Tree of Life.**

✦**EAST WIND, ANGEL OF THE:** See **Winds.**

✦**EBED:** One of the seventy-eight names of **Metatron.**

✦**EBLIS:** A variation of the name **Iblis.** Iblis is the Islamic name for Satan.

✦**ECKHART, JOHANNES "MEISTER":** Dominican mystical theologian

(c. 1260–c. 1328). Eckhart had the ability to communicate his feelings of God's presence and nearness to men. During the fourteenth century in Germany, he began a movement centering around mysticism. He held that the angels assisted humans in their personal experiences and perceptions of God. About angels, Eckhart once wrote, "The soul at its highest is found like God, but an angel gives a closer idea of Him. That is all an angel is: an idea of God."

✤**EDEN:** See **Garden of Eden.**

✤**EDEN, BARBARA:** Actress Barbara Eden played the lovable genie in the popular sitcom *I Dream of Jeannie.* Genies are a form of guardian angel in Arabic and Islamic folklore.

✤**EDOM, ANGEL OF: Sammael.**

✤**EDUCATION AND KNOWLEDGE, MUSE OF:** In Greek mythology, Clio was the **muse** of education and knowledge.

✤**EGIBIEL:** One of the angels who preside over the twenty-eight **lunar mansions.**

✤**EGOROI:** A variation of the name **Grigori.** The Grigori were a class of angels assigned to watch over mankind.

✤**EGREGORI:** A variation of the name **Grigori.**

✤**EGRUMIAL:** An angel who stands guard over the palace of Makon, the **Sixth Heaven.**

✤**EGYPT(IANS), ANGELS OF:** In ancient Egypt, angels and winged gods and goddesses were found in the Egyptian pantheon. There was **Isis,** the goddess of fertility and nature. She is depicted in art both with and without wings. There was also **Horus,** who was portrayed as a falcon. There was also Nut, the goddess of the sky, also depicted with wings. Angels called **Serefs** carried the bodies of Egyptian kings to Heaven. ANGELIC LORE. Egypt is mentioned quite frequently in angelic lore. The fallen angel **Abezi** fought against **Moses** in Egypt and aided **Pharaoh** in his attempts to keep the Hebrews in bondage. The demon **Asmodeus** was banished to Egypt by the archangel **Raphael. Mastema** used the guise of the angel of death and killed the firstborn of Egypt. **Astarte,** a she-demon, was known as **Athtar** to the Egyptians. **Dumah** was the guardian angel of Egypt during the Hebrews' Exodus. The angel **Rahab** replaced him in this position.

✤**EIGHTH ORDER:** The eighth order of angels found in the angelic hierarchy are the **Archangels.**

✤**EILO:** One of the many aliases used by the she-demon **Lilith** when she works evil against mortals.

✤**EISHETH ZENUNIM:** A she-demon. She is also one of the angels of **prostitution.**

✤EISTIBUS: The angel of divination. Eistibus presides over crystal gazing, **palmistry, tarot cards, rune stones, I Ching,** and **tea leaves.**

✤EL: The word *el* is found at the end of many angel names. It means "shining." It is taken from the Sumerian word *el*, which means "brightness," the Akkadian word *ilu*, which means "radiant," and the Babylonian *ellu*, which means "the one who shines."

✤EL EL: An angel who watches over the north wind.

✤EL-KARUBIYAN: The Islamic word for **Cherubim.** It means "those brought near to God." The El-Karubiyan glorify God night and day, continuously.

✤ELDERS: The Book of **Revelation** speaks of twenty-four spirits called Elders that stand before the **throne of God.** The Elders praise God by singing, "You are worthy, our Lord and God, to receive glory and honor and power, for you created all things, and by your will they existed and were created" (Revelation 4:11).

✤ELECT ONE: A term used by **Enoch** when referring to the Messiah.

✤ELEMENTAL(S): Angelic beings that work with nature's four basic elements: earth, water, air and fire. The Elementals working with the earth are called **gnomes,** those working with water are called **undines,** those working with the air are **sylphs,** and those working with fire are **salamanders.** The **archangels** rule the Elementals. **Uriel** rules the gnomes, **Gabriel** rules the undines, **Raphael** rules the sylphs, and **Michael** rules the **salamanders.** They are thought by some to be projected energy of individuals who have evolved into spiritual beings. The projected energy of humans is said to be able to create Elementals that can be either angelic or demonic. The archangels create Elementals that are angels, and **Satan** creates Elementals that are demons.

✤ELIJAH: A biblical prophet who was transported to Heaven without ever seeing death. According to Jewish lore, Elijah became a great angel in Heaven. One Jewish prayer hails him as the "Angel of the **Covenant.**" The **Talmud** tells us that he is the angel in charge of recording the deeds of mankind. He is also said to be in charge of escorting the faithful from the earth to their places in Heaven. Elijah appeared as one of the angels in the Transfiguration.

✤ELIM: A superior order of angels.

✤ELOHIM: A high order of angels. They are sometimes referred to as shining beings. The angels of the **Divine Presence** are also called Elohim. According to lore, the great angel **Melchizedek** is said to be the father of the Elohim. (Note: Elohim is also a Hebrew word for God.)

✤ELVES: Small, helpful **fairies** with supernatural powers. They are said to inhabit forests and hills.

✦**EMBRYO, ANGEL OF THE:** Sandolphon.

✦**EMERSON, RALPH WALDO:** One of America's greatest thinkers and authors (1803–1882). About angels Emerson once wrote, "It is in rugged crises, in unweariable endurance, and in aims which put sympathy out of the question, that the angel is shown."

✦**EMMANOUEL:** A name used when referring to God the Almighty. In the Testament of **Solomon** it is a name used to thwart demons that are so strong that only God can render them powerless.

✦**ENAN:** A fallen angel who holds many dark titles including Genius of Satan, Genius of Arnan the Demon, Genius of the Place of Death, Genius of Rage, Genius of the Shadow of Death, Genius of Terror, Genius of Trembling, Genius of Destruction, Genius of Extinction, Genius of Evil-Name, Genius of Mocking, Genius of Plagues, Genius of Deceit, Genius of Injury, and Genius of Asmodeus.

✦**ENEDIEL:** One of the angels who preside over the twenty-eight **lunar mansions.**

✦**ENEPSIGOS:** A female demon able to change into many different forms. This is especially advantageous when she is working her evil against humans.

✦**ENERGY:** At the **throne of God,** angels are thought to have no form at all, but are said to be whirling balls of energy. In Rosicrucian writings, the archangels are described as being like small suns with auras of radiant energy that give off streamers of power.

✦**ENGINES OF WAR:** The angel **Exael** taught men to build engines of war. Because of revealing this knowledge, Exael was cast out of Heaven. He is now ranked among the fallen angels.

✦**ENOCH:** A great Hebrew prophet. He was the seventh descendant of Adam and Eve; the son of Jared, and father of Methuselah. In Islamic beliefs he is called Idris and is also a prophet. He is characterized in the Bible as being a righteous man who was devoted to God. Because of this devotion he never saw death. At the age of 365 God took him bodily up into the Heavens (Genesis 5:24). Legend has it that Enoch was transformed by God into the mighty angel **Metatron.** He also has a twin brother in Heaven, another angel named **Sandolphon.** When Enoch was exalted in the Heavens, he was given thirty-six pairs of wings and 365,000 eyes. BOOKS OF ENOCH. While on earth, Enoch is said to have composed 366 books. Three of those books have his name. The Books of Enoch relate secrets of the Heavens and of the future, which he witnessed in visions and while journeying through the seven Heavens. One of the books dates back to the first two centuries B.C. and gives some insight and understanding of the New Testament and its backgrounds.

The Books of Enoch are a part of the **Pseudepigrapha.** They are full of information about the angels, including their names and responsibilities. They list the angels of hail, lightning, storms, comets, windstorms, hurricanes, thunder, earthquakes, snow, rain, daylight, night, sun, moon, and the heavenly bodies. They give information on the fall of the angels, of their sexual relationships with mortal women, their corruption of humankind, Enoch's unsuccessful attempt to act as mediator for them, and the foretelling of their demise. There is also Enoch's account of a journey he took to the seven Heavens where he witnessed gigantic angels in a confined penal area. Enoch ranked the angels in the following order: (1) **Cherubim,** (2) **Seraphim,** (3) **Ophanim,** (4) all the angels of power, (5) **Principalities,** (6) the **Elect One,** (7) the powers of earth and water.

✦**ENOCHIAN:** See **Angelic.**

✦**ENVIRONMENT ANGELS:** Angels who protect the earth's environment and natural resources such as the oceans, forests, rivers, mountains, and vegetation. They also work at solving environmental problems such as air and water pollution. They help environmentalists come up with new strategies to preserve nature.

✦**ENVY:** Envy is one of the seven deadly sins and is considered a demon **Archon** in gnosticism.

✦**EPIC POETRY, MUSE OF:** In Greek mythology, **Calliope** inspired men to write epic poetry.

✦**ERATO:** In Greek mythology, Erato was the muse who inspired men to write love verses in poetry and music.

✦**ERCLE:** An Etruscan angel who belonged to the group of angels called the **Novensiles.** The Novensiles ruled over the thunderbolts.

✦**ERELIM:** Another name for the order of angels called **Thrones.** The angel **Raziel** is Chief of the Erelim. Variations of the name Erelim are Aralim and Arelim.

✦**EREMIEL:** A great angel who watches over the **abyss** and **Hades.** He is in charge of the souls who are imprisoned in Hades.

✦**ERGEDIEL:** One of the twenty-eight angels of the **lunar mansions.**

✦**EROS:** The winged **god of love** in Greek mythology. He later became an **archetypal angel** of Judeo-Christian lore. According to legend, he was born at the beginning of time out of the chaos of the creation of the world. He brought about the marriage of father sky (Uranus) and mother earth (Gaia). He is the embodiment of the power that causes creatures to procreate. He is portrayed in art as a handsome, muscular young man. He later evolved through art and literature into a child with wings and bow and arrows. His Roman equivalent is **Cupid.** He is considered by many to be an angel.

✤**ERROR:** In the Testament of Solomon, Error is the name of a demon that King **Solomon** summons and interrogates. Error revealed to Solomon that he was a ruler in the world of darkness. He leads people into error and away from religion. He can be thwarted by the angel **Uriel**.

✤**ERTOSI:** Chief of the order of **Powers** and the angel of Mars.

✤**ESCORTS TO HEAVEN:** A title often used when referring to the **Psychopomp,** which are the celestial escort in Zoroastrianism. The idea of angels escorting the souls of the dead is not uncommon in Christianity. In the Book of Luke (16:22), the Bible speaks of angels carrying the soul of a dead man to Heaven: "The poor man died and was carried by the angels to sit beside Abraham at the feast in Heaven." During his ascension, Jesus was escorted to Heaven by two angels from the class of **Virtues** (Acts 1:10–11). See **Celestial Escort, Ascension of Christ.**

✤**ESKIMOS:** Most Eskimos believe in angels who assist mankind and who help in fighting evil spirits that roam the earth looking for a human to possess. The Copper Eskimos of the central Canadian Arctic believe that children have individual guardian angels.

✤**ESSENE(S):** An ancient Jewish religious sect that flourished from the first century B.C. through the first century A.D. They were the writers of the Dead Sea scrolls. According to the scrolls, the Essenes believed that the world was in the control of **Beliar** and his evil forces. They also believed that the final war against Beliar, whom they referred to as the Prince of Darkness, was near. In the scroll *The War of the Sons of Light Against the Sons of Darkness*, the archangel **Michael** is named the Prince of Light. He was believed to have led a host of angels against the dark forces of Beliar. GOOD VERSUS BAD ANGELS. The Essenes believed that the energy with which they existed came from good angels. They believed that within every individual dwells an angel of light and an angel of darkness. The angel of light was good, and the angel of darkness was evil. They believed that an individual's salvation depended upon his deeds in strengthening the good that dwelled within him. This angel of light, also called the spirit of truth, is portrayed as having a positive effect on humans. In the scroll *The Manual of Discipline*, the angel of light is referred to as righteous, humble, patient, and compassionate. By emulating this spirit one could obtain salvation. The angel of darkness had adverse effects on humans. *The Manual of Discipline* refers to the angel of darkness as the "spirit of perversity." He encourages the righteous to participate in such wrongdoing as greed, wickedness, lies, pride, deception, lewd conduct, and blasphemy. The Essenes believed that following the angel of darkness was detrimental to one's salvation.

✦**ESTHER:** The main character in the Book of Esther. Legend has it that the archangel **Gabriel** hindered Queen Vashti from appearing naked before King Ahasuerus and his guests, so that Esther would be chosen to replace Vashti as queen (Esther 1:1–22).

✦**ETERNAL PUNISHMENT, ANGELS OF:** Angels found in the Apocalypse of Zephaniah. They are angels of ungodly men. They have the faces of leopards, tusks like wild boars, and eyes mixed with blood. They have long hair, and in their hands are fiery whips. These are the angels who carry men to Hell for eternal punishment.

✦**ETERNITY:** The name of one of the ten **Holy Sefiroth,** which are angels found in the **Cabala.**

✦**ETHNARCHS:** Angels who are individually assigned to guard nations and large groups of people.

✦**ETRUSCAN(s):** The Etruscan god of the dead was named **Charon.** He had huge wings and a large, crooked nose resembling the beak of a bird. Charon carried the souls of the dead to Hades and was the overseer of the cities of the underworld. Nine angels of the Etruscan beliefs ruled the thunderbolts, called **Novensiles.** Their names were Tina, Menrva, Cupra, Vejovis, Summanus, Ercle, Sethlans, Mantus, and Mars.

✦**EUCHEY:** An angel called upon in exorcisms to ward off demons.

✦**EUPHRATES RIVER, ANGELS OF THE:** The Book of Revelation (9:13–15) mentions four angels who are bound in the great Euphrates River. They are let loose to kill sinful men during the last days of God's great war. The account states: "And the sixth angel sounded, and I heard a voice from the four horns of the golden altar which is before God, saying to the sixth angel which had the trumpet, loose the four angels which are bound in the great river Euphrates. And the four angels were loosed, which were prepared for an hour, and a day, and a month, and a year, for them to slay the third part of men."

✦**EUTERPE:** A muse of the arts in Greek mythology. She was believed to inspire men to write lyric poetry and song verses. She is depicted in art carrying a flute.

✦**EVE (LIFE):** The first human woman created and the wife of **Adam.** THE TEMPTATION OF EVE. Through the guise of a serpent Satan tricked Eve into disobedience to God, there in the **Garden of Eden.** When he spoke to her, he accused God of not telling her the truth and of holding back knowledge from her and Adam (Genesis 3:1–7). Satan said to her, "Did God really tell you not to eat fruit from any tree in the garden?" Eve replied, "We may eat the fruit of any tree in the garden. Except the tree in the middle of it. God told us not to eat the fruit of that tree or even touch it; if we do, we will die." Satan next said, "That's not true; you will not die. God said that because he knows that when you eat it, you will be like God and know what is good and what is bad." Because of what Satan had said to her, Eve ate from the tree, and later her husband, Adam, ate from it as well. The two were immediately cast out of Paradise and eventually died. The children of Adam and Eve have since been in constant turmoil deciding between good and evil. Other angels stand accused of deceiving Eve also. According to the chronicles of **Enoch,** it was **Gader'el** who deceived Eve. (Gader'el is sometimes referred to as the devil.) Legend has it that it was **Pistis-Sophia**'s idea to trick Eve into disobedience to God. LILITH. In Judaic lore Eve is the second wife of Adam, created after **Lilith,** Adam's first wife. Legend has it that Lilith forsook her place as Adam's wife to become a consort to the fallen angels. She later became a she-demon, declaring Eve and her children as her mortal enemies.

✤**EVENING STAR:** Because of the magnificent light that emanates from his body, **Lucifer** is sometimes referred to as the Evening Star.

✤**EVENING SUN, ANGEL OF THE: Aftiel.**

✤**EVIL, ANGEL OF:** A title held by **Satan** the Devil, the originator of evil.

✤**EVIL ANGEL(S):** Another name for the "angels of the **wrath** of God." They are sent to inflict punishment on humans for God. The term is taken from Psalms 78:49 where it says, "He cast upon them the fierceness of his anger, wrath, and indignation, and trouble, by sending evil angels among them." The phrase *evil angels* also refers to the **fallen angels.**

✤**EVIL EYE, ANGEL OF THE:** The angel **Abrid** is called upon to ward off the evil eye. See **Malochia.**

✤**EVIL GIANTS:** See **Nephillim.**

✤**EVIL ONE:** A term frequently used in literature when referring to **Satan** the Devil representing his opposition to God. According to religious beliefs, Satan is responsible for all of the evil and wicked acts in the world. See **Prince of Evil.**

✤**EVIL SPIRIT(S):** A phrase often used when referring to demons. In the chronicles of **Enoch,** the children of the **Watchers** (the **Nephillim**) are also referred to as evil spirits. Evil spirits often attack saints, holy people, and righteous individuals. The angels are often called upon to help individuals fight evil spirits. WARDING OFF EVIL SPIRITS. Evil spirits can be warded off in a variety of ways: through prayer, in asking God to send his angels to protect the individual; also through the use of the names of angels, such as the four archangels **Michael, Gabriel, Raphael,** and **Uriel.** These four names are very powerful in warding off evil spirits.

Also, through magical writings, and the wearing of an amulet charged for protection, often with the name of an angel inscribed upon it.

✤Exael: An angel from the order of angels called **Watchers.** According to the chronicles of **Enoch,** Exael taught men how to build engines of war. He also taught them to create works with precious metals such as silver and gold, and the usage of gems, stones. He instructed women on the use of perfumes and scents. Exael fell from grace because of teaching mankind this knowledge. He also lost favor with God because of his coming to the earth to pursue mortal women.

✤Executioner, The: A title held by the angel **Mastema.** According to lore, Mastema posed as an angel of death and slaughtered the firstborn of Egypt.

✤Existon: An angel invoked in the blessing of **salt.**

✤Exodus, Angels of the: The Book of Exodus 23:20–21 states, "Behold, I send an angel before you, to guard you on the way and to bring you to the place which I have prepared. Give heed to him and hearken to his voice." In the Bible, three primary angels are mentioned in relation to the Hebrews' exodus from Egypt. These include the angel of the **burning bush,** who spoke to **Moses,** informing him that he was to lead the Hebrews out of Egypt; the angel of the **pillar of cloud,** who led the Hebrews out of Egypt; and the angel of death, who slew the first-born of the Egyptians.

✤Exorcism: Angels are often summoned for help in exorcisms. The names of the archangels are powerful in exorcising demons. **Gabriel, Raphael, Michael,** and **Uriel** are the names that hold the most power. Other angels whose names are sometimes used in exorcisms are Bedaliel, Euchey, Iaeo, Iealo, Ioelet, and Sasgabiel.

✤*Expulsion from Paradise:* The name of an engraving by **Albrecht Dürer.** Painted in the fifteenth century, the engraving shows one of the **Cherubim** expelling the disobedient couple (**Adam** and **Eve**) from Paradise.

✤Extraterrestrials: It has been speculated by some that angels are really a superior race of beings who visit humans in the form that is most expected, based on religious and cultural beliefs. Some believe that humans are the offspring of a superior race of beings. Others contend that humans are an experiment and are being monitored by higher beings. It has also been said that **Ezekiel's** vision of angels in the Bible was actually a UFO, with extraterrestrial beings. In addition, there are ancient tales of "shining beings" who once visited and even lived on the earth. Some theologians have stated that the UFOs in the sky and other extraterrestrial phenomena are actually the work of demons (or fallen angels) attempting to lead mankind away from the belief in God.

✦**EYES, DEMON OF THE:** In the Testament of **Solomon,** Artosael is the demon who damages the eyes. He can be rendered powerless by calling on the archangel **Uriel.**

✦**EZEKIEL:** A major prophet of the Old Testament and author of the Book of Ezekiel. In Ezekiel 1:4–9 he writes about angels that he referred to as "living creatures": "I looked up and saw a windstorm coming from the north. Lightning was flashing from a huge cloud, and the sky around it was glowing. Where the lightning was flashing, something shone like bronze. At the center of the storm I saw what looked like four living creatures in human form, but each of them had four faces and four wings. Their legs were straight, and they had hoofs like those of a bull. They shone like polished bronze. In addition to their four faces and four wings, they each had four human hands, one under each wing. Two wings of each creature were spread out so that the creatures formed a square, with their wing tips touching. When they moved, they moved as a group without turning their bodies." According to angelic lore, the four living creatures hold up God's throne. They also represent the four directions, symbolizing that God is everywhere and all-seeing.

✦**EZEQEL:** One of the angels who led the **Watchers** to earth to have sexual relations with women. Ezeqel also taught meteorology to mankind.

F

Praise him, all his angels, praise him, all his host.
—PSALMS 148:2

✢FACE, ANGELS OF THE: The equivalent of the **Angels of the Presence**.
✢FAIRIES: Small, beautiful, angelic beings with wings who have supernatural powers. They belong to the family of **nature spirits** and are sometimes referred to as little angels. They are guardians of animals and
vegetation. In Persian mythology the Peri are beautiful fairies who reside in
Heaven. In Arabic lore, the **jinn** were considered a type of fairy. In German
mythology, fairies are called **Lorelei**. See **Fairy Godmother, Tooth Fairy**.
✢FAIRIES OF HEAVEN: In Persian mythology the Peri are known as the
beautiful fairies of Heaven.
✢FAIRY: See **Fairies**.
✢FAIRY GODMOTHER: A type of guardian angel. The fairy godmother
looks after and protects her charges, granting them wishes and appearing
to them in times of great need. The most famous fairy godmother is the
one in the classical tale *Cinderella*. Cinderella is a fairy-tale heroine who
escapes from a life of drudgery with the help of her fairy godmother and
marries a handsome prince.
✢FAIRY QUEEN: In Celtic lore, the fairy queen reigned over a realm
called the "land of the forever living" (a place that closely resembles
Heaven), where death did not exist, nor did sin or wrongdoing. See
Fairies.

✤**FAITHFUL SERVANT:** In Islam the archangel **Jibril** is referred to as the faithful servant.

✤**FAITHFUL SPIRIT:** In Islam the archangel **Jibril** is referred to as the faithful spirit for his dictating of the **Koran** to **Muhammad.**

✤**FAKR-ED-DIN:** An angel of the **Yezidics.**

✤**FALL, ANGEL OF:** Ardarcel.

✤**FALLEN ANGEL(S):** Regarding the fallen angels, William Shakespeare writes in his famous play *Macbeth*, "Angels are bright still, though the brightest fell." There are two definitions of fallen angels: (1) an angel who has lost God's favor because of disobedience; (2) an angel who opposed God and is a follower of **Satan** the Devil. According to the Cardinal Bishop of Tusculum (thirteenth century), there are 133,306,668 fallen angels. The names of the most notorious, and also the most interesting, are **Abezi, Adirael, Adramalec, Agniel, Agreas, Amy, Anan'el, Anituel, Anmael, Arakeb, Arakiba, Arazyal, Ariael,** Arioch, **Armaros, Armen, Arsiel, Asael, Asbeel, Asel, Asmodeus, Asta-**roth, **Astarte,** Atarculph, **Azael, Azza, Baal-Beryth, Baal-Peor, Ba-**lam, **Baraqijal, Baraqiyal,** Barbatos, **Barbelo, Bareschas, Baruel, Batanel, Batar'el,** Batarjal, **Beleth, Beqa,** Busasejal, **Carniveau,** Caym, Curson, Dagon, Dan'el, Danjal, **Dommiel, Dubbiel, Enan, Exael, Ezeqel, Forneus, Furcalor, Gader'el, Gressil, Haroth, Havras, Inias, Iuvart, Jomjael, Kasadya, Kasbel, Kokabi'el, Lahash, Levia-**than, **Makkiel, Mammon,** Marchocias, **Maroth, Mastema, Melchi Dael, Meririm,** Murmus, Nelchael, **Nisroch,** Nith-haiah, Oeillet, Pay-mon, **Penemuel, Pharzuph,** Pocel, **Rimmon, Salmael,** Sameveel, **Sam-mael, Sariel, Satan, Shemyaza,** Sonnillon, Tabaet, **Tam'el,** Tap, **Turiel,** Urakabarameel, **Usiel,** Verrier, Vual, Xaphan, **Yeqon, Zaphiel,** and Zavebe. See **Demons.**

✤**FALLEN STARS:** According to the chronicles of **Enoch,** in the heavenly Book of Angels, the fallen angels are referred to as fallen stars.

✤**FALSEHOOD:** Falsehood is one of the seven deadly sins and considered a demon **Archon** in gnosticism. He represents the planet Mercury. His antithesis is the archangel **Michael.**

✤**FAMILIARS:** In Native American beliefs, Familiars are spirit helpers believed to manifest in the form of animals. Familiars is also the name of the guardian spirits of witches.

✤**FANUEL:** A variation of the name **Phanuel.** Phanuel is the angel of penance.

✤**FARLAS:** The angel who presides over **winter.**

✤**FARMING, ANGEL OF:** Risnuch.

✤**FASTING, ANGEL OF:** Sangariah.

✤FATE: In the Testament of Solomon, Fate is a demon that King **Solomon** summons and interrogates. Fate reveals to Solomon that he is a ruler in the world of darkness. He causes men to fight rather than make peace. He can be thwarted by the angel Marmaroth.

✤FATE, ANGEL OF: **Manu.**

✤FATHER OF THE LIE: A title held by **Satan** the Devil.

✤FATIMA: In 1917 in Fatima, Portugal, the **Virgin Mary** appeared to three shepherd children. Through these children she warned the world of coming punishments on mankind if people did not change their sinful lives. Fatima, Portugal, is now a site of religious pilgrimages.

✤FAUNUS: A guardian spirit in Roman mythology. He protected the herds and crops.

✤FAUST, JOHANN: Sixteenth-century German doctor and magic practitioner. Legend has it that Faust sold his soul to **Mephistopheles** (another name for Satan) in exchange for magical powers, wisdom, and eternal youth. He is said to have died a mysterious death. His story was portrayed in Goethe's masterpiece, *Faust*, in which angels were portrayed as heroic figures.

✤FEAR, ANGEL OF: **Yrouel.**

✤FEAST OF GUARDIAN ANGELS, THE: A holiday of Catholicism, celebrated on October 2. The purpose of the feast is to celebrate all of the angels at once. In the old days there was a holiday for each archangel. The exception now is for the archangel **Michael,** who is celebrated in a feast called **Michaelmas.**

✤FEBRUARY, ANGEL OF: **Barakiel.**

✤FEMALE ANGEL(S): The top-ranking female angels are **Pistis-Sophia,** the **Virgin Mary, Gabriella, Achamoth,** and Al Ussa (from Arabic lore).

✤FEMALE DEMON(S): The Queen of the She-Demons is **Proserpina.** Top-ranking female demons are **Astarte,** Ruler of the Spirits of the Dead; **Leviathan,** the she-dragon of the **bottomless pit; Agrat-bat-Mahlaht,** Eisheth Zenunim, and **Naamah,** the angels of prostitution; and **Lilith,** Adam's first wife. Others include **Barbelo,** one of the daughters of **Pistis-Sophia;** Enepsigos, who has the ability to change into different forms; **Obyzouth,** who causes harm and pain to the bodies of humans; and **Onoskelis,** who has the body of a woman and the legs of a mule.

✤FERESHTA: A variation of the name **Fereshteh.**

✤FERESHTEH: The Persian word for angel. A variation of the name Fereshteh is Fereshta. The Fereshteh are winged spiritual counselors that praise and worship God.

✤**FERTILITY, ANGEL OF:** According to Mandaean mythology, the angel of fertility is named Samandiriel. In Arabic mythology it was Manah. In Egyptian mythology it was the winged goddess **Isis.**

✤**FETUS, ANGEL OF:** The angel who guards the fetus is **Armisael.**

✤**FIERY AND MERCILESS ANGEL: Pusiel,** whose name means "fire," is known as the fiery and merciless angel. He is in charge of interrogating and torturing sinful souls in Hell.

✤**FIERY-COLORED DRAGON:** A phrase used in the Bible when referring to **Satan** the Devil. Revelation 12:3–4 of the New World translation of the Holy Scriptures states, "And another sign was seen in heaven, and look! a great fiery-colored dragon, with seven heads and ten horns and upon its head seven diadems; and its tail drags a third of the stars of heaven, and it hurled them down to the earth."

✤**FIERY SERPENT:** A title held by the archangel **Uriel.** According to Judaic lore, Uriel appeared to **Moses** as a fiery serpent, punishing him for not observing the rite of circumcision for his son.

✤**FIFTH ANGEL OF THE TRUMPETS:** In the Book of Revelation, there are seven angels with **trumpets.** Each angel sounds his trumpet, one at a time, and an apocalyptic event takes place. The Bible states that when the fifth angel sounded his trumpet, "a star [angel] fell from Heaven unto the earth: and to him was given the key of the bottomless pit. And he opened the bottomless pit; and there arose a smoke out of the pit, and the sun and the air were darkened by the smoke. And there came out of the smoke locusts upon the earth: and unto them was given power, as the scorpions of the earth have power. And it was commanded them that they should not hurt the grass of the earth, neither any green thing, neither any tree; but only those men which have not the seal of God in their foreheads. . . . And they had a king over them, [which is] the angel of the bottomless pit, whose name in the Hebrew tongue is **Abaddon,** but in the Greek tongue hath his name Apollyon." (Revelation 9:1–4,11)

✤**FIFTH HEAVEN, ANGELS OF THE:** The angel Satqi'el is prince of the Fifth Heaven, also called Maon. It is the dwelling place of the avenging angels. The northern part of the Fifth Heaven is where the Watchers are eternally imprisoned for their sin of coming to the earth and having sexual relations with mortal women; the chronicles of **Enoch** portray it as a fiery place. The southern part of the Fifth Heaven is where the **Trisagion** is chanted by angels at night. In addition, the Islamic angel Kalka'il is said to dwell there. Kalka'il is ruler of the **Huri.** The angels who guard the great palace of the Fifth Heaven are Drial, Gamrial, Garfial, Gmial, Grial, Paltrial, Sefrial, Techial, and Uzial.

✦FIFTH ORDER: The fifth order of angels in the angelic hierarchy are the Virtues.

✦FINANCIERS, ANGEL OF: Anauel.

✦FIORETTI: A term referring to situations where angels intercede in the lives of mankind.

✦FIRE: The word *fire* is often used when referring to angels. It can be found in many of the names of angels, and when describing the makeup of angels. Fire symbolizes the passion that the angels carry for their assigned duties. It also represents their divine powers, as well as the pure raw energy that their spiritual bodies are made of. The Koran states that angels have bodies of fire. In Judaism the archangels are referred to as fire spirits. The archangel **Gabriel** is said to be made of fire; the archangel **Michael** represents the "element of fire"; and the archangel **Uriel**'s name means **"fire of God."** **Pusiel,** whose name means "fire," is known as the "fiery and merciless angel." In scripture the **Watchers** are referred to as "angels of fire" and are said to have bodies made up of fire. **Chasmal** is the "fire-speaking angel." The Angel of the Lord first appeared to Moses as fire in a **burning bush** (Exodus 3:2).

✦FIRE, ANGEL OF: In ancient Jewish lore the angel of fire was named Nathanel. Because of his association with fire sacrifices, **Adramelec** is known as the angel of fire. In Zoroastrianism, Atar was the protector of fire. In Vedic beliefs it was **Agni.** In ancient occult beliefs Ardarel was summoned to guard the fire, and in rabbinic lore Atuniel was an angel of fire.

✦FIRE OF GOD: The meaning of the name **Uriel,** who is one of the seven archangels in Judeo-Christian beliefs. The symbol of an open hand holding a flame represents Uriel.

✦FIRE SACRIFICES: In Samaria the fallen angel **Adramalec** was a god to whom children were sacrificed by fire. Because of this he obtained the titles angel of fire and **ruler of fire.**

✦FIRE-SPEAKING ANGEL: A phrase used when referring to the angel **Chasmal.**

✦FIRE SPIRITS: A term sometimes used in angelology when referring to the archangels. The term refers to their nature, as they are thought by some to be made of fire.

✦FIRST ANGEL OF THE TRUMPETS: In the Book of Revelation, there are seven angels with **trumpets.** Each angel sounds his trumpet, one at a time, and an apocalyptic event takes place on earth. When the first angel sounds his trumpet, hail and fire mixed with blood were cast down upon the earth. As a result trees and vegetation were destroyed (Revelation 8:7).

✤**FIRST CHOIR OF ANGELS:** See **First Triad of Angels.**

✤**FIRST-CREATED ANGELS:** Legend has it that the first five angels created by God were, in order, **Satan, Michael, Gabriel, Uriel,** and **Raphael.** All other angels were created after these.

✤**FIRST HEAVEN, ANGELS OF THE:** The ruling angel of the First Heaven (also called **Wilon**) is Sidri'el. The angels who dwell in Wilon include the angels of astronomy, the angels of ice, the angels of snow, and the angels of the morning dew. At the border dwells the order of angels called the **Powers.** The angels who stand guard over the great palace of the First Heaven are Adririon, Ashrulyai, Dahariel, Deheboryn, Huzia, Jekusiel, Khabiel, Maskiel, Mufgar, Nahuriel, Sabriel, Sheviel, Shoel, Shokad, Suria, Tandal, Tashriel, Tufiel, Tutrechial, Tutrusiai, Zahabriel, and Zortek.

✤**FIRST ORDER OF ANGELS:** The first order of angels found in the angelic hierarchy are the **Seraphim.** The Seraphim are the angels who dwell closest to God in Heaven.

✤**FIRST RECORDS OF ANGELS:** In the Euphrates Valley, in the city of **Ur,** archaeologists found a stele with an angel carved on it. The angel is portrayed as descending from the **Seventh Heaven** carrying a jar overflowing with water and pouring it into the cup of a mortal king. It is recognized as the earliest known depiction of an angel. Other sources state that the first recorded reference to angels was over 10,000 years ago.

✤**FIRST TRIAD OF ANGELS:** The first triad of angels in the angelic hierarchy consists of the **Seraphim, Cherubim,** and **Thrones.**

✤**FIRSTBORN OF EGYPT:** In the Book of Exodus, God sends the prophet **Moses** to free the Hebrews from bondage to the Egyptians. After a series of plagues brought on by God to force the Egyptians to release the Hebrews, **Pharaoh** finally relents after the firstborn of Egypt, including his son, are slaughtered by the angel of death. According to lore, it was **Mastema** (God's executioner) who slew the firstborn of Egypt.

✤**FISH, ANGELS OF: Gagiel** is the angel who presides over fish. In the Book of Tobit, the angel Azarias instructs young **Tobias** on the medicinal uses of the parts of a fish.

✤**FIT MINDEDNESS:** Another name for the Zoroastrian archangel named **Armaiti.**

✤**FLAME, ANGELS OF THE:** The symbol of an open palm holding a flame represents the archangel **Uriel,** who is called the fire of God. In Zoroastrianism, **Asha** is represented in rituals by the flame because of her title as the protector of fire.

✤**FLAMES:** An order of angels.

✤**FLAMING ONE:** The angel **Lahatiel** carries the title of the flaming one. This title represents his position in Hell as a wrathful angel of punishment.

✤**FLAMING SWORD:** A turning, flaming sword was posted outside the **Garden of Eden,** along with two **Cherubim,** to prevent **Adam** and **Eve** from reentering Paradise after their disobedience to God (Genesis 3:24).

✤**FLETCHER, JOHN:** English dramatist (1579–1625). In his play *The Honest Man's Fortune*, Fletcher wrote, "Our acts our angels are, or good or ill, Our fatal shadows that walk by us still."

✤**FLIES:** In some ancient beliefs, flies were thought to bear the souls of the dead to the underworld. The Lord of the Flies later became known as **Beelzebub,** who carried the souls of the dead to Hades.

✤**FLOOD, ANGELS OF THE:** According to 1 **Enoch** 10:1–2, Asuryal was the messenger sent by God to warn **Noah** of the impending flood: "And he [God] sent Asuryal to the son of Lamech [Noah], saying, 'Tell him in my name, Hide yourself! The Deluge is about to come upon all the earth; and all that is in it will be destroyed.' " In addition to Asuryal other angels have been named in association with the flood. The angel **Raziel** authored the Book of Raziel, from which Noah followed instructions on the building of the ark. The angels in charge of releasing the water of the flood were the angels of punishment. Also the angel in charge of drying up the water was Charavah, whose name means "dryness."

✤**FLORENTINE PAINTERS:** The most famous Florentine painters who featured angels in their art include **Benozzo Gozzoli, Fra Angelico, Domenico Ghirlandaio,** and **Giotto di Bondone.**

✤**FLOWERS, ANGELS OF:** In Zoroastrianism the angel of flowers is **Ameretat.** In addition, flowers are also nurtured and protected by **nature spirits.**

✤**FLYING, ANGEL OF: Ampharool.**

✤**FOOD, ANGEL OF: Manna.** In Islam, **Mikhail** provides men with food and sustenance.

✤**FOOD OF ANGELS:** The food of angels is called manna. According to the Bible, it is a granular substance. It is the same substance that was rained down upon the Hebrews after they fled from Egypt. The Bible states, "And he [the Lord] spoke to the sky above and commanded its doors to open; he gave them grain from heaven, by sending down manna for them to eat. So they ate the food of angels, and God gave them all they wanted" (Psalms 78:23–25). It is said to taste like wafers and honey.

✤*FOR HEAVEN'S SAKE:* A 1950 movie starring Clifton Webb as an angel named Charles, and Edmund Gwenn as his companion angel, Arthur. The two are sent to earth to assist the prospective parents of a child called Item. Item is an angel who has waited seven years to be born to earthly parents. While on earth Charles experiences some of earth's more sinful pleasures.

✤FORCE, ANGEL OF: The archangel **Raphael.**

✤FORCE FIELD: A term sometimes used when referring to the luminous **light** surrounding angels. It is described as a glowing light that starts at the crown of their head, surrounding their body. The light gives them an appearance of having wings of light. It is said that the angels project themselves by maneuvering this force field.

✤FORESTS, ANGEL OF: The angel Zulphas presides over all of nature within the forests and sees to its preservation.

✤FORETELLING OF BIRTHS, ANGEL OF THE: The archangel **Gabriel,** who is also called the "angel who presides over childbirth." He holds this title because of his announcement of important births. In the New Testament, the archangel Gabriel foretold the births of both **John the Baptist** (to Zechariah), and Jesus Christ (to the **Virgin Mary**). In apocryphal lore he foretold the **births** of **Samson** and the Virgin Mary.

✤*FOREVER DARLING:* A 1956 movie starring Lucille Ball as Susan Bewell, a young woman who is visited by her guardian angel, played by James Mason. The movie also starred Desi Arnaz as the husband of Susan Bewell.

✤*FORGETFUL ANGEL:* A drawing by **Paul Klee.**

✤FORGETFULNESS, ANGEL OF: Poteh.

✤FORMS: See **Appearance.**

✤FORNEUS: A fallen angel from the order of angels called **Thrones.** He later became a marquis in the underworld. When he is invoked, he appears to men as a sea monster.

✤FORNICATION, ANGEL OF: **Pharzuph.** He is also called the angel of **lust.**

✤FORTUNE-TELLING, ANGEL OF: **Eistibus.**

✤FOSTERING, ANGEL OF: The archangel **Gabriel.**

✤FOUNDATION: The name of one of the ten **Holy Sefiroth** (angels of the **Cabala**).

✤FOUR SEASONS, ANGELS OF THE: The angels of the seasons are Ardarcel, the angel of fall; Farlas, the angel of winter; Talvi, the angel of spring; and Casmaran, the angel of summer.

✤FOUR WINDS, ANGELS OF THE: See **Winds.**

✤FOURTH ANGEL: According to angelic lore, the archangel **Uriel** was the fourth angel created by God. See **First-Created Angels.**

✤FOURTH ANGEL OF THE TRUMPETS: In the Book of **Revelation,** there are seven angels with **trumpets.** One at a time, each angel sounds his trumpet, and an apocalyptic event takes place. The apostle **John,** to whom the vision was given, tells us that when the fourth angel sounded his trumpet, "the third part of the sun was smitten, and the third part of the moon, and the third part of the stars; so as the third part of them was darkened. And I beheld, and heard an angel flying through the midst of Heaven, saying with a loud voice, Woe, woe, woe, to the inhabiters of the earth by reason of the other voices of the trumpet of the three angels, which are yet to sound!" (Revelation 8:12–13)

✦**FOURTH HEAVEN, ANGELS OF THE:** Sahaqi'el is the ruling prince of the Fourth Heaven, which is named **Zebul.** It is where the "heavenly Jerusalem" is located. The orders of angels called the **Phoenixes** and the **Kalkydra** dwell there. The angels that stand guard over the grand palace of the Fourth Heaven are Almon, Anfial, Avial, Gvurtial, Kfial, Kzuial, Pachdial, Shchinial, and Shtukial.

✦**FOURTH ORDER:** The fourth order of angels in the angelic hierarchy are the **Dominations.**

✦**FOWL, ANGEL OF: Trigiaob.**

✦**FRA ANGELICO:** See **Angelico, Fra.**

✦**FRANCE:** The fallen angel **Baal-Peor** is known as the Demonic Ambassador to France and the Guardian Demon of Paris.

✦**FRANCESCA, PIERO DELLA:** A major Italian Renaissance painter (1420–1492) who specialized in religious paintings that featured angels. Two of his most famous works portraying angels are the paintings of the archangel **Michael,** entitled, *St. Michael* (ca. 1469) and his depiction of the archangel **Gabriel** (painted in 1455). In his depiction of Gabriel, he gave him very human qualities. It was a way in which Gabriel, a popular figure in art history, had not been seen before.

✦**FRANCESCO FORGIONE (PADRE PIO DA PIETRALCINA):** Italian priest and mystic. He felt the calling to become a priest at age five when he was already experiencing mystical powers and seeing visions of angels. In his life he had angelic visitations and battles with demons. During his bouts with the demons he was comforted by an angel who encouraged him and strengthened him. He is said to have even been washed by angels. In addition, the **Virgin Mary** and the Sacred Heart of Jesus both appeared to him in visions.

✦**FRANCIS (SAINT):** See **Saint Francis of Assisi.**

✦**FRANCIS DE SALES, SAINT:** See **Saint Francis de Sales.**

✦**FRAVASHI:** Angels in Zoroastrianism. A Fravashi is a cross between ancestral spirits, guardian angels, and the immortal higher self of individuals. It was believed that each individual had a Fravashi to protect and defend him or her against demons. In ancient Zoroastrian legend, the Fravashi assisted **Ohrmazd** (God) in his battle against **Ahriman** (Satan).

✤FREE WILL, ANGEL OF: Tabris.

✤FREEMAN, EILEEN ELIAS: The best-selling author of *Touched by Angels*, *Angelic Healing*, and *The Angel's Little Instruction Book*. She is also the director of the AngelWatch Foundation, an organization dedicated to providing information on the topic of angels; and the creator of *AngelWatch*, a bimonthly newsletter about angels. *AngelWatch* includes angel stories, angel experiences, and is a resource guide on angels. For more information send a letter and a self-addressed, stamped business-size envelope to *AngelWatch*, P.O. Box 1362, Mountainside, NJ 07092, Attention: President of the AngelWatch Foundation.

✤FRIDAY, ANGEL OF: **Haniel.** The angels who preside over the hours of the day on Friday are 1:00-Haniel, 2:00-**Raphael**, 3:00-**Gabriel**, 4:00-**Casziel**, 5:00-**Sachiel**, 6:00-**Sammael**, 7:00-**Michael**, 8:00-Haniel, 9:00-Raphael, 10:00-Gabriel, 11:00-Casziel, 12:00-Sachiel. The angels who preside over the hours of the night are 1:00-Sammael, 2:00-Michael, 3:00-Haniel, 4:00-Raphael, 5:00-Gabriel, 6:00-Casziel, 7:00-Sachiel, 8:00-Sammael, 9:00-Michael, 10:00-Haniel, 11:00-Raphael, 12:00-Gabriel.

✤FRIENDS OF LIGHTS: The name of a group of angels in **Manichaeism.**

✤FRIENDSHIP, ANGEL OF: In Persian mythology, the angel **Mihr** was the angel of friendship.

✤FRUIT, ANGEL OF: Sofiel.

✤FRUITFULNESS, ANGEL OF: **Zidkiel.** In Zoroastrianism it is **Ardvi Sura Anahita.**

✤FULLNESS OF GOD'S KNOWLEDGE: The meaning of the name **Cherubim.** From the Cherubim emanates the knowledge of God to the world below.

✤FURCALOR: A fallen angel from the order of angels called **Thrones.** After his fall he became a high-ranking demon of Hell who enjoys slaying men. When he manifests, he comes as a man with huge griffin wings.

✤FURNACE, ANGEL OF THE: The angel that rescued three faithful Hebrew men from a blazing, fiery furnace. The three men, named Shadrach, Meshach, and Abednego, were thrown into a fiery furnace for not worshiping King **Nebuchadnezzar's** golden idol. Daniel 3:22–23 of the Bible tells us, "Now because the king had given strict orders for the furnace to be made extremely hot, the flames burned up the guards who took the men to the furnace. Then Shadrach, Meshach, and Abednego, still tied up, fell into the heart of the blazing fire." However, God sent an angel to rescue them. Daniel 3:24–25 states, "Suddenly Nebuchadnezzar leaped to his feet in amazement. He asked his officials, 'Didn't we tie up three men and throw them into the blazing furnace?' They answered, 'Yes, we did, Your Majesty.' 'Then why do I see four men walking around in the fire?' he asked. 'They are not tied up, and they show no sign of being hurt—and the fourth one looks like an angel.' " Daniel 3:27 states, "Their hair was not singed, their clothes were not burned, and there was no smell of smoke on them." Nebuchadnezzar was so impressed with this that he stated, "Praise the God of Shadrach, Meshach, and Abednego! He sent his angel and rescued these men who serve and trust him. There is no other god who can rescue like this" (Daniel 3:28, 29). This biblical tale of the angel in the furnace has been a source of inspiration in Judaism and Christianity. It is taught that if people will stand for what is right and remain faithful to God, then God will send an angel to rescue them.

✤FUTURE, ANGEL OF THE: Teiaiel.

✤FYLGIR: The plural form of **Fylgja.**

✤FYLGJA: A type of angel in German mythology. A Fylgja is a cross between a guardian angel and one's immortal higher self. A Fylgja was usually met outside of one's body, or it would come to an individual in his dreams. When appearing, it came in the form of an animal that mirrored the individual's personality. In dangerous situations the Fylgja acted as a guardian angel. It also came to the aid of a person dying, to help through the transition of death. If a person saw his Fylgja die in a dream, it meant that that person's life was nearing its end. The plural form of Fylgja is Fylgir.

*For He will give His Angels charge concerning you,
To guard you in all your ways.*

—PSALMS 91:11

✤GABRIEL (GOD IS MY STRENGTH): One of the seven **archangels.** He is one of the two highest-ranking angels in Judaism, Christianity, and Islam He is best known for bringing important announcements to mankind. He is first encountered in the Bible's Old Testament when he appears to **Daniel** (8:16) to explain a vision. He later appears to Daniel a second time to announce the coming of the Messiah. In the New Testament he announces the birth of **John the Baptist** to Zechariah (Luke 1:11–22) and the birth of Jesus to **Mary** (Luke 1:26–33). In Islam, Gabriel is called **Jibril.** It was Jibril who revealed the **Koran** to **Muhammad.** For this reason he is also called the faithful spirit, the faithful servant, and the bringer of good news. He is also the guardian angel of Muhammad. During the Middle Ages, Christians believed him to be the angel of light. In **Essene** beliefs he was the angel of life and the angel of **Monday.** In ancient Judaic lore, Gabriel was thought to be female, the only female to be listed in the archangel class. In the Book of Raziel, he is listed as an angel whose name can be found on charms worn by pregnant women for help in childbirth. He is also listed as one of the ruling angels of the twenty-eight **lunar mansions.** TITLES. **Gabriel** holds many titles including Ruler of the **Sixth Heaven,** Chief Ambassador to Humanity, Chief Ambassador of God, Ruling Prince of the **Cherubim,**

Divine Herald, Angel of Revelation, Angel of Aspirations, Angel of **Truth,** Divine Husband, Prince of Justice, Angel of **Joy,** Angel of Child-birth, Archangel of the **Holy Sefiroth,** Trumpeter of the Last Judgment, Governor of Eden, Angel of Vengeance, Angel of Death, Angel of the Annunciation, Angel of the Resurrection, Angel of Revelation, Angel of Mercy, Angel of Aquarius, Angel of Judgment, and Angel of the **Apple Tree.** He is referred to as the voice of God. Because of this, he is symbol-ized by the trumpet, which represents God's voice. He is represented by the colors **silver** and **white.** Variations of the name Gabriel are Gavriel and **Gabriella.**

✤**GABRIELLA:** The female form of **Gabriel.** In Judaic lore, Gabriel is believed to be a female angel, the only female in the Archangel class.

✤**GADER'EL:** The prophet **Enoch** named Gader'el as the angel who deceived **Eve.** He also taught mankind how to manufacture arms and is sometimes referred to as the devil. Variations of the name Gader'el are Gadriel and Gadreel. He is also known as **Aramaic.**

✤**GADREEL:** A variation of **Gader'el.**

✤**GADRIEL:** A variation of **Gader'el.**

✤**GAGIEL:** The angel who presides over **fish.**

✤**GALGALIEL:** A variation of **Galgalliel.**

✤**GALGALLIEL:** A chief angel in Heaven. He is ruler of the **Galgallin,** an elite order of angels, and is one of two ruling angels of the sun. He holds the title Angel of the Orb of the Sun. Variations of Galgalliel are Gal-galiel and Galgliel.

✤**GALGALLIM:** A variation of the name **Galgallin.**

✤**GALGALLIN:** Another name for the class of angels called **Thrones.** It comes from the Hebrew word *galgal,* which means **wheels.** The Thrones are said to wheel around the **throne of God.** Their role is to inspire confidence in the power of God. A variation of the name Galgallin is Galgallim.

✤**GALGLIEL:** A variation of the name **Galgalliel.**

✤**GALLISUR YHWH:** A great angelic prince in Heaven. He is said to have revealed all of the secrets of the Torah to mankind.

✤**GALLIZUR:** Another name for **Raziel.**

✤**GALRAZYAH:** One of the seventy-eight names of the great angel **Metatron.**

✤**GAMALIEL:** One of the **Cabala**'s ten **Unholy Sefiroth.**

✤**GAMBLING, ANGEL OF:** Aclahaye.

✤**GAMCHICOTH:** One of the **Cabala**'s ten **Unholy Sefiroth.**

✤**GAMRIAL:** An angel who polices the palace of Maon (the **Fifth Heaven**).

✦**GANDHARVAS:** The Gandharvas were heavenly musicians in classical Hinduism. In art they are depicted as winged men.

✦**GANZ:** The name of an angel from the popular film *Wings of Desire.* Ganz travels about the city of Berlin listening to people's thoughts. He eventually becomes tired of observing the pain of humans and of not having his love returned. In time he decides to give up his position as an angel and reenter the world as a mortal.

✦**GARDEN FRUIT, ANGEL OF:** Sofiel.

✦**GARDEN OF EDEN:** The name of the earthly Paradise and the first home of humans. God created the garden for **Adam** and **Eve** to live in. According to lore, three attending **angels** were assigned to serve Adam in the Garden of Eden: **Aebel,** Anush, and Shetel. These three angels took care of the first couple until, having eaten of the forbidden fruit, they were banished. **Iophiel** is said to be the angel whom God sent to expel the couple from the garden. After their expulsion, God posted two **Cherubim** and a turning, flaming sword east of the garden to guard the way to the **Tree of Life.** When God created the Garden of Eden, he instructed the archangel **Michael** to assemble two hundred thousand and three angels to plant the garden. The olive tree was planted by **Michael, Uriel** planted the nut tree, **Gabriel** the apple tree, **Raphael** the melon bush, and **Satanael** the vine. The angel **Dohel** holds the keys to the Garden of Eden. Only by means of him can other angels enter.

✦**GARDEN OF GETHSEMANE:** The Garden of Gethsemane was located east of Jerusalem near the Mount of Olives. **Jesus** and his disciples often visited this garden. On the eve of his death, an angel of the Lord appeared to Jesus in the Garden of Gethsemane to strengthen him. The Bible tells us, "And there appeared to him an angel from heaven strengthening him" (Luke 22:43). This mysterious angel is believed to be **Chamuel** who is one of the seven **archangels.**

✦**GARFIAL:** An angel who polices the halls of the palace of Maon, the **Fifth Heaven.**

✦**GARSHANEL:** An angel who wards off evil spirits.

✦**GARZANAL:** An angel who wards off evil spirits.

✦**GATES OF HELL:** The archangel **Uriel** is keeper of the keys to the gates of Hell.

✦**GATHAS:** The name of the twenty-one hymns found in the **Avesta** (the Zoroastrian holy book). Zoroaster wrote these hymns to his angels.

✦**GAUGUIN, PAUL:** French painter and woodcut artist of modern art (1848–1903). Gauguin included angels in many of his works. One of his most famous portrays the famous account of **Jacob** wrestling with an angel.

✦**GAVRIEL:** A variation of the name **Gabriel.**

✦**GAZARNIEL:** An angel of fire who voluntarily left Heaven after opposing **Moses** when he visited Heaven. Moses was able to overpower him by stating God's holy name. He is also one of the angels of **destruction.**

✦**GAZRIEL:** See **Childbirth.**

✦**GEBURAH:** One of the ten **Holy Sefiroth** (angels) found in the **Cabala.** He is also called Strength.

✦**GEBURATI'EL:** A great angelic prince in Heaven.

✦**GEDIEL:** See **Childbirth.**

✦**GEHEGIAL:** An angel who stands guard over the palace of Makon, the **Sixth Heaven.**

✦**GEHENNA, ANGEL OF:** Gehenna (also called Hell) has three fallen angels that rule it. **Satan** the Devil ranks highest. Next are Arsiel, who is the Dark Prince of Gehenna, and **Dumah,** the Chief of the Demon Princes of Gehenna.

✦**GELIEL:** One of twenty-eight angels who preside over the **lunar mansions.**

✦**GEMINI, ANGEL OF: Ambriel.**

✦**GEMS:** Gems and precious stones are often used in the descriptions of angels. In the Bible, the account at **Ezekiel** 28:13 is believed by some to refer to Satan's beauty, before his fall from grace: "Every precious stone was your covering, ruby, topaz, and jasper; chrysolite, onyx, and jade; sapphire; turquoise, and emerald; and of gold was the workmanship of your settings and your sockets in you." In addition, angels are often depicted in scripture and in art as wearing gems as a sign of their majesty. In the Koran, **Jibril,** dictating the Koran to Muhammad, wears a necklace of rubies. Judaic lore tells us that mankind learned about precious gems from the angel **Exael.**

✦**GENESIS:** In a number of stories in the Book of Genesis, angels are principal players: (1) **Eve** is tricked into eating the forbidden fruit by the fallen angel **Satan** the Devil. (2) God places two **Cherubim** outside the **Garden of Eden** to prevent **Adam** and Eve from reentering Paradise once they have been cast out. (3) **Abraham** is visited by three angels, who announce that his wife, **Sarah,** will conceive and give birth to a son. (4) **Hagar,** the maidservant of Sarah, is visited twice by angels while in the wilderness. (5) **Lot** is visited by two angels, who warn him of the destruction of **Sodom.** (6) An angel prevents Abraham from sacrificing his son, **Isaac.** (7) **Jacob** dreams of a heavenly ladder with angels coming and going between Heaven and earth. (8) Jacob wrestles with an angel.

✦**GENIE(S):** A variation of the name jinni. **Jinn** are a form of guardian angel in Arabic and Islamic folklore. They have been portrayed in art both with and without wings.

✤**GENIEL:** One of the angels of the twenty-eight **lunar mansions.**

✤**GENII:** A variation of the name **jinni.**

✤**GENIUS:** Guardian spirits of people, nations, and cities. The word *genius* originated in ancient Rome. There, every family had its own genius called a **lare** watching over it. The word *genius* was also used when referring to the guardian spirit of men and boys (Juno were the guardian spirits of women and girls). It later became a term used interchangeably when referring to guardian angels. It was a tradition in Rome to give thanks at every meal to the genius of the house. Some families went as far as setting a place during mealtime for the genius. The Romans also paid tribute to the genius during their birthday festivities.

✤**GEOGRAPHY, ANGEL OF: Araqiel.** Araqiel taught the secrets of earth's geography to humankind.

✤**GERMAN SOLDIERS:** In World War I, during a battle between German and British soldiers, German troops reported that spectral riders, knights on horseback and shining beings with bows, arrows, and swords, were fighting in the sky over the British soldiers. The soldiers claimed that the angels were impeding their attack on the British.

✤**GEYOR'EL:** One of the seventy-eight names of **Metatron.**

✤**GHIRLANDAIO, DOMENICO:** Domenico Ghirlandaio was a great Florentine painter (1449–1494) who often featured angels in his art. Ghirlandaio painted religious narrative paintings, such as the famous *Madonna with the Vespucci Family* and the *Adoration of the Magi.* Along with **Botticelli** he decorated parts of the **Sistine Chapel,** which feature spectacular portrayals of angels. **Michelangelo** was a student of Ghirlandaio's and assisted him with the fresco cycle of the lives of the **Virgin Mary** and **John the Baptist,** in Santa Maria Novella, Florence.

✤**GHOSTS:** In her book *A Book of Angels,* **Sophy Burnham** writes, "Ghosts are the spirits of the dead, but angels are messengers of the divine." Whether humans become angels after their death has been debated for centuries. Some think that once humans have passed on, they are given the choice of becoming angels. However, many agree that angels are not the spirits of the dead, but existed long before creation. The Book of Job supports this idea. At Job 38:1–7, God reveals to **Job** that the angels were present at the creation of the world: "In the dawn of that day the stars sang together, and the heavenly beings shouted for joy." The "heavenly beings" are the angels.

✤**GIANTS:** See **Nephillim.**

✤**GIBBORIM:** The Gibborim were giants on the earth during the preflood era. Their name means "mighty ones." They constructed temples to make names for themselves. The dark angels are said to have rescued them from the flood. The **Gibborim** are also thought to be the **Nephillim.**

✤GIDEON: In the Bible, he was the youngest son of Joash, from the Abierzite line of Manasseh. Gideon was called to be a judge during the seven years that the Hebrews came under the rule of Midian. The Midianites would attack the Hebrews and destroy their crops, leaving them with nothing. Out of fear for their lives, and as a means of shielding themselves, they made their homes in dens and caves in the mountains. They begged God to deliver them. God, who had heard their prayers from Heaven, chose Gideon to deliver them. He sent an angel to inform Gideon of his divine appointment and to assure him that God would be with him during the war with the Midianites. The account in the Book of Judges (6:11–14) tells us, "Then the Lord's angel came to the village of Ophrah and sat under the oak tree that belonged to Joash, a man of the clan of Abiezer. His son Gideon was threshing some wheat secretly in a wine press, so that the Midianites would not see him. The Lord's angel appeared to him there and said, 'The Lord is with you, brave and mighty man! Go with all your great strength and rescue Israel from the Midianites.' "

✤GIOTTO DI BONDONE: Florentine painter (1266–1337) who featured angels in his art. Some of his greatest works featuring angels include the fresco cycle (ca. 1300) that decorates the Arena Chapel in Padua. There he painted an unclothed angel and angelic musicians. Another famous painting of Giotto's is *Bust of an Angel*.

✤GIOVANNI DA FIESOLE: See **Angelico, Fra.**

✤GLOBAL HEALING, ANGEL OF: The angel of global healing is the archangel **Raphael,** whose name means "the brilliant one who heals."

✤GLORY, ANGEL OF: **Sandolphon.**

✤GLORY, ANGELS OF: The angels of glory are the equivalent of the angels of the **presence** and the angels of sanctification.

✤GLORY, THE: In art the circle of light surrounding the body of an angel is called the glory.

✤GLORY OF GOD: The meaning of the name **Haniel.** Haniel is one of the seven **archangels** of Judaic and Christian beliefs.

✤GMIAL: An angel who polices the palace of Maon (the **Fifth Heaven**).

✤GNOMES: **Elemental** spirits that rule the element earth. According to legend, the gnomes dwell in the forests of the earth. They manifest in the form of elderly dwarfs. They are the protectors and healers of the animals of the forests. They are also protectors of earth's treasures. The archangel **Uriel** is their ruler. They are also called trolls.

✦**GNOSTICISM:** A system of belief blending ideas taken from Greek philosophy, oriental mysticism, and Christianity; and emphasizing salvation through gnosis. In gnostic beliefs the world was created by the **Demiurge.** The high-ranking orders of angels found in gnosticism are called **Aeons** and **Archons.** The Aeons are superior angels said to be the first beings created by **God.** Their rulers include **Dynamis, Pistis-Sophia,** and **Abraxis.** The Archons stand guard over the nations of the material world. The names of these Archons are Jaldabaoth, Jao, Sabaoth, Adonaios, Astanphaios, Ailoaios and Oraios. The Pistis-Sophia is the mother of the Aeons and the **Schechinah,** the **Queen of Angels.** The gnostics believed that God gave the angels free will. He recognized that if they were to exercise their free will, he would have to remove himself so that they could pursue their own destinies. He then decided to withdraw, leaving the angels on their own. Spores of God's divine light were left after His withdrawal. From these spores, the Demiurge is thought to have created the universe.

✦**GOD:** The Supreme Being. He is known by a variety of names. In Zoroastrianism he is called **Ahura Mazda** and Ohrmazd. In Judaism and Christianity he is Yahweh (also **YHWH**), and **Jehovah.** In Islam he is called **Allah.** In both Judaism and Christianity, God maintains a relationship with humans through the angels. The angels act as intercessors between God and mankind and perform various functions on behalf of God toward humans. This is because God is too overwhelming a force for man to come face-to-face with. According to the Bible, no man can see God's face and live. It says, "I will not let you see my face, because no one can see me and stay alive" (Exodus 33:20). However, Jesus said that the angels are always in the presence of God: "See that you don't despise any of these little ones. Their angels in heaven, I tell you, are always in the presence of my Father in heaven" (Matthew 18:10). Therefore the angels are thought to be a necessary link between God and humankind. God is believed to have many angels surrounding him at all times. These include the **Seraphim, Cherubim, Thrones,** seven **Archangels,** and thousands of **ministering angels,** who attend to God's immediate wishes. This is supported in 1 Enoch 14:22–23 where it says, "No one could come near unto him from among those that surrounded the tens of millions that stood before him. He needed no council, but the most holy ones who are near to him neither go far away at night nor move away from him." In addition, God is described in 1 Enoch as "the Great Glory," "the Excellent One," and "the Glorious One."

✤**GOD, ANGEL OF:** The equivalent of the Angel of the **Lord.**

✤**GOD BLESSES:** The meaning of the name **Baruch,** the Guardian of the Tree of Life.

✤**GOD HEALS:** The meaning of the name **Raphael,** who is the angel of healing.

✤**GOD IS MY HELPER:** The meaning of the name **Gadriel.** Gadriel is the angel who taught mankind how to manufacture **weapons.**

✤**GOD IS MY STRENGTH:** The meaning of the name **Gabriel.**

✤**GOD OF COINCIDENCE:** The winged god **Kairos** is also known as the God of Coincidence.

✤**GOD OF LIGHT:** In Persian lore, the God of Light was **Mithra.** Legend has it that he was once one of the twenty-eight angels (izeds) that surrounded **Ahura Mazda.** He later became the God of Light.

✤**GOD OF LOVE:** In Roman mythology **Cupid** was the winged god of love. In Greek mythology it was **Eros.** Both gods served as **archetypal angels** for Judaism and Christianity.

✤**GOD OF THE DEAD:** In Etruscan lore, **Charon** was the god of the dead. He carried the souls of the dead to **Hades.** The angel of death was later patterned after him.

✤**GOD OF THE UNDERWORLD:** A title held by **Satan.**

✤**GOD OF WAR:** The angel **Camael** served as the god of war for the Druids.

✤**GODDESS OF DEATH:** A title held by the she-demon **Lilith.**

✤**GODS:** Angels are sometimes referred to in scripture and literature as "gods."

✤**GOD'S ADVERSARY: Satan** is God's Adversary. He became the Adversary when he rebelled against God. Once a beautiful angel in Heaven, Satan thought so much of himself that he believed that he should be worshiped as a god. He sought out the mortals of earth for them to become his subjects. Since then he has been competing with God for the worship of humans. He has been successful in his endeavor. The Bible says that Satan was able to offer Jesus all of the kingdoms of the world if he would perform an act of worship to him. In Zoroastrianism, the Adversary is called **Angra Mainyu.** Zoroastrians hold him responsible for all of mankind's sorrows. Some Zoroastrians believed that he was created by **Ahura Mazda** (God) himself. They believe that Angra Mainyu eventually turned against him and became his chief opponent. In Islam he is named Iblis. Iblis is said to have loved God most out of all the angels. When God created **Adam,** he told the angels to bow down and worship him. Iblis refused. Because of this disobedient act, God cast him out of Paradise.

✤**GODS AND GODDESSES:** The gods and goddesses of the ancient world were the archetypal angels of Western religious beliefs. In the mythology of the Greeks and Romans, the gods and goddesses traveled back and forth between Heaven and earth. Some were messengers, some had wings, and most aided humanity in some way. Later, when the monotheistic religions came along, these gods and goddesses metamorphosed into the angels that we know today. Some of the gods and goddesses that the angels were patterned after included **Hermes, Iris, Eros, Cupid,** and the Greek **muses** of inspiration.

✤**GOD'S CHILDREN:** The meaning of the name **Bene ha-Elohim.** They are angels who sing praises of God both night and day.

✤**GOD'S COMMAND:** The meaning of the name **Sariel,** one of the archangels. "God's command" refers to his God-given duty of deciding the fate of the angels who sin against God's law.

✤**GOD'S DESERTER:** The angel **Asbeel** holds the title God's Deserter. This is because of his role as instigator in the **Grigori** coming to the earth and taking wives for themselves.

✤**GOD'S EXECUTIONER:** A title held by **Mastema.** According to lore, God sent Mastema to slay the firstborn of Egypt.

✤**GOD'S FRIEND:** The meaning of the name **Raguil.** Raguil watches over the behavior of the other angels.

✤**GOD'S FULLNESS:** The meaning of the name **Machidiel.** Machidiel is angel of March and the angel of Aries.

✤**GOD'S LIGHT:** Both angels and mankind are said to carry the light of God within them. This light is to remind the angels and humans of God's love.

✤**GOD'S LIGHTNING:** The meaning of the name **Barakiel.**

✤**GOD'S LION:** See **Lion of God.**

✤**GOD'S MERCY:** The meaning of the name Jeremiel. Jeremiel once presided over the souls awaiting the resurrection. He was later named **Raziel.**

✤**GODS OF HIDDEN KNOWLEDGE:** Another name for the **Ahuras,** who are angels in Aryan mythology.

✤**GOD'S PERFECTION:** The meaning of the name **Tam'el.** Tam'el is the angel of the deep.

✤**GOD'S SERVANT:** The angel **Abdiel.**

✤**GOD'S SERVANTS:** A title held by the angels. It was taken from the Book of Hebrews 1:14 where it says, "What are the angels, then? They are spirits who serve God and are sent by him to help those who are to receive salvation."

✤**GOD'S SPOKESMAN:** In the Bible, the Angel of the **Lord** is God's personal spokesman. He is sometimes referred to as Angel of God. In the New Testament he is personalized as both **Gabriel** and the **Holy Spirit.**

✦**GOD'S SPY:** A title held by the angel Zaphiel. According to angelic lore, he worked as a double agent between Heaven and Hell. Eventually, his loyalties went completely to Hell. He later became known as the **Herald of Hell.**

✦**GOD'S STRENGTH:** The angel **Usiel.**

✦**GOD'S VOICE:** The archangel **Gabriel** is the personification of the voice of God.

✦**GOD'S WARRIOR:** A title held by the archangel **Michael.**

✦**GOETHE, JOHANN WOLFGANG VON:** A German poet (1749–1832) who authored *Faust*, one of the greatest works of world literature. The poem is about the life of Johann Faust, a sixteenth-century German doctor who practiced magic and died a mysterious death. Legend has it that he sold his soul to **Mephistopheles** (Satan) in exchange for magical powers, wisdom, and eternal youth. In the poem angels are portrayed as heroic figures.

✦**GOLAB:** One of the **Unholy Sefiroth** of the **Cabala.**

✦**GOLD, ANGELS OF:** According to **Enoch,** the angel named **Exael** (one of the **Watchers**), taught men how to create various works and items with gold. In angelic lore, the color gold represents the archangel **Michael**.

✦**GOLDEN ALTAR:** The magnificent **altar** that stands before the **throne of God.** It is where the prayers of the saints are offered up to God. Around the altar the angels gather to listen to these prayers.

✦**GOLDEN CENSER, ANGEL OF THE:** The censer carried by an angel to the golden altar, which stands before God's throne. The incense inside is to be offered with the prayers of the saints to God. The Book of Revelation 8:3 states, "Another angel with a golden censer came and stood at the altar; he was given a great quantity of incense to offer with the prayers of all the saints on the golden altar that is before the throne."

✦**GOLDEN IDOL:** See **furnace.**

✦**GOLDEN SPEAR, ANGEL OF THE:** According to **Saint Teresa of Avila,** an angel once visited her and pierced her body with a long golden spear that caused a sharp pain. The pain, she said, was so sweet that one would never wish to lose it.

✦**GOLDEN TABLETS, ANGEL OF THE:** The ancient tablets to which the angel Moroni led Joseph Smith. The tablets contained information that eventually led to the **Book of Mormon.** With these golden tablets Smith founded the Church of Jesus Christ of the Latter-Day Saints.

✦**GOLDEN VIAL OF BALM, ANGEL OF THE:** The archangel **Raphael** is said to carry a golden vial of balm. This golden vial of balm symbolizes his position as the angel of healing.

✤GOLIATH: In the Bible, Goliath was a giant Philistine who challenged the Israelites. He was slain by young David at Ephesdammim with a slingshot (1 Samuel 17). According to apocryphal lore, **Cervihel,** the angel of strength, and guardian angel of David, assisted David in the slaying of Goliath.

✤GONAEL: An angel who watches over the north wind.

✤*GOOD AND EVIL ANGEL(S):* The title of two famous paintings by **William Blake.** Each painting depicts an angel of light protecting a child from the clutches of an angel of darkness. The angels of darkness are depicted shackled with chains, leaping out from the fires of Hell, attempting to take the child from the arms of the angel of light.

✤GOOD ANGEL: The meaning of the name **Zeus,** the supreme being in Greek mythology.

✤GOOD FORTUNE, ANGEL OF: **Shemyaza.**

✤*GOOD HEAVENS:* A 1976 television show that featured an angel as the hero. The angel was played by Carl Reiner. In the show Reiner granted the wishes of the guest stars. The show ran for one season.

✤GOOD MIND: The name of one of the **Amesha Spentas** (archangels) in Zoroastrianism. In some writings "Wisdom" or "Good Thought" are used in place of "Good Mind." He is also called Vohu Manah.

✤GOOD NEWS, ANGEL OF: A title held by the archangel **Gabriel.** Gabriel is sometimes referred to as the **Bringer of Good News** because of his joyful announcements.

✤GOOD SPIRITS: A phrase sometimes used when referring to the angels.

✤GOOD THOUGHT: One of the **Amesha Spentas** (archangels) in Zoroastrianism. In some writings "Wisdom" or "Good Mind" are used in place of "Good Thought." Good Mind is also called Vohu Manah.

✤GOSPEL, ANGEL OF THE: The angel who oversees the preaching of the gospel on earth. He makes sure that the gospel of Jesus is preached in every nation of the earth before the end comes. The account of Revelation 14:6 states, "And I saw another angel fly in the midst of heaven, having the everlasting gospel to preach unto them that dwell on the earth, and to every nation, and kindred, and tongue, and people."

✤GOVERNANCE, ANGELS OF: The angels of governance include the **Seraphim, Cherubim,** and **Thrones.**

✤GOVERNMENTS: An order of angels. They are also referred to as Governors.

✤GOVERNOR OF EDEN: A title held by the archangel **Gabriel.**

✤**GOVERNOR OF THE PLANETS:** A title held by Rahatiel, the angel who oversees the **planets.**

✤**GOVERNOR OF VENUS:** A title held by the angel **Haniel.**

✤**GOVERNORS:** See **Governments.**

✤**GOZZOLI, BENOZZO:** A Florentine painter (1420–1497) who featured angels in his art. He apprenticed under **Fra Angelico,** who also portrayed angels in his work. One of Gozzoli's most famous paintings featuring angels is his portrait of Heaven, entitled *Paradise.* He portrayed Heaven as a beautiful paradise garden, with angels singing, praying, and smiling.

✤**GRACE:** The name of one of the ten **Holy Sefiroth** (angels) listed in the **Cabala.**

✤**GRACE, ANGELS OF:** Another name for the order of angels called **Virtues.** They are referred to as angels of grace because they grant blessings from on high.

✤**GRAHAM, BILLY:** American evangelist (1918–). Billy Graham was ordained in 1939 as a minister in the Southern Baptist Church and began evangelizing in 1944. He is the author of the best-selling angel book *Angels: God's Secret Agents.* The book chronicles his experiences with angels, as well as those of others who believe that angels came to their aid in moments of need. Graham ranked the orders of angels as follows: (1) **Archangels,** (2) **Angels,** (3) **Seraphim,** (4) **Cherubim,** (5) **Principalities,** (6) **Authorities,** (7) **Powers,** (8) **Thrones,** (9) **Mights,** (10) **Dominions.** Of angels Graham once wrote, "I believe in angels because the Bible says there are angels; and I believe the Bible to be the true Word of God."

✤**GRAIL, ANGEL OF THE:** See **Holy Grail.**

✤**GRANT, CARY:** In the 1947 film *The Bishop's Wife,* Grant plays an angel named Dudley who comes to earth to help a bishop in need of a new church.

✤**GRANTER OF WISHES: Haniel** is the angel who grants the heart's desire.

✤**GRAY, ANGELS OF:** A **color** that represents the angels **Auriel,** the angel of night, and **Casziel,** the angel of tears.

✤**GREAT BEAR:** The demon **Asmodeus** is also known as the Great Bear.

✤**GREAT DRAGON:** A title held by **Satan.** In the Book of Revelation 12:3, 7–9, Satan is referred to as the "great *dragon.*"

✤**GREAT EAGLE:** The Assyrian god **Nisroch** is also called the great eagle and the eagle-headed deity.

✤**GREAT LAW COURT:** See **Court of Heaven.**

✤**GREAT REBELLION, THE:** According to Christian lore, the great rebellion in Heaven occurred when **Satan,** who was once the most beautiful of all angels, fell from God's favor because of **pride.** He then started a rebellion in Heaven against God. He and his rebellious followers were cast out of Heaven by the archangel **Michael** and his celestial army and thrown down to the vicinity of earth. See **God's Adversary.**

✦**GREATEST ANGEL:** The archangel **Metatron** is believed to be the greatest angel in Heaven. He is called the Lesser Yahweh (God's name in ancient Hebrew). He is also considered to be the **Demiurge** (creator of the universe). Before his fall, **Satan** was considered the greatest angel in Heaven.

✦**GREECE, ANGELS OF:** In Greek mythology there were gods and goddesses who performed angelic functions. These gods and goddesses later became **archetypal angels** of later religious systems such as Judaism and Christianity. They include the Horae, winged spiritual beings that guided and protected the Greeks; the winged god **Hermes,** who ran messages between Heaven and earth for **Zeus;** the goddess **Iris,** who was a messenger for Hera; **Eros,** the winged god of love; and **Proserpina,** Queen of Hades. Javan is the guardian angel of Greece. The Horae were also considered guardian protectors of Greece.

✦**GREED:** Greed is one of the seven deadly sins and is considered a demon **Archon** in gnosticism. His antithesis is **Raphael.** The demon **Mammon** is called the angel of greed. He is equated with **Satan** the Devil.

✦**GREEN, ANGEL OF:** The **color** green represents the angel **Ariael,** the Lord of the Earth.

✦**GREGORY OF NAZIANUS:** See **Saint Gregory Nazianzen.**

✦**GREGORY THE GREAT:** See **Saint Gregory the Great.**

✦**GRESSIL:** A **fallen angel.**

✦**GRIAL:** An angel whose name can be found on charms worn by pregnant women to ensure a successful labor. He also polices the halls of the palace of Maon (the **Fifth Heaven**).

✦**GRIGORI:** Another name for the order of angels called **Watchers.** The chief of the Grigori is **Azaz'el.**

✦**GRIM REAPER:** Another name for the angel of death.

✦*GRIMORIUM VERUM:* A magic book that includes many names of angels that are invoked in magical practices.

✦**GROUPS, ANGELS OF:** The angels who work with groups of people are called guardian companions of groups. These angels work to help groups of people to stay together. They are also referred to as collecting angels, coordinating angels, and connecting angels.

♣GUABAREL: One of four angels considered the angel of autumn. **Gabriel, Michael,** and **Tarquam** are the other three.

♣GUARDIAN ANGEL OF
    ARYANS: **Dyeus.**
    CATTLE: **Vohu Manah.**
    EARTH: **Armaiti.**
    EDOM: **Sammael.**
    EGYPT: **Rahab.**
    GREECE: Javan.
    ISRAEL: **Michael.**
    KING DAVID: **Cervihel**
    MARS: **Ertosi.**
    MOSES: Animastic.
    MUHAMMAD: **Jibril.**
    ORIGINALITY: **Raziel.**
    PEACE: The archangel **Michael.**
    PERSIA: **Dubbiel.**
    PLANTS: **Ameretat.**
    ROME: **Sammael.**

♣GUARDIAN ANGEL OF THE ROMAN CATHOLIC CHURCH: The archangel **Michael.**

♣GUARDIAN ANGEL OF THE SKY: **Khshathra.**

♣GUARDIAN ANGEL OF THE UNBORN: **Armisael.**

♣GUARDIAN ANGEL OF THE UNDERWORLD: **Abbaton.**

♣GUARDIAN ANGEL PRAYER: A prayer taught to children in Catholicism: "Angel of God, my guardian dear, To whom His love commits me here; Ever this day [or night] be at my side, To light and guard, to rule and guide."

♣GUARDIAN ANGELS: The **Koran** states, "He [God] sends forth guardians who watch over you and carry away your souls without fail when death overtakes you." Guardian angels are angels assigned by God for protection. There are guardian angels for almost everything including people, nations, planets, plants, animals, and governments. RELIGIONS AND CULTURES. The concept of guardian angels can be found in both the ancient and modern worlds. Ancient Romans believed that guardian spirits called **lares** protected each family. Romans also believed in the **Genius,** spirits who protected men and boys, and **Juno,** spirits who guarded women and girls. Pakistani and Burmese people believe in guardian spirits called **Nats.** Nats were thought to dwell next to the people they were guarding. In Islam there are the **Malaika,** known as the guardians of mankind, and the **Hafazah,** who protect humans against the **jinn** (demons). Guardian spirits called genies are found throughout the Near East. In Zoroastrianism there are the **Fravashi,** ancestral spirits who are also guardian angels. The **Native Americans** believe in guardian spirits, much like the guardian angels of other religious beliefs. Each clan or tribe has a guardian that is believed to remain with them forever. Personal guardian spirits are sought after by individual members of a tribe. In Catholicism it is taught that every child has two guardian angels, one good and one bad sitting on either shoulder. CHILDREN. It has been suggested that children have several guardian angels. This is because children are more vulnerable and in need of more protection when they are young. As they grow, they are thought to need less angelic protection as they become aware of the dangers around the them. Some, not all, of the angels leave a child as he matures. The famous German clairvoyant **Rudolph Steiner** believed that the guardian angels are with a person through each incarnation and carry the complete history of the soul of the person. Once the individual has finished the last incarnation, the guardian angel's role is completed and he leaves that individual. PERSONAL ANGELS. The guardian angels of individuals come from the order of angels called **Angels.** They rank last in the angelic hierarchy and are the closest angels to mankind. They are assigned to individuals at birth to protect and guide them. They are sometimes referred to as personal angels and companion angels. Guardian angels use a variety of ways to reach individuals, including their intuition, thoughts, and dreams. Sometimes, they work through people and manipulate circumstances in order to relay messages. Although guardian angels do appear from time to time, most of their work is done invisibly. When they do appear, however, they may take on a variety of forms including people, animals, lights, etc. When appearing as humans they appear in forms that are in accord with the beliefs of the individual, disguising themselves in the appropriate cultural clothing. There are many reports, too, of angels appearing in full angel regalia, including halos and wings. October 2 is the feast day of guardian angels.

✦**GUARDIAN ANGELS OF JORDAN RIVER: Nidbai** and **Shelmai.**

✦**GUARDIAN ANGELS OF KEYS:** See **Keys.**

✦**GUARDIAN ANGELS OF NATIONS:** The **Principalities** are the order of angels that are in charge of protecting the nations of the earth.

✦**GUARDIAN ANGELS OF THE BOOKS OF ENOCH:** God assigned the angels Ariukh and Pariukh to guard the Books of **Enoch.**

✦**GUARDIAN ANGELS OF THE TREE OF LIFE: Raphael** and **Baruch.**

✦**GUARDIAN COMPANIONS OF GROUPS:** Angels featured in the book *Ask Your Angels* by Alma Daniel, Timothy Wyllie, and Andrew Ramer. They are angels who work to help groups of people to stay together. They are also called connecting angels and coordinating angels.

✤Guardian Spirit(s): Guardian spirits are the equivalent of **guardian angels.**

✤Gvurtial: An angel who stands guard over the palace of Zebul, the **Fourth Heaven.**

God sends forth the angels as His messengers with two, three, or four pairs of wings.

—The Koran

✤**Hadarniel (God's grandeur):** An angel who stands guard over the gates of Heaven. In Jewish legend, he is the angel who prevented Moses from entering Heaven. He is believed to be a tall and imposing figure. However, when God's name is mentioned, he is said to tremble.

✤**Hades, Angels of:** In ancient legends, Hades was believed to be beneath the earth and was home to the dead. In apocryphal lore, the ruler of Hades was the archangel **Uriel,** who was believed to hold the keys to the gates of Hades. In the Apocalypse of **Zephaniah,** the angel **Eremiel** is listed as the overseer of Hades. **Baal-Beryth** is the "master of ceremonies" in Hades.

✤**Hadraniel:** A variation of the name **Hadarniel.**

✤**Hadrial:** An angel who stands guard over the palace of Sehaqim, the **Third Heaven.**

✤**Hafazah:** Guardian angels in Islam who protect humans against the jinn (demons). According to lore, every person has four Hafazah protecting them, two for the day and two for the night. In addition to acting as guardian angels, the Hafazah also record the good and bad deeds of humans.

✤**Hagar:** In the Bible, Hagar was the maidservant to Abraham's wife, **Sarah.** Hagar was visited twice by an angel of the Lord. The first came after she had fled into the wilderness to escape the wrath of Sarah. The angel told her that she was going to give birth to a son and that she should call him **Ishmael** (Genesis 16:1–14). The second visitation occurred when she wandered into the wilderness after Abraham sent her away at Sarah's request. Exhausted and dehydrated, Hagar put her son, Ishmael, under a bush and walked away, asking God not to let her see it when the child died. From Heaven, God heard the child crying and sent an angel to speak to Hagar. The angel called out to her, telling her not to be afraid, that God would one day turn Ishmael's seed into a great nation (Genesis 21:17–19). See **Beerlahairoi, Beersheba.**

✦**HAHHAHYAH:** One of the seventy-eight names of **Metatron.**

✦**HAIL, ANGEL OF:** Bardiel.

✦**HALL OF HEROES, ANGELS OF THE:** See **Valhalla.**

✦**HALLELUJAHS:** Songs of praise sung by the angels to God.

✦**HALOS(S):** A ring of white light shown around the head of an angel in art. The halo symbolizes virtue and innocence. It also represents God's glory and the angel's service to him.

✦**HALOS (HELPING ANGEL LOVERS OWN STORES):** An organization dedicated to helping people set up angel stores. It was founded by Denny Dahlmann, who in 1993 found phenomenal success when he opened his angel outlet, Angel Treasures, located in Royal Oak, Michigan. For more information, write to HALOS, 31700 W. 12 Mile Road, Suite 202, Farmington Hills, MI 48334. The phone number is 1-810-553-9111; fax, 1-810-553-7744.

✦**HALQIM:** An angel who rules over the north **wind.**

✦**HAMALATAL-'ARSH:** Angels of the **Koran.** The Hamalatal-'arsh are the four throne bearers of God. They are symbolized by a man, a bull, an eagle, and a lion.

✦**HAMALIEL:** An angel who holds the titles of the Angel of August, the Angel of Virgo, and Chief of the **Virtues.**

✦**HAMIEL:** The angel who transported the prophet **Enoch** to Heaven. In **Chaldean** lore he was the deity called Ishtar. The name Hamiel is also a variation of the name **Haniel.**

✦**HAMON:** A great angelic prince in Heaven.

✦**HAMSHALIM:** A variation of the name **Hashmallim.**

✦**HAMWAKIL:** An angel summoned in Arabic ceremonies involving exorcism.

✦**HANAEL:** A variation of the name **Haniel.** Haniel is one of the seven archangels of Judaism and Christianity.

✦**HANAN'EL:** One of the angels who brought the secret knowledge of Heaven to earth.

✦**HANGING MAN, ANGEL OF THE:** The angel **Azaz'el** is said to represent the hanging man in the tarot. This idea is taken from the story of the **Grigori.** The Grigori were angels who came to earth to take wives for themselves from among mortal women. Out of these unions came children. Among these angels was Azaz'el, the leader of the Grigori, who had also fathered children. When the angels of vengeance came to destroy the children of these unions, Azaz'el became so upset over the death of his children that he threw himself into the constellation of Orion. He is said to hang there forever upside down.

✦**HANIEL (GLORY OF GOD):** One of the seven **archangels** of Judaism and Christianity. He is also one of the ten archangels of the **Holy Sefiroth.** Considered a great prince in Heaven, Haniel was one of the few angels privileged with serving in the creation of the world. He was later appointed to rule over Raquia, the **Second Heaven.** He has influence over kings and presidents of the nations on earth. He also holds the titles of Prince of **Virtues,** Governor of Venus, Angel of Love, Angel of December, Angel of Capricorn, Prince of **Principalities,** Leader of the **Innocents,** Prince of Love and Harmony, and Angel of the Quince Tree. He is also the angel who grants wishes of the heart. He can be called upon to help fight against evil forces. Variations of this name include Anael, Aniel, Aniyel, Aufiel, Hamiel, Hanael, and Onoel.

✦**HAOMA:** In Zoroastrian rituals, the Haoma plant is used to represent the angel named **Ameretat.** Ameretat is the protector of vegetation.

✦**HAR-MAGEDON:** See **Armageddon.**

✦**HARAB SERAP:** One of the **Unholy Sefiroth.**

✦**HARABAEL:** An angel of the **earth.**

✦**HARBONAH:** The angel of annihilation. He annihilates the evildoers in the world. He is also one of the angels of **confusion** and is a leader of the angels of **destruction.**

✦**HARHAZIAL:** An angel who stands guard over the palace of Sehaqim, the **Third Heaven.**

✦**HARIEL:** An angel who presides over **domestic animals.**

✦**"HARK THE HERALD ANGELS SING":** A traditional Christmas song.

✦**HARLOTS:** The notorious she-demons of the underworld are sometimes referred to as harlots and harlots of Hell. They include **Agrat-bat-Mahlaht,** Eisheth Zenunim, **Lilith,** and **Naamah.** They are also known as the angels of prostitution.

✦**HARMONY, ANGEL OF:** The archangel **Haniel** is the Prince of Love and Harmony.

✦**HARON-PEOR:** One of the angels of **destruction.**

✤**HAROODA:** In ancient Persian lore Harooda was the angel that presided over **water.**

✤**HAROTH:** See **Haroth and Maroth.**

✤**HAROTH AND MAROTH:** Two angels who are found in both Persian and Islamic lore. In Persian mythology they were two angels who knew the secret name of God. According to Islamic lore, they are angels who gave in to sexual temptation, taught humans the secret knowledge of Heaven, and relayed the secret name of God to a beautiful woman whose name is thought to be Zuhrah. This account closely resembles the story of the **Watchers** in Judaism (where two hundred angels gave in to sexual temptation, taught mankind forbidden secrets, and their leader **Shemyaza** told a beautiful woman the secret name of God). They chose to be disciplined by being hung upside down in an abyss in Babil. Variations of the names Haroth and Maroth are Harut and Marut.

✤**HARP(S):** In art angels are often depicted playing harps. The harp symbolizes the angel's special role of making beautiful music in Heaven.

✤**HARPIES:** Winged birdlike female figures.

✤**HARUT AND MARUT:** See **Haroth and Maroth.**

✤**HARVEST, ANGEL OF THE:** In the Book of Revelation 14:14–16, **John** sees in a vision an angel holding a sickle, ready to reap the harvest. The account says, "Then I looked, and there was a white cloud, and sitting on the cloud was what looked like a human being, with a crown of gold on his head and a sharp sickle in his hand. Then another angel came out from the temple and cried out in a loud voice to the one who was sitting on the cloud, 'Use your sickle and reap the harvest, because the time has come; the earth is ripe for the harvest!' Then the one who sat on the cloud swung his sickle on the earth, and the earth's harvest was reaped." The angel with the sickle has been interpreted as being Jesus. The harvest is Jesus separating the good people from the bad at the end of the world.

✤**HASDIEL:** An angel of **charity.**

✤**HASHASYAH:** One of the seventy-eight names of the mighty angel **Metatron.**

✤**HASHMAL:** A variation of the name Chasmal, a chief of the **Hashmallim** (also known as the **Dominations**). He is also known as the firespeaking angel.

✤**HASHMALLIM:** Another name for the order of angels known as the **Dominations.** The leaders of the Hashmallim are **Muriel, Hashmal,** Yahriel, and **Zadkiel.** Variations of the name Hashmallim are Hamshalim and Bashmallin.

✤**HASRIEL:** The name of the angel who protects individuals from evil spirits.

✤**HAURVATAT:** One of the **Amesha Spentas** in Zoroastrianism. He is the protector of **water.** In rituals he is represented by holy water. He is also referred to as Wholeness and Hordad.

✤**HAVRES:** A **fallen angel.**

✤**HAYLI'EL YHWH:** A great angelic prince in Heaven. He flogs the **Seraphim** with "lashes of fire" if they do not chant the **Trisagion** on time.

✤**HAYYAL:** An angel who presides over **wild animals.**

✤**HAYYOTH:** Also called heavenly beasts, the Hayyoth are angels of fire who reside in the **Seventh Heaven** with God, supporting God's throne. According to apocryphal lore, **Raziel** spreads his wings over the Hayyoth so that their fiery breath does not incinerate the attending angels around God's throne. They are also credited with holding up the universe. Each time their wings spread they break out in hallelujahs to God. The prophet **Ezekiel** saw them in a vision (Ezekiel 1:23–24) and wrote, "There under the dome stood the creatures, each stretching out two wings toward the ones next to it and covering its body with the other two wings. I heard the noise their wings made in flight; it sounded like the roar of the sea, like the noise of a huge army, like the voice of Almighty God. When they stopped flying, they folded their wings, but there was still a sound coming from above the dome over their heads." They are the equivalent of the order of angels called the **Cherubim.** They are also called Divine Beasts.

✤**HE WHO DESPISES LIGHT:** The meaning of the name **Mephistopheles,** who is listed in some writings as **Satan.**

✤**HE WHO GIVES LIGHT:** The meaning of the name **Lucifer.** Lucifer is said to be so glorious that he radiates a great light around him.

✤**HE WHO KEEPS HELL:** The meaning of the name Tartaruchus. Tartaruchus is in charge of the torments and punishments conducted in Hell.

✤**HE WHO SEARCHES FOR GOD:** The meaning of the name **Chamuel.**

✤**HE WHO SEES GOD:** The meaning of the name **Camael,** who is the chief of the order of angels called **Powers.**

✤**HEALING, ANGELS OF:** The official angel of healing is the archangel **Raphael.** According to lore, Raphael carries a golden vial of balm for healing ailments. In addition, the **Seraphim** are angels of healing. The name Seraphim means "healer." Their symbols are dragons and serpents, which represent the "powers of healing." The **caduceus** is the modern symbol of the medical profession and also represents the **Seraphim.** In addition, there are healing angels, who aid in curing both the physical and emotional ailments. These angels help us to be healed from sickness by transmitting healing rays of energy from God. They take care of the sick and work in hospitals and hospices. They also work directly with doctors, nurses, and healers.

✦HEALTH, ANGEL OF: **Raphael.**

✦HEART, ANGEL OF THE: **Haniel** is the angel who grants wishes of the heart.

✦HEAT, ANGEL OF: **Raphael** is the angel of the heat of the **sun.**

✦HEAVEN(s): A place of great beauty and pleasure, and the dwelling place of God and the angels. In John Milton's *Paradise Lost,* the walls of Heaven are made of "crystal." According to tradition, the streets of Heaven are paved with gold. The seven realms of Heaven are sometimes referred to as the seven Heavens. According to the Book of **Enoch,** the names of the angelic princes ruling the seven Heavens are **Michael,** Prince of the Seventh Heaven **(Arabot); Gabriel,** Prince of the **Sixth Heaven** (Makon); Satqi'el, Prince of the **Fifth Heaven** (Maon); Sahaqi'el, Prince of the **Fourth Heaven** (Zebul); Baradi'el, Prince of the **Third Heaven** (Sehaqim); **Barakiel,** Prince of the **Second Heaven** (Raquia); and Sidri'el, Prince of the **First Heaven** (Wilon).

✦*HEAVEN AND HELL:* A book written by Swedish mystic **Emanuel Swedenborg.** The book reveals information about Heaven, Hell, and the angels. It is based on his experiences in the spiritual realm, and his conversations with the angels. It covers such topics as the clothing angels wear; the homes of angels; the language of angels; how angels communicate with humans; and the power of angels. It has been held up as Swedenborg's greatest work.

✦*HEAVEN CAN WAIT:* A 1978 movie starring Warren Beatty as Joe Pendleton, a quarterback who has an accident and meets with an untimely death. Joe teams up with two angels who help him to search for a suitable earthly replacement for Joe's spirit. The film also stars Julie Christie, Jack Warden, Dyan Cannon, Charles Grodin, James Mason, Buck Henry, and Vincent Gardenia. It was directed by Warren Beatty and Buck Henry.

✦HEAVENLY ACADEMY: The name of a group of angels who judge the souls of men.

✦HEAVENLY ARCHIVIST: **Radweri'el YHWH.**

✦HEAVENLY ARMY: Another name for the **Celestial Army.**

✦HEAVENLY BEASTS: A name given to the order of angels called the **Hayyoth.** They are angels of fire who reside in the **Seventh Heaven** with God, supporting God's throne.

✤HEAVENLY BEINGS: In scripture, angels are sometimes referred to as **heavenly beings.**

✤HEAVENLY BODIES: In scripture, angels are sometimes referred to as heavenly bodies. In 1 Corinthians 15:40, the apostle **Paul** in referring to angels calls them "heavenly bodies." Paul states, "And there are heavenly bodies and earthly bodies; the beauty that belongs to heavenly bodies is different from the beauty that belongs to earthly bodies." (Note: In some translations "heavenly bodies" is interpreted as "celestial bodies.") In the Testament of Solomon, thirty-six demons are listed. They are referred to as the **"thirty-six heavenly bodies."**

✤HEAVENLY CHOIRS: Tag'as, who is a great lord in Heaven, is in charge of the heavenly choirs.

✤HEAVENLY COURT: See **Court of Heaven.**

✤HEAVENLY PALACES, ANGELS OF THE: See **First Heaven, Second Heaven, Third Heaven, Fourth Heaven, Fifth Heaven, Sixth Heaven, Seventh Heaven.**

✤HEAVENLY PASSAGEWAYS, ANGELS OF THE: The heavenly passageways are corridors in the spiritual realm that lead to Heaven. According to apocryphal lore, these passageways are patrolled on a regular basis by angels of the order of angels called the **Powers.** They are on the lookout for demons trying to enter. The angel **Anapiel YHWH** holds the keys to the heavenly passageways.

✤HEAVENLY SCRIBE: The scribe of Heaven is **Metatron.**

✤HEAVENLY SONGS: In Judaism, the **Master of Heavenly Songs** is thought to be either **Metatron** or Shemiel.

✤HEBREW PATRIARCHS: Founders of ancient Hebrew families. According to lore, the Hebrew patriarchs **Abraham, Isaac,** and **Jacob** became angels of the **Ophanim** class when they reached Heaven.

✤HEBREWS, ANGEL OF THE: The archangel **Michael** is the guardian angel of the Hebrews. See **Israel.**

✤HELEL: Leader of the **Nephillim** (offspring of angels).

✤HELL: According to religious thought, Hell is the place where sinners go after death to be punished and tormented forever. It is a fiery place ruled by **Satan** and his demons. Some religions believe that Hell exists beneath the earth. Others believe that it is a spiritual realm separated from Heaven. In Hell there exist all sorts of hideous demons who were once angels in Heaven but rebelled, sinned, or fell away from God's laws. ANGELS OF HELL. The angel of Hell in Islam is **Malik.** In Judeo-Christian lore Satan presides over Hell. According to Judaic lore, the archangel **Uriel** holds the keys to Hell. In addition, the *Sibylline Oracles* speak of Uriel doing away with the gates of Hell on **Judgment Day.** The angel **Tartaruchus** is called the Keeper of Hell. GUARDIANS OF HELL. In the Koran the **Al-Zabaniya** (also referred to as the Violent-Thrusters) are guardians of Hell. CHIEF DEMONS OF HELL. Chief demons of Hell include **Satan, Anituel, Asmodeus, Astarte, Balam, Beleth, Belphegor, Dumah, Furcalor, Kokabiel, Salmael, Haroth, Forneus, Raym, Lahash,** and **Gazarniel.** HERALD OF HELL. The **Herald of Hell** is **Zaphiel,** who was once a double agent between **Heaven** and **Hell.** After grieving over his decision to warn the heavenly army that the demons were planning a fierce attack, he eventually chose Hell over Heaven and later received the title of the Herald of Hell. PRIME MINISTER OF HELL. **Rofocale** is the Prime Minister of Hell.

✤**HEMAH:** A fear-inspiring angel from Judaic lore. He is an angel of wrath, an angel of **punishment,** an angel of death (in rabbinical lore), and he holds the exceedingly unpleasant title of the angel of the death of domestic animals. Legend has it that he along with his brother **Af** made an attempt on the life of **Moses.** However, God intervened, and Moses was given permission to slay him.

✤**HERA:** In Greek mythology Hera was the queen of the Olympian gods, and the wife and sister of **Zeus.** The goddess **Iris** ran messages for Hera between Heaven and earth. In Judaism and Christianity, the idea of angels acting as messengers to God was patterned after the goddess Iris.

✤**HERALD OF HELL:** A title given to Zaphiel. Zaphiel was once a double agent between Heaven and Hell. After grieving over his decision to warn the heavenly army that the demons were planning a fierce attack, he eventually chose Hell over Heaven and thus received the title Herald of Hell.

✤**HERBS, ANGEL OF:** The angel **Pharmoros** taught mankind to use herbs for medicinal purposes. Teaching humans the secrets of using herbs was considered a grave sin in Heaven.

✤**HERMES:** A winged god of Greek mythology. He carried messages for **Zeus,** the Supreme Being. He also conducted souls to Hades and gave aid to humans. He wore a winged hat and sandals and carried a **caduceus.** The angels of Judaism were later patterned after Hermes. He is equated with the Roman god **Mercury,** the Egyptian god Thoth, and the archangel **Michael.** He is thought to be a Seraph because of his carrying a caduceus (a symbol of the **Seraphim**). In the *Odyssey* (a Greek epic poem attributed to Homer), Hermes acts as a guardian angel to **Ulysses.**

✤**HERO OF GOD:** The archangel **Gabriel** is sometimes referred to as the Hero of God.

✤**HEROD:** In the Book of Acts (12:22–23), an angel of the Lord strikes

Herod down for not giving glory to God. The account states, "On ar appointed day Herod put on his royal robes, took his seat on the platform, and delivered a public address to them. The people kept shouting, 'The voice of a god, and not of a mortal!' And immediately, because he had not given the glory to God, an Angel of the Lord struck him down, and he was eaten by worms and died."

✦**HEROES, ANGELS OF:** In Judaic lore, the order of angels called **Virtues** are responsible for looking after the heroes of the world. In Germanic lore, the **Valkyries** would carry the souls of heroes to Valhalla, also known as the Hall of Heroes.

✦**HEROES OF HEAVEN:** A title for the good angels who dwell in Heaven.

✦**HEYWOOD, THOMAS:** See *Hierarchy of Blessed Angels.*

✦**HEZEKIAH:** In the Book of 2 Kings (19:35), Hezekiah prays to God for protection from King **Sennacherib** of Assyria. God hears his prayers and sends an angel of death to slay Sennacherib's army. The account states, "That night an Angel of the Lord went to the Assyrian camp and killed 185,000 soldiers."

✦**HIDDEN TREASURES, ANGEL OF:** Aziel.

✦**HIEL:** An angel who wards off evil spirits.

✦*HIERARCHY OF BLESSED ANGELS:* A treatise on angels, written by noted English dramatist Thomas Heywood in 1635.

✦*HIGHWAY TO HEAVEN:* A popular television show in which an angel was the hero. *Highway to Heaven* ran on NBC from 1984 to 1988. The show starred Michael Landon, who played Jonathan Smith, an angel sent from Heaven to teach humans love and compassion. The show also starred Victor French, who played an ex-policeman named Mark Gordon. Gordon sometimes aided Jonathan in his attempts to accomplish his God-given mission.

✦**HINDU FAIRIES:** See **Apsaras.**

✦**HINDUISM, ANGELS OF:** Hinduism is a diverse religion made up of the philosophy and culture of native India. The angels of Hinduism include the Apsaras, who are beautiful fairies of Heaven. They specialize in giving sensual pleasure to the gods. They were sometimes sent from Heaven to prevent wicked men from doing harm by distracting them with their beauty and sexual expertise. There are also the Shakti and the devi, who are the manifestations of God in the female form. Popular devi and Shakti include Durga, **Kali, Lakshmi,** and **Surasuti.** There are also the **Avatars,** angels who accompany the major gods of Hinduism.

✦**HIPHKADIEL:** The name of an angel who chases away evil spirits.

✦**HISTORY, MUSE OF:** In Greek mythology Clio was the **muse** of education and knowledge. She inspired men to study and record history.

❦HIWA: One of the **Nephillim.** He was the son of the angel **Shemyaza,** an angel from the class of **Watchers,** and Ishtarah, a beautiful earthly woman. He had a brother named Hiya.

✦HIYA: One of the **Nephillim.** He was the son of the angel **Shemyaza,** an angel from the class of **Watchers,** and Ishtarah, a beautiful earthly woman. He had a brother named Hiwa.

✦HOCUS POCUS: A powerful spirit who during medieval times appeared as an angel when invoked.

✦HOD: One of the **Holy Sefiroth** (angels in the **Cabala**). He is also called Splendor.

✦HODNIEL: An angel who has the power to cure the stupidity of humans.

✦HOLINESS, ANGEL OF: Ananchel. In Zoroastrianism the angel of holiness was **Asha.**

✦HOLY ANGELS: God's "holy angels" is a term that is often heard and also used in literature. The angels are considered holy because of their living in a constant state of perfection. Angels, unlike men, are not born into sin and are not in need of a savior. They are holy because they are free of sin. Ancient mystics contended that holy state of an angel comes through years of trial and error, of their repeating many lifetimes on the earth until they evolve to a perfect state of being. Only then are they worthy of becoming a holy angel of God.

✦HOLY BEASTS: Another name for the **Cherubim.**

✦HOLY BOOKS: Angels can be found throughout the holy books of the various religions around the world. In Zoroastrianism, the **Avesta** lists several angels including the **Amesha Spentas** and a number of **ministering angels.** Angels of the Bible include the **Angel of the Lord, Gabriel, Michael,** ministering angels, **Abaddon,** and several unnamed angels of the Book of **Revelation.** In the Koran there are **Jibril** and **Mikhail.** The Koran also speaks of ministering angels, and the **Al-Zabaniya** (guardians of Hell). The angel of the *Book of Mormon* is named Moroni.

✦HOLY DEVOTION: Another name for **Armaiti,** one of the **Amesha Spentas** in Zoroastrianism.

✦HOLY GHOST: In Christian doctrine, the Holy Ghost is the third person of the Trinity. The archangel **Michael** is often equated with the Holy Ghost. The Holy Ghost is sometimes referred to as the **Holy Spirit.**

✦HOLY GHOST, ANGEL OF THE: The archangel **Gabriel.**

✦HOLY GRAIL, ANGELS OF THE: In medieval legend, the Holy Grail was the chalice used by Christ at the Last Supper. According to tradition, the

Holy Grail was brought to earth by angels who, during the great rebellion of Heaven, remained neutral, as one-third of the angels sided with God and one-third sided with Satan.

✤HOLY HOUSE, ANGELS OF: Holy House is where the Virgin Mary was born and where the **Annunciation** took place. The house is believed to have been moved from Nazareth in 1291 by angels and taken to the coast of Illyria, where they placed it upon a hill. In 1294 the angels are said to have again moved the house, this time depositing it in the province of Ancona in Italy, where it was moved around several times before being taken to Loreto. According to sources, research has proved that the house did indeed originate in the Middle East.

✤HOLY MOTHER OF VIRTUES: A title held by the **Virgin Mary,** who is also called **Queen of Angels.**

✤HOLY ONES: A title sometimes used in literature when referring to the angels. It is also a name used when referring to the **archangels.**

✤HOLY SEFIROTH: The ten primary angels of the **Cabala.** Each is a manifestation of God, representing the ten divine characteristics that rule and shape the world. They are Kether (Crown), Chokmah (Wisdom), Binah (Understanding), Chesed (Mercy), Geburah (Strength), Tiphereth (Beauty), Netzach (Victory), Hod (Splendor), Jesod (Foundation), and Malkuth (Kingdom). Variations of the name Sefiroth are Sefirot and Sephiroth. Archangels of the Sefiroth include **Metatron, Raziel, Zadkiel,** Kamael, **Michael, Haniel, Raphael,** and **Gabriel.** See **Unholy Sefiroth.**

✤HOLY SPIRIT: In some religious beliefs the Holy Spirit is God's power (also referred to as the "force of God"). In others the Holy Spirit is God himself. In still others the Holy Spirit is thought to be a separate entity from God, a higher angelic being that is part of God, but separate from God. The Holy Spirit is also a part of the Trinity, which consists of God, Jesus, and the Holy Spirit. In the New Testament, the **Angel of the Lord** is personalized as the Holy Spirit. When Jesus was baptized, the Holy Spirit appeared in the form of a **dove** above his head. In the Book of Matthew 3:16 it states, "And when Jesus had been baptized, just as he came up from the water, suddenly the heavens were opened to him and he saw the Spirit of God descending like a dove and alighting on him." In Zoroastrianism the Holy Spirit is the Supreme Being, **Ahura Mazda.**

✤HOLY SPIRITS: A phrase used in Zoroastrianism when referring to the **Amesha Spentas** (archangels).

✤HOLY WATER: In rituals, the Zoroastrian angel **Haurvatat** is represented by holy water. Haurvatat is the protector of **water.**

✤HOME (OF THE ANGELS): **Heaven.** Heaven is made up of seven

Heavens in which the various **orders of angels** live. It has been suggested that the home of the angels is not a place but a state of being that coexists with the physical universe. German philosophic genius and clairvoyant **Rudolph Steiner** held that each order of angels dwells within its own kingdom (or realm).

✤**Homelessness, Angel of:** The archangel **Uriel.**

✤**Hope, Angel of:** **Phanuel.**

✤**Horae:** The Horae are winged spirits from Greek mythology. They were guardian protectors of the people of Greece.

✤**Hordad:** Another name for **Haurvatat.** Haurvatat is one of the **Amesha Spentas** (archangels) in Zoroastrianism.

✤**Horeb:** See **Mount Horeb.**

✤**Hori:** A variation of **Huri.**

✤**Horus:** The sky god in Egyptian mythology. He represented light and goodness. According to lore, he once battled Set, the god of darkness and evil. In art he is portrayed as a falcon.

✤**Host:** The word *host* means an assembly of angels. It is also the name of one of the **orders of angels** that reside in the **Seventh Heaven.** The archangel **Michael** rules over the heavenly "host." In Heaven the host of angels stand near God's throne. The Book of 1 Kings 22:19 states, "I saw the Lord sitting on his throne, and all the host of heaven standing beside him on his right hand and his left."

✤**Hostility, Angel of:** The angel of hostility is **Satan.**

✤**Hosts of Fury:** The name of a high order of angels.

✤**Houri:** A variation of the word **Huri.** The Huri are female spirits in Islam.

✤**Hours of the Day and Night, Angels of the:** See **Sunday, Monday, Tuesday, Wednesday, Thursday, Friday, Saturday.**

✤**Humankind, Angel of:** **Metatron** is the protector of humankind.

✤**Humans as Angels:** Whether humans become angels after they die has been debated for centuries. Some maintain that humans do not become angels, arguing that the angels are of the hierarchy of God, created on behalf of humans. According to the Bible, the angels were already in existence when humankind and the world were created, as stated in the Book of Job (38:4–7). However, some accounts of apocryphal lore tell of humans becoming angels after they reached Heaven. According to lore, **Enoch, Elijah,** and the **Virgin Mary** were all transformed into angels upon their arrival in Heaven. Enoch was transformed into the mighty archangel **Metatron.** Elijah became the angel of the **covenant,** and the Virgin Mary is an angel from the order of **Virtues.** In addition, the Hebrew patriarchs **Abraham, Isaac,** and

Jacob are said to have become angels of the **Ophanim** class upon their arrival in Heaven.

✦**HUNGER, ANGEL OF:** The archangel **Uriel.**

✦**HURI:** Beautiful, dark-eyed female spirits of Islamic lore. They give sensual pleasures to the male inhabitants of Paradise. After each night of fulfilling desires, the Huri once again become virgins. Kalka'il is the angel who presides over the Huri. Kalka'il is said to dwell in the **Fifth Heaven.** Variations of Huri are Hori and Houri.

✦**HURMIZ:** One of the daughters of the she-demon **Lilith.**

✦**HURRICANES, ANGEL OF:** **Za'apiel.**

✦**HUZIA:** An angel who stands guard over the palace of Wilon, the **First Heaven.**

✦**HYMNS:** In Greek mythology **Polyhymnia** inspired men to write sacred hymns. In Vedic mythology Vrihaspati was the guardian angel of hymns.

✦**HYPNOS:** A winged god of Greek mythology. He was the god of sleep, and a messenger to the gods. His sons were called dreams. The word *hypnosis* was taken from his name. A variation of the name Hypnos is Hypnus.

✦**HYPNUS:** A variation of the name **Hypnos.**

I

For every soul, there is a guardian watching it.
—The Koran

✤**I Ching, Angel of:** Eistibus.

✤*I Dream of Jeannie:* A television sitcom that featured a **genie** as the main character. The genie, played by Barbara Eden, provided protection for and granted the wishes of her master, played by Larry Hagman. (Note: Genies are a form of guardian angel in Arabic and Islamic folklore.)

✤**Iaeo:** An angel summoned for help in fighting evil spirits in exorcisms.

✤**Iameth:** An angel listed in the Testament of **Solomon.** He has the power to thwart **Kunopegos,** a demon of the sea.

✤**Iaoth:** One of the archangels listed in the Testament of **Solomon.** He thwarts the demon Kourtael, who causes pain in the bowels of humans.

✤**Iblis:** The spirit of darkness (**Satan**) in Islam. Iblis is said to have loved God most of all the angels. When God created **Adam,** he told the angels to bow down and worship him. Iblis refused. Because of this disobedient act, God ordered him from his presence. The Koran states that when Adam was created, God told the angels to prostrate themselves saying, "Fall ye prostrate before Adam! And they fell prostrate, all save Iblis, who was not of those who make prostration. He said: What hindered Thee that thou did not fall prostrate when I bid thee? [Iblis] said: I am better than he. Thou createdst me of fire, while him Thou didst create of mud. He said: Then go down hence! It is not for Thee to show pride here, so go forth! Lo! Thou art of Those degraded" (Koran, VII). A variation of the name Iblis is Eblis.

✦**ICHTHION:** A demon who causes **paralysis.**

✦**ICONOGRAPHY:** Angels in iconography are usually shown in the traditional forms. They may be either male or female with wings, a halo or aureole, and dressed in long, light-colored gowns. Symbols of angels in iconography may include the **lily, harp,** lute, **trumpet, codex,** or a **thurible.** The archangel **Michael** is often portrayed wearing **armor. Cherubs** are popular in angel iconography. They are often pictured nude, wearing garlands around the head, hovering around a beautiful woman.

✦**IEALO:** An angel summoned for help in fighting evil spirits in exorcisms.

✦**IEROPA:** A demon who causes convulsions.

✦*ILIAD:* A Greek epic poem credited to Homer. The poem is about circumstances growing from the anger of Achilles. It takes place in the tenth year of the Trojan War. In the *Iliad*, divine figures are given functions similar to those of the angels in Judaism and Christianity. In the first book of the *Iliad*, the goddess **Athena** behaves toward Achilles in a manner that closely resembles that of a guardian angel. The god **Nestor** is also portrayed as a guardian spirit to Agamemnon. He has been sent by **Zeus,** the Supreme Being, as a messenger. **Iris** also performs the function of an angel when she is sent by Zeus as a messenger to comfort the aged king Priam as he weeps over the body of his dead son Hector. The gods and goddesses portrayed in the literature of ancient Greece became the archetypal angels of Judaism and Christianity.

✦**ILLNESSES, ANGEL OF:** The archangel **Raphael** presides over cures for illnesses.

✦**ILLUMINATI:** The Illuminati are a group of people who professed to be unusually enlightened spiritually. In the writings of the Illuminati, angels were described as small suns with an aura of energy, radiating streamers of power.

✦**ILLUMINATION, ANGEL OF:** The archangel **Uriel.**

✦**IMBECILITY, ANGEL OF: Akriel.**

✦**IMMORTALITY:** The name of one of the **Amesha Spentas** in Zoroastrianism. She is also called **Ameretat.**

✦**IMMORTALITY, ANGEL OF: Zethar.**

✦**IMMORTALS:** A term used for humans who cheated the angel of death and were taken bodily to Heaven by God. Some of these people, such as the prophets **Enoch** and **Elijah,** later became angels in Heaven.

✤In Hii: An angel who watches over the north **wind**.

✤*In Search of Angels:* A 1994 PBS documentary examining the purpose of angels and the roles of angels in history and in art. It was narrated by actress Debra Winger.

✤Incantations, Angel of: The angel **Amasras** brought the knowledge of incantations to the earth. This knowledge was forbidden to humankind.

✤Incarnations, Angels and: According to **Rudolph Steiner,** every person has a companion angel that guards the soul. This angel stays with the individual through all of his incarnations. He also keeps track of all of that person's former lives. At a certain point in their spiritual development the individual may ask his angel to reveal his former incarnations. The angel also works with the individual, assisting him in the development of the soul. At the end of that person's earthly evolution the angel leaves. The individual has by then evolved to the consciousness of an angel, and to a higher spiritual plateau.

✤Incubi: A variation of **Incubus**.

✤Incubus: A demon who has intercourse with sleeping women. In medieval times they were believed to take on the forms of handsome men, who would then seduce beautiful women. They later became thought of as invisible spirits who would climb into bed with women to have sexual intercourse. They are thought to especially pursue single women and those dedicated to a life of celibacy. A variation of the name Incubus is Incubi. See **Succubus.**

✤Indivisible, Angel of the: In gnosticism the angel Aphredon governs the indivisible.

✤Indra: One of the **Adityas** (angels) of Vedic beliefs. In Zoroastrianism, Indra is the spirit of apostasy. His opponent is **Asha** the angel of truth.

✤Infertility, Angel of: **Akriel** and **Zidkiel** are both angels of infertility. See **Barrenness.**

✤*Influence of Spiritual Beings on Mankind:* A book by German philosophic genius and clairvoyant **Rudolph Steiner.** In the book Steiner speaks about the angels and their role in mankind's evolution.

✤Information Angels: Angels who help humans by providing needed information. They are present most often when humans have questions and cannot find the answer. They are also the keepers of the celestial records (also called **Akashic Records**), a heavenly library that contains the recorded history of the universe from creation to the present day.

✤Inias: A fallen angel who willingly left Heaven for Hell after he was reprobated by the Church of Rome in 745 C.E.

✤INNER CIRCLE: The Talmud states that before the creation, God held a consultation with His inner circle of angels for their advice on his intended plan to create man. That inner circle consisted of the angels of **truth, justice, peace,** and **charity.**

✤INNOCENTS: An order of angels found in Francis Barrett's book *The Magus.* The Leader of the Innocents is **Haniel.**

✤INSOLENCE, ANGEL OF: **Rahab.**

✤INSOMNIA, ANGEL OF: The archangel **Michael.**

✤INSPIRATION, ANGELS OF: Many great artists have claimed that angels inspired their work. These angels are sometimes referred to as the angels of inspiration. In Greek mythology, nine **muses** were credited with inspiring the ancient masters of history, art, science, and religion. These muses were the **archetypal angels** of inspiration.

✤INSTANT TRAVEL, ANGEL OF: **Ampharool.**

✤INTEGRATING ANGELS: Another name for the order of angels called **Principalities.**

✤INTELLIGENCE, MUSE OF: In Greek mythology **Thaleia** was the **muse** of intelligence.

✤INTELLIGENCES: Another name for the **Holy Sefiroth** (angels of the **Cabala**).

✤INTERMEDIARIES: Angels appear in numerous religious traditions in the role of intermediaries between humans and God. In ancient times, gods and goddesses such as the winged god **Hermes** and the goddess **Iris** of Greek mythology carried messages from Heaven to earth. Later, with the development of the monotheistic religions, angels, too, stood in place of God as intermediaries in the carrying out of God's divine will. In the Bible, the archangel **Gabriel** served as an announcer of births and an interpreter of visions and prophecies. Other angels, such as the **Angel of the Lord,** served in other intermediary roles such as ushering **Lot** and his family out of **Sodom** before its destruction, and rescuing three Hebrew men from a fiery **furnace.** God is believed to need such intermediary help because he is too powerful a force for humankind to come face-to-face with. The Bible explains that no man can see God's face and live (Exodus 33:20). Therefore, the angels are needed to stand in place of God. In some religious traditions, angels are believed to carry the prayers of humans to God and to deliver messages from God to humans. The angels who act as intermediaries generally come from the orders of **Archangels** and **Angels.**

✤INTERPRETATION, ANGELS OF: The angel of interpretation is the archangel **Uriel.** He is said to bring the knowledge of God to men. As a symbol of this title, Uriel is often depicted in art carrying a scroll. In the

Bible the archangel **Gabriel** interpreted a vision and also a prophecy for the prophet **Daniel.**

✤**Intuition, Angels of the:** The intuition is a person's ability to understand or know things without conscious reasoning. Guardian angels often work through the intuition of individuals to assist them in making decisions, solving problems, and as a way of protecting them from dangerous situations. The intuition is sometimes referred to as the inner voice. In his book *Divine Love and Wisdom*, **Emanuel Swedenborg** writes about angels and the intuition: "Do not believe me simply because I have discoursed with angels. . . . Believe me because I tell you what your consciousness and intuitions will tell you if you listen closely to their voice."

✤**Invention, Angel of: Liwet.**

✤**Invisibility, Angel of:** Almiras.

✤**Ioelet:** An angel summoned for help in fighting evil spirits in exorcisms.

✤**Iofiel:** A variation of the name **Iophiel.**

✤**Iophiel (Beauty of God):** A high-ranking angel of Heaven who works closely with the mighty angel Metatron. He is a ruling prince of **Saturn,** and an angel of the Torah. He is believed to be the angel who drove **Adam** and **Eve** out of Paradise after they sinned. Variations of the name Iophiel are Iofiel, Jofiel, and **Jophiel.**

✤**Iouda Zizabou:** An angel from the Testament of **Solomon.**

✤**Iran(ians), Angels of:** See **Persia.**

✤**Irateness, Angel of:** Zkzoromtiel.

✤**Irin:** The Irin are the angels that the prophet **Daniel** refers to as "alert and watchful angels," in Daniel 4:17. Legend has it that while **Moses** visited Heaven the mighty angel **Metatron** pointed out the **Irin** to him in the **Sixth Heaven.** In addition, the name Irin is another name for the order of angels called **Watchers.**

✤**Iris:** In Greek mythology, Iris was the goddess of the rainbow and acted as a messenger for the gods. She ran errands and delivered messages to humans for **Zeus** (the Supreme Being) and **Hera** (wife to Zeus). As goddess of the rainbow, she was believed to connect the sky and the earth. She was depicted by Callimachus as sleeping under Hera's throne, shod and ready to carry Hera's messages at her bidding. Homer portrayed her as carrying messages for Zeus. In the *Iliad,* Iris is a guardian angel. In book 24 she is sent by Zeus in the role of a comforter to the aged king Priam as he weeps over the body of his dead son Hector. Her functions closely resembled the role of angels later found in Judaism and

Christianity. She is considered to be an **archetypal angel** of the mono-theistic religions.

✤**ISA:** The name of **Jesus** in Islam. In the Koran, Isa stands with the host of angels nearest to God. He is considered a semi-angelic character.

✤**ISAAC:** The son of the prophet **Abraham.** His birth was announced to Abraham by one of three angels who visited him. The angel informed an elderly Abraham and his barren wife, **Sarah,** that they would conceive and give birth to a son. Later, after the child was born, God tested the faith of Abraham by commanding him to offer Isaac as a sacrifice. An angel stopped Abraham from carrying out the deed by calling to him from Heaven, saying, "Abraham, Abraham, do not hurt the boy or do anything to him" (Genesis 22:12).

✤**ISAIAH:** A prophet from the Old Testament of the Bible. In a vision Isaiah saw flaming angels above the **throne of God.** Each had six wings. Two wings covered the face, two covered the feet, and two were used for flying. These angels are generally thought to be the **Seraphim.** In addition, Isaiah was touched on the lips by a Seraph who was carrying a live coal. The coal was to cleanse him in order that he might speak to God without sin. Says Isaiah, "Then one of the Seraphs flew to me, holding a live coal that had been taken from the altar with a pair of tongs. The Seraph touched my mouth with it and said: Now that this has touched your lips, your guilt has departed and your sin is blotted out" (Isaiah 6:6–7).

✤**ISCHIM:** A variation of the name **Izachim.** Izachim are angels who sing praises to God.

✤**ISHIM:** A variation of the name **Izachim.**

✤**ISHMAEL:** The son of **Abraham** and **Hagar** (the maidservant of Abraham's wife, **Sarah**). Angels twice appeared to Hagar when she was in distress on Ishmael's behalf. The first angel appeared to her after she had fled into the wilderness to escape the wrath of Sarah (Genesis 16:1–14). The second angel came after she had wandered into the wilderness, after Abraham had sent her away at Sarah's request (Genesis 21:17–19).

✤**ISHTAR:** A **Chaldean** deity. In Judaism Ishtar became Hamiel. Hamiel was the name of the angel who transported the prophet **Enoch** to Heaven.

✤**ISHTARAH:** A beautiful earthly woman who seduced the angel **Shemyaza** and had him reveal the secret name of God to her. She also had sons by Shemyaza, who became giant mutants known as the **Nephillim.** Their names were Hiwa and Hiya.

✤**ISIAIEL:** A variation of the name Teiaiel, the angel of the future.

✤**Isis:** Egyptian goddess of fertility and nature. She is depicted in art both with and without wings. In John Milton's poem *Paradise Lost* she is a fallen angel. In some traditions, she is considered a Seraph. Others believe her to be a high-ranking demon in Hell.

✤**Islam(ic), Angels of:** Islam is a religion based on the teachings of the prophet **Muhammad.** In Paradise, **Allah** (God) sits on his throne in the **Seventh Heaven** surrounded by angels who minister to him. There are four archangels in Islam. The Koran lists only two, **Jibril** (Gabriel), the "faithful servant," and **Mikhail** (Michael), "who provides men with food and knowledge." The other two are **Azrael,** the angel of death, and **Israfel,** the angel of music, who praises Allah in many languages. It was Jibril who revealed the Koran to Muhammad. He also took Muhammad on a tour of the seven Heavens. There are also the **El-Karubiyan** (Cherubim); the **Hafazah,** guardian angels; the **Huri,** a group of female angels who inhabit Paradise (Heaven); the **jinn** which are demons; the **Al-Zabaniya,** nineteen guardians of Hell; the **Malaika,** angels who record mankind's deeds. Other angels include **Harut and Marut,** angels who gave in to sexual temptation; **Malik,** the ruler of Hell; **Isa** (Jesus), who is a semi-angelic character; and **Iblis** (Satan). According to early Muslim lore, the El-Karubiyan were created from the tears of Mikhail when he cried over the sins of the faithful. In Islam, angels are said to sit in the mosques listening to and recording the prayers of men. The archangels in Islam are believed to record the good and bad deeds of humankind.

✤**Isphan Darmaz:** In Persian mythology Isphan Darmaz is the angel of earth and the angel of February.

✤**Israel:** The name of one of the **throne angels.**

✤**Israel(ites), Angels of:** The archangel **Michael** is the guardian protector of Israel. The angel **Metatron** assisted Israel in their escape from bondage. According to lore, angels fall silent at daybreak to hear the praises and prayers of Israel. In the Book of Revelation 21:10–12, **John** tells of seeing gates that have the names of the twelve tribes of Israel written on them. Angels stand guard over these gates. The account states, "The angel carried me to the top of a very high mountain. He showed me Jerusalem, the Holy City. The city shone like precious stone. It had a great, high wall with twelve gates and with twelve angels in charge of the gates. On the gates were written the names of the twelve tribes of the people of Israel."

✤**Israfel:** The Islamic angel of music. According to Islamic lore, Israfel glorifies **Allah** in a thousand languages. Israfel looks daily to Hell and cries so hard that his tears would flood the earth if Allah did not intercede and stop their flow. About Israfel the Koran says, "And the angel Israfel, whose heart-strings are a lute, and who has the sweetest voice of all God's creatures." **Edgar Allan Poe** wrote about Israfel in a poem entitled *Israfel.* In the poem Poe wrote, "None sing so wildly well, As the angel Israfel. And the giddy stars (so legends tell), Ceasing their hymns, attend the spell, Of his voice, all mute." A variation of the name Israfel is Israfil.

✤**ISRAFIL:** A variation of **Israfel.**

✤*IT HAPPENED ONE CHRISTMAS:* See **Christmas Movies.**

✤**ITA:** One of the many aliases used by the she-demon **Lilith.**

✤**ITMON:** One of the seventy-eight names of **Metatron.**

✤**ITRAIL:** An angel summoned in Arabic exorcism ceremonies.

✤*IT'S A WONDERFUL LIFE:* See **Christmas Movies.**

✤**IUVART:** A **fallen angel.**

✤**IZACHIM:** A superior order of angels who reside in Maon, the **Fifth Heaven.** The Izachim sing songs of praise to God. Variations of the name Izachim are Aishim, Ischim and Ishim.

✤**IZEDS:** Angels in Persian mythology. In Persian lore, twenty-eight izeds surround the great god **Ahura Mazda.**

✤**IZORPO:** An alias used by the she-demon **Lilith** when working evil against humans.

✤**IZRAIL:** A variation of the name **Azrael,** the angel of death in Islam.

Millions of spiritual creatures walk the earth
unseen, both when we wake, and when we sleep.

—ADAM TO EVE, JOHN MILTON, *Paradise Lost*

✤**JABRAIL:** A variation of the name **Jibril,** one of the four **archangels** of Islam.

✤**JACHNIEL:** An angel who safeguards the south **wind.**

✤**JACOB:** One of the patriarchs of the Hebrew pedigree. He is the younger of the twin sons of **Isaac.** In a dream Jacob saw angels ascending and descending a ladder as they went about their work between Heaven and earth. At Genesis 28:11–12, it states, "In time he came across a place and set about spending the night there because the sun had set. So he took one of the stones of the place and set it as his head supporter and lay down in that place. And he began to dream, and, look! there was a ladder stationed upon the earth and its top reaching up to the heavens; and, look! there were God's angels ascending and descending on it." Jacob was also met by angels on his return home to Canaan from Haran. He named the place where he met the angels Mahanaim. "And as for Jacob, he got on his way, and the angels of God now met up with him. Immediately Jacob said, when he saw them: 'The camp of God this is!' Hence he called the name of that place Mahanaim" (Genesis 32:1–2). On another occasion Jacob wrestled with an angel in order to receive a blessing from him. At Genesis 32:24–26 it states, "Then a man came and wrestled with him until just before day break. When the man saw that he was not winning the struggle, he hit Jacob on the hip, and it was thrown out of joint. The man said, 'Let me go; daylight is coming.' 'I won't, unless you bless me,' Jacob answered." It has been said that it was the angel **Camael** with whom he wrestled. The archangel **Uriel** is also thought to have been the angel that wrestled with Jacob. This angel is also called the Dark Angel. Jacob named the spot where he wrestled with the angel **Peniel.** The archangel **Raphael** reportedly healed his hip joint. The story of Jacob wrestling with an angel later became popular in art. Three of the most popular portrayals were painted by **Paul Gauguin, Gustave Doré,** and nineteenth-century painter **Eugène Delacroix.**

✤**JACOB-ISRAEL:** Jacob-Israel is another name for the archangel **Uriel.** According to legend, Uriel is the mysterious Dark Angel who wrestled with **Jacob** (Genesis 32:25–30). Legend has it that when the two wrestled, they merged and became one man. It is the only listing in angelic lore where an angel became a man. Because of this merging, Uriel took the name Jacob-Israel.

✤**JAHOEL:** A high-ranking angel of Heaven. He is one of the ruling princes of the **Seraphim.** A variation of the name Jahoel is Jehoel.

✤**JALDABAOTH:** One of the seven **Archons** of gnosticism.

✤**JANNES AND JAMBRES:** Egyptian wizards from the Book of Exodus. According to legend, Jannes and Jambres magically gained entry into Heaven and refused to leave. God set the archangels **Michael** and **Gabriel** against them, but the two were unable to remove them. God then set **Metatron** against them and they were immediately ousted. Jannes and Jambres were reportedly aided by **Mastema** in working magic against the Hebrews during their **exodus** from Egypt.

✤**JANUARY, ANGEL OF:** The archangel **Gabriel.**

✤**JAO:** One of the seven **Archons** (angels) of gnosticism.

✤**JAPHKIEL:** A leader of the order of angels called **Thrones.**

✤**JAVAN:** The guardian angel of Greece.

✤**JAZERIEL:** One of the angels of the twenty-eight **lunar mansions.**

✤**JEDUHIEL:** Thought to be one of the three unnamed **archangels** of Judeo-Christian lore.

✤**JEFEFIYAH:** The angel who instructed **Moses** on the mysteries of the **Cabala.** A variation of the name Jefefiyah is Yefehfiah.

✤**JEHIEL:** The angel who presides over **animals** in the wild.

✤**JEHOEL:** A variation of the name **Jahoel.**

✤**JEHOVAH:** The name of **God** the Almighty in Judaism and Christianity. In the Bible, the angels act as intermediaries between Jehovah and mankind. According to the Book of **Revelation,** Jehovah is ministered to by myriads of angels. The angel of Jehovah is **Metatron.**

✦Jehudiel: A prince of the **Archangels**. He also governs the movements of the planets.

✦Jekusiel: An angel who stands guard over the palace of Wilon, the **First Heaven.**

✦Jeremiel (God's Mercy): Jeremiel was once an angel who presided over the souls awaiting the **resurrection**. He was later renamed **Raziel** and assigned greater duties in Heaven. A variation of the name Jeremiel is Remiel.

✦Jerome, Saint: See **Saint Jerome.**

✦Jesod: One of the ten **Holy Sefiroth** found in the **Cabala.** He is also called Foundation.

✦Jesus: In Judaism he is a prophet. In Christianity he is the son of God. In Islam he is called **Isa** and is also a prophet. The birth of Jesus was announced by the archangel **Gabriel** to the **Virgin Mary** (Luke 1:26–33). That famous event is now referred to as the **Annunciation.** When Jesus was born, an angel appeared to **shepherds** in a field announcing his birth (Luke 2:9–15). As a man, Jesus was tempted by **Satan,** who said he would give Jesus all of the kingdoms of the world if he would perform an act of worship to him (Matthew 4:8–9). After Jesus refused Satan, angels came and ministered to him. (Matthew 4:11). Once when he was feeling distressed, an angel came and strengthened him (Luke 22:43). After his death two angels escorted him to Heaven (Acts 1:9–11). He once revealed that he could call on several armies of angels to give him aid, stating, "Don't you know that I could call on my Father for help, and at once he would send me more than twelve armies of angels?" (Matthew 26:53). The angels are said to have had no prior knowledge of the incarnation and the death of Jesus. His being born into the world and the events that followed during his time on earth are as extraordinary to them as they are to humans.

✦Jewelry, Angel of: The angel **Azaz'el** taught women to adorn themselves with jewelry.

✦Jewish Patriarchs: The founding fathers of **Judaism.** According to Judaic lore, the patriarchs were transformed into angels of the **Ophanim** class upon reaching Heaven. In the **Cabala** each patriarch had an angel who acted as his guide. **Adam**'s guide was **Raziel;** Shem's guide was **Jophiel;** Noah's guide was **Zaphkiel;** Abraham's guide was **Zadkiel;** Isaac's guide was **Raphael;** Joseph's guide was **Joshua;** Daniel's guide was **Gabriel;** Jacob's guide was **Peliel;** Moses' guide was **Metatron;** Elijah's guide was **Maltiel;** Samson's guide was **Camael;** David's guide was **Cervihel;** and Solomon's guide was **Michael.**

✦Jibreel: A variation of **Jibril.**

✤**JIBRIL:** The Islamic name for the archangel **Gabriel.** Legend has it that he has sixteen hundred wings with hair of saffron. Daily he enters the ocean, and when he comes out, a million drops of water fall from his wings and become angels who sing praises to God. He is called the faithful spirit and also the faithful servant. **Jibril** dictated the **Koran** to **Muhammad.** He first appeared to Muhammad when he was meditating on a mountain near Mecca. Stunned, Muhammad turned away. However, everywhere he turned, Jibril's face appeared. On another occasion, Jibril appeared and ordered Muhammad to call men to God. One night, angels appeared to Muhammad to prepare him for a journey through Heaven. Jibril awakened Muhammad and removed his heart. After washing and purifying the heart, Jibril put it back into Muhammad's body. Muhammad was then filled with wisdom and faith. On the **Night of Glory,** when Jibril dictated the Koran to Muhammad, his wings were outstretched, his face illuminated, and between his eyes was written, "There is no God, but God, and Muhammad is the prophet of God." Jibril is also the guardian angel of Muhammad. Variations of the name Jibril are Djibril, Jibreel, and Jabrail.

✤**JINEE:** A variation of **jinni.**

✤**JINN:** The plural form of *jinni.* In Arabic folklore the jinn are guardian angels with supernatural powers. They use these powers to grant wishes and protect their charges. They were popular in Near Eastern literature and were portrayed in art both with and without wings. Famous stories that included jinn are the *Arabian Nights* and *Thousand and One Nights.* The television show *I Dream of Jeannie* featured a jinni in its story line. In Islam jinn are considered demons.

✤**JINNI:** The singular form of **jinn.** Variations of the name *jinni* are *jinee, genii,* and *genie.*

✤**JOAN OF ARC:** A national heroine of France who was canonized a saint in 1920. She was born in Domrémy, a little town of Champagne that sat on the banks of the Meuse. Her neighbors were later witnesses of her pious conduct and her love of God, Church, and prayer. Often referred to as the Maid of Orleans, Joan (Jeanne in French) began to hear the voices of angels at the age of fourteen. In the beginning, she heard only one voice, which was sometimes accompanied by a brilliant light. Later, as she began to hear more voices, she began to see the angels behind the voices, which turned out to be Saint **Michael, Saint Catherine,** and Saint Margaret. Joan reported that the angels visited her many times during the week. She said that she could see, hear, and touch them. She stated that she felt such love and peace when she was with them that she used to cry when they left and wished that they would take her with them. When she was sixteen, the voices admonished her to go and help the **Dauphin.** The Church claimed her revelations regarding hearing voices and seeing angels were satanic and sentenced her to death. She was burned at the stake on May 30, 1431, for heresy.

✤**JOB:** A faithful servant of God whose life account is recorded in the Bible. In the account, Job's faith is tested as Satan strips him of his health, family, and all of his worldly possessions. In the end Job refuses to curse God and die and continues as a faithful servant of God, whom God blessed with renewed health, children, and wealth. His experience has served for centuries as encouragement to people who have suffered and who feel that they are being tested by the fallen angel Satan (Job 1:6–22; 2:1–10). The Book of Job also attests that the angels existed long before humankind. As God queries Job on his knowledge about the creation of the world, God states that the angels were there to witness the creation. Speaking of the angels witnessing the creation, God says to Job, "In the dawn of that day the stars sang together, and the heavenly beings shouted for joy" (Job 38:4–7). The "stars" and the "heavenly beings" are the angels.

✤**JOBS, ANGEL OF:** The archangel **Uriel.**

✤**JOEL:** The name of one of the **Cherubim** that are depicted on the **Ark of the Covenant.**

✤**JOFIEL:** A variation of the name **Iophiel.** Iophiel is a ruler of **Saturn,** and an angel of the Torah.

✤**JOHN:** An apostle of Jesus Christ who received a vision from the angels. This vision later came to be called the **Revelation** of **John.** It is the last book of the Bible's New Testament. In the Book of Revelation, John is shown a vision by an angel of the last days. He is instructed to write down what he has seen in the vision (Revelation 22:10). Angels are present throughout the revelation.

✤**JOHN OF DAMASCUS:** See **Saint John of Damascus.**

✤**JOHN THE BAPTIST:** A biblical prophet. John the Baptist was a cousin of **Jesus** Christ. He was also the messenger chosen by God to prepare the way for Jesus and is called the "forerunner" of Jesus. His birth was foretold by the archangel **Gabriel** who appeared to his father, Zechariah, to inform him that he and his wife, Elizabeth, would have a son. The Bible tells us, "An angel of the Lord appeared to him standing at the right side of the altar." The angel informed Zechariah that Elizabeth, who was old and barren, would give birth to a son, and that they were to name him John. Zechariah said to the angel, "How shall I know if this is so? I am an old man, and my wife is old also." The angel replied, "I am Gabriel. I stand in the **presence** of God, who sent me to speak to you and tell you this good news. But you have not believed my message which will come true at the right time. Because you have not believed, you will be unable to speak; you will remain silent until the day my promise to you comes true." (Luke 1:5–19)

✦JOMJAEL: A **fallen angel** from the **Watchers** class.

✦JONATHAN SMITH: See *Highway to Heaven*.

✦JOPHIEL: An archangel, he is a ruling prince of the order of **Thrones**. He is also one of twelve archangels listed by modern angelologists. The name Jophiel is also a variation of the name **Iophiel**.

✦JORDAN RIVER, ANGELS OF THE: **Nidbai** and **Shelmai** are angels who watch over the Jordan River.

✦JOSEPH: The husband of **Mary** (the mother of **Jesus**). After Joseph found out that Mary was pregnant, he decided to divorce her secretly because he did not wish to embarrass her publicly. However, an angel prevented him from doing so by appearing to him in a dream to inform him that Mary was pregnant by the **Holy Spirit.** Matthew 1:20 tells us, "But just when he had resolved to do this, an angel of the Lord appeared to him in a dream and said, 'Joseph, do not be afraid to take Mary as your wife, for the child conceived in her is from the Holy Spirit.' " An angel of the Lord later appeared to Joseph in a dream to warn him that **Herod** was planning to kill the baby Jesus. The angel commanded Joseph to take Mary and Jesus and flee to Egypt where Herod would not reach them. Matthew 2:13 states, "An angel of the Lord appeared to Joseph in a dream and said, 'Get up, take the child and his mother, and flee to Egypt, and remain there until I tell you; for Herod is about to search for the child, to destroy him.' "

✦JOSHUA: The successor to **Moses**. Joshua was nervous at the prospect of succeeding Moses. To increase his confidence, God sent an angel to appear to him. The angel appeared in the form of a man and stood before him with a sword drawn. Joshua asked the angel if he was one of them or one of the enemies. The angel replied, "Neither; but as commander of the army of the Lord I have now come." Joshua immediately prostrated himself and asked what the angel commanded of him. The angel asked only that he remove his sandals, because the place where he was standing was holy. After the appearance of the angel, Joshua had the courage needed to lead the Hebrews.

✦JOY, ANGEL OF: According to lore, the archangels **Gabriel** and **Raphael** both carry the title of angel of joy. To the **Essenes** the angel of joy was **Camael**.

✦JUDAISM, ANGELS OF: Judaism is the religious beliefs, practices, and way of life of the Jews, founded circa 2000 B.C. by **Abraham, Isaac,** and

Jacob. Judaism espouses belief in monotheism, which was embraced by biblical Hebrews. It is a primary source of angelic lore. It also founded much of the beliefs in angels later adopted by Christianity and Islam. Angels can be traced in Judaism dating back three thousand years. They are usually portrayed as masculine and are believed to be caretakers of the universe and guardians of humankind. There are seven **archangels** of Judaism. The four most recognized are **Raphael, Gabriel, Michael,** and **Uriel.** Angels also act as messengers of God and have very humanlike qualities. In the Old Testament, they appear as ordinary men and eat and drink as humans do. They also show weakness when they fall from grace because of giving in to **sexual temptation.** In angelology, primary sources for studying the angels come from Apocryphal books of Judaism. These books offer an in-depth look at the characteristics, qualities, and activities of the angels. See **Bible.**

✤**JUDGMENT:** The twentieth card in the major arcana of the **tarot.** Judgment is depicted in most decks of tarot cards as an angel blowing a **trumpet,** heralding the coming of God's judgment.

✤**JUDGMENT, ANGELS OF:** In Judaism the angel of judgment is the archangel **Gabriel. Phalgus** and **Zehanpuryu YHWH** are also referred to as angels of judgment. The angels of judgment judge the deeds of humankind. They sometimes apply the deserved punishment for the misdeed.

✤**JUDGMENT DAY, ANGEL OF:** The angel of Judgment Day is the archangel **Uriel.** Uriel holds the keys to Hell and, according to the *Sibylline Oracles*, will do away with the gates of Hell on Judgment Day. Five angels will lead the souls of man to stand before God on Judgment Day. They are referred to as the "angels of the judgment of God." They are **Araqiel, Rumael, Samiel, Uriel,** and **Aziel.**

✤**JULY, ANGEL OF: Verchiel.**

✤**JUNE, ANGEL OF: Muriel.**

✤**JUNO:** Female guardian spirits of ancient Rome.

✤**JUPITER, ANGEL OF: Zadkiel.**

✤**JUSTICE, ANGEL OF: Tzadkiel.** In Zoroastrianism Rashnu and **Asha** were both angels of justice. In the Talmud the angel of justice is listed as one of the angels in God's **inner circle.** God consulted the angels of the inner circle on his idea of creating mankind. The angel of justice was in favor of this idea, unlike some of the other angels.

K

Every time a bell rings, an angel gets its wings.
—It's a Wonderful Life

✤**Kabaiel:** A variation of the name **Kokabi'el.**

✤**Kabbalah, Angels of the:** See **Cabala.**

✤**Kachina:** The **kachina** are **nature spirits** whose characteristics resemble those of angels. They are found in the belief system of the Pueblo peoples, who reside in America's Southwest. They are considered sacred spirits, believed to connect the physical realm with the spiritual. Kachina dolls are given to children to remind them of the invisible spiritual realm surrounding them.

✤**Kadal:** See **Childbirth.**

✤**Kadashiel:** An angel of the south **wind.**

✤**Kadashim:** The Kadashim are high-ranking angels who dwell in the **Sixth Heaven.** They praise God continuously.

✤**Kadir-Rahman:** An angel of the **Yezidics.**

✤**Kadmiel:** See **Childbirth.**

✤**Kafziel:** An angel of death, and the ruling angel of **Saturn.** In Geonic lore he is listed as one of the seven archangels.

✤**Kairos:** The term *kairos* means the "right moment" for angels to accomplish their God-given missions. Kairos is also a winged god who holds the scales of chance. A depiction of him dates back to 300 B.C., long before any Judaic or Christian portrayals of angels. He was also known as the god of coincidence.

✤KAIROXANONDALON: A demon who causes ear obstructions. He is thwarted by the angel **Uriel.**

✤KAKABEL: A chief demon of Hell. The name Kakabel is also a variation of the name **Kokabi'el.**

✤KAL: The guardian angel of King **Nebuchadnezzar.**

✤KALAZAEL: An angel from the Testament of **Solomon.**

✤KALI: One of the **Shakti** in Hinduism. She is often referred to as the Black One because she is the cosmic energy in which colors fuse into formless darkness. She brings into being innumerable universes. She is analogous with both destruction and grace. Kali is also one of the aliases used by she-demon **Lilith.**

✤KALKA'IL: The angel who presides over the **Huri,** the beautiful female spirits of **Islamic** lore who give sensual pleasures to the male inhabitants of Paradise. Kalka'il is said to dwell in the **Fifth Heaven.**

✤KALKI: One of the **avatars** of Hindu lore.

✤KALKYDRA: A high order of angels ranked along with the **Seraphim** and **Cherubim.** They dwell in Zebul, the **Fourth Heaven.** They are odd in appearance, with heads like a crocodile's and bodies like a lion's. Each has twelve wings. According to lore, the Kalkydra sing praises to God when the sun rises. A variation of the name Kalkydra is Chalkydri.

✤KAMAEL: One of the archangels of the **Holy Sefiroth.** Variations of the name Kamael are **Camael** and Khamael.

✤KAMI: In the Far East, the word Kami signifies the deities of Heaven and the spirits of the shrines where they are worshiped.

✤KAMUEL: A variation of the name **Chamuel.** Chamuel is believed to be one of the seven **archangels.**

✤KANIEL: See **Childbirth.**

✤KAPHKAPHIEL: An angel who frightens away evil spirits. His name can be found on oriental amulets.

✤KARAEL: An angel who is able to thwart the powerful demon Belbel.

✤KARIBU (ONE WHO INTERCEDES): The Akkadian word for **Cherubim.**

✤KARKIEL: See **Childbirth.**

✤KARMIEL: An angel who presides over the east **wind.**

✤KARNIEL: An angel who presides over the west **wind.**

✤KAROZ: **Reporting angels** of Judaism.

✤KASADYA: A fallen angel from the class of angels called **Watchers.** He taught women how to perform abortions. A variation of the name Kasadya is Kasdaye.

✤KASBEL (DECEIVER OF GOD): Another name for the angel Beqa.

According to legend, Beqa, whose name meant "virtuous perso⌐ rebelled against God the day he was created. After his fall, he took tℏ name Kasbel, which means "deceiver of god" or "the one who lies tℴ God." He received this title because he attempted to trick the archangel **Michael** into revealing the secret name of God. A variation of the name Kasbel is Kazbeel.

❖**KASDAYE:** A variation of the name **Kasadya.** Kasadya is the angel of abortion.

❖**KASHDEJAN:** An angel from the class of **Watchers.** He taught men psychiatry and how to cure various diseases.

❖**KASHIEL:** An angel who presides over the west **wind.**

❖**KATANIKOTAEL:** A demon who causes dissension in the home.

❖**KATCHIEL:** See **Childbirth.**

❖**KATMIAL:** An angel who stands guard over the palace of Makon, the **Sixth Heaven.**

❖**KATRAX:** A demon who causes fever.

❖**KATZHIEL:** See **Childbirth.**

❖**KAZBEEL:** A variation of **Kasbel.**

❖**KAZIEL:** A variation of the name **Casziel.** Casziel is the angel of Saturday.

❖**KEA:** One of the many aliases used by the she-demon **Lilith** when working evil against mortals.

❖**KEMUEL:** An angel who attempted to prevent Moses from entering Heaven to receive the Torah. He was said to have had twelve thousand angels of destruction under his command. However, Moses was able to thwart him, preventing his interference. Kemuel is also a variation of the name **Camael.**

❖**KENUNIT:** See **Childbirth.**

❖**KEPHAREL:** An angel of several titles including the Angel of **Saturday,** the Angel of the Pomegranate Tree, and the Angel of Completeness.

❖**KEPLER, JOHANNES:** German astronomer (1571–1630). Kepler became professor of mathematics at Graz in 1593. He was also the court mathematician to the Holy Roman Emperor Rudolf II. He wrote Kepler's Laws, which were three mathematical expositions describing the rotations of the planets around the sun. Kepler believed that angels move the planets and act as coordinators of the enormous and complex actions of the entire universe.

❖**KERMES OAK, ANGEL OF THE: Sammael.**

❖**KERUB:** A Hebrew variation of the word **Cherub.** It means "one who intercedes."

❖**KERUBIEL:** See **Kerubi'el YHWH.**

KERUBI'EL YHWH: A powerful and majestic angel in Heaven. He is a princely ruler of the **Cherubim.** He is described in 3 Enoch as being as large as the seven heavens. His tongue is like fire, his body full of eyes and wings. Legend has it that he is so forceful that when he's angry the earth trembles and the **Seventh Heaven** (the dwelling place of God) quakes. A shortened version of Kerubi'el YHWH is Kerubiel.

✦**KERUBIM:** An Islamic word for **Cherubim.** According to lore, the Kerubim are created from the tears of **Mikhail.**

✦**KESEF:** In Judaism he is listed as an angel of **destruction** and an angel of death. He is said to have attacked the prophet **Moses** at Mount Horeb and was later captured and locked inside the Holy Tabernacle by the high priest **Aaron.** A variation of the name Kesef is Kezef.

✦**KESTAR'EL:** One of the leaders of the **Watchers** who came to earth to have sexual relations with women.

✦**KETHER:** One of the ten **Holy Sefiroth** of the **Cabala.** He is also called Crown and Ancient of Days.

✦**KEY(S), ANGELS OF:** The New Testament of the Bible lists **Abaddon** (the Angel of the **Abyss**) as the keeper of the key to the Abyss (Revelation 9:1). This key will lock **Satan** and his demons away for a thousand years (Revelation 20:3). The keys to God's kingdom are held by the archangel **Michael.** The keys to the gates of Hell are held by the archangel **Uriel. Anapiel YHWH** is keeper of the keys to the palaces of **Arabot.** He is also the guardian of the keys to the **heavenly passageways.** The angel **Dohel** holds the keys to the four corners of the earth. In Muslim lore, Riswan guards the keys to the earthly paradise. In the Middle East, the **owl goddess** was believed to carry keys of life.

✦**KEZEF:** A variation of the name **Kesef.**

✦**KFIAL:** An angel who stands guard over the palace of Zebul, the **Fourth Heaven.**

✦**KHABIEL:** An angel who stands guard over the palace of Wilon, the **First Heaven.**

✦**KHAMAEL:** An archangel of the **Holy Sefiroth.** Variations of the name Khamael are Kamael and **Camael.**

✦**KHARURAIL:** An angel summoned in Arabic exorcism ceremonies.

✦**KHSHATHRA:** A shortened version of **Khshathra Vairya.**

✦**KHSHATHRA VAIRYA:** In Zoroastrianism he is one of the **Amesha Spentas** and guardian of the sky. He is also called Dominion and Shahrevar.

✦*KID WITH THE BROKEN HALO, THE:* A 1982 film about a young African-American angel, played by Gary Coleman, and his skeptical elder, played by Robert Guillaume, who come to earth to aid three ethnic families.

✦**KIDNEYS, DEMON OF: Metathiax** is the demon who causes pain in the kidneys. In the Testament of **Solomon, Adonael** is the angel capable of overpowering him.

✦**KIDUMIEL:** See **Childbirth.**

✦**KINDNESS, ANGELS OF:** The angels of kindness are Achsah, Hasdiel, and **Zadkiel.**

✦**KING OF ANGELS:** In Judaism, the archangel **Metatron** is the King of Angels. Legend has it that he was placed above the archangels **Michael** and **Gabriel** after ousting **Jannes and Jambres** (the magicians of Egypt who had mysteriously gained entry into Heaven) from God's **presence.** Michael and Gabriel had tried to remove the magicians but were unsuccessful.

✦**KING OF FIRE:** A title held by **Adramelec,** a throne angel who stands in the **presence** of God. Adramelec received this title because of his association with fire sacrifices.

✦**KING OF FRANCE:** See **Charles VII of France.**

✦**KING SOLOMON:** See **Solomon.**

✦**KINGDOM OF HEAVEN:** The word *kingdom* is used when referring to the place in Heaven in which God dwells. The archangel **Uriel** holds the keys to the Kingdom. In Judaism and Christianity the Kingdom of Heaven is the dwelling place of not only God, but also the **Seraphim, Cherubim, throne angels,** and the righteous souls of individuals who once lived on earth.

✦**KINGDOM OF THE ANGELS:** The angelic kingdom consists of the nine **orders of angels,** which include the **Seraphim, Cherubim, Thrones, Dominations, Virtues, Powers, Principalities, Archangels,** and **Angels.** There are also the **throne angels** and the **ministering angels.** There are rulers over the various groups of **angels.** They include the rulers of the Seraphim: **Michael, Serapiel,** Jahoel, **Uriel, Camael, Metatron,** and Nathanael. Rulers of the Cherubim: **Gabriel, Kerubiel,** Ophaniel, **Raphael, Uriel,** and Zophiel. Rulers of the Thrones: Japhkiel, **Oriphiel, Zaphkiel,** Zabkiel, **Jophiel** and **Raziel.** Rulers of the Dominations: **Zadkiel,** Hashmal, Yahriel, and **Chasmal.** Rulers of the Virtues: **Haniel, Michael, Raphael, Barbiel, Uzziél,** Tarshish, and **Peliel.** Rulers of the Powers: **Camael, Gabriel, Verchiel,** and **Mother Mary.** Rulers of the Principalities: **Nisroch,** Amael, **Haniel, Cervihel,** and Requel. Rulers of the Archangels: **Metatron, Raphael, Michael, Gabriel, Barbiel, Jehudiel,** and **Barakiel.** Rulers of the Angels: Phaleg, **Adnachiel, Gabriel,** and Chayyliel.

✤**KINGDOMS OF THE EARTH:** The **Principalities** are the guardians of kingdoms (or governments) of the earth. The leader of kings (or government rulers) on earth is **Haniel.** In Christianity, **Satan** (once a magnificent angel in Heaven) is believed to have control over all of the kingdoms (or governments) on earth. This is revealed when Satan offers Jesus all of the kingdoms of the world in order to tempt Jesus into bowing down and performing an act of worship to him. In addition, the book of Revelation (11:5) mentions an angel who blows a trumpet announcing that the **Kingdom of Heaven** will become one with the kingdoms of the earth. It states, "And the seventh angel sounded his trumpet; and there were great voices in heaven, saying, 'The kingdoms of this world have become [the kingdoms] of our Lord, and of his Christ; and he shall reign forever and ever.' "

✤**KINGS, ANGEL OF: Haniel.** See **World Leaders.**

✤**KINPURU'SH:** Winged spirits in Hinduism who dwell near the gods. They hover around the gods in reverence and adoration.

✤**KISMET, ANGEL OF: Manu.**

✤**KLAHA:** An angel who watches over the south **wind.**

✤**KLEE, PAUL:** Swiss abstract painter and art theorist (1879–1940). He painted the famous *Angelus Novus*, which now hangs in the Israel Museum.

✤**KNIGHT, MICHAEL E.:** Star of the romantic comedy *Date With an Angel.*

✤**KNOWLEDGE, ANGELS OF:** The angel of science and knowledge in Judeo-Christian lore is the archangel **Raphael.** In Islam, **Mikhail** is the angel who provides men with knowledge. Knowledge is also the name of one of the ten **Holy Sefiroth** (angels found in the **Cabala**). In Greek mythology Clio was the **muse** of knowledge. The essence of the **Cherubim** is "God's knowledge."

✤**KOCHAB:** A variation of the name **Kokabi'el.**

✤**KOCHBIEL:** A variation of the name **Kokabi'el.**

✤**KOK:** An angel from the Testament of **Solomon.**

✤**KOKABI'EL (STAR OF GOD):** A fallen angel. Kokabi'el was once a great lord in Heaven who was an expert in astrology and astronomy. He passed this knowledge on to humankind. He later became a high-ranking demon of Hell who continued to practice astrology. Variations of the name Kokabi'el include Kabaiel, Kakabel, Kochab, Kochbiel, Kokabriel, Kokbiel, and Kokarer'el.

✤**KOKABRIEL:** A variation of the name **Kokabi'el.**

✤**KOKARER'EL:** A variation of the name **Kokabi'el.**

✤**KOKBIEL:** A variation of the name **Kokabi'el.**

✦**KOKOS:** One of many aliases used by the she-demon **Lilith.**

✦**KOLAZANTA (THE PUNISHER):** A mighty destroying angel. He is also listed as one of the leaders of the angels of **destruction.**

✦**KORAN, ANGELS OF THE:** The Koran (also Qu'ran) is the Holy Book of **Islam.** There are one hundred and four references to angels in the Koran. The Koran was dictated in its entirety to the prophet **Muhammad** by the archangel **Jibril (Gabriel)** on what is called the **Night of Glory.** Angels of the Koran include Jibril and **Mikhail.** There are also the Hamalatal-'arsh, the four throne bearers of God, symbolized by a man, a bull, an eagle, and a lion. **Allah** (God) is praised by many angels, who are created from his breath to glorify and exalt him. He is also praised by **Israfel,** the angel of music, in many different languages. There are the **Hafazah,** who are guardian angels, and the **Malaika,** angels who record mankind's deeds. Other angels include **Haroth and Maroth,** angels who gave in to sexual temptation; **Malik,** the ruler of Hell; and the Al-Zabaniya, nineteen guardians of Hell, also known as the Violent-Thrusters. About angels the Koran says, "You shall see the angels circling around the Throne, giving glory to their Lord."

✦**KORNIEL:** An angel who watches over the south **wind.**

✦**KOURTAEL:** A demon.

✦**KRISHNA:** One of the **avatars** of Hindu lore.

✦**KSIEL:** An angel of God who smote the sinful nations with a long, fiery whip.

✦**KUAN YIN:** A female spirit of compassion in ancient Chinese lore.

✦**KUNOPEGOS:** A demon of the sea. He is called the cruel sea-horse demon in the Testament of **Solomon.** In the front, he resembles a horse, in back, a fish. He causes ships to crash and seasickness. He is thwarted by the angel Iameth.

✦**KURIOTETES:** Another name for the class of angels called **Dominations.**

✦**KURMA:** One of the **avatars** of Hindu lore.

✦**KYRIEL:** One of the twenty-eight angels who preside over the **lunar mansions.**

✦**KZUIAL:** An angel who stands guard over the palace of Zebul, the **Fourth Heaven.**

For it is written, "he will command his angels concerning you, to protect you."

—Luke 4:10

✤**LABBIEL:** The archangel **Raphael** was known as Labbiel in **Chaldea.** God changed his name to Raphael when he took a stand on God's side regarding the creation of humankind (some of the angels opposed this idea). The name Raphael means "the shining one who heals."

✤**LACTANTIUS:** A writer from the fourth century. In his writings Lactantius referred to the angels as "breaths of God." He believed that the angels are made up of a very fine, ethereal substance.

✤**LAHAL:** See **Childbirth.**

✤**LAHARIEL:** See **Childbirth.**

✤**LAHASH:** A fallen angel. Lahash was expelled from the **presence** of God and was severely punished with fire for leading a group of one hundred and eighty-four angels against **Moses,** in an effort to prevent his prayers for Israel from reaching God.

✤**LAHATIEL (FLAMING ONE):** An angel of punishment. In Hell he is an overseer of the gates of death. He is also in charge of punishing entire nations for their sins.

✤**LAILA:** A variation of the name Lailah.

✤**LAILAH:** The angel of birth, conception, and pregnancy. She is the guardian of spirits at their birth. She also aids women desirous of having children to conceive. Variations of the name Lailah include Laila, Leliel, Lailahel, and Lala.

✤**LAILAHEL:** A variation of the name **Lailah.**

✤**LAILIEL:** The angel of **night.**

✤**LAKSHMI (ABUNDANCE):** The most popular **devi** in Hinduism. She is also a goddess of **luck.** Lakshmi takes on many forms. She is Radha, a peasant girl; Rukmini, queen of Krishna's sixteen thousand wives; and Sita, wife of Rama (Rama was a hero in the epic tale the *Ramayana*).

✤**LALA:** A variation of the name **Lailah.**

✤**LAMASSU:** In Assyrian beliefs the angel Lamassu was called upon for the exorcism of demons.

✤**LAMECH:** The father of **Noah.** Legend has it that Lamech was fearful of Noah when he was a baby because he looked different. When Noah was born, a light surrounded him. The light was so brilliant that it was said to fill a dark room. Lamech believed that the baby was a prodigy of the angels and not his own child. In another legend surrounding Lamech, the angel **Azael** came to the earth and had a sexual relationship with Lamech's granddaughter **Naamah.** She later gave birth to a son named **Azza,** who was one of the **Nephillim.**

✤**LAMECHIEL:** An angel found in the *Testament of Solomon.* Lamechiel is able to overpower the demon named **Deception.**

✤**LANDON, MICHAEL:** Popular actor who starred in the hit television series *Highway to Heaven.* In the show Landon played an angel named Jonathan Smith, whose divine mission is to teach humans love and compassion. *Highway to Heaven* ran on NBC from 1984–1988.

✤**LANGUAGE(S):** According to Judaic lore, the official language of the angels is Hebrew. The Catholic Church maintains that it is Latin. Others have stated that it is Greek. When angels visit humans, they speak the native language of that particular individual. In their pure and natural form, the angels are said to communicate by telepathy. HUMAN LANGUAGE. The angels taught humankind language. *The Testament of Naphtali* states that seventy angels taught mankind the seventy languages of the world's nations. The archangel **Michael** taught the Jews the Hebrew language. According to lore, the angels also taught mankind to communicate through the written word. One legend states that humans learned the various languages while building the Tower of Babel. God sent the angels to scramble the language of the builders, who were attempting to build a tower to Heaven.

✤**LARE(S):** Guardian spirits of ancestors who watch over homes and cities. In ancient Rome each household was believed to have a lare watching over the family. The lare was believed to be the spirit of the family's founder. It was traditional to thank the lare during meals (much like the Christians give thanks to God during meals). Some households even set a place for the lare at the table. The lare was credited as the source of the family's creativity and considered a part of their everyday life.

✤**LASHES OF FIRE:** According to legend, the great angelic prince Hayli'el YHWH flogs the **Seraphim** with "lashes of fire" if they do not chant the **Trisagion** on time.

✤**LAST JUDGMENT, ANGEL OF THE:** The angel who will lead the souls of men to stand before God on judgment day, the final day of God's great war on the wicked, otherwise known as **Armageddon.** He will also weigh the good and the evil deeds of the souls of mankind on judgment day. This angel is traditionally said to be the archangel **Michael.** LAST JUDGMENT IN ART. The Last Judgment has been a source of inspiration for several great artists. Among the most famous paintings are those of **Michelangelo** on the **Sistine Chapel,** in which he portrays angels without wings; and **Giotto,** who portrayed a scene of the Last Judgment that was inspired by the Irish Knight Tundale's idea of judgment day.

✤**LATTER-DAY SAINTS, ANGEL OF:** Moroni. See **Mormon; Smith,** Joseph.

✤**LAW OF THE TORAH, ANGEL OF: Dina.**

✤**LEACHMAN, CLORIS:** In the 1977 remake of *It's a Wonderful Life,* entitled *It Happened One Christmas,* actress Cloris Leachman stars as an angel.

✤**LEADER OF THE DEMONIC HORDES:** A title held by the angel **Angra Mainyu** in Zoroastrianism.

✤**LEGIONS OF ANGELS:** A phrase used in literature when referring to God's myriads of angels, and also God's army of angels. They are also called legions of Heaven. Jesus is said to have had legions of angels at his command. Legions of angels fought **Satan** and his demons. And the archangel **Michael** is commander of the legions of angels. According to lore, each of the nine **orders of angels** has 6,666 legions. Each of these legions has 6,666 angels.

✤**LEGIONS OF HEAVEN:** A phrase used in literature when referring to God's army of angels in Heaven.

✤**LEIKOURGOS:** An angel from the Testament of **Solomon.**

✤**LELIEL:** A variation of the name **Lailah.**

✤**LEMURES:** In Rome they were spirits of the dead. They were considered to be both good and evil.

✤**LEO, ANGEL OF: Verchiel.**

✤**LEOPARD:** When invoked, the angel **Camael** appears in the form of a leopard.

✤**LEROEL:** A demon who causes chills, shivering, and sore throat in humans.

✤**LESSER YAHWEH:** The word Yahweh is the original Hebrew spelling of God's name. The angel **Metatron** holds the title of the Lesser Yahweh, making him the highest-ranking angel in Heaven, and the closest angel to God. In his role as the Lesser Yahweh he acted as mediator between God and the Hebrews in their exodus from Egypt.

✤**LEVIATHAN:** A female demon from the Books of **Enoch** (1 Enoch 60:7). She is the female equivalent of the dragon of the **abyss** (Satan). Medieval authors portrayed her as a king who governed "the children of pride" (the fallen angels). When invoked, she manifests as a large crocodile. In rabbinical lore, Leviathan is an angel of death.

✤**LIBRA, ANGEL OF:** Uriel.

✤**LIE, ANGEL OF THE:** The creator of the lie is **Satan** the Devil. He is also called the Father of Lies and Prince of Lies. He created the first lie when he used the guise of a serpent to trick **Eve** into disobedience to God in the **Garden of Eden.** He accused God of not telling her the truth and of holding back knowledge from her and her husband, **Adam.** This was a lie and it made him a devil (slanderer) and a satan (opposer).

✤**LIE, THE:** In Zoroastrianism, **Angra Mainyu** is referred to as the Lie. In Christianity it is **Satan.**

✤**LIFE, ANGEL OF:** The angel of life can be found in **Essene** beliefs. The personification of the angel of life is the archangel **Gabriel.**

✤*LIFE OF ADAM AND EVE:* One of the books found in the Pseudepigrapha. It relates the tale of the fall of the angels. According to the account, when **Adam** was created, God placed him above the angels and instructed the angels to bow down to him. This was because Adam had been created in the image of God. **Satan** refused to bow down to the newly created man. Afterward, Satan became the leader of other angels who also refused to bow down to Adam. Because of this act of disobedience, Satan and his followers were cast out of the Heavens and thrown downward to the earth. Satan blamed Adam for his ousting and set out for revenge. He assumed the guise of the serpent, entered the **Garden of Eden,** and tricked **Eve** into sin.

✤*LIFE OF ANTHONY:* The name of a book written by **Saint Athanasius** of Alexandria in 360. It is about a monk named Anthony and his struggles with **Satan** and the demons. It was an effort by Athanasius to help monks in their battles with the demons.

✤**LIFE SPAN OF THE ANGELS:** How long an angel lives has been a subject of debate by religious scholars, theologians, and mystics for centuries. Some believe the angels to be immortal. Others believe that they are created for only a specific time and purpose. Some say that when humans die, they become angels. Some religions teach that angels can only die or be destroyed by God. Most religions believe that the angels are finite, meaning that they had a beginning. The Koran tells us that angels are formed from the breath of God. Some believe that some of the angels are immortal, but that some have a limited life span, lasting only until their assigned duty has been completed. Eastern thought holds that the soul of an angel grows and evolves through many lifetimes and life-forms. Origen (a Greek theologian) held that the angels die and are reborn into a higher level of spirituality. Swedish mystic **Emanuel Swedenborg** believed that angels were once men. **Rudolph Steiner** held that humankind would one day evolve to the state of being to which the angels now belong, and that angels would then evolve to an even higher spiritual state.

✤**LIGHT:** See **Aureole.**

✤**LIGHT, ANGELS OF:** In the *War of the Sons of Light Against the Sons of Darkness* (one of the Dead Sea scrolls), the archangel **Michael** is referred to as the Prince of Light. In Judaic lore, **Isaac, Jesus, Gabriel,** and **Satan** have also been referred to as angels of light. The Persian angel of light was **Mithra.** In the **Third Heaven** there are said to dwell three hundred angels of light. They continuously sing praises to God as they guard the **Garden of Eden** and the **Tree of Life.**

✤**LIGHT AND MERCY, ANGEL OF:** In Zoroastrianism, **Meher** is the angel of light and mercy. Meher sustained and comforted the soul during the transition of dying.

✤**LIGHT BLUE, ANGEL OF:** Light blue is the **color** representing the archangel **Raphael.**

✤**LIGHT OF GOD:** A phrase used when referring to the archangel **Uriel.**

✤**LIGHTNING, ANGEL OF:** The angel of lightning is **Barakiel,** whose name means "God's lightning." Barakiel uses the power of lightning to thwart the great demon **Murder.** Murder strikes humans so that they become mutes.

✤**LILIM:** The daughters of **Lilith.** They are also known as **Succubus.** They are spiritual **harlots** who copulate with monks while they are sleeping. To ward them off, monks tie crosses to their genitals in an attempt to prevent them from attempting arousal.

✤**LILITH:** A notorious she-demon. In Judaic lore, Lilith was originally Adam's first wife. Claiming that she was equal to **Adam,** she rebelled against his superiority and forsook her position by his side to become a consort to the fallen angels. She is also said to be the mother of Cain. When **Eve** was created for Adam, Lilith became a mortal enemy of Eve and Eve's daughters. She was especially upset with them for showing submissiveness to men. Lilith went about exacting her revenge on Eve's daughters with various torments. Amulets and talismans have been created to keep her and her evil female demons away. **Senoy,** Sansenoy, and Semangelof are names used in magic to protect women who are pregnant, and infants, from Lilith. Men needed protection from Lilith as well. It is said that she sometimes would get into bed with a man alone in his bedroom and arouse him sexually and emit semen. She used this semen to impregnate herself and her female hosts. This, it is said, is where demons come from. After becoming a consort of demons, she became the bride of the fallen angel **Sammael** (Satan). In the **Zohar** she is identified with the Queen of Sheba. Her daughters are referred to as **Lilim.** According to lore, the prophet **Elijah** forced her to tell him the aliases she used in her treachery against mortals. These aliases are Abeko, Abito, Amizo, Batna, Eilo, Ita, Izorpo, Kali, Kea, Kokos, Odam, Partasah, Patrota, Podo, Satrina, and Talto. Lilith is also listed as one of the **Unholy Sefiroth** of the **Cabala.** She is also known as the goddess of death.

✤**LILY:** The symbol of purity. It is the emblem of the archangel **Gabriel,** who is often portrayed carrying a lily in art. It was once the symbol of **Lilith, Adam**'s first wife.

✤**LINEN:** See **Man Clothed in Linen.**

✤**LION(S):** In Assyrian art **Cherubim** were portrayed with wings. They had a body of either an eagle, a bull, or a sphinx, with a lion's face. When invoked, the demon **Ornias** manifests as a lion.

✤**LION OF GOD:** A phrase used when referring to the angel **Ariael.** He is also known as the Lord of the Earth and Prince of Waters.

✤**LION-SHAPED DEMON:** A demon found in the Testament of **Solomon.** He is the leader over a region of demons. He prevents the recovery of people who are ill. He can be overpowered by **Emmanouel.**

✤**LIONS' DEN, ANGEL OF THE:** In the Old Testament's Book of Daniel, the king's edict ordered everyone to pray only to either the king or the king's gods. Daniel refused and continued to pray to the Hebrew God. For this he was thrown into the lions' den. He was rescued by an angel sent by God to close the mouths of the lions. In Daniel 6:22, Daniel says to the king, "My God sent his angel and shut the lions' mouths so that they would not hurt me."

✤**LIPIKA:** A high order of angels. The Lipika record world history and the individual experiences of the people of earth. These records then become a part of the **Akashic Records** (the heavenly library).

✤**LITERATURE, ANGELS IN:** Throughout history angels have been a popular subject in literature. The three most famous works of literature featuring angels include **Johann Wolfgang von Goethe**'s masterpiece, *Faust*, in which angels are portrayed as heroic figures. There is also **John Milton**'s epic poem *Paradise Lost.* It is considered Milton's greatest work as well as the best epic ever written in the English language. It is the tale of **Satan**'s rebellion against God, and the banishment of **Adam** and **Eve** from Paradise. And there is **Dante Alighieri**'s poem *The Divine Comedy,* which is an account of a poet's journey through Heaven, Purgatory, and Hell, and his many encounters with angels along the way.

✤**LITTLE ANGELS:** A term sometimes used when referring to **fairies.**

✤**LITTLE BOOK, ANGEL OF THE:** See **Little Scroll.**

✤**LITTLE SCROLL, ANGEL OF THE:** In the Book of Revelation 10:8–10, the apostle **John** relates his experience with an angel who holds a little scroll: "Then the voice from heaven spoke to me saying, 'Go and take the open scroll which is in the hand of the angel standing on the sea and on the land.' I went to the angel and asked him to give me the little scroll. He said to me, 'Take it and eat it: it will turn sour in your stomach, but in your mouth it will be sweet as honey.' I took the little scroll from his hand and ate it, and it tasted sweet as honey in my mouth. But after I swallowed it, it turned sour in my stomach." (Note: In some translations it is called the "little book.")

✤*LITTLEST ANGEL, THE:* A made-for-television movie. *The Littlest Angel* aired in 1969. It starred Johnny Whitaker as a shepherd boy who dies and then fights to become an angel. Eventually, he becomes an angel, but not before learning a few pointed lessons.

✤**LIVESTOCK, ANGEL OF:** In Zoroastrianism, the archangel **Vohu Manah** is the protector of livestock.

✤**LIVING CREATURES:** A phrase used when referring to the **Seraphim.** It is taken from the book of Revelation 4:8. There the apostle **John** refers to them: "And the four living creatures, each of them with six wings, are full of eyes all around and inside. Day and night without ceasing they sing, Holy, holy, holy, the Lord God the Almighty, who was and is and is to come." In his vision, the prophet **Ezekiel** also saw angels whom he referred to as living creatures: "I looked up and saw a windstorm coming from the north. Lightning was flashing from a huge cloud, and the sky around it was glowing. Where the lightning was flashing, something shone like bronze. At the center of the storm I saw what looked like four living creatures in human form, but each of them had four faces and four wings" (Ezekiel 1:4–6).

✤**LIWET:** In Mandaean mythology Liwet was the angel who inspired ideas for new inventions. He is also an angel of love.

✦LIX TETRAX: The demon of the wind. His demonic activities include causing divisions among men, creating whirlwinds, setting fires, and creating dysfunctional households. He carries out his deeds mostly during the summer, creeping in under the corners of houses. He can be thwarted by the angel **Azael.** In the Testament of Solomon, **Solomon** captures and interrogates him through the use of a **magic ring.**

✦LOBKIR: An angel of the west **wind.**

✦LOCUSTS, ANGEL OF: **Apollyon.** Apollyon (his Greek name. In Hebrew he is called **Abaddon**) presides over the locusts that God sets loose to destroy the wicked people of earth in the last days. These locusts are kept in the great **abyss,** found in the Book of Revelation.

✦LOEL: An angel who safeguards the south **wind.**

✦LONGFELLOW, HENRY WADSWORTH: Famous American poet (1807–1882). He is author of the popular poem "Golden Moon." In the poem, Longfellow refers to the archangel **Gabriel** as the "angel of the moon, who brings the gift of hope to mankind." In his play *The Nativity*, Longfellow refers to the archangel **Raphael** as the "angel of the sun."

✦LORBER, JAKOB: Australian musician (1800–1864), author of *The New Revelation*, which was dictated to him by unseen spiritual beings. On March 15, 1840, Lorber heard a voice that told him to pick up a pen and write. From that day forward, he spent every day writing what the voice dictated. Part of the manuscript contains scientific information. The second part contains spiritual information and is called *The New Revelation*. It tells of God's divine purpose and reveals the meaning behind the scriptures. It talks extensively about the fall of **Satan,** and the fall of the angels. It also speaks of a divine plan to bring back the fallen angels into a favored state with God.

✦LORD: A designation for **God.**

✦LORD, ANGEL OF THE: In the Book of Judges 6:22 we read, "For now I have seen the Angel of the Lord face-to-face." The Angel of the Lord is God's personal spokesman. He is also referred to as the Angel of God. He has no individual characteristics except that he is a mediator for the Almighty. In the New Testament he is personalized as both **Gabriel** and the **Holy Spirit.** In various parts of the Bible he has different roles. He judges and destroys disobedient people, delivers the righteous ones from harm, and brings important announcements. When he appears to men, he is sometimes mistakenly addressed as "God." (Note: It is a misconception to think that the Angel of the Lord is one angel. God has myriads of angels to perform various deeds and functions for him. Therefore, the Angel of the Lord more than likely is several different angels that God calls on to represent him.)

✤**LORD OF CHAOS:** A title held by **Beelzebub.**

✤**LORD OF SOULS:** A title held by **Beelzebub.** Beelzebub was once considered a **Psychopomp.** As Lord of Souls he was responsible for escorting the souls of the dead to the underworld.

✤**LORD OF SPIRITS:** In the Book of Enoch the Lord of Spirits is **God.**

✤**LORD OF THE EARTH: Ariael.**

✤**LORD OF THE FLIES: Beelzebub.**

✤**LORD OF THE SHADOW OF DEATH:** A title held by **Shaftiel.**

✤**LORD OF THE SPIRITS:** In his writings **Enoch** refers to God as the Lord of the Spirits. The spirits are the angels and other spiritual beings that reside in Heaven.

✤**LORDS:** A word sometimes used to refer to the order of angels called **Dominations.**

✤**LORDS OF DREAD:** An unusual term used for angels who surround God's throne and sing praises.

✤**LORDS OF SOULS:** The **Psychopomp** are the lords of souls, who carry the souls of men to **Hades.**

✤**LORDSHIPS:** An order of angels.

✤**LORELEI: Fairies** of German lore.

✤**LOS ANGELES:** A city in southern California that sits on the Pacific Ocean. It was founded by a Spanish missionary in 1781 who had first visited the area in 1769. It was named Los Angeles (which means "the angels") after the angels.

✤**LOT:** The nephew of **Abraham.** In the Bible, angels visited Lot because he was the nephew of the prophet Abraham. He was also a good and faithful servant of God. He was the only godly man to be found in the city of **Sodom.** The angels came to remove Lot and his family from Sodom because God had decided to destroy it. When the angels arrived, Lot insisted that they stay with him and his family. He invited them in, served them dinner, and offered them a place to sleep. However, before they could lie down, the men of Sodom surrounded the house and formed a mob. They called out to Lot to send out the men who were visiting him, so that they could have sex with them. Finally, Lot went outside and begged the mob to disperse and leave the visiting angels alone. He even offered them his two virgin daughters to have sex with instead. He explained to the mob that their conduct was the reason the angels had come. Angrily, the mob accused Lot of judging them. They threatened to do worse to him than what they had planned for his guests. The mob moved toward Lot, nearly breaking in his door. The angels put out their hands and the door opened. They brought Lot quickly back inside the house and closed the door. They then struck the men with blindness.

The angels told Lot to take his family out of Sodom because God had condemned the city and all in it, and they were going to destroy it. At dawn the angels told Lot to take his wife and daughters and leave Sodom. Lot lingered for a time. The angels finally grabbed hold of his hand and the hands of his wife and two daughters and escorted them out of the city. They told him to escape to the mountains. Lot said that he did not want to go to the mountains, but that he wanted to go to a nearby city. The angels gave their consent but told him to hurry because they could not destroy the city until he and his family were clear of danger. Once they were safe, fire and sulfur were rained upon Sodom. (Genesis 19:1–26) (Note: The angels who were sent to destroy Sodom would have been the angels of **destruction.**)

✤**LOVE, ANGELS OF:** In Judeo-Christian lore several angels have held the title of the angel of love. Among them are **Haniel, Donquel, Liwet, Rahamael, Raphael,** and Theliel. In Persia, **Mihr** was the angel of love. To the Cabalists, it was Rome's goddess Venus. In Greek mythology **Eros** was the winged god of love; in Roman mythology it was **Cupid.** The **Seraphim** are called angels of love because love is their essence. See **Love Charms.**

✤**LOVE AND HARMONY, ANGEL OF:** Haniel.

✤**LOVE CHARMS, ANGELS OF:** In Aramaic beliefs the names of the angels **Opiel** and **Salbabiel** were inscribed on love charms. It was believed that they would help individuals obtain the love of a desired one.

✤**LOVE VERSES, MUSE OF:** In Greek mythology Erato inspired men to write verses of love. Today she is considered an archetypal angel of **inspiration.**

✤**LUCIFER (HE WHO GIVES LIGHT):** Lucifer is known as the Prince of Darkness and Prince of the Power of Air. The name Lucifer was once the Latin name for the planet Venus (Venus was also called the **Morning Star** and was considered the brightest luminary in the Heavens). Lucifer is said to be one of the many names of **Satan** the Devil, which is why in some literature Satan is referred to as the Morning Star and the **Bringer of Light.**

✤**LUCK, ANGEL OF:** **Barakiel.** In Hindu beliefs, **Lakshmi** was believed to bring luck to individuals.

✤**LUMAIL:** An angel summoned in Arabic exorcism ceremonies.

✤**LUMAZI:** In Assyrian cosmology the Lumazi are spiritual beings who created the universe.

✤**LUMINARIES:** A term sometimes used in literature and scripture in referring to the angels.

✤**LUMINOUS SONS:** A term used in the Tibetan *Book of Dzyan* when speaking of people in the ancient world who had shining faces and huge, luminous eyes. They were believed to be angels who had descended to earth.

✤LUNAR MANSIONS: The lunar mansions represent the day-to-day phases of the **moon.** The angel **Sariel** brought the knowledge of these phases to earth. Twenty-eight angels preside over the lunar mansions. They are Abdizuel, Abrinael, Adriel, Amnediel, Amnixiel, Amutiel, Anixiel, Ardifiel, Atheniel, Atliel, Azariel, Azeruel, **Aziel, Barbiel,** Bethnael, Dirachiel, Egibiel, Enediel, Ergediel, Gabriel, Geliel, Geniel, Jazeriel, Kyriel, Neciel, Requiel, Scheliel, and **Tagriel.**

✤LURIA, ISAAC BEN SOLOMON: Isaac ben Solomon Luria was a Jewish Cabalist (1534–1572) who started a school of mysticism. He combined messianism with old doctrines found in the **Cabala.** Lurianic mystics had many visitations with their guardian angels, who visited them mainly in their dreams.

✤LUST, ANGELS OF: The angel of lust is named Pharzuph. He enjoys tempting those who have proclaimed a life of celibacy, such as nuns and priests. In gnosticism, **Lust** is the name of one of the demon **Archons.** Priapus is another angel of lust. In addition, lust was the reason for the fall of two hundred angels from the class of **Watchers,** also known as the Grigori.

✤LUTHER, MARTIN: Martin Luther was a German leader of the Protestant Reformation (1483–1546). Luther often made reference to the angels who guided his life. He believed that the angels were God's warriors, and that they were defenders, guides, and guardians over mankind. He believed that without Satan there would be no need for Jesus Christ.

✤LYING SPIRITS, ANGEL OF: **Python.**

✤LYRE: An ancient stringed instrument. Angels are sometimes shown in art playing the lyre. It symbolizes praise.

✤LYRIC POETRY, MUSE OF: In Greek mythology **Euterpe** inspired men to create lyrics for poetry and songs.

And the angels said, "I have learned that every man lives, not through care of himself, but by love."

—LEO TOLSTOY

✤MACHIDIEL (GOD'S FULLNESS): The angel of March and the angel of Aries. In magic he is called upon to aid men in obtaining the love and affections of a desired woman. Variations of the name Machidiel include Malahidael, Malchedael, Malchidiel, Melkeial, and Melkejal.

✤MACHKIAL: An angel who stands guard over the palace of Makon, the **Sixth Heaven.**

✤MACHNIA: See **Childbirth.**

✤MACLEAN, DOROTHY: Author of the popular book *To Hear the Angels Sing.* It is about the author's experiences with angels within the **devic kingdom.** From her telepathic communications with the angels, she developed the Findhorn Garden (a beautiful garden that grew from sand in adverse conditions) and the Findhorn Community in Scotland.

✤MADE BY GOD: The meaning of the name Asael. Asael was one of two hundred **Watchers** who came to earth to have sexual relations with women.

✤MADGABIEL: An angel who safeguards the north **wind.**

✤MADONNA: The name used in Catholicism when referring to the **Virgin Mary.** The Madonna is one of the highest angels in Heaven. She belongs to the class of angels called the **Virtues.** She is also called Blessed Mother, **Queen of Angels,** and **Queen of Peace.**

✤**MAGDALENE, MARY:** A prostitute in the Bible's New Testament. **Jesus** exorcised seven demons (fallen angels) from her (Luke 8:2). She was also one of the women who witnessed an angel sitting outside of the **tomb of Jesus** (Matthew 28:1–8).

✤**MAGGID:** The Hebrew word meaning "guardian angel."

✤**MAGIC, ANGELS OF:** In most magical settings, five **archangels** are usually called upon. They include **Raphael, Michael, Gabriel, Uriel,** and **Metatron.** In ceremonial magic Raphael represents the east, **Michael** the south, **Gabriel** the west, **Uriel** the north, and **Metatron** the center. In talismanic magic, seven archangels are invoked. Their names are **Zaphkiel, Zadkiel, Camael, Raphael, Haniel, Michael,** and **Gabriel.** Angels are also invoked in magic depending upon their specific function in the universe. For love, the angel of love would be called upon; for rain the angel of rain would be called upon; and so on. The knowledge of and the practice of magic was brought to the earth by the **fallen angels.** It was knowledge that was forbidden to mankind.

✤**MAGIC RING:** A ring that had power over the demons. According to the Testament of Solomon, God sent the archangel **Michael** to deliver the ring to King **Solomon,** to help him to fight demons who were interfering with the building of his temple.

✤**MAGICAL MEDICINE:** The order of angels called **Watchers** brought the knowledge of magical medicine to the earth.

✤**MAGICAL WRITINGS:** Ceremonial magic requires the use of magical alphabets for writing spells and incantations within the ceremony. Through the centuries, the names of angels written in various magical alphabets have turned up on talismans and amulets and other magical tools. A few of the writings that have been used to communicate with and invoke angels include the Arabs' Rihani, the Jewish **Cabala,** and medieval magical writings such as **Angelic,** the Theban, and Malachim. Angelic is the most widely used in magical practices. A powerful alphabet, it is used almost exclusively by ceremonial magicians. It is believed that it can open doors to other realms and open up communications with the angels and other spiritual entities.

✤*MAGUS OF STROVOLOS, THE: The Magus of Strovolos* is a book written by Kyrialos Markides about a mystic in modern Greece. In the story, the Magus alludes to the idea that demons are more humanlike than the good angels. The book claims that good angels can only do God's will. However, Satan and his followers operate from their own ideas and have established free will. It is suggested that the nature of the fallen angels is more human than spiritual.

✤**MAH:** The angel of the moon in Persian mythology.

✦MAHALEL: An angel who chases away evil spirits.

✦MAHALKEL: An angel who chases away evil spirits.

✦MAHANAIM, ANGELS OF: In the Bible, Mahanaim is the place where angels met **Jacob** on his return to Canaan from Haran. When Jacob saw the angels, he said "This is God's camp." He named the place Mahanaim, which means "two camps." (Genesis 32:1–2).

✦MAHANANEL: An angel who safeguards the north **wind.**

✦MAHKAIL: An angel summoned in Arabic exorcism ceremonies.

✦MAIMONIDES, MOSES: A great Hebrew scholar (1135–1204) who was a rabbi, philosopher, and doctor. He wrote that angels "are consecrated and devoted to the service of the Father and Creator, whose wont is to employ them as ministers and helpers, to have charge and care of mortal man." He ranked the **orders of angels** as follows: (1) **Hayyoth,** (2) **Ophanim,** (3) **Arelim,** (4) **Hashmallim,** (5) **Seraphim,** (6) **Malakim,** (7) **Elohim,** (8) **Bene ha-Elohim,** (9) **Cherubim,** (10) **Izachim.**

✦MAINYU, ANGRA: See **Angra Mainyu**

✦MAIRYA: The angel of death in Zoroastrianism.

✦MAKER OF CHANGES: A title held by the archangel **Gabriel.**

✦MAKKIEL: A fallen angel who is known as the Plague of God.

✦MAKON, ANGEL OF: Makon is the name of the **Sixth Heaven.** It is ruled by the archangel **Gabriel.**

✦MALACH HA-MAVET: An angel of death in rabbinical lore.

✦MALACH-RE: An angel who is mistakenly thought of as evil. He is called upon by God to destroy the wicked and to mete out harsh punishments to evildoers.

✦MALACHE HABBALAH: Hebrew for "the angels of **destruction.**"

✦MALACHIM: A variation of **Malakim.** Malakim are a class of angels equated with the **Virtues.** It is also the name of a magical writing that is used to contact and communicate with the angels.

✦MALAHIDAEL: A variation of the name **Machidiel.**

✦MALAIKA (MESSENGERS): Angels in Islam. They are protectors of mankind. They also record the good and bad deeds of men. In Islam they are neither male nor female, but are thought to be androgynous. A variation of the name Malaika is Malaka.

✦MALAKA: A variation of **Malaika.**

✦MALAKH: See **Mal'akh.**

✦MAL'AKH: The Hebrew word for angel. It originally meant "shadow of God," but later became known as "messenger." A variation of Mal'akh is Malakh.

✦MALAKIM: An order of angels equated with the **Virtues.** The archangels **Uriel** and **Raphael** are both governing princes of the Malakim.

✤MALAKU 'L-MAUT: An angel of death in Islam (Koran 32:11).

✤MALCHEDAEL: A variation of the name **Machidiel.**

✤MALCHIDIEL: A variation of the name **Machidiel.**

✤MALCHIEL: See **Childbirth.**

✤MALIK: The ruler of hell in Islam. In the Koran those in Hell cry for mercy from his painful torments.

✤MALKIEL: See **Childbirth.**

✤MALKUTH: One of the ten **Holy Sefiroth** from the **Cabala.** He is also called Kingdom.

✤MALOCHIA: **Abrid** is the angel called upon in magical practices to ward off Malochia (the evil eye).

✤MALTIEL: An angel from Judaic lore. He was the preceptor of the prophet **Elijah.**

✤MAMMON: A fallen angel and arch-demon, known as the angel of greed. He is equated with **Satan.** During medieval times he was a Syrian god. He holds the title of the Prince of Tempters.

✤MAMRE, ANGELS OF: In the Bible, Mamre was a place in the district of Hebron associated with **Abraham.** Under the oaks of Mamre, Abraham was visited by three angels, who informed him of the coming birth of his son **Isaac** and the destruction of **Sodom and Gomorrah.**

✤MAN CLOTHED IN LINEN: In the ancient world, linen symbolized purity. The priest wore linen in the temple. The angels wore linen to stand out among the men of earth and to symbolize their holy position. The Old Testament of the Bible mentions two accounts of angels who are dressed in linen. The first account is found in Ezekiel 9:3–4. The angel had been sent by God to mark the righteous people of Jerusalem so that they would be saved from destruction. The Bible says, "The Lord called to the man clothed in linen and said to him, 'Go through Jerusalem, and put a mark on the foreheads of those who sigh and groan over all the abominations that are committed in it.'" The second account occurs in Daniel 10:5–6, when a man in linen appears to **Daniel:** "I looked up and saw a man clothed in linen, with a belt of gold from Uphaz around his waist. His body was like beryl, his face like lightning, his eyes like flaming torches, his arms and legs like the gleam of burnished bronze, and the sound of his words like the roar of a multitude." The angel had come in answer to Daniel's prayers, and to inform him about the future of the Hebrews.

✤MANAH: The angel of fertility in Arabic mythology.

✤MANAKEL: The angel of marine life.

✤MANES: Revered spirits of people who have died. They are believed to become guardian angels of surviving relatives. When the living relatives finally die, the Manes evolve to higher states of being.

✦**MANICHAEISM:** A religion founded by a Persian visionary and prophet named Manes. During ancient times Manichaeism was popular in Rome and Asia. It carried elements of Zoroastrianism, gnosticism, and Christianity. Manichaeism taught that there is a universal struggle between good and evil. Angels were a large part of the struggle for the good. Angels of Manichaeism included the Twelve Aeons, the Twelve Light Diadems, and the Friends of Lights.

✦**MANIFESTATION ANGELS:** Angels found in the book *Ask Your Angels* by authors Alma Daniel, Timothy Wyllie, and Andrew Ramer. They are angels who manifest spirit and thought into the physical domain. Another name for the manifestation angels are transformation angels.

✦**MANKIND, ANGEL OF: Metatron.** In Zoroastrianism, **Ahura Mazda** is the protector of mankind.

✦**MANNA:** The name of the angel of food. See **Food of Angels.**

✦**MANOAH:** The father of **Samson.** In the Book of Judges 13:1–5, Manoah and his wife received two visitations from an angel of the Lord. The angel informed them that they would have a son who was to be "dedicated to God as a Nazirite." The angel told them that Samson would deliver the Israelites from the Philistines.

✦**MANTUS:** An Etruscan angel who belonged to the group of angels called the **Novensiles.** The Novensiles ruled over thunderbolts.

✦**MANU:** The angel of destiny in ancient Assyrian and Babylonian lore.

✦**MANY-EYED ONES:** A phrase used in scripture when referring to the **Cherubim.** The Book of Revelation 4:8 describes the Cherubim as being full of eyes: "And the four living creatures, each of them with six wings, are full of eyes all around and inside." The many eyes symbolize God's all-seeing power. (Note: The **Seraphim** are also believed to be the Many-Eyed Ones.)

✦**MAON, ANGELS OF:** Maon is the name of the **Fifth Heaven.** It is where the sinful **Watchers** are imprisoned. It is also home to the avenging angels. The ruling prince of Maon is Satqi'el.

✦**MARA:** The Buddhist Satan. Mara keeps individuals imprisoned in the cycle of reincarnation, a cycle that all Buddhists are struggling to be free of. This to the Buddhist believer is the equivalent of Hell.

✦**MARCH, ANGEL OF: Machidiel.**

✦**MARCHOCIAS:** A **fallen angel.**

✦**MARDERO:** A demon who causes incurable fevers.

✦**MARGAY'EL:** One of the many names of **Metatron.**

✦**MARINE LIFE, ANGEL OF:** Manakel.

✦**Mariokh:** Another name for the angel Pariukh. Pariukh was one of two angels that God assigned to be a guardian over the writings of **Enoch** (Ariukh was the other).

✦**Marmaraoth:** An angel found in the Testament of **Solomon.** He can thwart the evil demons **Rhyx Anoster** and **Fate.**

✦**Marniel:** An angel who chases away evil spirits.

✦**Maroth:** See **Haroth and Maroth.**

✦**Marranos:** Spanish Jews. During the Inquisition the Marranos were burned at the stake. Wanting desperately to escape their torment, they prayed for "savior angels" to come and rescue them. During that period, a woman named Ines (also referred to as the Damsel of Herrera) was often visited by angels. The angels escorted her to Heaven where she heard beautiful music. The angels informed her that the people who had been burned at the stake were now happy in Heaven and were making music.

✦**Marriage and the Angels:** According to the Bible, the angels do not marry. In the Book of Matthew 22:30, Jesus responds to a question regarding resurrected ones marrying. In doing so, he makes reference to angels. He says, "For in the resurrection they neither marry, nor are given in marriage, but are like angels in Heaven." The only known account of angels marrying is that of the **Watchers** who came to the earth to take wives for themselves. This was considered a great sin in Heaven. The Book of Genesis 6:2 speaks of this: "Then the sons of the true God began to notice the daughters of men, that they were good-looking; and they went taking wives for themselves, namely, all whom they chose." At 1 Enoch 7:1 it states, "And they took wives unto themselves, everyone chose one woman for himself." In the book of 1 Enoch 15:3–7, 10, God responded to their great sin: "For what reason have you abandoned the high, holy, and eternal Heaven; and slept with women, taking wives, acting like the children of the earth, and begetting giant sons? Formerly you were spiritual, having eternal life. That is why I did not make wives for you, for the dwelling of the spiritual beings of Heaven is Heaven."

✦**Mars:** An Etruscan angel who belonged to the group of angels called the **Novensiles.** The Novensiles ruled over thunderbolts.

✦**Mars, Angels of:** The ruler of Mars is **Sammael. Camael** is also an angel of Mars.

✦**Martyrs:** An order of angels. The archangel **Gabriel** is ruler of the Martyrs.

✦**Mary:** See **Virgin Mary.**

✦**Masculine Angels:** In Judaic lore, angels are masculine. All of the angels that appear in the Hebrew scriptures (the Old Testament) are depicted as male.

✤**MASHHIT:** An angel of death in rabbinical lore.

✤**MASHITH:** An angel who was appointed to look after children at their death.

✤**MASIM:** A guardian of the east **wind.**

✤**MASKIEL:** An angel who stands guard over the palace of Wilon, the **First Heaven.**

✤**MASKIM:** Demons in Akkadian beliefs.

✤**MASMASYAH:** One of the seventy-eight names of the great angel **Metatron.**

✤**MASON, JAMES:** A veteran screen actor. James Mason played angels in two separate movies. The first was the popular 1956 film *Forever Darling* starring Lucille Ball. In the film Mason played the guardian angel of the wacky socialite Susan Bewell (Ball). In 1978 he is a heavenly messenger in the film *Heaven Can Wait.*

✤**MASPAD:** One of the seventy-eight names of **Metatron.**

✤**MASPIEL:** An angel who stands guard over the palace of Raquia, the **Second Heaven.**

✤**MASTEMA (HOSTILITY):** A fallen angel. According to lore, Mastema holds a strong disliking for the Jews. So much so that he is said to have made an attempt on the life of **Moses.** It was Mastema who hardened **Pharaoh**'s heart against the Israelites. In addition, he helped Pharaoh's magicians **Jannes and Jambres** to fight against the Hebrews. Mastema also slew the firstborn of Egypt. He holds such titles as the Accuser, the Tempter, the Destroyer, and the Shadow of God. He is equated with **Satan.**

✤**MASTER OF BALANCE:** A title held by the archangel **Michael.**

✤**MASTER OF HEAVENLY SONG:** A phrase sometimes used when referring to the angel of **music.** In Judaic lore both Shemiel and **Metatron** are called the Master of Heavenly Song. In Christianity it is the archangel **Uriel.** In Islam it is **Israfel.**

✤**MASTER OF INFERNAL CEREMONIES:** The fallen angel named Baal-Beryth is called the Master of Infernal Ceremonies. Before his fall, Baal-Beryth was a member of the **Cherubim** class. Later he became a high-ranking demon of Hell, where he officiated over ceremonies.

✤**MATAREL:** A variation of the name **Matriel.**

✤**MATARIEL:** A variation of the name **Matriel.**

✤**MATRIEL:** The angel of rain. Variations of the name Matriel are Matariel, Matatriel and Matarel.

✤**MATSGA:** One of the **avatars** of Hindu lore.

✤MAVET: An angel of death.

✤MAVKIEL: An angel who can be called upon for protection against evil spirits.

✤MAY, ANGEL OF: Ambriel.

✤MEBARGAS: One of the seventy-eight names of Metatron.

✤*MECCAN REVELATIONS:* A book of poetry written by Ibn Arai, a notable Sufi poet. He held that the *Meccan Revelations* were given to him by the angel of inspiration.

✤MEDIATOR(S): The angels act as mediators between God and humankind. As mediators they listen to the prayers of mankind and present them to God. They also act as mediators to God's faithful ones and the Devil. In Judaism and Christianity, it is the guardian angels who act as personal mediators. In Judaism, Christianity, Islam, and Zoroastrianism, the archangels are mediators between God and nations of people. The archangel Michael mediated for the Hebrews. Gabriel mediated for the Christians and the Muslims. In Zoroastrianism, the Amesha Spentas were mediators for the Persians.

✤MEDICINE, ANGELS OF: The angels have given humankind a wealth of information regarding medicine. In the Book of Tobit the angel Azarias instructs young Tobias on the medicinal uses of the parts of a fish. The angel Kasadya taught women how to perform abortions. The angel Kashdejan taught men how to cure various diseases and also taught psychiatry. The angel Pharmoros taught men about herbs, pharmacy, general medicine, and how to diagnose diseases. The Book of Raziel is said to have contained useful medical information that would benefit mankind. According to legend it was written by the angel Raziel.

✤MEDICINE MAN: See Shamanism.

✤MEDIEVAL SYMBOLS: In medieval times, angels were often depicted in art with symbols. The most popular symbols included the lyre, trumpet, wings, halos, aureoles, and diadems. The lyre symbolized praise; the trumpet symbolized God's voice; wings symbolized the angels' roles as messengers and also their speed; halos symbolized purity; aureoles symbolized holiness; and diadems symbolized the angels' royal positions in Heaven.

✤MEDIUMS, ANGEL OF: Phaldor.

✤MEDJUGORJE, ANGELS OF: A small town in Yugoslavia. Since 1981 the Virgin Mary has been appearing daily to six young people who have become known as the visionaries. Through these visionaries, the Virgin Mary communicates with the world. She brings revelations and messages of hope and encouragement. She also shares extraordinary secrets about the final outcome of the history of the world. She appears to the visionaries every day at 6:40 P.M. When she comes, she is said to be surrounded by angels.

✦**MEHABIAH:** The angel of morals.

✦**MEHER:** The angel of light and mercy in Zoroastrianism. He is charged with sustaining the soul during the transition from life to death. Meher is also a variation of the name **Mithra.**

✦**MEHUMAN:** The angel of **confusion.**

✦**MEKARKAR:** One of the seventy-eight names of **Metatron.**

✦**MELAKMELAPYAH:** One of the seventy-eight names of **Metatron.**

✦**MELCHI DAEL:** A fallen angel. Melchi Dael provides men with the women of their desires. Payment for his services is the loss of one's soul.

✦**MELCHISEDANS:** A group of heretics during the third century A.D. They are said to have been in touch with **Melchizedek,** a mighty angel from the class of **Virtues.** They claimed that Melchizedek was more powerful and more magnificent than Jesus.

✦**MELCHISEDEC:** A variation of the name **Melchizedek.**

✦**MELCHIZEDEK:** A great and powerful angel from the class of **Virtues.** Melchizedek is to the angels what Jesus Christ is to humankind. Legend has it that around two thousand years prior to the coming of Christ, Melchizedek descended to earth in the form of a man. He set up a school in which he taught for a hundred years. He also started an evangelist school in Salem in which he trained students for missionary work. From his school hundreds of missionaries graduated and were sent to preach around the world about God. **Dionysius the Pseudo-Areopagite** once wrote that Melchizedek was the angel most loved by God. Later, during the third century A.D., a group called the **Melchisedans** said that they were in communication with a great power named Melchizedek. He is credited with delivering God's covenant to the prophet **Abraham;** bringing light to the world during a spiritually dark period on earth; and for laying the foundation for Christ's coming. According to one account, Melchizedek is the father of the seven Elohim, also known as angels of the **Divine Presence.** In Phoenician mythology he was called Sydik. Variations of the name Melchizedek are Melchisedec and Melchzodok.

✦**MELCHZODOK:** A variation of the name **Melchizedek.**

✦**MELKEIAL:** A variation of the name **Machidiel.**

✦**MELKEJAL:** A variation of the name **Machidiel.**

✦**MELON BUSH, ANGEL OF:** When the **Garden of Eden** was first created, the archangel **Raphael** planted the melon bush.

✦**MELPOMENE:** One of the nine **muses** of Greek mythology. She inspired writers to write tragedies.

✦**MEMLING, HANS:** Flemish religious painter (c. 1430–1494) who sometimes featured angels in his art. One famous work is the *Musician Angels,* in which several angels are depicted with wings and diadems, playing a variety of instruments. This painting is preserved in Antwerp, at the Fine Arts Museum.

✤MEMORY, ANGEL OF: Zadkiel.

✤MEN, ANGELS AS: In the Bible, the first angels to appear on earth came in the form of men. They were wingless and ate and drank just as regular men. In the Book of Genesis, **Abraham** was visited by three of these angels. Genesis 18:1–2 says, "As he sat at the entrance of his tent in the heat of the day, he looked up and saw three men standing near him." Although the Bible does not tell how these angels looked or what they were wearing, we can assume that they had some differentiating characteristic that set them apart in order for Abraham to have immediately recognized them. Perhaps they were dressed in white as were so many other angels in accounts in the Bible. However, we can assume that they were not the traditional winged angels in long robes. In fact these angels enjoyed a meal with Abraham and held a rather lengthy discussion with him. The same occurred with Abraham's nephew **Lot,** who was visited by two angels who appeared as regular men. At Genesis 19:1 it states, "The two angels came to Sodom in the evening, and Lot was sitting in the gateway of Sodom." At Genesis 19:4–5 we read of the men of Sodom calling to Lot to send out the "men," to them: "But before they lay down, the men of the city, the men of Sodom, both young and old, all the people to the last man, surrounded the house, and they called to Lot, 'Where are the men who came to you tonight? Bring them out to us, so that we may know them.' " We can assume that if the angels looked the way we view angels today, the men of Sodom would have been more fearful. In Ezekiel 9:3, God refers to an angel as "the man clothed in linen." **Daniel** (10:5) also spoke of an angel to whom he referred as a man: "I looked up and saw a man clothed in linen." Angels as men is further indicated by Jacob's dream. In Jacob's dream (which was divinely sent), **Jacob,** too, saw angels not with wings, but as regular men going up and down a ladder that went from Heaven to earth. In Genesis 28:12, it states, "And he began to dream, and, look! there was a ladder stationed upon the earth and its top reaching up to the heavens; and, look! there were God's angels ascending and descending on it." The idea of angels with wings and halos, flying around the heavens, was patterned after the winged gods of the polytheistic religions such as the Roman god **Mercury** and the Greek god **Hermes.**

✤MEN AS ANGELS: Some men have walked the earth and later become great angels in Heaven. The most noted include **Enoch, Elijah,**

Moroni, and **Aaron.** Among women, the **Virgin Mary** is the most noted woman who became a great angel in Heaven. It has been speculated that the men who were taken from earth and made into angels were actually angel incarnates. This means that when they left the earth, they simply shed their physical bodies and returned to the spiritual realm, their real home. Although **Jacob** was not taken bodily to Heaven, it has been suggested that he was actually an angel who descended to earth in the flesh to help God's chosen people.

✤**MEN IN WHITE:** During his ascension, Jesus was escorted to Heaven by two angels. The Bible describes them as "two men in white garments" (Acts 1:10–11). The angels informed the apostles who were watching Jesus ascend that he would return in the same manner. These angels are said to have been from the class of angels called the **Virtues.** According to lore, it took Jesus and the angels three days to ascend to Heaven.

✤**MENRVA:** An Etruscan angel who belonged to the group of angels called the **Novensiles.** The Novensiles ruled over thunderbolts.

✤**MEPHISTOPHELES (HE WHO DISLIKES LIGHT):** Once a magnificent angel in Heaven, from the **Archangel** class, he now serves as a high-ranking demon of Hell. He is also known as the deceitful destroyer. The name Mephistopheles was originally Hebrew. It is taken from the words *mephiz*, which means "executioner," and *tophel*, which means "deceiver." The name Mephistopheles is also an alias of Satan's.

✤**MERCURY:** A messenger to the gods in Roman mythology. He wore a winged hat and delivered messages to humans from Jupiter (God). He also gave aid to humans on Jupiter's behalf. He was the equivalent of the Greek god **Hermes** and the Egyptian god Thoth. He was later identified with the archangel **Michael.**

✤**MERCURY, ANGEL OF:** The archangel **Michael** is the ruling angel of the planet Mercury.

✤**MERCY, ANGELS OF:** The archangel **Gabriel** is the official angel of mercy. **Saint Francis of Assisi** was transformed into an angel of mercy upon reaching Heaven. His name was then changed to Rhamiel. When God sits on the throne of judgment, the angels of mercy stand on his right-hand side.

✤**MERCY OF GOD, ANGEL OF THE:** **Remiel.** He is the angel who grants God's mercy to humans.

✤**MERIRIM:** A fallen angel. He is known as the Lord of the Strength of the Air. He is believed to be an angel of the **Apocalypse** who is sent to do damage to the oceans and the earth.

✤**MERKABAH:** The group of angels that dwell closest to God in the Heavens. They include the **Seraphim, Cherubim, Ophanim, Galgallim,** and the **Hayyoth.** The name Merkabah is also a name found in the Jewish **Cabala** for the class of angels called **Thrones.**

✤**MERMAIDS:** In art, Balinese angels are sometimes depicted in the forms of winged mermaids. Mermaids also represent the **undines,** which are female water spirits. They are also referred to as angels of the waters.

✤**MERRATON:** A variation of the name **Metatron.**

✤**MESAMYAH:** One of the seventy-eight names of **Metatron.**

✤**MESHABBER:** An angel of **punishment.**

✤**MESHACH:** One of three Hebrew men in the Book of Daniel (3:1–30) who were rescued from a fiery **furnace** by an angel.

✤**MESOPOTAMIA, ANGELS OF:** Mesopotamia was an ancient country in Southwest Asia between the Tigris and Euphrates Rivers, now in Iraq. Winged **gods** and **goddesses** were first depicted in Mesopotamian art, in which they were portrayed as giant creatures. The wings indicated the belief that the gods dwelled in the sky. The wings were patterned after those of birds. The winged gods of Greek and Roman mythology were copied from the depictions of the gods of the Mesopotamians. Later the Hebrews and Christians adopted the idea of spiritual beings with wings into their beliefs.

✤**MESSAGES FROM THE ANGELS:** Angels deliver messages from God to humankind. Most of the messages offer hope, comfort, and encouragement. Some warn of impending danger. Others are prophetic messages. In the Bible messages were delivered from God to humans by the Angel of the Lord. Later the **archangels** also delivered divine messages. In the modern era, people have received messages from their guardian angels and spirit guides. The **Virgin Mary,** who is one of the highest angels in the Heavens, brings messages of hope to humankind daily. She brings these messages to six visionaries in a little town in Yugoslavia called **Medjugorje.**

✤**MESSENGER(S):** Angels have long been thought of as messengers of God. Dionysius stated that angels are "messengers which carry Divine Decrees." The idea of angelic messengers can be found in the ancient religious traditions of many cultures. In Judaic lore the angels brought messages to the prophets such as **Abraham** and **Daniel.** The Christians had **Gabriel,** the angel of revelation, who delivered messages regarding important births such as those of **John the Baptist** and **Jesus** Christ. In Islam, **Jibril** brought **Muhammad** messages from God. The Babylonians had the Sukalli, which translates into "angelic messengers." The Greeks had **Hermes,** the winged messenger of **Zeus.** The Greeks also had **Iris,** who was messenger for **Hera.** In Rome there was **Mercury,** the messenger of Jupiter. In Vedic beliefs, Agni, the angel of fire, is a messenger between God and mankind.

✦**METARPITAS:** One of the many names of **Metatron.**

✦**METATHIAX:** A demon who causes disease and pain in the kidneys.

✦**METATRON:** According to Judaic lore, Metatron is the greatest angel in Heaven. The Third Book of Enoch tells us that Metatron was once the biblical prophet **Enoch.** God took Enoch bodily from earth because he was a righteous man. When he reached Heaven, he was immediately transformed into a mighty angel and renamed Metatron. According to lore, God blessed him with 1,365,000 blessings; enlarged his size until he was as large as the world; gave him seventy-two wings, each the size of the world; gave him 365,000 eyes, a crown of precious stones, and a majestic throne that sits in the seventh palace. God called him the **Lesser Yahweh** (God's name) and placed him over all of the princes of Heaven. He is responsible for the welfare and provisions of mankind and is mankind's direct connection to God. In one account he is put above the archangels **Michael** and **Gabriel** for ousting **Jannes and Jambres** (**Pharaoh**'s Egyptian wizards) from Heaven. The **Cabala** states that it was Metatron who led the Hebrews through the wilderness after they fled Egypt. The Cabala lists him as an archangel of the **Holy Sefiroth.** He holds many titles including Chancellor of Heaven, Prince of the Divine Presence, Prince of the Torah, Prince of the Divine Face, Angel of the Covenant, Prince of the Seraphim, King of Angels, Prince of Princes, the **Demiurge,** the Angel of Death, the Angel of Music, the Angel of Humankind, and Heavenly Scribe. According to the chronicles of Enoch, he has seventy-eight names. All of these names are based on the name of God. They are Yaho'el Yah; Yoppie'el; Apap'el; Margay'el; Geyor'el; Tandu'el; Tatnadi'el; Tatri'el; Tabtabi'el; Ozahyah; Zahzahyah; Ebed; Zebuli'el; Sapsapi'el; Sopri'el; Paspasi'el; Senigron; Sarpupirin; Mitatron; Sigron; Adrigon; Astas; Saqpas; Saqpus; Mikon; Miton; Ruah Pisqonit; Atatyah; Asasyah; Zagzagyah; Paspasyah; Mesamyah; Masmasyah; Absannis; Mebargas; Bardas; Mekarkar; Maspad; Tasgas; Tasbas; Metarpitas; Paspisahu; Besihi; Itmon; Pisqon; Sapsapyah; Zerah Zerahyah; Ab'abyah; Hahhahyah; Pepatpalyah; Rakrakyah; Hashasyah; Taptapyah; Tamtamyah; Sahsahyah; Ar'aryah; Al'alyah; Zazruyah; Aramyah; Sebar Suhasyah; Razrazyah; Tahsanyah; Sasrasyah; Sabsebibyah; Qeliqalyah; Warwahyah; Zakzakyah; Titrisyah; Sewiryah; Zehapnuryah; Za'za'yah; Galrazyah; Melakmelapyah; Attaryah; Perisyah; Amqaqyah; Salsalyah. When invoked, Metatron becomes a pillar of fire.

✦**METEOROLOGY, ANGEL OF: Ezeqel,** who taught the science of meteorology to humans.

✦**METEORS, ANGEL OF: Ziquiel.**

✤**Methathiax:** A demon who causes pain in the kidneys. He can be thwarted by the angel **Adonael.**

✤**Metratton:** A variation of the name **Metatron.**

✤**Michael (Who Is as God):** One of the seven **archangels.** He is God's warrior who leads the **Celestial Army,** and the ruler of the **Seventh Heaven.** In art he is depicted as muscular, youthful, handsome, and is usually suited in armor. The bible tells us that Michael and his army defeated **Satan** and his angels in the war in Heaven, throwing them out of Heaven and down to the earth. The Bible states, "And war broke out in heaven: Michael and his angels battled with the dragon and the dragon and its angels battled but did not prevail, neither was a place found for them any longer in heaven. So down the great dragon was hurled, the original serpent, the one called Devil and Satan, who is misleading the entire inhabited earth; he was hurled down to the earth, and his angels were hurled down with him" (Revelation 12:7–9). It is also Michael who will descend from heaven with the key to the **abyss** and will lock Satan away for a thousand years: "And I saw an angel coming down out of heaven with the key of the abyss and a great chain in his hand. And he seized the dragon, who is the Devil and Satan, and bound him for a thousand years. And he hurled him into the abyss and shut it and sealed it over him" (Revelation 20:1–3). According to Judaic lore, it was Michael who prevented **Abraham** from sacrificing his son **Isaac.** Legend has it that it was also Michael who appeared to **Moses** in the **burning bush.** He has been credited with freeing the apostle **Peter** from prison, and rescuing **Daniel** from the **lions'** den (Acts 5:19, Daniel 6:22). In Islam, Michael is called **Mikhail.** In the Koran the **Cherubim** are created from the tears of Mikhail. During the Middle Ages the Church portrayed Michael as a Psychopomp (an escort of souls to the spiritual world, an idea found in the ancient beliefs of Zoroastrianism and Greece) in order to attract non-Christians into the Church. In the **Dead Sea scrolls** Michael is the Prince of Light battling against the sons of darkness. He leads the good angels against the fallen angels, which are led by **Beliah. Joan of Arc** named him as one of the angels who encouraged her to help the **Dauphin.** In 1950, Pope Pius XII declared him protector of police officers. In the **Book of Raziel** he is listed as an amulet angel who is summoned in **childbirth** for a safe delivery. Titles. The archangel Michael holds many titles including Prince of God, Leader of the Archangels, Ruler of the East, ruling angel of the planet Mercury, Captain of the Heavenly Host, Prince of the Heavenly Host, Viceroy of Heaven, Guardian Angel of the Roman Catholic Church, Guardian of Israel, Commander in Chief of the Celestial Army, Prince of the **Virtues,**

Divine Protector, Prince of Light, Guardian of Peace, Angel of Sunday, Master of Balance, Angel of Earth, Angel of the **Olive Tree,** and Angel of the **Almond Tree.** Michael is represented by the colors gold, yellow, and rose red. A variation of the name Michael is Michail. MICHAEL AND THE DRAGON. The archangel Michael battling the great dragon (Satan) has been portrayed by several artists. Among them are Martin Schongauer, from 1470, and Lubok in nineteenth-century Russia. Their paintings were inspired from the account in the Book of Revelation 12:7–9, where Michael battles the **dragon** and casts him out of Heaven.

✦**MICHAELMAS:** A festival in honor of the archangel **Michael.** It is mainly celebrated in England, on September 29.

✦**MICHAIL:** A variation of the name **Michael**. Michael is the commander in chief of the Celestial Army.

✦**MICHELANGELO BUONARROTI:** Major Italian sculptor, poet, and painter (1475–1564). Michelangelo featured angels in much of his work. This includes his most famous work, entitled the *Last Judgment.* His vision of the Last Judgment (taken from the Book of Revelation) takes up one entire wall of the **Sistine Chapel.** There he portrays the seven angels of the **Apocalypse** blowing their trumpets from the four corners of the earth and calling the dead to the Last Judgment. The angels are portrayed without wings.

✦**MIDDLE AGES, ANGELS OF THE:** During the Middle Ages, angels were named for every function of the universe. There were angels representing the **four seasons,** the **planets,** the twelve **months of the year,** the twelve signs of the **zodiac,** the **seven days of the week,** the **hours of the day and night,** and more. In addition, angels flourished in art and took on a feminine appearance. They were portrayed in poetry, paintings, sculpture, and architecture. People lost their fascination with angels during the fourteenth century when the black plague struck, killing nearly half of Europe's population. The people of that time felt that the angels had not protected them and began to question their existence.

✦**MIDDLE TRIAD:** The middle triad of the angelic hierarchy consists of the **Dominations,** the **Virtues,** and the **Powers.**

✦**MIGHTS:** Another name for the order of angels called **Virtues.**

✦**MIGHTY, THE:** A term sometimes used in literature when referring to the angels.

✦**MIGRATION, ANGEL OF:** Nadiel.

✦**MIHR:** In Persian lore Mihr was the angel of love, brotherhood, and friendship. Mihr is also a variation of the name **Mithra.**

✦**MIKAEL:** A variation of **Michael.**

✦**MIKAIL:** A variation of **Mikhail.**

✦**MIKAL:** A variation of **Mikhail.**

✦**MIKHAIL:** One of the four archangels of **Islam.** It is the Islamic name for the archangel **Michael.** In Islam, Mikhail is the angel "who provides men with food and knowledge." The Koran describes him as having wings of green emerald and hair of saffron. Each hair has a million faces with a million mouths and tongues. He is said to speak in many languages. In these languages, he begs Allah for the pardon of mankind's many transgressions. Variations of the name Mikhail are Mikail and Mikal.

✦**MIKON:** One of the seventy-eight names of the mighty angel **Metatron.**

✦**MILK, ANGEL OF:** In Zoroastrianism a glass of milk symbolizes **Vohu Manah.** He is the guardian angel of cattle.

✦**MILTON, JOHN:** Noted English poet (1608–1674) who portrayed angels in many of his writings. His most recognized poem featuring angels is *Paradise Lost.* It has been hailed as the greatest epic ever written in the English language. It is the tale of **Satan** the Devil's rebellion against God, and the banishment of **Adam** and **Eve** from Paradise. In *Paradise Lost*, Milton writes, "Millions of spiritual creatures walk the earth unseen, both when we wake and when we sleep."

✦**MINISTERING ANGEL(S):** Angels who attend to God's immediate wishes. God is said to have ministering angels surrounding his throne day and night to do his bidding. According to lore, there are many hundreds of thousands of ministering angels. They act as messengers and mediators between God and humans. They are considered by some to be a separate class of angels. It is the duty of the ministering angels to instruct the nations who are the offspring of **Noah.**

✦**MINISTERING SPIRITS:** Another name for the **ministering angels.**

✦**MINISTERS:** One of the many titles of the angels.

✦**MIRACLES, ANGELS OF:** The order of angels called **Virtues** bestow miracles from on high and are called angels of grace.

✦**MITATRON:** One of the seventy-eight names of **Metatron.**

✦**MITHRA:** In Zoroastrianism, **Mithra** was the angel of light. He was also the angelic mediator between God and mankind and held the title of guardian of the world. In addition, he was one of the twenty-eight **izeds** of **Ahura Mazda,** and one of the **Adityas** (angels of Vedic beliefs). He later became the Persian god of light and wisdom. In ancient art he was portrayed as young, handsome, and strong and was often shown slaying bulls. A religion titled Mithraism started in the second century A.D It was based on the worship and following of Mithra. Mithraism taught the dualistic conflict between the celestial forces of good and evil. Variations of the name Mithra include Mihr and **Meher.**

✦**MITHRAISM, ANGELS OF:** See **Mithra.**

✦**MITON:** One of the seventy-eight names of **Metatron.**

✦**MITTRON:** A variation of the name **Metatron.**

✦**MOAKIBAT:** A **recording angel** in Muslim lore.

✦**MODEBEL:** A demon who causes fights between married couples.

✦**MODERN ANGELS:** See **Twentieth Century.**

✦**MODIEL:** An angel who safeguards the east **wind.**

✦**MOLECH:** A cruel and brutal fallen angel featured in John Milton's poem *Paradise Lost.* He was also a Canaanite god. Tribes sacrificed their firstborn to him in a temple near Jerusalem. Variations of the name Molech are Moloc and Moloch.

✦**MOLOC:** A variation of the name **Molech.**

✦**MOLOCH:** A variation of the name **Molech.**

✦**MONACO, LORENZO:** A fifteenth-century Italian painter (c. 1370–1425) who featured angels in his art. One of his most famous paintings is a depiction of the archangel **Gabriel,** painted in 1420.

✦**MONARCHS, ANGELS OF:** The angels in charge of protecting the world's monarchs are the **Principalities.**

✦**MONDAY, ANGELS OF:** The archangel **Gabriel** is the official angel of Monday. The angels who preside over the hours of the day on Monday are: 1:00-Gabriel, 2:00-**Casziel,** 3:00-**Sachiel,** 4:00-**Sammael,** 5:00-**Michael,** 6:00-**Haniel,** 7:00-**Raphael,** 8.00-Gabriel, 9:00-Casziel, 10:00-Sachiel, 11:00-Sammael, 12:00-Michael. The angels who preside over the hours of the night are: 1:00-Haniel, 2:00-Raphael, 3:00-Gabriel, 4:00-Casziel, 5:00-Sachiel, 6:00-Sammael, 7:00-Michael, 8:00-Haniel, 9:00-Raphael, 10:00-Gabriel, 11:00-Casziel, 12:00-Sachiel.

✦**MONKS:** See **Angel Monks.**

✦**MONOTHEISM:** The belief in one God. In the monotheistic religions such as Judaism, Christianity, and Islam, angels are separate entities that dwell apart from God. Their roles are to mediate for God, and to act as his servants, ministers, and messengers.

✦**MONS, ANGELS OF:** In August of 1914, German troops claimed that while fighting in World War I at Mons in Belgium, spectral riders, with bows, arrows, and swords, were battling in the sky above the British soldiers, hampering the German attack on the British.

✦**MONTHS OF THE YEAR, ANGELS OF THE:** During the Middle Ages, angels were named for every month of the year. They are as follows: January-**Gabriel;** February-**Barakiel;** March-**Machidiel;** April-**Asmodel;** May-**Ambriel;** June-**Muriel;** July-**Verchiel;** August-**Hamaliel;**

September-**Uriel;** October-**Barbiel;** November-**Adnachiel;** December-**Haniel.**

✤**MOON, ANGELS OF:** In his poem "Golden Moon," **Longfellow** refers to the archangel **Gabriel** as the "angel of the moon, who brings the gift of hope to mankind." In the occult the angel of the moon is Tsaphiel. **Opanni'el YHWH** is the angel of the orb of the moon. The angel named **Abuzohar** is also an angel of the **moon.** In Persian mythology the angel of the moon was Mah. In ancient African beliefs **Yemaya** governed the moon. Asder'el brought the knowledge of the phases of the moon to the earth. The **Canaanite priestesses** were taught the power of the moon and how to utilize its phases from **Sariel.**

✤**MORALS, ANGELS AND:** Angels are naturally considered moral beings because of their Divine association. However, history shows that angels can become immoral. This is exemplified in the behavior of the angels known as the **Watchers.** The Watchers left their positions in Heaven to come to earth and have sexual relations with women. Another case of immoral behavior among the ranks of the angels includes the tale of **Satan.** Satan became immoral when he rebelled against God. One-third of the angels followed him in his immoral conduct. It is believed that the closer the angels are to the physical realm and humankind, the more apt they are to be tempted to do wrong. The story of the Watchers is an example of this. The Watchers were charged with watching over humans. To carry out their heavenly duties they dwelled close to the earthly realm. In the end they became tempted into immorality and sin. The order of angels called **Powers** are also said to be subject to immorality and falling away from God's laws.

✤**MORMON:** The earthly father of Moroni, the angel of Mormons. It was Mormon's ancient ancestral records that make up The **Book of Mormon.** The records tell of a visitation from Jesus Christ to Mormon's ancestors after Jesus' crucifixion. These ancient ancestral records were buried by Moroni while he was still on earth. They were later revealed to **Joseph Smith** by Moroni, who came back to the earth as an angel.

✤**MORMONS, ANGEL OF: Moroni.**

✤**MORNING, ANGELS OF:** The archangel **Uriel** holds the title of the angel of the morning. The **Zafrire** are also angels of the morning. **Lucifer** is sometimes referred to as the son of the morning.

✤**MORNING DEW, ANGELS OF:** The angels of the morning dew dwell in the **First Heaven.** The First Heaven is the heavenly realm in the closest proximity to the earth.

✤**MORNING STAR:** A phrase used when referring to **Lucifer.** Lucifer was formerly the Latin name of the planet Venus. Venus was once called the

Morning Star. **Jesus** is referred to as the "morning star" in the Book of Revelation 22:16: "I Jesus have sent mine angel to testify unto you these things in the churches. I am the root and the offspring of David, [and] the bright and morning star."

✦**MORNING STAR OF HEAVEN:** In Aramaic the she-demon **Astarte** is referred to as the Morning Star of Heaven.

✦**MORNING STARS:** A term used when referring to the angels.

✦**MORONI:** The angel of the Mormons. See **Mormon.**

✦**MORS:** The god of death in Roman mythology, and the equivalent of the Greek god **Thanatos.** Mors carried the souls of humans to Hades after they died. He was the **archetypal angel** of death.

✦**MOSES:** The deliverer of the Hebrews. He first encountered the Angel of the Lord in a **burning bush** on **Mount Sinai** (Exodus 3:2). The angel informed him that he was the one to deliver the Hebrews from bondage to the Egyptians. According to Jewish lore, the angel in the burning bush was the archangel **Michael.** Lore also has it that it was Michael who appeared at Moses' burial and argued with Satan over the ownership of the body of Moses. The angel **Zagzagel** is credited with giving Moses his wisdom and knowledge (although some authorities believe it was **Sariel**). According to the *Midrash Aggada Exodus*, Moses was once attacked by a fiery serpent for not having his son circumcised. This serpent is believed to have been the archangel **Uriel.**

✦**MOSQUES:** In Islam angels are believed to sit in the mosques listening to and recording the prayers of men.

✦**MOT:** The angel of death in Babylonian lore.

✦**MOTHER MARY:** A title held by the **Virgin Mary.** The Virgin Mary is one of the highest angels in Heaven. She holds the title of **Queen of Angels.**

✦**MOTHER OF ALL PEOPLE:** A title held by the **Virgin Mary.**

✦**MOTHER OF GOD:** A title held by the **Virgin Mary.**

✦**MOUNT HARAITI, ANGEL OF:** Mount Haraiti is where the Zoroastrian angel **Sraosha** is said to dwell. According to legend, Sraosha has a house of a thousand pillars that sits on top of the mountain.

✦**MOUNT HERMON, ANGELS OF:** Mount Hermon is a 9,200-foot mountain in the Anti-Lebanon Range. It is the highest mountain in the neighborhood of Palestine. According to 1 Enoch 6:6, it is where **Watchers** descended when they came to earth to have sexual relations with mortal women.

✦**MOUNT HOREB, ANGELS OF:** See **Mount Sinai.**

✦**MOUNT MORIAH, ANGEL OF:** Mount Moriah is where **Abraham** took his son **Isaac** to offer him as a sacrifice to God. Just as Abraham was about to slay his son, the Angel of the Lord called out to him from Heaven, to stop him. This angel is sometimes referred to as the Angel of Mount Moriah (Genesis 22:11–14).

✤MOUNT OLYMPUS: The home of the gods in Greek mythology. The winged god and goddess **Hermes** and **Iris** delivered messages between Mount Olympus and the earth for **Zeus** and **Hera.**

✤MOUNT SINAI: The mountain in the Old Testament where **Moses** first encountered the Angel of the Lord in a **burning bush.** It is also the place where Moses received the tablets that held the Ten Commandments from God. According to lore, the archangel **Raziel** stands on top of Mount Sinai announcing the secrets of men for all to hear. About Mount Sinai, Psalms 68:17 says, "The chariots of God are twenty thousand, even thousands of angels: the Lord is among them, as in Sinai, in the holy place." It is also called Mount Horeb and the Mountain of God.

✤MOUNT VERNA, ANGEL OF: The mountain where **Saint Francis of Assisi** received the stigmata from an angel. As he was meditating, he saw a **Seraph** swiftly descending from Heaven. The Seraph had six fiery wings. An image of a crucified man appeared between the wings. Saint Francis grieved at the sight of the crucified man. As he watched, wounds opened in Saint Francis's hands, feet, and chest. The wounds looked as though they had been caused by nails.

✤MOUNTAIN OF GOD, ANGEL OF THE: See **Mount Sinai.**

✤MOUNTAINS, ANGEL OF: **Rampel.** In an ancient Hawaiian legend, the great female spirit named **Pele** presided over the mountains.

✤MOVEMENTS OF THE PLANETS, ANGEL OF THE: **Jehudiel.**

✤MOVIES: Angels are a popular subject in movies. The most popular movies in which angels have been featured include *All That Jazz* (1979), *Almost an Angel* (1990), *Always* (1989), *The Angel Levine* (1970), *Angel on My Shoulder* (1980), *The Angel Who Pawned Her Harp* (1954, Great Britain), *Angelic Conversations* (1985), *Angels in the Outfield* (1951, remake 1994), *Barbella* (1968), *The Bible* (1966), *The Bishop's Wife* (1947), *Cabin in the Sky* (1943), *Charley and the Angel* (1973), *Dad, the Angel and Me* (1994), **Date with an Angel** (1987), *Faraway, So Close* (1993, Germany,) **For Heaven's Sake** (1950), **Forever Darling** (1956), *The Greatest Story Ever Told* (1965), *Green Pastures* (1936), *A Guy Named Joe* (1993), *Heart and Soul* (1993), **Heaven Can Wait** (1978), *Heaven Only Knows* (1947), *The Heavenly Kid* (1985), *Here Comes Mr. Jordan* (1941), *The Horn Blows at Midnight* (1945), *Human Feelings* (1978), *I Married an Angel* (1942), **It Happened One Christmas** (1977), **It's a Wonderful Life** (1946), *Jesus of Nazareth* (1976), **The Kid with the Broken Halo** (1982), *King of Kings* (1961),

L'Ange (*The Angel*, 1982), *The Littlest Angel* (1969), *Made in Heaven* (1987), *The Marvelous Visit* (1974, France), *Montana Mike* (1947), *Mr. Destiny* (1990), *One Magic Christmas* (1985), *Sodom and Gomorrah* (1963), *Stairway to Heaven* (1946), *The Ten Commandments* (1956), *That's the Spirit* (1945), *Two of a Kind* (1983), *Waiting for the Light* (1990), *Wholly Moses* (1980), **Wings of Desire** (1988, Germany), *Yolanda and the Thief* (1945).

✦**MTNIEL:** The angel of **wild animals.**

✦**MUFGAR:** An angel who stands guard over the palace of Wilon, the **First Heaven.**

✦**MUHAMMAD:** The founder of **Islam.** The archangel **Jibril** appeared to Muhammad while he was meditating on a mountain near Mecca and gave him a revelation from God. This revelation turned into Islam's holy book, the **Koran.** As Jibril dictated the Koran to Muhammad, his wings were outstretched, his face was illuminated, and between his eyes was written, "There is no God, but God, and Muhammad is the prophet of God." Jibril later appeared to Muhammad and told him to call men to God. On another occasion, angels washed and purified Muhammad's heart and filled him with wisdom and faith. They then took Muhammad on a tour of Paradise. The guardian angel of Muhammad is Jibril. See **Night of Glory.**

✦**MUNKIR:** See **Munkir and Nakir.**

✦**MUNKIR AND NAKIR:** Angels in Islam who visit the tombs of those who have recently died. They are to determine where the deceased will go, to Paradise or to Hell. They ask questions regarding the religious beliefs of the individual, and also their good and evil deeds on earth. The good are shown what life will be like in Heaven. The bad are shown the torments of Hell.

✦**MURDER:** A demon from the Testament of **Solomon.** He is responsible for humans becoming mute. He can be thwarted by **Barakiel,** the angel of lightning.

✦**MURIEL:** The angel who presides over the month of June. He is also the angel of the zodiac sign Cancer, and one of four ruling lords over the **Dominations** (also called **Hashmallim**).

✦**MURMUS:** A **fallen angel.**

✦**MUSE(s):** In Greek mythology muses were thought to inspire men in areas of education, religion, history, and the arts and sciences. The names of the muses are **Calliope,** the muse of epic poetry; **Clio,** the muse of history; **Erato,** the muse of love verses: **Euterpe,** the muse of lyric poems and song verses; Melpomene, the muse of tragedy; **Polyhymnia,** the muse of hymns; **Terpsichore,** the muse of dance; Thaleia, the muse of comedy, creativity, and intelligence; and **Urania,** muse of astronomy. Many people consider muses to be angels. They are the **archetypal angels** of inspiration.

✤MUSIC (ANGELS AND): The noted English poet **John Milton** wrote, "Speak ye who best can tell, ye sons of light, Angels, for ye behold him and with songs, and choral symphonies, day without night, circling his throne rejoicing." In Judaism, Christianity, and Islam, angels are believed to sing praises to God. They are mentioned in scripture as playing musical instruments. In Judaic lore, **Metatron** and Shemiel both hold the title of the angel of music. In Christianity, it is **Uriel;** in Islam, it is **Israfel.** The angel in charge of the heavenly chorus is named Tag'as. In classical Hinduism the Gandharvas were winged men who made beautiful music in Heaven. MUSICIAN ANGELS IN ART. In art, angels are often depicted playing **trumpets, harps,** cymbals, flutes, and violas. The instruments symbolize the angels praising God. Some of the most famous paintings depicting angels as musicians include (1) three paintings by Melozzo da Forli entitled *Angel Musicians.* These paintings show angels playing the violin and lyre. They were painted in 1480, in Rome; (2) a painting by **Hans Memling** from the fifteenth century, entitled *Musician Angels;* (3) a painting of angel musicians by Baldassare Franceschini entitled *Il Volterrano,* painted in 1644.

✤MUSICAL INSTRUMENTS: Angels are often portrayed in art and scripture playing musical instruments, which symbolize the angels praising God.

✤*MUSICIAN ANGELS:* The name of a famous painting by **Hans Memling** in which angels are depicted playing musical instruments.

✤MUSLIMS, ANGELS OF: See **Islam.**

✤MY MOON IS GOD: The meaning of the name **Araziel.** Araziel was one of the **Watchers** who came to earth to have sexual relations with mortal women.

✤MYSTERIES, ANGEL OF: **Raziel.**

✤MYSTERIES OF HEAVEN: The *mysteries of heaven* is a term used in scripture when referring to knowledge that is known only by higher beings that exist in the spiritual realm. In the chronicles of **Enoch,** God informs Enoch that the "mysteries of Heaven" were no longer accessible to the group of angels called **Watchers** because of their sin with the women of the earth. He accused the Watchers of broadcasting to women the mysteries of Heaven. Some of these mysteries God referred to as mysteries that were "rejected" in Heaven. God said that the people of earth would use this knowledge to perform evil deeds. These mysteries are referred to in the chronicles of Enoch as "eternal secrets." In 1 Enoch the angels **Michael,** Surafel, and **Gabriel** tell God about the events on the earth after the angels had descended to earth to be with women. They say to God, "You see what Azaz'el [Chief of the Watchers] has done; how he has taught all forms of oppression upon the earth. And they [the Watchers] revealed eternal secrets which are performed in heaven and which man learned."

✦MYSTICAL ALPHABETS: See **Angelic.**

✦*MYSTICAL THEOLOGY:* A book written in the sixth century on angels. It was once (along with its companion, *The Celestial Hierarchy*) the absolute resource on angels. The authorship of the book is questionable. It is believed to have been written by either Dionysius the Areopagite or **Dionysius the Pseudo-Areopagite.**

✦MYSTICS: Throughout history mystics have claimed to be in contact with the angels. Famous mystics who had experiences with the angels include Jacob Boehme, who had visions of angels; **Emanuel Swedenborg,** who communicated directly with the angels and learned a great deal about Heaven and Hell; **Rudolph Steiner,** who conversed regularly with angels and learned much about the spiritual realm and mankind's evolution; **William Blake,** who had visions of angels and believed that his work was guided by them and credited his creative genius to them; and **Teresa Palminota,** who regularly received visits from angels. See **Saints, Visionaries.**

Make yourself familiar with angels, and behold them frequently in spirit; for, without being seen, they are present with you.

—SAINT FRANCIS DE SALES

✤NAAMAH (PLEASURABLE): The daughter of **Lamech** and the sister of **Noah.** According to lore, **Azael** (an angel from the class of **Watchers**) came to earth and had sexual relations with Naamah. From that union, Naamah gave birth to a son whom they named Azza, who was called the Strong One. According to lore, Naamah later became a bride of Satan and an angel of **prostitution.**

✤NA'ARIRI'EL YHWH: A great angelic prince in Heaven.

✤NABU (THE ANNOUNCER): A **recording angel** in Heaven. He records the deeds and the history of mankind. To the Babylonians Nabu served as a god. To the Sumerians he was a great angel of God's. Variations of the name Nabu are Nebu and Nebo.

✤NACHMIEL: An angel who safeguards the south **wind.**

✤NADIEL: The angel of **migration.**

✤NAFRIEL: An angel who oversees the south **wind.**

✤NAHURIEL: An angel who stands guard over the palace of Wilon, the **First Heaven.**

✤NAKIR: See **Munkir and Nakir.**

✤NAKRIEL: An angel who oversees the south **wind.**

✤NAGAZDIEL: A lion-headed angel who carries the souls of ungodly men to Hell.

✤**NARASIMHA:** One of the **avatars** of Hindu lore.

✤**NASR-ED-DIN:** An archangel of the **Yezidics.** He is also known as Mulla Nasrudin in Muslim lore. To Georges Gurdjieff he was Mulla Nassr Eddin.

✤**NATHANAEL:** A ruling prince of the **Seraphim.**

✤**NATHANEL:** According to ancient Hebrew lore, Nathanel is the angel of fire.

✤**NATIEL:** An angel called upon for protection against demons.

✤**NATIONS, ANGELS OF:** The order of angels in charge of protecting the world's nations and their leaders are the **Principalities.** As protectors of nations they are responsible for seeing to it that no one group of people are wiped completely off the earth. In addition, each nation is assigned a guardian angel by God. These individual guardians are called Ethnarchs. The **Archons** were also considered protectors of nations. The archangels **Gabriel, Michael, Raphael,** and **Uriel** are among some of the angels of this order.

✤**NATIVE AMERICAN(S):** Native Americans believe in spirit helpers they call "guides" and **"familiars."** These spirits help with problems and chores. When in need of help or guidance, Native Americans commune with these spirits privately. In addition, each tribe is said to be protected by a guardian spirit. Personal guardian spirits are sought after by individual members of a tribe. Through vision-questing they are able to learn their power animal and the names of their spirit helpers and guardians.

✤**NATS:** The guardian spirits of the Burmese and Pakistani people. They are called upon through propitiatory ceremonies for protection, and to give assistance when needed. Nats can be either good or evil spirits.

✤**NATURE, ANGELS OF:** The angels of nature include **nature spirits, devas, elves,** and **fairies.** They work with the four elements, which are earth, water, fire, and air. They are responsible for nurturing and guarding plant and animal life. According to legend, they dwell in caves, underwater, near lakes, and in or around bushes and trees.

✤**NATURE OF ANGELS:** The nature of angels has been a source of debate for theologians and religious scholars for centuries. Most religious scholars agree that angels are ethereal beings, made up of pure energy, and have the ability to take on **assumed bodies.** The celebrated twentieth-century American thinker and author **Mortimer J. Adler** wrote in his book *The Angels and Us* that angels take on bodies as guises, but do not inhabit bodies. He believed that their corporeal forms are merely assumed bodies. **Rudolph Steiner** believed that the consciousness of an angel is superior to that of mortal man. **Saint Thomas Aquinas** believed that angels are pure intellect, but can assume bodies at will. Some scholars have speculated that angels are composed of elements less dense than those of humans. The Bible supports this idea. In 1 Corinthians the apostle **Paul** states, "For not all flesh is alike. There are celestial bodies and there are terrestrial bodies." When angels return to their heavenly position, they must discard the assumed physical body. Fourth-century writer Lactantius said that "angels are the breaths of God." He believed them to be made of fine ethereal matter. The Koran says that angels have "bodies of fire."

✤**NATURE SPIRIT(S):** Angels of nature (aka **fairies**). From the blueprints of nature that are carried by the **devas,** the nature spirits take the structure of nature and "flesh it out" into physical existence. They are also responsible for the physical requirements of nature.

✤**NAZARETH, ANGEL OF:** Nazareth was a city in Galilee where the archangel **Gabriel** appeared to the **Virgin Mary** in the **Annunciation.**

✤**NEAR-DEATH EXPERIENCES:** In published accounts of near-death experiences, people often tell of leaving their bodies and meeting beings of light, angels, guardian angels, and friends and relatives who have passed on. These beings escort them to Heaven, show them around the heavenly realm, and in some cases help them to understand why they should return to earth. An example of this is found in the best-selling book *Embraced by the Light* by Betty J. Eadie. In the book Eadie tells of leaving her body and seeing three men whom she referred to as "monks." These three men informed Eadie that they had been her guardian angels while on earth.

✤**NEBO:** A variation of **Nabu.**

✤**NEBU:** A variation of **Nabu.**

✤**NEBUCHADNEZZAR, ANGELS OF:** The king of Babylon. The guardian angel of Nebuchadnezzar was named Kal. In the Book of Daniel, Nebuchadnezzar ordered all of his officials to bow down and worship a golden idol. Anyone who refused would be thrown into a fiery **furnace.** Out of faithfulness to their God, three Hebrew men refused to worship the idol. (Their names were Shadrach, Meshach, and Abednego.) Angrily, Nebuchadnezzar had them thrown into the blazing furnace. To Nebuchadnezzar's amazement, the three men were rescued from the fire by an angel. (Daniel 3:28, 29)

✤**NECIEL:** One of twenty-eight angels who preside over the **lunar mansions.**

✤**NEGATIVITY:** Ancient mystics believed that individuals who harbored strong negative emotions and passions drove the angels away from them.

✤**NELCHAEL:** A **fallen angel.**

✤**NEPHILIM:** A variation of the word **Nephillim.**

✤**NEPHILLIM:** The offspring of the group of angels called **Watchers,** who came to earth to have sexual relations with women. Their children, the Nephillim, became fierce, evil, giant mutants, who were hated by the people. They were said to have consumed so much food that the people grew tired of feeding them They then began to eat birds, large and small animals, reptiles, fish, and they drank blood. They eventually turned on the people to eat them. In 1 Enoch, God referred to them as "evil spirits." The Book of Genesis 6:4 also speaks of the Nephillim: "In those days, there were giants on the earth who were descendants of human women and the heavenly beings." The First Book Enoch 15:8 tells us, "But now the giants who are born from the [union of the] spirits and the flesh shall be called evil spirits upon the earth, because their dwelling shall be upon the earth and inside the earth." The Nephillim are also said to be responsible for the building of the Tower of Babel. Four hundred and nine thousand of them were destroyed during the great **flood.** Once their physical bodies were destroyed, their spiritual bodies continued to dwell on earth. They are thought to be some of the evil spirits that roam the earth. They are also called Anakim. A variation of the name Nephillim is Nephilim.

✤**NEQA'EL:** One of the angels who brought the secret knowledge of Heaven to earth.

✤**NERGAL:** The angel of **pestilence.** He was also one of four genii (guardian angels) found in Chaldean mythology. In the occult he is known as the leader of the secret police of Hell.

✤**NERIAH:** See **Childbirth.**

✤**NESTOR:** A Greek god who is portrayed in the *Iliad* as a guardian angel to Agamemnon. He appears to him in a dream and gives him suggestions on how to succeed in combat.

✤**NETZACH:** One of the ten **Holy Sefiroth** (angels in the **Cabala**). His abstract name is Victory. A variation of the name Netzach is Netzael.

✤**NETZAEL:** A variation of the name **Netzach.**

✤**NEUMANN, TERESA:** Modern mystic (1898–1962). Neumann desired to become a nun. However, an accident left her blind and paralyzed and prevented her from fulfilling her spiritual ambition. After many years of being bedridden, she was visited by Saint Teresa and told that she would be cured. After the appearance of Saint Teresa, Neumann began having mystical experiences. These experiences included receiving the stigmata, seeing Jesus Christ in visions, seeing her guardian angel and the guardian angels of others, and receiving visions of angels going about their heavenly duties. She had a unique relationship with her guardian angel, whom she described as being a brilliant figure on her right side. She held that her angel protected her from Satan and helped her in difficult situations. Her angel also took her place in instances of bilocation, when she left her body and could be seen in two places at once. In one vision she saw the **Annunciation,** where **Mary** was told by the archangel **Gabriel** that she would give birth to the Messiah. She also had a vision of the **shepherds** when the Angel of the Lord approached them with the news that their savior had been born.

✤**NEUTRAL ANGELS:** Angels who would not choose either God's side or Satan's side. According to Christian theologian and scholar **Origen,** some angels were uncertain which side to take and therefore remained neutral. Legend has it that humans originated from these neutral angels.

✤**NEW AGE ARCHANGELS:** According to New Age angelologists, there are twelve **archangels** as opposed to the traditional seven. These include Anthriel, Aquariel, **Chamuel, Gabriel, Jophiel, Michael,** Omniel, Perpetiel, **Raphael, Uriel,** Valeoel, and **Zadkiel.**

✤**NICHBADIEL:** An angel who safeguards the south **wind.**

✤**NIDBAI:** One of the **Uthri** (guardian angels) who preserve the Jordan River.

✤**NIGHT, ANGEL OF THE:** Lailiel and **Auriel** both hold the title of angel of the night.

✤**NIGHT OF GLORY, ANGEL OF THE:** In Islam the term Night of Glory refers to the evening that the archangel **Jibril** brought a revelation to the prophet **Muhammad.** That revelation turned into the **Koran,** the Holy Book of Islam. About the Night of Glory the Koran XCVII says, "The Night of Glory, more opulent than a thousand moons! Then angels and revelations waft down by the grace of their Lord."

✤**NIKE:** Greek winged goddess of **victory.** She was the daughter of Pallas and Styx and oversaw all of the Greek championships. One famous representation of Nike in her winged form is the *Victory* (*Nike*) *of Samothrace* (Louvre), which is one of Greece's finest sculptures. Nike's winged figure later became a pattern for artists depicting **angels** in the **Renaissance.**

✤**NIMBI:** The plural of **Nimbus.**

✤**NIMBUS:** A bright light that surrounds angels when they appear to humans on earth.

✤**NINHURSAG:** A variation of the name **Ninkharsag.**

✤**NINKHARSAG:** A Sumerian mother goddess who is identified with **Gabriella** (the female form of **Gabriel**). She has also been identified with the she-demon **Lilith.** Variations of Ninkharsag are Ninhursag and Ninkhursag.

✤**NINKHURSAG:** A variation of the name **Ninkharsag.**

✦**NINTH ORDER:** The ninth **order of angels** in the angelic hierarchy is the **Angels.**

✦**NISROC:** A variation of the name **Nisroch.**

✦**NISROCH:** In the Bible, Nisroch is an Assyrian deity worshiped by King **Sennacherib.** In John Milton's *Paradise Lost,* he is a prince of the **Principalities.** Nisroch is also known as the great eagle and the eagle-headed deity.

✦**NITH-HAIAH:** A **fallen angel.**

✦**NOAH:** In the Bible, Noah was the builder of the ark that saved his family and various animals from the great **flood.** According to Judaic lore, God sent the angel Asuryal to warn Noah of the impending flood. Noah is said to have patterned the ark after instructions laid out in the **Book of Raziel.** The book had been given to him by **Enoch.** After the flood the angel **Sarasael** spoke to Noah. Sarasael told Noah to plant the **vine** and change its name. (Note: When the **Garden of Eden** was first created, each **archangel** planted a **tree.** Satan planted the vine. After Satan's fall, God evidently wanted the vine renamed.) According to the book of Enoch, as a baby, Noah was surrounded by a brilliant light that glowed in the darkness and would light up an entire room. His father, **Lamech,** believed that the baby was fathered by the angels and was not his own child. According to the Cabala, Noah's preceptor was the angel **Zaphkiel.**

✦**NOAH'S ARK, ANGELS OF:** See **Noah.**

✦**NOHARIEL:** An angel of the east **wind.**

✦**NONTRADITIONAL ANGELS:** A term used for angels outside the mainstream religions. The mainstream religions use the term *angels.* However, other religious systems believe in spiritual beings who protect, guard, and help mankind. These nontraditional angels are usually called by other names. Examples of this would be the **Bodhisattvas,** heavenly beings of Buddhism; and the **shen,** angelic beings of Chinese lore.

✦**NOON-DAY HEAT, ANGEL OF:** In Persian mythology the angel of the noon-day heat was called **Rapithwin.**

✦**NORSEMEN, ANGELS OF THE:** The Norsemen were Scandinavian Vikings who invaded and settled on the coasts of northwest Germany, France, Spain, and also the Low Countries, during the ninth and tenth centuries. Angels of Norse beliefs included the Valkyries. These were female angels of death in German mythology. They were also called the Northern Angels of Death. In Germanic lore the Valkyries under **Brunnhilde**'s direction oversaw wars and chose who would live and who would die. They also carried the souls of the heroes to the hall of heroes called Valhalla.

✤NORTH, ANGEL OF THE: The archangel **Gabriel.**

✤NORTH STAR, ANGEL OF THE: **Abyatur.**

✤NORTH WIND, ANGEL OF THE: See **Wind.**

✤NORTHERN ANGELS OF DEATH: Another name for the **Valkyries.** Their leader was **Brunnhilde.** See **Norsemen.**

✤NOVEMBER, ANGEL OF: In Hebrew lore the angel of November was **Adnachiel.** In ancient Persia it was Azur.

✤NOVENSILES: There are nine **Etruscan** angels that rule over thunderbolts. The names of these angels are Tina, Menrva, Cupra, Vejovis, Summanus, Ercle, Sethlans, Mantus, and Mars.

✤NUMBER OF ANGELS: In his 1635 treatise on angels entitled *The Hierarchy of Blessed Angels,* English dramatist Thomas Heywood wrote, "Of the angels, th' exact number who shall undertake to tell, he shall grow from ignorance to error; yet we may conjecture." Exactly how many angels there are is unknown. However, that has not stopped human speculation on the subject, and down through the ages various numbers have been given. In the Book of Psalms, King **David** says that there are "twenty thousand angels." Jesus once stated that he could ask God for more than "twelve legions of angels." The prophet **Enoch** wrote that when he visited Heaven, he saw countless angels. He said there were a "hundred thousand times a hundred thousand, ten million times ten million angels." The Bible tells us that in a vision, **Daniel** saw "thousands upon thousands" of ministering angels. He also saw "ten thousand times a hundred thousand" angels standing before God. During the Middle Ages a group of Cabalists came up with the number of 301,655,722, and 133,306,668 of those were thought to be fallen angels. **Saint Thomas Aquinas** counted each of the nine **orders of angels** as having 66,666 legions of angels. Within each legion were 6,666 angels, totaling 444,395,556. Each of the seven **archangels** are said to command 496,000 angels. The Talmud says that every Jew is assigned eleven thousand guardian angels when he is born. The Jewish Cabala gives the number as 49 million angels. An Islamic legend tells us that the archangel **Mikhail** is covered from head to foot with hair and has a million faces for each hair, and for each face a million eyes. When he cries, from each eye comes seven hundred thousand **tears.** From these tears, the **Cherubim** are created. If those numbers are multiplied, we find that there are 700,000,000,000,000,000 angels. FALLEN ANGELS. According to lore, the number of fallen angels varies. During the fifteenth century, the cardinal bishop of Tusculum estimated that there are 133,306,668 fallen angels. One sixteenth-century estimate was 7,405,926.

✦**Nuriel:** See **Childbirth.**

✦**Nut:** Winged goddess of ancient Egypt. She presided over the sky.

✦**Nut Tree, Angel of the:** When the **Garden of Eden** was first created, each of the archangels planted a tree. The archangel **Uriel** planted the nut tree.

✦**Nymphs:** A type of **nature spirit.** In art they are portrayed as beautiful young maidens and are said to be musically inclined and amorous. They dwell in rivers, mountains, and trees.

✦**Nymphs of Paradise:** A term sometimes used when referring to the Persian **Houri.**

Angels are spirits, but it is not because they are spirits that they are angels. They become angels when they are sent.

—Saint Augustine

OBEDIENCE: The name of one of the seven archangels in **Zoroastrianism.**

OBIZUTH: A variation of **Obyzouth.**

OBLIVION, ANGEL OF: Poteh.

OBYZOUTH: A she-demon from the Testament of **Solomon** who kills children. She also causes harm and pain to the bodies of humans. She can be rendered powerless by calling on the archangel **Raphael.** In addition, the angel Afarof is said to be able to stop Obyzouth. She can also be thwarted by writing her name on papyrus. A variation of Obyzouth is Obizuth.

OCEANS, ANGEL OF: Rahab.

OCH: An angel best known in occult lore. He holds the title of the angel of **alchemy** and is said to have 35,536 angels that accompany him.

OCTOBER, ANGEL OF: In Judaic lore the angel of October is **Barbiel.** In Persian mythology it was **Aban.**

ODAM: One of many aliases used by the she-demon **Lilith** when she works evil against mortals.

ODDBODY, CLARENCE: See **Clarence.**

ODYSSEY: A Greek epic poem attributed to Homer. It is about the wanderings of **Ulysses** after the fall of Troy. In the poem, **Athena** and the winged god **Hermes** act as guardian angels to Ulysses.

✤**OEILLET**: A **fallen angel.**

✤**OFANIEL**: A variation of the name **Ophaniel.** Ophaniel is one of the ruling angels of the **Cherubim.**

✤**OFANIM**: A variation of the name **Ophanim.** They inspire humans to have confidence in God's love and also his great power.

✤**OFIEL**: See **Childbirth.**

✤**OGDOAS**: A class of superior angels. They are equal to **Archons.**

✤**OHRMAZD**: Another name for **Ahura Mazda,** the Supreme Being in **Zoroastrianism.**

✤**OLD DRAGON**: Another name for **Satan.** See **Dragon.**

✤**OLIVE BRANCH, ANGEL OF THE**: The archangel **Gabriel** is often depicted in art carrying an olive branch. The olive branch has been a symbol of **peace** since ancient times.

✤**OLIVE TREE, ANGEL OF THE**: When the **Garden of Eden** was first created, the archangel **Michael** planted the olive tree.

✤**OMNIEL**: One of twelve **archangels** listed by New Age angelologists.

✤**ONE WHO DECEIVES GOD**: A title given to the angel **Kasbel.** He received this title because of his attempt to trick the archangel **Michael** into revealing the secret name of God.

✤**ONES WHO NEVER SLEEP**: A title held by the **Watchers.** The Watchers were angels assigned to watch over humans night and day.

✤**ONOEL**: A variation of the name **Haniel,** the Prince of Love and Harmony.

✤**ONOSKELIS**: A female demon said to be beautiful. She has the body of a woman and the legs of a mule. She dwells in the dens and caves of the earth.

✤**OPANNIEL**: A variation of **Opanni'el YHWH.**

✤**OPANNI'EL YHWH**: The Prince of the **Ophanim.** He also carries the title of the angel of the disk of the moon. His appearance is like lightning. He is so brilliant that no man can look at him without being incinerated. According to legend, he has sixteen faces (four on each side). He also has one hundred wings on each side of his body. A shortened version of Opanni'el YHWH is Opanniel.

✤**OPHANIEL**: One of the ruling princes of the **Cherubim.** A variation of the name Ophaniel is Ofaniel.

✤**OPHANIM**: A high order of angels. The Prince of the Ophanim is Opanni'el YHWH, to whom God has entrusted their care and keeping. Daily Opanni'el YHWH tends to them to increase their brilliance and beauty. He also teaches them to be swift in praising God. The Ophanim are full of eyes and wings. Each wears seventy-two sapphires in his robe. Each wears four emeralds in his crown. They are so brilliant that their light illuminates **Arabot,** the Seventh Heaven (the dwelling place of God). The Jewish prophets became angels of the Ophanim when they reached Heaven. The Ophanim are equated with the order of angels called **Thrones.**

✦**OPIEL:** An angel who aids individuals in obtaining the love of a desired one. His name can be found written on Aramaic **love charms.**

✦**OPPOSER(S) OF GOD:** According to accounts in both Judaic and Islamic lore, some angels opposed God's plan to create man. After God created **Adam,** he told the angels to bow down to him. **Satan** adamantly refused and became an opposer of God. Other angels followed him and they, too, became opposers of God. In Islam it was **Iblis** who refused to bow down to Adam. Iblis is the Islamic name for Satan.

✦**OPUS SANCTORUM ANGELORUM:** See **Religious Groups.**

✦**ORACLE:** See **Angel Oracle.**

✦**ORACLES, ANGEL OF:** Phaldor.

✦**ORAIOS:** One of the seven **Archons** (a high order of angels) of gnosticism.

✦**ORANGE, ANGEL OF:** The **color** orange represents the archangel **Raphael.**

✦**ORB:** A small globe with a cross on top, sometimes held by angels in art. The orb represents the angels' heavenly sovereignty.

✦**ORB OF THE SUN, ANGEL OF:** Galgalliel.

✦**ORDER:** A term used when referring to any of the nine groups of angels found within the angelic hierarchy. For example, the **Seraphim** is the first order, the **Cherubim** is the second order, etc.

✦**ORDERS OF ANGELS:** The nine orders of angels listed in the angelic hierarchy are the (1) **Seraphim,** (2) **Cherubim,** (3) **Thrones,** (4) **Dominations,** (5) **Virtues,** (6) **Powers,** (7) **Principalities,** (8) **Archangels,** and (9) **Angels.** RULING ANGELS. The ruling angels of the nine orders of angels are: *Seraphim:* Jahoel, **Metatron, Michael,** Nathanael, **Serapiel,** Shemuel, and **Uriel.** *Cherubim:* Cherubiel, **Gabriel,** Ophaniel, **Raphael, Uriel,** and Zophiel. *Thrones:* **Oriphiel, Raziel,** Zabkiel, **Zaphkiel,** Zophiel. *Dominations:* **Hashmal, Muriel,** Yahriel, **Zadkiel.** *Virtues:* **Barbiel, Hamaliel, Haniel, Gabriel, Michael,** Peliel, **Sabriel,** Tarshish, and Uzziel. *Powers:* **Camael, Gabriel,** and **Verchiel.** *Principalities:* Amael, **Cervihel, Haniel, Nisroch,** and **Requel.** *Archangels:* **Barakiel, Barbiel, Gabriel, Jehudiel, Metatron, Michael,** and **Raphael.** *Angels:* **Adnachiel,** Chayyliel, **Gabriel,** and Phaleg. The names of various orders of angels found outside of the traditional nine include **Abalim, Abdals, Adityas, Aeons, Aishim, Ambassadors, Animastics,**

Apparitions, Aralim, Archai, Archons, Ardours, Arelim, Armies, Auphanim, Authorities, Bene ha-Elohim, Chariots of God, Confessors, Degalim, Devas, Elim, Elohim, Erelim, Flames, Governors, Grigori, Hashmallim, Hayyoth, Holy Sefiroth, Hosts, Innocents, Izachim, Kalkydra, Lordships, Malakim, Martyrs, Ofanim, Ogdoas, Ophanim, Phoenixes, Regents, Sarim, Sin'anim, Sovereignties, Tarshishim, Voices, Warriors, Watchers.

✦ORDIBEHESHT: The angel of **April** in ancient Persian mythology (the Persian month of April runs between April 21 and May 21).

✦ORIEL: A variation of the name **Uriel.** The name Oriel can be found in the **Book of Raziel,** where he is listed as an angel whose name can be found on charms worn by pregnant women. It is believed that the charm will aid them in having a safe and successful delivery.

✦ORIENTAL AMULETS: Angels can frequently be found on oriental amulets to frighten away evil spirits. Some of the most frequent names found are Achathriel, Akzariel, Avartiel, **Azariel,** Bethuel, Buchuel, Busthariel, Garshanel, Garzanal, Hasriel, Hiel, Hiphkadiel, Kaphkaphiel, Mahalel, Mahalkel, Marniel, Mavkiel, Natiel, Urpaniel, Yehemiel, Yephiel, and Zamarchad.

✦ORIFIEL: A variation of the name **Oriphiel.**

✦ORIGEN: Origines Adamantius (185?–254?), better known as Origen, was a Christian philosopher and scholar. Origen taught in Alexandria, Egypt, for twenty-eight years. He became famous for his interpretation of the scriptures. He wrote that angels were placed over the four elements, earth, water, air, and fire, and also the plants and animals. He taught that every person has two angels to protect and watch over them, one good and one evil.

✦ORIGIN OF ANGELS: See **Creation of Angels, The.**

✦ORIGINAL FORCES: Another name for the order of angels called the **Archai.**

✦ORIGINALITY, ANGEL OF: **Raziel.**

✦ORION, ANGEL OF: **Shemyaza.**

✦ORIPHIEL: An angel of the **apocalypse.** He is also one of the rulers of the order of angels called **Thrones.** A variation of the name Oriphiel is Orifiel.

✦ORNIAS: A demon found in the Testament of Solomon. Ornias interfered with the building of King **Solomon**'s temple, by stealing the wages of a young artisan. In addition, he would suck the thumb of the boy until he began to grow thin and weak. He was later rendered powerless by King Solomon's **magic ring.** He can be thwarted by **Uriel.**

✦OROPEL: A demon from the Testament of **Solomon.** He takes delight in causing sore throats in humans. He can be thwarted by the archangel **Raphael.**

♣**OURIEL:** A variation of the name **Uriel.**

♣**OWL GODDESS:** A winged goddess who is part bird, serpent, and human. She was once worshiped in the Middle East (and some parts of Europe). She was believed to carry the sacred **keys** of life.

♣**OZAHYAH:** One of the seventy-eight names of **Metatron.**

P

Every visible thing in this world is put in the charge of an angel.

—Saint Augustine

✤**Pachdial:** An angel who stands guard over the palace of Zebul, the **Fourth Heaven.**

✤**Padiel:** See **Childbirth.**

✤**Painters of Angels:** See **Art.**

✤**Pairimaiti:** An angel from Zoroastrian beliefs. She is also referred to as the angel of crooked mindedness. Her opponent is Taromaiti, the angel of presumption.

✤**Palm(s):** Angels in art are sometimes depicted carrying palms, a symbol of victory.

✤**Palminota, Teresa:** An Italian mystic who regularly received visitations from the angels. She had ESP, received the stigmata, and once fasted for three years. A mysterious fire emanated from her breast and would burn anyone who came near her. Because of this she led a solitary life. Palminota communicated regularly with her guardian angel, whom she called her "little angel." Eventually, she went deaf and her angel would communicate to her information she needed to know. She also called upon her angel for help in other areas of her life. Her guardian was with her even while she took walks. When she would stop to rest, a butterfly would come to play with her. She believed the butterfly to be her guardian angel. She conveyed to her confessor that she had seen it change into a small angel.

✤PALMISTRY, ANGEL OF: Eistibus.

✤PALMYRA, NEW YORK, ANGEL OF: Palmyra, New York, is the place where the angel Moroni led Joseph Smith (founder of the Church of Jesus Christ of Latter-Day Saints) to the golden tablets that held the text to what is now called the **Book of Mormon.**

✤PALTRIAL: An angel who stands guard over the palace of Maon, the **Fifth Heaven.**

✤PAN: Traditionally known in Greek mythology as the god of the forests, who danced with **nymphs.** He was portrayed as a jovial, ugly man with the horns, ears, and legs of a goat. He is also referred to as Old Pan. He is identified by some as Satan.

✤PARADISE: There are two paradises, the earthly Paradise (the **Garden of Eden**) and the heavenly Paradise. God created the earthly Paradise for the first humans to dwell in. It was in there that Satan tricked **Eve** into eating the forbidden fruit. Later, after **Adam** and Eve were cast out of Paradise, God placed two **Cherubim** and a turning, flaming sword as guards to the entrance. The heavenly Paradise is where God and the highest **orders of angels** dwell.

✤PARADISE, ANGEL OF: In Persian mythology the angel of paradise was named **Surush.**

✤*PARADISE LOST:* An epic poem written by **John Milton.** It has been hailed as the greatest epic ever written in the English language. It is the story of **Adam** and **Eve**'s expulsion from Paradise. In it Milton writes about the fallen angels and the effect their rebellion had on mankind's destiny. It begins with **Satan**'s revolt against God and the banishment of Adam and Eve from the **Garden of Eden.** It also tells how **Jesus** overcame the temptations of the Devil. It describes the great war in Heaven, which Milton depicts as occurring for three days; after which the Son of God intervened. Satan is then cast out of Heaven, taking with him one-third of the angels, whom Milton portrays as being angels from the Cherubim and Seraphim classes. According to Milton, after he was cast out of Heaven, Satan recovered for nine days. He then went after Adam and Eve. The sequel to *Paradise Lost* was named *Paradise Regained.*

✤PARALYSIS, DEMON OF: A demon from the Testament of **Solomon.** Ichthion is the name of the demon who causes paralysis in humans. The angel Adonaeth can be called upon to ward off Ichthion.

✤PARASIEL: The angel of treasures.

✤PARASURANA: One of the **avatars** of Hindu lore.

✤PARI: A variation of the name **Peri.**

✤**PARIUKH:** An angel assigned by God to guard the writings of **Enoch.**

✤**PARTASAH:** One of the many aliases of the she-demon **Lilith.**

✤**PARZIAL:** An angel who stands guard over the palace of Makon, the **Sixth Heaven.**

✤**PASPASI'EL:** One of the seventy-eight names of **Metatron.**

✤**PASPASYAH:** One of the seventy-eight names of **Metatron.**

✤**PASPISAHU:** One of the seventy-eight names of **Metatron.**

✤**PASSIONS:** Ancient mystics believed that humans who possess strong negative passions drive the angels away from themselves.

✤**PATIENCE, ANGEL OF: Achaiah.**

✤**PATRIARCHS:** See **Jewish Patriarchs.**

✤**PATROTA:** An alias used by the she-demon **Lilith.**

✤**PATTERN ANGELS:** Angels that hold the blueprints of universal creation.

✤**PAUL:** One of the twelve **apostles** of **Jesus.** On a ship to Rome, the apostle Paul found himself in a severe storm. The storm continued for several days, and Paul began to fear for his safety and the safety of others on board. An angel appeared to Paul to comfort him, saying, "Do not be afraid, Paul, God has granted safety to all those who are sailing with you." The angel informed him that all aboard would be saved (Acts 27:23–24). Paul writes about angels in the Book of Hebrews 1:14: "What are the angels then? They are spirits who serve God and are sent by him to help those who are to receive salvation."

✤**PAYMON:** A **fallen angel.**

✤**PEACE, ANGELS OF:** The archangel **Michael** is the guardian of peace. Michael kept peace in the Heavens by ousting **Satan** and his followers. According to prophecy, Michael will again lead a war in the interest of peace, when he locks Satan and the rest of the fallen angels in the **abyss** for a thousand years. In addition to Michael, other angels serve the interest of peace. The **order of angels** called **Ambassadors** are known as angels of peace. They promote peace within the universe. The archangel **Gabriel** is often depicted in art carrying an olive branch, symbolizing his position as an emissary of peace. The "angel of peace" is the name of one of the angels who escorted **Enoch** on his journey through earth and **Sheol.** In the Talmud, God consulted the angel of peace on his decision to create mankind. When God sits on the **throne of judgment,** the angels of peace stand on his left side.

✤**PELE:** A great female spirit of Hawaiian lore who watches over the earth's mountains. She causes new land masses to form when the old ones are swept away.

✤**PELIEL:** A prince of the order of **Virtues.**

✤PENANCE, ANGEL OF: **Phanuel.**

✤PENEME: A variation of the name **Penemuel.**

✤PENEMUE: A variation of the name **Penemuel.**

✤PENEMUEL: The angel who taught humans to write, and to use ink and paper. This was considered a great transgression in Heaven, because writing was forbidden to mankind. According to lore, God believed that mankind would use writing for evil purposes. On account of this, it is said that humans have sinned from eternity to eternity. Variations of the name Penemuel include Penemue, Peneme, and Pinem'e.

✤PENIEL, ANGEL OF: The name of the place where **Jacob** wrestled with an angel. According to some sources, Peniel is also the name of the angel that wrestled with Jacob. However, it has been speculated that it was either **Uriel, Camael,** or **Sammael** who wrestled with Jacob. Peniel is believed to dwell in Sehaqim, the **Third Heaven.** A variation of Peniel is Penuel.

✤PENTATEUCH, ANGEL OF THE: **Zagzagel.** The angel of the Pentateuch is credited with teaching **Moses** all of his knowledge and wisdom.

✤PENUEL: A variation of **Peniel.**

✤PEPATPALYAH: One of the seventy-eight names of **Metatron.**

✤PERFUME, ANGEL OF: **Exael.**

✤PERI: In Persian mythology the Peri are beautiful fairies of Heaven. A variation of the name Peri is Pari.

✤PERISYAH: One of the seventy-eight names of **Metatron.**

✤PERPETIEL: One of **twelve archangels** named by New Age angelologists.

✤PERSIA(NS), ANGELS OF: Ancient Persia's rich religious background was deeply rooted in the beliefs in God and the angels. During ancient times, Persians' belief in angels came from their Muslim, Zoroastrian, and **Aryan** backgrounds. Among the angels are the **Ahuras** (angels of Aryan beliefs also called the gods of hidden knowledge), the **Amesha Spentas** (archangels of Zoroastrian beliefs), and the angels of the **Koran.** Most modern Persians base their beliefs in angels on their beliefs in Islam. The guardian angel of Persia was **Dubbiel.**

✤PERSONAL ANGELS: A term sometimes used when referring to guardian angels and spirit guides. Both of these groups of angels work with humans on a personal level, acting as both their protectors and their teachers.

✤PERSONAL HEALING, ANGEL OF: The archangel **Raphael** is the angel of **healing.** If personal issues need resolving or mending, Raphael is the angel to call upon for assistance and guidance.

✤PERUGINO: An Umbrian painter (c. 1445–1523). He was a student of **Leonardo da Vinci**'s and later taught **Raphael.** He assisted with the decoration of the **Sistine Chapel.** As did many of the artists during his period, he painted religious scenes and incorporated angels into his work. One particularly famous painting is *The Virgin*, from which the detail of the three angels has been reproduced for centuries.

✤**PERVERSITY, ANGEL OF:** See **Spirit of Perversity.**

✤**PESTILENCE, ANGEL OF: Nergal.**

✤**PETER:** One of **Jesus'** apostles. In the Bible, King **Herod** had the apostle Peter arrested and planned to kill him. Peter was put under the guard of four squads of soldiers. While Peter was in prison, his congregation prayed for him. On the eve of his death, an Angel of the Lord appeared to him. His light illuminated the cell. He tapped Peter on the side and woke him, saying, "Get up quickly." When he said this, the chains fell off Peter's wrists. The angel said to him, "Fasten your belt and put on your sandals." Peter did so. Then the angel said, "Wrap your cloak around yourself and follow me." The angel led Peter past the guard stations and through an iron gate leading into the city. After they had passed through the gate and Peter was safe, the angel suddenly vanished (Acts 12:6–10).

✤**PHADIEL:** One of the angels of the **covenant.**

✤**PHALDOR:** The angel who presides over oracles.

✤**PHALEG:** A prince of the order of **Angels.**

✤**PHALGUS:** One of the angels of **judgment.**

✤**PHANUEL (FACE OF GOD):** A high-ranking angel of Heaven. He is the angel of penance and one of the angels of the **presence.** His name is sometimes used in magic to ward off evil spirits. He is said to come from either the **Seraphim** or **Cherubim** class. He is equated with the archangel **Uriel.** A variation of the name Phanuel is Fanuel.

✤**PHARAOH:** The Egyptian monarch who kept the Israelites as slaves. It is said that Pharaoh's heart was hardened against freeing the Hebrews by **Mastema,** a fallen angel whose name means "hostility." It was also Mastema who assisted Pharaoh's wizards **Jannes and Jambres** in performing magic against the Hebrews. Mastema is equated with Satan.

✤**PHARMACY, ANGEL OF:** Pharmoros, who taught men pharmacy.

✤**PHARMOROS:** The angel who taught men the usage of herbs, pharmacy, general medicines, and how to diagnose diseases. A variation of the name Pharmoros is **Armaros.**

✤**PHARZUPH:** The angel of lust, and the angel of fornication. Pharzuph enjoys tempting those who have proclaimed a life of celibacy, especially priests and nuns.

✤**PHEDISMOS:** An angel from the Testament of **Solomon.**

✤**PHENIEL:** A variation of the name **Uriel.**

✤PHILANGELI: See **Religious Groups.**

✤PHILIP: An evangelizer in the New Testament. In the Book of Acts 8:26, Philip was guided by an angel to an Ethiopian eunuch who wanted to learn more about the scriptures. Because of the guidance from the angel, Philip was able not only to explain the scriptures, but also to baptize the eunuch.

✤PHILO JUDAEUS: A Jewish philosopher of Alexandria, Egypt. His writings include philosophical works that examine the nature of the cosmos and human responsibility. He held that God revealed himself to mankind as an angel. He also believed that every person had two angels watching over him, one good and one evil.

✤PHOBOTHEL: According to the Testament of **Solomon,** Phobothel is a demon who causes loosening of the tendons.

✤PHOENICIA(NS): The **Phoenicians** worshiped the god Sydik. Sydik was another name for the great and powerful angel **Melchizedek.**

✤PHOENIX: In apocryphal lore, the Phoenix is a bird in Heaven who guards the world. Every day he goes before the sun and spreads his wings to cover the flaming rays of the sun. If he did not do so, all living creatures on earth would be incinerated.

✤PHOENIXES: A high order of angels ranked with the **Seraphim** and **Cherubim.** From their dwelling place in the **Fourth Heaven,** they can be heard singing praises to God.

✤PHOUNEBIEL: An angel from the Testament of **Solomon.**

✤PHYSICAL BODIES, ANGELS AND: See **Assumed Bodies.**

✤PHYSIKORETH: A demon from the Testament of **Solomon.**

✤PIETY: One of the angels of **Zoroastrianism.**

✤PHILALAEL: An angel who presides over the west **wind.**

✤PILGRIMAGES, ANGEL OF: The archangel **Raphael.** Raphael looks after all people who are on pilgrimages relating to God.

✤PILGRIM'S STAFF: Angels are sometimes depicted in art carrying a pilgrim's staff. The pilgrim's staff is a symbol of their being ready to do God's bidding.

✤PILLAR OF CLOUD, ANGEL OF THE: By day an angel led the Hebrews out of Egypt with a huge pillar of cloud. The book of Exodus 14:19 says, "The Angel of God, who had been in front of the army of Israel, moved and went to the rear. The pillar of cloud also moved until it was between the Egyptians and the Israelites. The cloud made it dark for the Egyptians, but gave light to the people of Israel, and so the armies could not come near each other all night."

✤PILLAR OF FIRE, ANGEL OF THE: By night an angel led the Hebrews out of Egypt with a huge pillar of fire so that they could have light at night as they traveled. The angel put the pillar of fire in front of the Hebrews and kept it between them and the soldiers, as a protection from **Pharaoh**'s army. The book of Exodus 13:21 states, "The Angel of the Lord went in front of them in a pillar of cloud by day, to lead them along the way, and in a pillar of fire by night." The mighty angel **Metatron,** also known as the **Lesser Yahweh,** is believed to be that angel who led the Hebrews out of Egypt. Metatron is said to become a pillar of fire when invoked.

✤**PILLAR OF SALT, ANGEL OF THE:** In the Book of Genesis, an angel instructed **Lot** to take his family and leave the city of **Sodom** because it was about to be destroyed. The angel warned Lot and his family not to look back after fleeing the city. God later sent angels to rain burning sulfur on the city to destroy it. However, Lot's wife looked back. When she did so, she was turned into a pillar of salt, for not adhering to the warnings of the angel (Genesis, 19:17, 26).

✤**PINEM'E:** A variation of the name **Penemuel.**

✤**PISCES, ANGEL OF: Barakiel.**

✤**PISQON:** One of the seventy-eight names of **Metatron.**

✤**PISTIS-SOPHIA:** A great female angel from the class of **Aeons.** She is the personification of God's divine wisdom. She is said to be so beautiful that she outshines **Satan,** once considered the most beautiful angel in Heaven. Many tales and legends surround Pistis-Sophia. In gnosticism she was the **Schechinah,** the **Queen of Angels,** and mother of the high class of angels called Aeons. In Jewish legend she is equated with the female principle. In ancient Christian beliefs she was the **Bride of Christ** mentioned in Revelation 21:9. In the **Dead Sea scrolls** of Nag Hammaddi, she is described as the first and the last, the honored and the hated, the prostitute and the holy one, the wife and the maiden, the **infertile** and the fertile. In some beliefs she is an angel who fell from grace because of an extreme interest in sex. In addition, she displayed an intense jealousy of the other Aeons. She is said to have been the one who sent the serpent to tempt **Eve.**

✤**PIT, ANGEL OF: Beliar.**

✤**PITARAH:** Guardian spirits of Indian lore. It was believed that each household had a Pitarah to protect the family from such misfortunes as sickness, hunger, and many other calamities.

✤**PIXIES:** A type of **fairy.** According to legend, pixies have pointed ears, nose, and high, arched eyebrows. They usually are wearing green, with long, pointed caps. They often help people with chores around the house. However, they can also be mischievous and are said to enjoy playing jokes on people.

✦**PLAGUE OF GOD:** The fallen angel Makkiel.

✦**PLAGUES, ANGEL OF: Nergal.** See **Seven Plagues.**

✦**PLANET OF LOVE, ANGEL OF: Haniel.**

✦**PLANET OF WAR, ANGELS OF THE: Sammael** and **Camael** are both angels who rule the Planet of War (Mars).

✦**PLANETS, ANGELS OF THE:** During the Middle Ages, angels were placed over the planets. The angel who oversees all planets is Rahatiel. Individual angels of the planets include sun-**Raphael;** moon-**Gabriel;** Venus-**Aniel;** Mercury-**Michael;** Saturn-**Kafziel;** Jupiter-**Zadkiel;** Mars-**Sammael.**

✦**PLANTS, ANGELS OF:** According to Judaic lore, the **Watchers** taught humans to use plants for medicinal purposes. In Zoroastrianism, **Ameretat** is the guardian angel of plants. In rituals she is represented by plants and flowers. The angel of plants is **Sachluph.**

✦**PLATO:** A Greek philosopher (427?–347 B.C.). In his writings, Plato referenced mediating spirits that existed in both the physical and spiritual realms. He believed that there are many spirits of different kinds. One of these spirits was **Eros.** According to Plato, Eros (the god of love in Greek mythology) had the duties of translating and showing the gods the thoughts of humans. He also communicated to humans what the gods required. According to Plato, the gods would not communicate directly with humans. He held that **mediators** were necessary to converse between the two.

✦**PLEASURABLE:** The meaning of the name **Naamah.** According to some sources, Naamah is a she-demon who is proficient in giving sexual pleasure.

✦**POCEL:** A **fallen angel.**

✦**PODO:** One of the many aliases used by the she-demon **Lilith** when she works evil against mortals.

✦**POE, EDGAR ALLAN:** Brilliant American writer (1809–1849). He authored the famous poem *Israfel,* about Islam's angel of music. See **Appendix 6.**

✦**POETRY, ANGEL OF:** In Judaic lore, **Radweriel** and **Uriel** are both angels of poetry. In Islam, it is **Israfel.**

✦**POETS:** Throughout history angels have been a popular subject in poetry. Famous poets who have included angels in their work include **Dante Alighieri, Johann Wolfgang von Goethe, Henry Wadsworth Longfellow, John Milton,** and **Edgar Allan Poe.**

✦**POISON, ANGEL OF: Sammael.**

✦**POLICE OFFICERS, ANGEL OF:** In 1950, Pope Pius XII declared the archangel **Michael** the protector of police officers.

✦**POLITICAL REFORM, ANGEL OF:** The archangel **Uriel.**

✤**POLYHYMNIA:** In Greek mythology she was a muse of the arts. She inspired men to create sacred and religious music.

✤**POLYTHEISM:** The worship of more than one God. In ancient polytheistic religions such as those of ancient Egypt, Rome, and Greece, there were several winged **gods and goddesses.** In Egypt there was the nature goddess **Isis.** In Greece there was **Nike,** the goddess of **victory; Hermes,** who was messenger to the gods; and **Eros,** the god of love. The Romans had **Cupid,** the god of love; **Victoria,** the goddess of war; and **Mercury,** who was messenger to the gods.

✤**POMEGRANATE TREE, ANGEL OF THE: Kepharel.**

✤**POPE JOHN PAUL II:** In the summer of 1986, Pope John Paul II made references to angels in one of his discourses. He said that angels are "discussed with ignorance." He stated that for people to doubt that angels exist is to "radically revise Holy Scripture and with it the whole history of salvation." He also said the angels are "free and rational purely spiritual beings."

✤**PORTENARI:** An angel in **Dante's** *Divine Comedy.* She is also called **Beatrice.**

✤**PORTUGAL, ANGELS OF:** See **Fatima.**

✤**POTEH:** The angel of forgetfulness.

✤**POTENTATES:** Another name for the class of angels called **Powers.**

✤**POWER:** The name of one of the ten **Holy Sefiroth** (angels found in the **Cabala**). Power is also the name of a demon found in the Testament of Solomon. **Solomon** summoned and interrogated him with the aid of a **magic ring.** Power revealed to **Solomon** that he is a ruler in the world of darkness. He also stated that he raises up tyrants and deposes kings. He can be thwarted by the angel Asteraoth.

✤**POWERS:** An order of angels that rank sixth in the angelic hierarchy. The Powers are said to be the first angels created by God. They reside between the **First** and **Second Heavens.** They are guardians of the passageways leading to Heaven. They also act as guides to lost souls. The Powers bring balance to the earth. Because of them, humans are able to maintain balance within their spirits. The Powers also record the history of mankind. They are said to prevent the efforts of demons to take control of the world. Ruling princes of the Powers are **Camael, Gabriel, Verchiel,** and the **Virgin Mary.** Satan was also one of the ruling princes before his fall from God's favor. They are also called Authorities, Dynamis, Dunamis, and Potentates.

✤**PRAISING ANGELS:** One of the many functions of the angels is to praise God. In fact it is believed by some to be the sole purpose of God's creating the angels. However, others contend that the angels do not praise

God out of duty, but out of love for their creator. Many **orders of angels** praise God regularly. The **Seraphim** sing praises to God unceasingly day and night. The **Phoenixes** and **Kalkydras** sing praises to God when the sun rises. In Islam angels are created from the breath of Allah to sing praises to him. The Islamic archangel **Israfel** praises God in a thousand languages. In the Bible, the angels stand before God's throne praising him. The **Izachim** are a superior order of angels whose duty is to praise God.

✦**Prayer(s), Angels of:** In Judaic lore the angels are said to carry the prayers of the righteous to God. Judaic lore also gives **Akatriel, Metatron, Michael, Raphael,** and **Sandolphon** as angels of prayer. In Jewish occult lore, the angel Abuliel is listed as an angel of prayer. In one Jewish legend the prayers of the righteous spout wings and become angels. In Persian lore the angel of prayer was **Sizouze.** In Islam angels are said to sit in the mosques listening to and recording the prayers of men. In Greek mythology the winged god **Hermes** and the goddess **Iris** speeded between earth and Heaven carrying prayers to the gods. In Roman mythology it was **Mercury.** In Mandaean beliefs, the angel **Sanasel** stood at the entrance to Heaven and offered up prayers for souls. In the Bible the prayers of the saints are offered up to God by angels who stand at a golden altar in front of God's throne.

✦**Pre-Mortal Existence:** See **Creation.**

✦**Precipices, Angel of:** Zarobi.

✦**Pregnancy, Angels of:** The angel of conception and pregnancy is named **Lailah.** She aids women desirous of having children. In Judaic lore, the angels of pregnancy make certain that male infants look like their father. This is to protect the mother from being accused of adultery. See **Childbirth.**

✦**Pregnant Angel:** In the Book of Revelation 12:1–2 an angel appears in a vision as a pregnant woman: "Then a great and mysterious sight appeared in the sky. There was a woman, whose dress was the sun and who had the moon under her feet and a crown of twelve stars on her head. She was soon to give birth, and the pains and suffering of childbirth made her cry out." The woman is said to symbolize Heaven and the angels, and the child symbolizes God's kingdom waiting to be born. This vision has also been interpreted as the **Virgin Mary** giving birth to **Jesus.**

✦**Premature Babies, Angels of:** Premature babies are protected by **caretaker angels.**

✦**Presence, Angels of the:** In Judaism, twelve angels were given the privilege of existing in the presence of God. They include **Michael,**

Metatron, **Suriel, Sandolphon,** Astanphaeus, Saraqael, **Phanuel, Ja-hoel, Zagzagel, Uriel, Jafefiyah,** and **Aktriel.** They are the equivalent of the Angels of Glory, the Angels of Sanctification, and the Angels of the Face. Some sources name four angels of the presence. They include **Gabriel,** Michael, **Raphael,** and Phanuel. The **Schechinah** are also considered angels of the presence. In Phoenician lore the angel of the presence is Adonay.

✤**PRESIDENTS, ANGELS OF:** See **World Leaders.**

✤**PRESUMPTION:** A female angel of Zoroastrian beliefs. She is also called Taromaiti. Her opponent is Pairimaiti, the angel of crooked mindedness.

✤**PRIAPUS:** An angel of **lust.**

✤**PRIDE:** The name of a demon **Archon** in gnosticism. He represents the planet Jupiter. His antithesis is **Zadkiel.**

✤**PRIDE, ANGEL OF:** Pride was the cause of the downfall of **Satan** the Devil. Satan thought so much of himself that he desired to be worshiped as a god. Because of this pride he rebelled against God. Another account states that when **Adam** was created, God instructed the angels to bow down to him. Satan refused saying, "How can a Son of Fire bow to a Son of Clay?" Out of pride he rebelled against God's wishes that mortal man be placed above him and was cast out of Heaven.

✤**PRIESTS, ANGEL OF:** Sachiel-Meleck.

✤**PRIME MINISTER OF HELL:** A title held by the fallen angel **Rofocale.**

✤**PRIMORDIAL SEAS, ANGEL OF THE:** **Rahab.**

✤**PRINCE OF ACCUSERS:** A title held by **Sammael.**

✤**PRINCE OF DARKNESS:** Both **Satan** and **Beliar** are called the Prince of Darkness. In some accounts Satan and Beliar are the same.

✤**PRINCE OF DECEPTION:** A title held by **Satan** because of his deception of **Eve** in the **Garden of Eden.** It is also because of his many aliases, which include **Abaddon, Sammael, Beliar, Beelzebub, Azaz'el,** and **Mastema.** They are all names that Satan is said to hide behind when performing evil deeds.

✤**PRINCE OF DEMONS:** In the Testament of **Solomon, Beelzebub** is referred to as the Prince of Demons.

✤**PRINCE OF DEVILS: Beelzebub.**

✤**PRINCE OF EVIL:** A title held by **Satan** the Devil. Satan is believed to be the originator of evil.

✤**PRINCE OF EVIL SPIRITS:** A title held by **Satan** the Devil. Considered to be the primary evil spirit, Satan is the leader of the other evil spirits, also known as the **demons.**

✤**PRINCE OF GEHENNA:** A title held by the angel Arsiel.

✤**PRINCE OF GOD:** A title held by the archangel **Michael.**

✤**PRINCE OF JUSTICE:** A title held by the archangel **Gabriel.**

✤**PRINCE OF LIES:** A title held by **Satan.**

✤**PRINCE OF LIGHT:** In the Dead Sea scroll *The War of the Sons of Light Against the Sons of Darkness*, the archangel **Michael** is referred to as the Prince of Light. As the Prince of Light, Michael sets a legion of angels against the Prince of Darkness **(Beliar)** and his army.

✤**PRINCE OF LOVE AND HARMONY:** A title held by **Haniel.**

✤**PRINCE OF PRINCES:** A title held by the great angel **Metatron.** He is called King of Angels.

✤**PRINCE OF SHADOWS:** A title held by **Satan.**

✤**PRINCE OF SPIRITUAL LOVE AND FAIRNESS:** A title held by **Shemyaza.**

✤**PRINCE OF TEMPTERS:** The fallen angel Mammon. Mammon is thought by some to be the Devil.

✤**PRINCE OF TERROR AND TREMBLING:** A title held by **Dommiel.**

✤**PRINCE OF THE AEONS: Abraxis.**

✤**PRINCE OF THE DARK SPIRITS:** A title held by **Anituel.**

✤**PRINCE OF THE DIVINE FACE:** A title held by **Metatron.** Metatron is the closest angel to God and is continuously in his presence.

✤**PRINCE OF THE HEAVENLY HOST:** A title held by the archangel **Michael,** who leads the heavenly host in battle.

✤**PRINCE OF THE LYING SPIRITS:** A title held by the demon named **Python.**

✤**PRINCE OF THE OPHANIM:** The archangel **Raphael.**

✤**PRINCE OF THE POWER OF AIR:** A title held by **Lucifer.**

✤**PRINCE OF THE PRESENCE: Metatron.**

✤**PRINCE OF THE PRIMORDIAL SEAS: Rahab.**

✤**PRINCE OF THE STARS:** The archangel **Michael** holds this title because of his position as leader of the **Celestial Army.** (Note: Angels are sometimes referred to as stars.)

✤**PRINCE OF THE TORAH: Metatron.**

✤**PRINCE(S) OF WATER:** Both **Anapiel YHWH** and **Ariael** are referred to as the Prince of Water.

✤**PRINCE OF WHEELS:** In 1 Enoch 19:1 **Rikbiel YHWH** is listed as the Prince of Wheels.

✤**PRINCEDOMS:** Another name for the class of angels called the **Principalities.** The Principalities are the guardians of all large groups on the earth.

✤**PRINCES WHO GUIDE THE WORLD:** In 3 Enoch, **Metatron** names the princes who guide the world. They are **Barakiel,** the angel of lightning; Bardiel, the angel of hail; **Gabriel,** the angel of fire; **Galgalliel,** the angel of the orb of the sun; **Kokabi'el,** the angel of stars; Lailiel, the angel of

night; Matriel, the angel of **rain; Opanniel,** the angel of the disk of the moon; Ra'amiel, the angel of thunder; **Ra'asiel,** the angel of **earthquakes; Rahatiel,** the angel of the **constellations;** Ruhiel, the angel of the **wind;** Shalgiel, the angel of snow; Shamshiel, the angel of day; Za'amiel, the angel of tornadoes; **Zaapiel,** the angel of **hurricanes;** Zi'iel, the angel of tremors; Ziquiel, the angel of the comets.

✦**PRINCIPALITIES:** An order of angels that ranks seventh in the angelic hierarchy. The Principalities are the guardians of all large groups on the earth including nations, great cities, religions, and large corporations. They are also called Princedoms and Integrating Angels. Ruling princes include **Nisroch,** Amael, **Haniel, Cervihel,** and Requel.

✦**PROCLAMATIONS, ANGEL OF:** The archangel **Gabriel.**

✦**PROCREATION:** Most religions teach that the angels came into being through **creation** and that they do not procreate. In the various religions of polytheism, there are many stories of the **gods and goddesses** producing offspring with mortals. However, this belief is not commonplace among the monotheistic religions. One account in Judaism does speak of angels procreating. However, this was done only after the angels took on fleshly bodies. It is the account of the **Watchers** who came to the earth to take wives and produce children. The children of these angels became giant mutants on earth and were referred to as evil spirits. They did not become angels.

✦**PROCREATION, ANGEL OF:** The archangel **Gabriel.**

✦**PROPHECY, ANGEL OF:** The archangel **Uriel.**

✦**PROSERPINA:** A she-demon who has several identities. In Rome she was a goddess. In Greece she was the Queen of Hades. In India she was **Kali.** To Christians she is Queen of the She-Demons.

✦**PROSERPINE:** A variation of the name **Proserpina.**

✦**PROSTITUTION, ANGELS OF:** Although they are demons, they are referred to as the angels of prostitution. They include **Agrat-bat-Mahlaht,** Eisheth Zenunim, **Lilith,** and **Naamah.**

✦**PROVIDENCE, ANGEL OF:** The archangel **Raphael.**

✦**PSALMS:** Scriptures from the Book of Psalms that reference angels are as follows: Psalms 8:5, "For you have made him a little lower than the angels, and have crowned him with glory and honor." Psalms 34:7, "The Angel of the Lord encamps around those who fear him, and delivers them." Psalms 35:5, "Let them be as chaff before the wind: and let the Angel of the Lord chase them." Psalms 35:6, "Let their way be dark and slippery: and let the Angel of the Lord persecute them." Psalms 68:17, "The chariots of God are twenty thousand, even thousands of angels: the Lord is among them, as in Sinai, in the holy place." Psalms 78:25, "Man did eat angels' food: he sent them meat to the full." Psalms 78:49, "He cast upon them the fierceness of his anger, wrath, and indignation, and trouble, by sending evil angels among them." Psalms 91:11, "For he will command his angels concerning you to guard you in all your ways." Psalms 103:20, "Bless the Lord, O you his angels, you mighty ones who do his bidding, obedient to his spoken word." Psalms 104:4, "Who makes his angels spirits; his ministers a flaming fire." Psalms 148:2, "Praise him, all his angels; praise him, all his host!" The angel **Asaph** is credited with writing Psalms 50 and Psalms 73–83 of the Bible.

✤**PSEUDEPIGRAPHA:** A group of scriptures not included in the Holy Canon. The Pseudepigrapha contain a substantial amount of information on angels, such as the fall of the angels, the names of angels, and their roles and functions in the Heavens. The scriptures were left out of the Holy Canon because of their questionable authorship. There is speculation that the scriptures were left out also because of the number of angels listed. The rabbis of the period thought the writings bordered on paganism because angels represented every function of the universe, just as the pagan **gods and goddesses** of the day did.

✤*PSEUDO MONARCHIA DAEMONIUM:* A book by Johann Weyer written in the sixteenth century. In it Weyer writes extensively about the underworld and the fallen angels that reside there.

✤**PSISYA:** See **Childbirth.**

✤**PSYCHIATRY, ANGEL OF: Kashdejan,** who taught mankind how to heal the mind.

✤**PSYCHOMPOI:** A variation of **Psychopomp.**

✤**PSYCHOPOMP:** The celestial escort in Zoroastrianism. The Psychopomp escort the souls of the dead to Heaven. Variations of Psychopomp are Psychompoi, Psychopompoi, and Psychopompus.

✤**PSYCHOPOMPOI:** A variation of **Psychopomp.**

✤**PSYCHOPOMPUS:** A variation of **Psychopomp.**

✤**PUNISHER, THE:** The angel Kolazanta is called the Punisher. He is one of the leaders of the angels of **destruction.**

✤**PUNISHMENT(S), ANGELS OF:** The Book of 2 Maccabees 15:23 states, "Sovereign of heaven, send a good angel before us to spread terror and dismay." The angels of punishment are angels that discipline the wicked on earth and in Hell. It was the angels of punishment who released the waters to **flood** the earth. They are also called angels of **destruction.** Their names are **Af,** Chitriel, **Dumah, Hemah, Kesef, Ksiel, Lahatiel, Makkiel, Mashhit,** Meshabber, **Pusiel,** and **Shaftiel.** In the Book of Ezekiel the angels of punishment are sent to the city of Jerusalem to punish the people for their sins. The account states, "And I heard God say to the other men, 'Follow him through the city and kill. Spare no one; have mercy on no one. Kill the old men, young men, young women, mothers, and children. But don't touch anyone who has the mark on his forehead.' " These would have been the angels that got sent to destroy **Sodom and Gomorrah.**

✤**PURE THOUGHT, ANGEL OF:** A title held by **Raziel.**

✤**PURIEL:** A variation of the name **Pusiel.**

✤**PURPLE, ANGEL OF:** One of two **colors** representing the angel **Sachiel.**

✤**PURPOSE ANGELS:** Angels who are called upon to aid people in finding their purpose in life.

✤**PURPOSE OF ANGELS:** According to Judaism, Christianity, and Islam, the purpose of angels is to praise and glorify God, to act as **mediators** between humankind and God, and to be administrators of the universe.

✤**PURUEL:** A variation of the name **Pusiel.**

✤**PUSIEL (FIRE):** An angel of punishment who has a reputation for being merciless in his torments of the wicked. Variations of the name Pusiel are Puriel and Puruel.

✤**PUTTI:** Baby angels. They are usually portrayed in art with wings, hovering around a beautiful woman. They became popular in art during the later part of the **Renaissance.** They were extremely popular during the Victorian era, and there has been a resurgence of them in artwork during the twentieth century. The **visionaries** of Medjugorje have reportedly seen them surrounding the **Virgin Mary** during her appearances. They are also called **Cherubs.**

✤**PYTHON:** An arch-demon. He is the Prince of the Lying Spirits. In Greek mythology he was a dragon.

There is a joy in the presence of the angels of God over one sinner who repents.

—LUKE 15:10

♣**QADDISIN:** High-ranking angels who are judges of the wicked in Heaven.

♣**QALBAM:** An angel who oversees the south **wind.**

♣**QAMIEL:** An angel who oversees the south **wind.**

♣**QANIEL:** An angel who oversees the south **wind.**

♣**QASPI'EL:** A guardian of the entrance to the seventh palace of Heaven, the palace of God. In 3 Enoch, Qaspi'el prevents the High Priest Rabbi Ishmael from entering the seventh palace and coming into the **presence** of God.

♣**QASPIEL:** An angel of **destruction.**

♣**QELIQALYAH:** One of the seventy-eight names of **Metatron.**

♣**QEMUEL:** A variation on the name **Camael,** a celestial prince of Heaven.

♣**QESEP:** A variation of the name **Qaspiel.**

♣**QUEEN OF ANGELS:** In Catholicism the **Virgin Mary** is the Queen of Angels. She was pronounced the Queen of Angels in 1954 by Pope Pius XII. In the Cabala the **Schechinah** (the female manifestation of God) is the Queen of Angels. The gnostics believed her to be the **Pistis-Sophia.**

♣**QUEEN OF FAIRIES:** See **Fairy Queen.**

✦**QUEEN OF HADES:** In Greece, Proserpina was the Queen of Hades. She later became a she-demon in Christian lore.

✦**QUEEN OF HEAVEN:** A title held by the **Virgin Mary.** In ancient times **Astarte** was called the Queen of Heaven.

✦**QUEEN OF PEACE:** A title held by the **Virgin Mary.** Daily the Virgin Mary brings messages of peace to six young **visionaries** in Medjugorje, a small town in Yugoslavia.

✦**QUEEN OF PROPHETS:** A title held by the **Virgin Mary.**

✦**QUEEN OF THE NORTHERN ANGELS OF DEATH: Brunnhilde,** who is the leader of the **Valkyries.**

✦**QUEEN OF THE SEA:** A title held by **Yemaya,** a guardian spirit of ancient African beliefs.

✦**QUEEN OF THE SHE-DEMONS: Proserpina.**

✦**QUEEN OF THE STARS:** A title held by the **Virgin Mary.**

✦**QUEEN OF THE UNDERWORLD: Proserpina.**

✦**QUEMEL:** A variation of the name **Camael.**

✦**QUESTHAVEN:** See **Religious Groups.**

✦**QUINCE TREE, ANGEL OF THE: Haniel.**

✦**QU'RAN, ANGELS OF THE:** See **Koran.**

God will put his angels in charge of you to protect you wherever you go.

—PSALMS 91:11

✢**RA'AMIEL:** The angel of thunder. A variation of the name Ra'amiel is Ra'miel.

✢**RA'ASIEL:** The angel of **earthquakes.** A variation of the name Ra'asiel is Rashiel.

✢**RACHMIAH:** See **Childbirth.**

✢**RACHMIEL:** See **Childbirth.**

✢**RACHSIEL:** Sec **Childbirth.**

✢**RADUERIEL:** A variation of the name **Radweri'el YHWH.**

✢**RADWERIEL:** A variation of **Radweri'el YHWH.**

✢**RADWERI'EL YHWH:** A **recording angel.** He is the heavenly archivist, the angel of the registry and keeper of the Book of Records. He is also angel of poetry, and the angel of muses. From every utterance of his mouth an angel is formed. These angels join the **ministering angels** in singing praises to God. Another name for Radweri'el YHWH is **Vrevoil.** Variations of the name Radweri'el YHWH are Radweriel and Radueriel.

✢**RAGIEL:** An angel who stands guard over the palace of **Raquia,** the **Second Heaven.**

✢**RAGUEL:** A variation of Raguil.

✢**RAGUIL (GOD'S FRIEND):** An angel who watches over the behavior of the angels. He was one of the angels who escorted **Enoch** on his tour of

Heaven and **Sheol**. According to the chronicles of Enoch, Raquil is one of the seven **archangels**. He was also assigned by God to guard the **Second Heaven**. In addition, he is listed as one of the angels that the Church of Rome reprobated in A.D. 745. Variations of his name are: **Akrasiel**, Raguel, **Rasuil**, and **Rufael**.

✤**RAGUILA:** An angel who served as an escort to **Enoch** on his journey to Heaven.

✤**RAHAB (VIOLENT TEMPERAMENT):** The angel of insolence. He is also the angel of the oceans. According to legend, God destroyed Rahab for attempting to prevent the Hebrews from crossing the **Red Sea** in their escape from **Pharaoh**'s soldiers.

✤**RAHAMAEL:** The angel of mercy and an angel of love. A variation of Rahamael is Rahmiel.

✤**RAHATIEL:** The angel of the **constellations**.

✤**RAHMIEL:** A variation of the name **Rahamael**.

✤**RAIN, ANGEL OF:** In Judaic lore it is **Matriel**. In Persian lore it is **Tishtrya**.

✤**RAINBOW, ANGEL OF THE:** See **Angel Crowned with a Rainbow**.

✤**RAIOUOTH:** An angel from the Testament of **Solomon**.

✤**RAKRAKYAH:** One of the seventy-eight names of **Metatron**.

✤**RAMA:** One of the **avatars** of Hindu lore.

✤**RAMAL:** See **Childbirth**.

✤**RAMAMIEL:** An angel who presides over the east **wind**.

✤**RAME'EL:** One of the leaders of the **Watchers** who came to earth to have sexual relations with women. A variation of the name Rame'el is Ram'el.

✤**RAM'EL:** A variation of **Rame'el**.

✤**RAMIAL:** One of the **Watchers** who came to the earth to have sexual relations with women.

✤**RA'MIEL:** A variation of the name **Ra'amiel**.

✤**RAMIEL:** From the **Book of Raziel**, he is an angel whose name can be found on charms worn by pregnant women. It is believed that the charm will aid them in having a safe and successful delivery. Ramiel is also a variation of the name **Rumael**.

✤**RAMPEL:** The angel of mountains and deep waters.

✤**RAMUEL:** See **Childbirth**.

✤**RAPHA:** The Hebrew word for "healer." The name **Raphael** derives from it and means "shining one who heals."

✤**RAPHAEL (SHINING ONE WHO HEALS):** One of the seven **archangels**. According to legend, his original name was Labbiel. God changed his name from Labbiel to Raphael when he sided with God on the issue of creating man. He is charged with healing mankind and the earth. It was Raphael who healed **Abraham** of the pain from being circumcised. He also cured **Jacob** after his hip was disjointed while wrestling with an angel. He is said to have given **Noah** a medical book containing cures for diseases, which legend says was the **Book of Razier.** In the Book of Tobit, Raphael travels under the alias of Azarias with the young **Tobias.** Azarias acts as a guide and protector of Tobias while on the journey. The Book of Raziel lists him as an amulet angel who is summoned at the time of **childbirth.** In his play *The Nativity*, **Longfellow** refers to Raphael as the "angel of the sun." He is said to be especially concerned about those who make religious pilgrimages for God. TITLES. Raphael holds many titles including the Angel of Love, Chief of the Guardian Angels, Ruler of the Sun, the Angel of Heat, the Guide of **Sheol,** Prince of the **Virtues,** the Angel of Science and Knowledge, Guardian of the **Tree of Life,** the Angel of **Sunday,** the Angel of Compassion, the Angel of Force, the Angel of the Sun, the Angel of the **Melon Bush,** the Angel of Baptismal Water, and the Angel of **Wednesday.** He is represented by the serpent, which is a symbol of **healing.** Other symbols for him include a vial of balm and an arrow. He is represented by the **colors** orange and light blue.

✦**RAPHAEL SANTI:** Major Italian **Renaissance** painter (1483–1520) who featured angels in his art. Some of his most famous paintings including angels are *Saint Michael Victorious*; *Triumph of Galatea*; *Sistine Madonna*; *Expulsion of Heliodorus from the Temple*; *Coronation of the Virgin*; *Virgin and Child with Saint Raphael and Saint Michael*; *Vision of Ezekiel*; and the frescoes of the Vatican.

✦**RAPITHWIN:** In Persian mythology he is the angel of the noon-day heat, and the months of summer. When the demon of **winter** comes, Rapithwin goes beneath the earth and warms the subterranean waters, to prevent the vegetation from dying. In Zoroastrianism, **Ahura Mazda** created the world at noon, and at the end of the world's history, the dead will be resurrected at noon. Because of this, Rapithwin is considered the angel of restoration.

✦**RAQUIA, ANGEL OF:** Raquia is the name of the **Second Heaven. Barakiel** is the ruling prince.

✦**RAQUIEL:** An angel who oversees the west **wind.**

✦**RARIDERIS:** An angel whose name can be found in the Testament of **Solomon.**

✦**RASH:** A variation of the name **Rashnu.**

✦**RASHIEL:** A variation of the name Ra'asiel, the angel of **earthquakes.**

✦**RASHIN:** A variation of the name **Rashnu.**

✢**RASHNU:** The angel of **justice** in Zoroastrianism. He weighs the deeds of the souls of humankind at their death. Variations of the name Rashnu are Rash, Rashin, and Rast.

✢**RAST:** A variation of the name **Rashnu.**

✢**RASUIL:** A variation of the name Raguil.

✢**RATHANAEL:** An angel from the Testament of **Solomon.** He is able to thwart the female demon Enepsigos, who changes form.

✢**RATZIEL:** A variation of the name **Raziel.**

✢**RAUM:** A variation of the name **Raym.**

✢**RAYM:** A fallen angel from the order of angels called the **Thrones.** He later became a chief demon of hell. He has a hatred for cities and goes about demolishing them with the thirty legions that he commands. He has been spotted among the ruins of desolated cities, in the form of a crow. A variation of the name Raym is Raum.

✢**RAZIEL:** An **archangel.** He holds many titles including Angel of the Secret Regions, Angel of Supreme Mysteries, Chief of the **Erelim,** and the Angel of Originality. He is also one of the ruling princes of the order of angels called **Thrones.** He is author of the famous **Book of Raziel,** which had cures for diseases and other information useful to mankind. It contained secrets to the mysteries of the universe, and fifteen hundred keys to the answers to these mysteries. **Noah** is said to have received information on how to build the Ark from it. In Heaven, Raziel spreads his wings over the **Hayyoth** so that their fiery breath does not incinerate the attending angels around God's throne. In early records he is called Jeremiel, which means "God's mercy." As Jeremiel he presided over the souls awaiting the **resurrection.** A variation of the name Raziel is Ratziel. Other names that Raziel is called by are Gallizur and Saraguil.

✢**RAZRAZYAH:** One of the seventy-eight names of **Metatron.**

✢**RECORDING ANGEL(S):** The famous American poet **Henry Wadsworth Longfellow** once wrote, "There are two angels that attend unseen each one of us, and in great books record our good and evil deeds." These angels are known as recording angels. They are the angels who write down both the good and wicked deeds of humans. In Judaism and Christianity, the recording angel is **Radweriel.** In Babylonian lore it was **Nabu.** In Muslim lore it is Moakibat. In Islam the **archangels** also act as recording angels.

✢**RECTORES MUNDORUM:** Divine spirits in **Chaldean** beliefs.

✢**RED, ANGEL OF:** The **color** red represents **Sammael.** Red is also the color of martyred saints.

✢**RED DRAGON:** A phrase used in some translations of the Bible when referring to **Satan** the Devil. The phrase is taken from Revelation

12:3–4. The *Good News Bible* states, "Another mysterious sight appeared in the sky. There was a huge red dragon with seven heads and ten horns and a crown on each of his heads. With his tail he dragged a third of the stars out of the sky and threw them down to the earth."

✤**Red Planet, Angel of the: Sammael.**

✤**Red Sea, Angel of the:** In the Bible, God parted the Red Sea so the Hebrews could cross as they fled **Pharaoh**'s soldiers. According to legend, the angel **Rahab** was destroyed for attempting to prevent the Hebrews from crossing the Red Sea. **Abezi,** a fallen angel who hates the Hebrews, is also a demon of the Red Sea.

✤**Reese, Della:** The costar of the 1995 television show *Touched by an Angel*. In the show Reese plays a wise heavenly messenger who brings the angel (played by Roma Downey) assignments from Heaven.

✤**Regent of God:** A title held by **Satan** the Devil.

✤**Regent of the Sun:** The archangel **Uriel.**

✤**Regents:** An order of angels found in **John Milton**'s poem *Paradise Regained*.

✤**Reiner, Carl:** In 1976, Carl Reiner starred in *Good Heavens*, a situation comedy that featured an angel as its hero. Reiner played the angel, who would grant the wishes of the guest stars on the show. The show ran one season.

✤**Reivtip:** An angel who works closely with the angel **Alimon** to prevent individuals from being harmed by **weapons** of war.

✤**Rekbiel:** A ruling angel of the **Ophanim.**

✤**Relationships, Angel of: Camael.**

✤**Religion(s), Angels of:** The order of angels called **Principalities** are in charge of protecting all of the great religions of the earth.

✤**Religions:** Angels play an important role in all of the world's great religions. In **Judaism,** angels guided **Abraham** and helped lead the Hebrews into the promised land. In **Christianity,** the archangel **Gabriel** announces to **Mary** that she will bear a son and will name him **Jesus.** Angels also rolled away the stone from the tomb of Christ and escorted him to Heaven. In **Islam,** angels are said to be present in the mosques recording the prayers of the righteous. The archangel **Jibril** appeared to **Muhammad** and dictated the **Koran** to him. Angels took Muhammad on a tour of Paradise. The polytheistic religions of the ancient world also had various winged beings and messengers among their pantheons. Eastern religions had angels among their beliefs as well. The various religions in which angels and angel-type deities can be found include **Buddhism,** Christianity, **Hinduism,** Islam, Judaism, **Manichaeism,** Shintoism and **Zoroastrianism.** The following cultures all included angels in their religious beliefs: the Arabs, **Aryans, Babylon**ians, **Chaldeans, Chinese,** Germans, Greeks, **Norsemen, Persians,** Romans and the Russians. See **Rome, Greece.**

✤**RELIGIOUS GROUPS:** Popular religious groups around the nation that focus on angels include *Angel Walk*, a nondenominational religious-metaphysical center, P.O. Box 1027, Riverton, WY 82501; *Opus Sanctorum Angelorum*, a Catholic organization, Marian Center, 134 Golden Gate Avenue, San Francisco, CA 94102; *Philangeli* (Friends of the Angels), a Catholic organization, 1115 E. Euclid Street, Arlington Heights, IL 60004; *Questhaven*, sponsors religious retreats and workshops that concentrate on angels, P.O. Box 20560, Escondido, CA 92029.

✤**RELIGIOUS MUSIC, MUSE OF:** In Greek mythology, the muse named Polyhymnia inspired men to write sacred and religious music.

✤**REMBRANDT HARMENSZOON VAN RIJN:** A major Dutch painter (1606–1669) considered one of Europe's greatest artists. He featured angels in many of his works. Some of his most famous paintings featuring angels include *The Angel and the Prophet Balaam; The Sacrifice of Isaac; The Angel Departing from the Family of Tobias; Presentation in the Temple; Jacob Wrestling with the Angel;* and *The Angel Appearing to the Shepherds* (etching).

✤**REMIEL:** A variation of the name **Jeremiel** and **Raziel.**

✤**RENAISSANCE:** The great revival of art, literature, and learning that took place in Europe during the fourteenth, fifteenth, and sixteenth centuries. During the Renaissance, angels in art flourished. They were portrayed as glorious beings and the embodiment of divine light. The depiction of angels with wings became popular, as did angels with **aureoles.** Artists began painting chubby little babies known as **Cherubs.** They also depicted angels playing musical instruments, such as **trumpets, harps,** cymbals, flutes, and violas, to symbolize the angels praising God.

✤**REORGANIZATION ANGELS: Angels** that assist individuals in making needed changes in their lives.

✤**REPENTANCE, ANGEL OF:** The archangel **Uriel.**

✤**REPLACEMENTS:** In Islam, seventy angels secretly oversee the administration of the world. They are selected by God, and their true identities are known only to God himself. At the death of one of these angels, God secretly selects another angel to replace him. The Islamic word for the **Replacements** is the Abdals.

✤**REPORTING ANGELS:** Angels who report to God the actions and conduct of humans on earth. The Karoz are reporting angels in Judaism. In

Islam, the reporting angels sit in the mosques listening to the prayers of men.

✦REPROBATED ANGELS: In 745 C.E. the Church of Rome reprobated seven angels. They are **Inias, Uriel, Raguel,** Saboac, Semibel, Tubuel, and Tubuas.

✦REQUEL: A ruling prince over the order of angels called **Principalities.**

✦REQUIEL: One of twenty-eight angels who preside over the **lunar mansions.**

✦RESCUERS: Guardian angels often appear at a moment's notice to rescue their charges from harm. They appear sometimes in human form, sometimes in the form of an animal, and sometimes as a voice or a vision. Many people have relayed experiences of being rescued by invisible hands, or through a dream that they had before the danger occurred.

✦RESTORATION, ANGEL OF: **Rapithwin,** an angel of Zoroastrian lore.

✦RESURRECTION, ANGEL OF THE: The archangel **Raziel. Raziel** presides over the souls who are awaiting the resurrection. **Gabriel** also is called the angel of the resurrection. At one time **Jeremiel** presided over the souls awaiting resurrection. In the Book of Matthew 22:30, Jesus compared the resurrected ones to the angels. He said, "For when the dead rise to life, they will be like the angels in Heaven and will not marry."

✦RESURRECTION OF JESUS: On the third day after the crucifixion of **Jesus,** two women by the name of Mary outside the sepulchre of Jesus witnessed an angel descending from Heaven. He had come to inform Jesus' followers that Jesus had been resurrected (Matthew 28:1–7). The Bible states, "After the Sabbath, as Sunday morning was dawning, Mary Magdalene and the other Mary went to look at the tomb. Suddenly there was a violent earthquake; an angel of the Lord came down from heaven, rolled the stone away, and sat on it. His appearance was like lightning, and his clothes were white as snow. The angel spoke to the women. 'You must not be afraid. I know you are looking for Jesus, who was crucified. He is not here; he has been raised, just as he said. Come here and see the place where he was lying. Go quickly now, and tell his disciples, he has been raised from death, and now he is going to Galilee ahead of you; there you will see him! Remember what I have told you.' "

✦RETRIBUTION, ANGELS OF: Twelve angels who mete out **punishment** to persons who sin against God. Only six are known: **Gabriel, Michael, Nathanel, Raphael, Uriel,** and **Satan** (before his fall from an act of rebellion).

✦RETSUTSIEL: An angel who stands guard over the palace of Sehaqim, the **Third Heaven.**

✤REVELATION, ANGEL OF: The archangel **Gabriel**. Gabriel brought a revelation of Islam to the prophet **Muhammad**.

✤REVELATION, ANGELS OF: Revelation is the twenty-seventh and last book of the Bible's New Testament. It was written circa A.D. 95 on Patmos by the apostle **John**. The Book of Revelation is a prophetic work given to John from God through an angel. Revelation tells of the great **war in Heaven** in which the archangel **Michael** and his army of angels battled against **Satan** and his demons. In the end Michael and the angels cast Satan and the demons out of Heaven and down to the earth (Revelation 12:7–10). The angels play important roles in the prophetic events outlined in Revelation. Primary angels include the Angels of the **Seven Trumpets.** As each of the seven angels sounds his **trumpet,** an apocalyptic event takes place on the earth (8:2, 6–13; 9:1–21; 11:15–19). There are the Angels of the **Seven Plagues** (15). The angels carry these plagues in **vials** (16:1). At God's command, each angel pours out the contents of these vials upon the earth. Other angels include the angels of the four winds (7:1); the **angel crowned with a rainbow** (10:1); the angel who carries the **little scroll** (10:8–10); the angel of the **Bottomless pit** (9:1, 11; 20:1); the angels of the **Euphrates River** (9:13–15); the Angel of the **gospel** (14:6); the angel who announces the fall of **Babylon the Great** (14:8); and the angel of the **harvest** (14:14–20). According to angel lore, the **Pistis-Sophia** is the **Bride of Christ** mentioned in Revelation 21:9 where it says, "Come, and I will show you the Bride, the wife of the Lamb." (Note: For a complete list of references to angels found in Revelation, see "Appendix 1: Biblical References to Angels.")

✤REVENGE, ANGELS OF: Angels who exact **punishment** on the wicked for God. They include **Gabriel, Michael, Nathanel, Raphael, Uriel,** and **Satan** (before his fall from an act of rebellion).

✤RHAMIEL: The name given to **Saint Francis of Assisi** when he was transformed into an angel in Heaven.

✤RHYX ACHONEOTH: The name of a demon listed in the Testament of **Solomon.**

✤RHYX AKTONME: A demon who causes pain in the ribs. He is listed in the Testament of **Solomon.**

✤RHYX ALATH: According to the Testament of **Solomon,** Rhyx Alath is a demon who causes the croup in infants.

✤RHYX ALEURETH: A demon whose name is found in the Testament of **Solomon.**

✤RHYX ANATRETH: A demon listed in the Testament of **Solomon.** He causes pain in the bowels of humans.

♣RHYX ANOSTER: A demon listed in the Testament of **Solomon.** He causes hysteria and also pains in the bladder.

♣RHYX AUDAMEOTH: A demon listed in the Testament of **Solomon.** He causes heart pain.

♣RHYX AUTOTH: A demon listed in the Testament of **Solomon.** He causes jealousy and arguments between lovers.

♣RHYX AXESBUTH: A demon listed in the Testament of **Solomon.** He causes hemorrhoids and diarrhea.

♣RHYX HAPAX: A demon listed in the Testament of **Solomon.** He causes **insomnia.**

♣RHYX ICHTHUON: A demon listed in the Testament of **Solomon.** He causes pain in the tendons.

♣RHYX MANTHADO: A demon listed in the Testament of **Solomon.** He causes pain in the kidneys.

♣RHYX MIANETH: A demon listed in the Testament of **Solomon.** He destroys houses and causes pains all over the body.

♣RHYX NATHOTHO: A demon listed in the Testament of **Solomon.**

♣RHYX PHTHENEOTH: A demon listed in the Testament of **Solomon.** He casts the **evil eye** on all men.

♣RHYX PHYSIKORETH: A demon listed in the Testament of **Solomon.** He causes long-term illness.

♣RHYX THE ENAUTHA: A demon listed in the Testament of **Solomon.** He alters hearts.

♣RIGAL: See **Childbirth.**

♣RIGHTEOUSNESS, ANGEL OF: The archangel **Michael.**

♣RIKBI'EL: A shortened version of **Rikbiel YHWH.**

♣RIKBIEL: A shortened version of **Rikbiel YHWH.**

♣RIKBIEL YHWH: One of the chief angels of Heaven, from the **Cherubim** class. He presides over the order of angels called **Wheels.** Shortened versions of the name Rikbiel YHWH are Rikbi'el and Rikbiel.

♣RILKE, RAINER MARIA: A notable German poet (1875–1926) who featured angels in his work. In his poem *Duino Elegies* (1923), angels represented a state of consciousness that surpassed the need for a physical existence, but found self-fulfillment in the invisible world. In this poem Rilke wrote, "Who if I cried out, would hear me among the angels' hierarchies? And even if one of them pressed me suddenly against his heart: I would be consumed in that overwhelming existence."

♣RIMMON (TO ROAR): A fallen **archangel** who became a demon of Hell. As an archangel he was the ruler of storms known throughout many different cultures. He was worshiped as an Aramaean god in Damascus; he was a deity in Syria; the god of thunder and lightning to the

Semites; a god called Barku in Assyria; a god named Tessub to the Kassites; and the god of storms in Babylon.

✤RISNUCH: The angel who presides over agriculture and farming.

✤RISWAN: An angel from Muslim lore. He guards the keys to the earthly paradise.

✤RITUAL ANGELS: Angels who assist humans with prayer time and other sacred periods established to build on spiritual pursuits. They are also called ceremonial angels.

✤RIVER OF FIRE: According to the Book of Enoch, the **ministering angels** all bathe in the river of fire.

✤RIVERS, ANGEL OF: In Persian mythology Dara is the angel of rivers.

✤RIZOEL: An angel from the Testament of **Solomon.**

✤ROCK OF GOD: The angel **Turiel** is also referred to as the Rock of God.

✤ROD OF GOD: The meaning of the name Chitriel. Chitriel is an angel of **punishment.**

✤ROFOCALE: A fallen angel. He is the Prime Minister of Hell and oversees all of the material wealth of mankind.

✤ROMAN CATHOLIC CHURCH, ANGEL OF THE: The archangel **Michael.**

✤ROME: Angelic-type deities can be found amongst the **gods and goddesses** of Rome. Two were **archetypal angels** for the monotheistic religions that came later. There was the winged god **Mercury,** who carried messages between Heaven and earth for Jupiter (the Supreme Being), and **Cupid,** the winged **god of love.** Romans also held the belief that a guardian spirit was assigned to each person at birth. This spirit was thought to protect the individual from harm. **Proserpina,** one of Christianity's most notorious she-demons, was once a goddess of Rome. Romans also believed that each household had a **lare** (guardian spirit) watching over the family. The lare was believed to be the spirit of the family's founder. The lare was credited as the source of the family's creativity and was considered a part of their everyday life. Centuries later Rome converted to Christianity and adopted the Christian beliefs in angels. In 745 C.E. the Church of Rome reprobated seven angels: **Inias,** the archangel **Uriel, Raguel,** Saboac, Tubuel, Tubuas, and Semibel. The guardian angel of Rome is **Sammael.**

✤ROOTS, ANGELS OF: The angel **Agniel** taught humans to use roots for magical purposes. In addition, **Amasras** brought the knowledge of the various uses of roots to mankind. This knowledge was forbidden to mortal man and was part of the reason these two angels fell from God's favor.

✤ROSA OF VITERBO: See **Saint Rosa of Viterbo.**

✤ROSE RED, ANGEL OF: Rose red is the color that represents the archangel **Michael.**

✤**Rosicrucian(s), Angels of the:** The Rosicrucians were a group of people from the seventeenth and eighteenth centuries who followed the esoteric teachings of Rosenkruetz. In Rosicrucian writings, angels were described as being like suns with an aura of brilliant energy, giving off streamers of power.

✤**Royal Blue, Angel of:** Royal blue is the **color** that represents the angel **Sachiel.**

✤**Rsassiel:** See **Childbirth.**

✤**Ruah Pisqonit:** One of the seventy-eight names of **Metatron.**

✤**Ruax:** A demon who takes pleasure in causing headaches in humans.

✤**Rudolph Steiner:** See **Steiner, Rudolph.**

✤**Rufael:** A variation of the name **Raguil.**

✤**Ruhiel:** The angel of the **wind.**

✤**Ruler of Evil Spirits:** A title held by the demon **Mastema.**

✤**Ruler of Fire: Adramalec.** He is called the **ruler of fire** because of his association with fire sacrifices.

✤**Ruler of Sheol: Beliar.**

✤**Ruler of the Demons: Beelzebub.** Beelzebub, who is sometimes equated with **Satan,** was referred to as the ruler of the demons three times in the Bible's New Testament. Matthew 12:24 says, "But when the Pharisees heard it, they said, 'It is only by Beelzebub, the ruler of the demons, that this fellow casts out the demons.'" Mark 3:22 says, "And the scribes who came down from Jerusalem said, 'He has Beelzebub, and by the ruler of the demons he casts out demons.'" Luke 11:15 states, "But some of them said, 'He casts out demons by Beelzebub, the ruler of the demons.'" (Note: In some translations Beelzebub is Beelzeboul.)

✤**Ruler of the Sun:** A title held by the archangel **Raphael.**

✤**Rulers:** An order of angels found in the hierarchy of angels conceived by **Saint John of Damascus.**

✤**Rumael:** One of five angels of **judgment** who lead the souls of man to the judgment of God, at the end of the world. A variation of the name Rumael is Ramiel.

✤**Rum'el:** One of the angels who brought the secret knowledge of Heaven to earth.

✤**Rumial:** An angel who stands guard over the palace of Makon, the **Sixth Heaven.**

✤**Rumiel:** See **Childbirth.**

✤**Rumyal:** One of the angels who went against God's wishes and brought the secret knowledge of Heaven to humans.

✤**Rune Stones, Angel of:** Eistibus.

✤**Ruyail:** An angel summoned in Arabic exorcism ceremonies.

Make friends with the angels.

—Saint Augustine

✤**Sabael:** An angel from the Testament of **Solomon.** He is the only angel able to overpower the demon Sphendonael, who causes tetanic recurvation (a disease that causes the body to draw back and stiffen).

✤**Sabaoth:** One of the seven **Archons** of gnosticism.

✤**Sabbath:** An high-ranking angel of Judaic lore. Other angels pay tribute to him as he sits upon his lofty throne. He is also the angel of the Sabbath.

✤**Sabbath, Angel of the:** Sabbath.

✤**Saboac:** One of seven angels that the Church of Rome reprobated in 745 C.E.

✤**Sabrael:** An angel listed as one of the seven **archangels** in the Testament of **Solomon.**

✤**Sabriel:** An angel who stands guard over the palace of Wilon, the **First Heaven.**

✤**Sabsebibyah:** One of the seventy-eight names of **Metatron.**

✤**Sachiel:** In **Essene** beliefs Sachiel was the angel of water. He is also one of the angels of the hours of the day and night.

✤**Sachiel-Meleck:** An angel who protects priests.

✤**Sachluph:** The angel who oversees **plants.**

✤**SACRED MUSIC, MUSE OF:** In Greek mythology, Polyhymnia inspired men to write sacred and religious music.

✤**SACRIFICE OF ISAAC, ANGEL OF THE:** As a test of faith, God commanded **Abraham** to offer his son, **Isaac,** as a sacrifice. Obediently, Abraham took Isaac to the designated spot, built an altar, bound him, and placed him on the altar. When he picked up the knife to slay him, an angel of the Lord called to him from Heaven saying, "Abraham, Abraham, do not hurt the boy or do anything to him. Now I know that you honor and obey God, because you have not kept back your only son from him" (Genesis 22:12). Abraham looked up and saw a ram caught in a thicket by its horns. He then took the ram and offered it as a sacrifice instead of his son.

✤**SAGITTARIUS, ANGEL OF: Adnachiel.** Ayil and Sizajasel are also angels of Sagittarius.

✤**SAHAQI'EL:** The ruling prince of the **Fourth Heaven** (Zebul).

✤**SAHAQUIEL:** The angel of the **sky.**

✤**SAHRIEL:** An angel who stands guard over the palace of Raquia, the **Second Heaven.**

✤**SAHSAHYAH:** One of the seventy-eight names of **Metatron.**

✤**SAINT(S):** According to the *American Heritage Dictionary,* a saint is "a person officially recognized by canonization, as being entitled to public veneration and capable of interceding for people on earth." In Heaven they are semi-angelic beings who minister to God and mediate between God and humans on earth. The **Virgin Mary** (an angel of the class of **Virtues**) is the chief saint. However, angels are also counted as saints. Saint **Michael** (the archangel **Michael**) is one of the most popular. Throughout history many saints, while still on earth, have communicated with angels. Many received visitations from angels regularly. Some of the most famous accounts are found among the Italian saints. **Saint Agnes of Montepulciano** communicated with angels throughout her life. She was even given Communion from angels so that her discussions with God would not be interrupted. An angel regularly visited **Saint Claire of Montefalco** at night, allowing her to listen to heavenly music. **Saint Frances of Rome** was regularly visited by her guardian angels. An angel often appeared to **Saint Rosa of Viterbo** to bring her predictions of the future. **Saint Francis of Assisi** received the stigmata from an angel. **Saint Catherine of Siena** entered public life after receiving a vision of angels. According to the Book of Revelation 8:3, the prayers of the saints are offered to God on a **golden altar**: "An angel with a golden censer came and stood at the altar; he was given a great quantity of incense to offer with the prayers of all the Saints on the golden altar that is before the throne."

✦**SAINT AGNES OF MONTEPULCIANO:** An Italian saint (1268–1317). Born in Gracchiano Vecchio, Tuscany, she entered the convent at Montepulciano when she was just nine years old. She became famous for her visions and her performance of miracles. Throughout her life she was visited by angels. She is said to have been given Communion from angels at least ten times in order to avoid having to interrupt her discussions with God. At troublesome points in her life, she was comforted by these visions of angels. In one vision she reportedly held the baby Jesus in her arms. In another vision the angels instructed her to build a monastery, and she complied. She died in the convent at Montepulciano. She was canonized in 1726.

✦**SAINT AMBROSE:** Bishop of Milan, and Doctor of the Church (340?–397). He authored many theological works including *Apologia Prophet David*, 5, in which he ranked the **orders of angels** as follows: (1) **Seraphim**, (2) **Cherubim**, (3) **Dominations** (4) **Thrones**, (5) **Principalities**, (6) **Powers**, (7) **Virtues**, (8) **Archangels**, (9) **Angels.**

✦**SAINT ANGELA OF FOLIGNO:** An Italian medieval mystic (c. 1248–1309) who frequently had visions of angels. Born in Foligno, Italy, she married a well-to-do man and had several children. In 1285 she was converted to Christianity after receiving a vision. Up to that point she had led a superficial life. The vision changed her entire life. After confessing her sins, she dedicated her life to God. She gave away all of her worldly possessions after her husband died and devoted herself to living a purely spiritual life. She often had vivid visions of the Passion and death of Jesus Christ. When she would see him, he was accompanied by angels.

✦**SAINT ATHANASIUS:** Patriarch of Alexandria, Doctor of the Church (c. 293–373). In 360 he authored the book *The Life of Anthony*, about a hermit named Anthony. It was designed to instruct monks on how to resist temptation and how to protect themselves against Satan and the demons.

✦**SAINT AUGUSTINE:** Doctor of the Church, bishop of Hippo (354–430). Saint Augustine believed that the angels were created simultaneously with the creation of Heaven and earth. He also believed that the angels bred like flies. He once wrote, "Every visible thing in this world is put in the charge of an angel." In defining the role of the angels, Saint Augustine wrote, "The name Angel refers to their office, not their nature. You ask the name of this nature, it is spirit; you ask its office, it is that of an Angel, which is a messenger."

✦**SAINT BONAVENTURE:** Italian scholastic theologian, known as the

Seraphic Doctor (c. 1217–1274). Bonaventure wrote theological doctrines on the angels, the spiritual world, and Heaven. He believed that angels, although belonging to the same species, were each different. He held that even though angels are spiritual in nature, they are still in need of sustenance from God. He believed that angels, just as humans, are subject to change.

✢**SAINT CATHERINE OF SIENA:** Italian Dominican mystic and diplomat (1347–1380). Saint Catherine entered public life after receiving a vision. Her love for God and humanity was so great that she desired to become "an earthly angel" to help those in need. At thirty-three she died from anorexia and malnutrition because she ate only Communion wafers. According to **Joan of Arc,** Saint Catherine was one of the angels who encouraged her to help the Dauphin.

✢**SAINT CLAIRE OF MONTEFALCO:** An Italian saint (c. 1268–1308) known as Sister Claire of the Cross because of her love of the crucified Christ. She was said to have been beautiful and from a wealthy family. However, because of her love of God, she chose to become a nun. She regularly received visions of angels, who appeared to her as youths. The angels appeared to her often accompanying Jesus in visions. They appeared to her in visions of the nativity, the crucifixion, and the **resurrection** of Christ. It is said that Jesus gave her Communion privately in her room, and when he came to do so, he was escorted by angels. An angel would come and visit Claire and her sister Joan (also a nun) at night, allowing them to listen to the music of Heaven. Nuns were said to have witnessed her room becoming illuminated when the angels appeared. She was canonized in 1881.

✢*SAINT DOMINIC:* The name of a famous painting featuring angels by Florentine painter **Fra Angelico.** Today the painting hangs in the Louvre.

✢**SAINT FRANCES OF ROME:** An Italian saint (1384–1440). Throughout her life Saint Frances of Rome experienced many visions and ecstasies that included angels. Angels are said to have accompanied her throughout her life. She saw her first guardian angel when he saved the lives of her and her sister-in-law Vannozza, when they fell into the Tiber River. She described him as having shining eyes, long hair, and wearing a white tunic. He stayed with her for twenty-three years. Afterward, a second guardian appeared to her. She believed him to be from a higher order of angels. He stayed with her until her death. Visible only to her, he sometimes appeared spinning a thread of gold. The thread represented her life. As her life neared its end, she could see the angel spinning faster, until finally, her life ended. She was canonized in 1608.

✤SAINT FRANCIS DE SALES: French Roman Catholic preacher (1567–1622), Doctor of the Church, key figure in the Catholic Reformation in France. About angels de Sales once said, "Make yourself familiar with angels, and behold them frequently in spirit; for, without being seen, they are present with you."

✤SAINT FRANCIS OF ASSISI: Roman Catholic saint (1182–1226), founder of the Franciscan order, patron saint of Italy. In 1224, Saint Francis of Assisi received the stigmata by an angel while meditating on Mount Verna. As he was meditating, he saw a **Seraph** swiftly descending from Heaven. The Seraph had six fiery wings. An image of a crucified man appeared between the wings. Two of the wings came from the angel's head, two were used for flying, and two covered the body of the angel. Saint Francis grieved at the sight of the crucified man. As he watched, wounds opened in Saint Francis's hands, feet, and chest. The wounds looked as though they had been caused by nails. Saint Francis also had other experiences with angels. Once as he lay ill in bed, the angels comforted him by appearing to him and playing music. Legend has it that after he died, he was transformed into an angel of mercy and renamed Rhamiel.

✤SAINT GABRIEL: See **Gabriel.**

✤SAINT GREGORY NAZIANZEN: Cappadocian theologian (c. 330–390), Doctor of the Church, one of the Four Fathers of the Greek Church. According to *Compton's Living Encyclopedia*, Saint Gregory's writings "contain the best statement of doctrine of Trinity in Greek Orthodox theology." It also calls him "a graceful and powerful expounder." About angels he once said, "The angel is then called spirit and fire: spirit, as being a creature of the intellectual sphere; fire, as being of a purifying nature; for I know that the same names belong to the first nature. But, relatively to us at least, we must reckon the angelic nature incorporeal, or at any rate as nearly so as possible."

✤SAINT GREGORY THE GREAT: Saint Gregory the Great (c. 540–604) was pope from 590 to 604. He had visions of the archangel **Michael.** In one famous account, during a scourge of Rome he saw Michael descending on top of the monument of the Emperor Hadrian. He interpreted the vision to mean that the scourge would cease. Because of this he named the monument the Castel Sant'Angelo. In addition, he authored many theological works, including *Homilia*, in which he ranked the **orders of angels** as follows: (1) **Seraphim,** (2) **Cherubim,** (3) **Thrones,** (4) **Dominations,** (5) **Principalities,** (6) **Powers,** (7) **Virtues,** (8) **Archangels,** (9) **Angels.**

✤SAINT JEROME: Christian scholar, Father of the Church, and Doctor of the Church (c. 347–420?). Saint Jerome ranked the **orders of angels** as follows: (1) **Seraphim,** (2) **Cherubim,** (3) **Powers,** (4) **Dominions,** (5) **Thrones,** (6) **Archangels,** (7) **Angels.**

❖**SAINT JOHN OF DAMASCUS:** Syrian theologian (c. 675–c. 749), Doctor of the Church, Father of the Church. In his writing *De Fide Orthodoxa*, Saint John ranked the **orders of angels** as follows: (1) **Seraphim,** (2) **Cherubim,** (3) **Thrones,** (4) **Dominions,** (5) **Powers,** (6) **Authorities,** (7) **Rulers,** (8) **Archangels,** (9) **Angels.**

❖**SAINT MICHAEL:** See **Michael.**

❖**SAINT PATRICK:** Christian missionary, the Apostle of Ireland (c. 385–461). An angel named Victorius is said to have visited Saint Patrick once a week to converse. The angel asked Saint Patrick to go to Ireland and convert the pagans to Christianity. Saint Patrick listened to the angel and went to Ireland, where he made many converts. Says the *Concise Columbia Encyclopedia*, "By his death, Ireland was Christianized."

❖**SAINT PAUL:** See **Paul.**

❖**SAINT RAPHAEL:** See **Raphael.**

❖**SAINT ROSA OF VITERBO:** An Italian saint (1234–1252). She had a vision of the **Virgin Mary** when she was just eight years old. At the age of twelve she started preaching in the streets. Throughout her life, an angel appeared to her bringing predictions of future events. She died at the age of seventeen. She was canonized in 1457.

❖**SAINT TERESA OF AVILA:** Spanish Carmelite nun (1515–1582), Doctor of the Church, and one of the great mystics. She was a leading figure in the Catholic Reformation. In 1562 she founded, at Avila, the convent of the Discalced Carmelites. In 1555 she began having visions and hearing voices. This greatly disturbed her. However, in 1557 she began seeing Saint Peter of Alcántara for spiritual advice and guidance. Saint Peter convinced her that the voices she heard were from the angels and were authentic. Afterward, she was visited regularly by the angels.

❖**SAINT THOMAS AQUINAS:** Italian philosopher (1225–1274), theologian, and Doctor of the Church. He was called the Angelic Doctor because of his discourses on angels. He authored the *Summa Theologica*, considered one of the foundational texts on the hierarchy of angels. Aquinas believed that the angels were necessary to fill the gap between God and mankind. He held that the angels were pure intellect, neither male nor female, but able to assume either form. He taught that both humans and angels have their places in the universe, that both have a duty in exemplifying God's glory. He contended that angels knew everything, except those decisions that depended on human choice, and knowledge held only by God. According to Aquinas, countless numbers of angels exist, and they are immortal.

✤SAKNIEL: An angel who safeguards the west **wind.**

✤SAKRIEL: An angel who stands guard over the palace of Raquia, the **Second Heaven.**

✤SALAMANDERS: **Elemental** spirits who rule fire. They manifest in the form of a lizard. The ruler of the salamanders is **Michael.**

✤SALBABIEL: An angel who aids individuals in obtaining the love of a desired one. His name can be found written on Aramaic **love charms.**

✤SALGIEL: A variation of the name **Shalgiel.**

✤SALMAEL: A **fallen angel** who has a strong hatred for the Hebrews.

✤SALSALYAH: One of the seventy-eight names of **Metatron.**

✤SALT, ANGELS OF: In ceremonial magic the angel Aboezra is considered a holy angel. He is invoked to consecrate **salt.** The angel Existon is also invoked in the blessing of salt.

✤SAMAEL: A variation of the name **Sammael.**

✤SAMANDIRIEL: The angel of fertility in Mandaean mythology.

✤SAMCHIA: See **Childbirth.**

✤SAMCHIEL: See **Childbirth.**

✤SAMEVEEL: A **fallen angel.**

✤SAMIEL: One of the five angels of **judgment.** He leads the souls of men to stand before the judgment of God.

✤SAMKI'EL: An angel of **destruction.** He is also responsible for escorting the souls of the wicked from Heaven to **Sheol.**

✤SAMMAEL: An angel from the **Seraphim** class who is considered both good and evil. In 3 Enoch, **Metatron** calls him the "greatest of all the princes of the kingdoms in Heaven." It was Sammael whom God sent to retrieve **Moses'** soul when he died. He is also said to be the angel who wrestled with **Jacob** at Peniel. As a good angel, he is responsible for strengthening the weak. He is also the ruler of the **Fifth Heaven,** the Ruler of Mars, and Angel of the Kermes Oak tree. As a dark angel he enjoys making the strong weak. In *The Sayings of Rabbi Elieze*, he is the serpent who tricked **Eve** in the **Garden of Eden.** He then seduced her and impregnated her with her firstborn son, Cain. In 3 Baruch he is the angel who planted the **vine.** In one legend he records the misdeeds of Israel so they can be accused before God. The Sumerians called him the **Bright and Poisonous One.** In the **Cabala,** he is one of the **Unholy Sefiroth.** In rabbinical lore, he is the Angel of Death. He is sometimes equated with **Satan.** Variations of the name **Sammael** are Samael and Samuel.

✤**SAMOILA:** An angel assigned by God to escort **Enoch** on his journey to Heaven. A variation of the name Samoila is Semeila.

✤**SAMSON:** An Israelite hero whose birth was foretold by an angel. In the Book of Judges, Samson's birth was foretold by an angel of the Lord who first appeared to Samson's mother. He told her that she would become pregnant and give birth to a son. He instructed her not to drink any alcohol and not to eat unclean foods. He told her never to cut the child's hair, and that the boy would be "dedicated to God as a Nazirite." He also told her that her son would deliver the Hebrews from the Philistines. Worried about what she had seen and been told by the angel, she told her husband, **Manoah.** Manoah prayed to God, and later the angel reappeared to Manoah and his wife together, bringing the same message that he had delivered earlier. When Manoah asked the angel what his name was, the angel said that it was "unknowable." Judges (13:1–18)

✤**SAMUEL:** A variation of the name **Sammael.**

✤**SANASEL:** In Mandaean beliefs, the angel Sanasel stood at the entrance to Heaven and offered up prayers for souls.

✤**SANCTIFICATION, ANGELS OF:** The equivalent of the angels of the **presence.**

✤**SANCTITY, ANGEL OF: ANANCHEL.**

✤**SANDALPHON:** A variation of the name **Sandolphon.**

✤**SANDOLFON:** A variation of the name **Sandolphon.**

✤**SANDOLPHON:** According to lore, Sandolphon was once the prophet **Elijah,** who is said to have been turned into this great angelic prince in Heaven. He is also the twin brother of **Metatron,** the King of Angels. He is the angel of **tears** and is said to be particularly concerned about the welfare of mankind. In Judaic lore he is one of the **Sarim. Longfellow** referred to him as the "angel of prayer" and the "angel of glory." Variations of the name Sandolphon are Sandalphon and Sandolfon.

✤**SANGARIAH:** The angel of fasting.

✤**SANSENOY:** One of the three angels sent to bring **Lilith** back to **Adam** (Senoy and Semangelof are the other two). The name Sansenoy appears on amulets made to protect pregnant women and infants from the revenge of Lilith, who hates all mortal women and their offspring.

✤**SANTI, RAPHAEL:** See **Raphael Santi.**

✤**SAPHTHORAEL:** A demon who causes dissension among men.

✤**SAPSAPI'EL:** One of the seventy-eight names of **Metatron.**

✤**SAPSAPYAH:** One of the seventy-eight names of **Metatron.**

✤**SAQPAS:** One of the seventy-eight names of **Metatron.**

✤**SAQPUS:** One of the seventy-eight names of **Metatron.**

✦**SARABOTES:** One of the rulers of the angels of **air.**

✦**SARAGAEL:** One of the angels of **earth.**

✦**SARAGUIL:** Another name for **Raziel.**

✦**SARAH:** The wife of **Abraham.** In the Book of Genesis, three angels visited Abraham. The angels informed him that his wife, Sarah, who was barren and old, would give birth to a son. One of the angels said, "Nine months from now I will come back, and your wife, Sarah, will have a son." When Sarah heard the angel reveal this to Abraham, she laughed, saying to herself, "Now that I am old and worn-out, can I still enjoy sex? And besides, my husband is old, too." The angel asked Abraham, "Why did Sarah laugh? Is anything too hard for God? As I said, nine months from now I will return, and Sarah will have a son." Because Sarah was afraid of the angel, she denied it, saying, "I didn't laugh." But the angel said, "Yes, you did. You laughed." (Genesis 18:9–15)

✦**SARAKIKAIL:** An Arabic angel summoned in ceremonies involving exorcisms.

✦**SARAKUYAL:** A **fallen angel.**

✦**SARAQAEL:** One of the **archangels.**

✦**SARAQUEL:** A ruling prince of the **Seraphim.** Saraquel is also a variation of the name **Sariel.**

✦**SARASAEL:** The angel who spoke to **Noah** after the flood. He told Noah to plant the **vine** and to change its name.

✦**SARHMAIL:** An Arabic angel summoned in exorcism ceremonies.

✦**SARIEL (GOD'S COMMAND):** One of the seven **archangels** listed in the chronicles of **Enoch.** He is also the angel of death and is sometimes called the Prince of the **Presence.** He is responsible for reprimanding angels who transgress God's laws. According to one legend, Sariel is a fallen archangel who was cast out of Heaven for revealing the secrets of the moon. He is said to have taught these secrets to the Canaanite priestesses. Sariel is also listed as one of the **Watchers** who came to earth to have sexual relations with women. Variations of the name Sariel are Saraquel, Suriel, Suriyel, and Zerachiel.

✦**SARIM:** A high order of angels. In Hebrew the word Sarim means "angelic princes." Their ruler is Tagas.

✦**SARPUPIRIN:** One of the seventy-eight names of **Metatron.**

✦**SASGABIEL:** An angel who overpowers evil spirits in exorcisms.

✦**SASNIGI'EL YHWH:** An angel from the **Seraphim** class. He is listed in 3 Enoch as a great prince of Heaven.

✦**SASOMASPE'EL:** One of the leaders of angels who came to the earth to have sexual relations with women.

✦**SASRASYAH:** One of the seventy-eight names of **Metatron.**

✤SATAN (OPPOSER): God's adversary, also known as the Devil. Satan and his followers are credited with causing all of the evil in the world. According to Christian lore, he was once one of God's perfect angels, who eventually came to think a great deal of himself. He was the Anointed Cherub and was considered the most beautiful of all the angels. He was so spectacular that he thought he should be worshiped as a god. To achieve this, he sought out the newly created mortals Adam and Eve. He knew that eventually the whole earth would be filled with people who worshiped God. He wanted this worship for himself. He used the guise of a serpent to trick Eve into disobedience to God. When he spoke to her, he accused God of lying to her and her husband, Adam. He also accused God of holding back knowledge from them. This was a lie and it made him a devil, which means "slanderer," and Satan, which means "opposer." Ever since then, Satan has been competing with God for the worship of humans. He does this by attempting to lead them into wrongdoing and away from God. He has been so successful in getting humankind to worship him that he was able to offer Jesus all the kingdoms of the world if he would fall down and perform an act of worship to him (Matthew 4:8–9). In 2 Corinthians 11:14 we read that Satan can appear as an angel of light. It says, "Even Satan disguises himself as an angel of light." In Islamic beliefs, Satan (Iblis) became the adversary because he refused to bow down and worship Adam, whom God had placed above the angels. In Dante's poem The Divine Comedy, Satan is portrayed as the greatest of all the Seraphim. In the Book of Revelation 12:3, 7–9, he is referred to as the "great dragon." According to the writings of Monsignor Corrado Balducci, Satan is a component in God's plan of salvation. Balducci believed that God is using Satan as a tool for the perfecting of humankind, through his temptations. He held that humankind, in the end, would triumph over Satan's temptations and achieve perfection. The titles held by Satan include the Angel of Evil, Father of the Lie, Prince of Darkness, Prince of Shadows, Prince of Evil, God of the Underworld, Prince of Lies, Prince of Deception, Prince of Evil Spirits, and Keeper of Hell. In the Cabala he is called Samael. In Zoroastrianism he is Ahaitin (also Angra Mainyu). He uses many aliases including Abaddon, Sammael, Beliar, Beelzebub, Azaz'el, and Mastema. The female equivalent of Satan is Leviathan. Variations of the name Satan are Satanel and Satanail.

✤SATANAEL: A variation of the name Satan.

✤SATANAIL: A variation of the name Satan.

✤SATANEL: A variation of the name Satan.

✤SATHARIEL: One of the Unholy Sefiroth of the Cabala.

✤SATQI'EL: The ruling prince of the **Fifth Heaven.**

✤SATRINA: One of many aliases used by the she-demon **Lilith.**

✤SATURDAY, ANGEL OF: **Kepharel** and **Casziel** are both angels of Saturday. The angels who preside over the hours of the day on Saturday are: 1:00-Casziel, 2:00-**Sachiel,** 3:00-**Sammael,** 4:00-**Michael,** 5:00-**Haniel,** 6:00-**Raphael,** 7:00-**Gabriel,** 8:00-Casziel, 9:00-Sachiel, 10:00-Samael, 11:00-Michael, 12:00-**Haniel.** The angels who preside over the hours of the night are: 1:00-Raphael, 2:00-Gabriel, 3:00-Casziel, 4:00-Sachiel, 5:00-Sammael, 6:00-Michael, 7:00-Haniel, 8:00-Raphael, 9:00-Gabriel, 10:00-Casziel, 11:00-Sachiel, 12:00-Sammael.

✤SATURN, ANGEL OF: Officially the angel of Saturn is **Kafziel.** However, in some sources **Haniel** and also **Tzaphqiel** are given as the angel of Saturn.

✤SAVITAR: One of the **Adityas** (angels) of Vedic beliefs.

✤SAVLIAL: An angelic prince who resides in the **Third Heaven.**

✤SCALES, ANGELS OF THE: **Abyatur** is the angel of the scales used to weigh the good and evil deeds of mortal men.

✤SCAPEGOAT, ANGEL OF THE: According to legend, every year on the **Day of Atonement,** the Jews pushed a goat off the desert cliff at Haradan. This was a scapegoat for the Jews, who believed that the goat transferred their sins to the fallen angel **Azaz'el,** who was believed to be trapped beneath a pile of boulders at the bottom of the cliff.

✤SCEPTER: An ornamental rod. **Archangels** are often depicted in art carrying a scepter, which symbolizes their authority. Scepter is also the name of a doglike demon from the Testament of **Solomon.** He plots evil deeds and leads men into stupidity. He is thwarted by the angel Briathos.

✤SCHACHNIEL: See **Childbirth.**

✤SCHECHINAH: The female manifestation of God. The Cabala names the Schechinah as the **Queen of Angels.** The gnostics believed her to be **Pistis-Sophia.** According to the **Zohar,** the world and all creatures within it were created by the Schechinah. Judaic lore tells us that the Torah was created to bring the Schechinah back into a relationship with God. A variation of the name Schechinah is Shekinah.

✤SCHELIEL: One of the twenty-eight angels who preside over the **lunar mansions.**

✤SCHOOL OF THE ANGELS: See **Angelic School.**

✤SCIENCE AND KNOWLEDGE, ANGEL OF: The archangel **Raphael.**

✤SCOLDING, ANGEL OF: **Amaliel.**

✤SCORPIO, ANGEL OF: **Barbiel.**

✤SCROLL(S): See **Codex, Little Scroll.**

✤SEA(S), ANGELS OF: In the Talmud, **Rahab** is the angel of the sea.

✤**SEA ANIMALS, ANGEL OF**: Manakel.

✤**SEA MONSTER, ANGEL OF THE**: When the fallen angel **Forneus** is invoked, he appears to men as a sea monster.

✤**SEAL RING**: The magical ring that God sent to King **Solomon** by the archangel **Michael** to give him power over the demons.

✤**SEALTIEL**: In Christian Gnostic beliefs, Sealtiel is one of the seven **archangels.**

✤**SEASICKNESS, DEMON OF**: In the Testament of **Solomon** Kunopegos is the demon of the sea. He delights in causing seasickness. He can be prevented from carrying out his evil deed by the angel **Iameth.**

✤**SEASONS**: See **Four Seasons.**

✤**SEBAR SUHASYAH**: One of the seventy-eight names of **Metatron.**

✤**SECOND ANGEL**: In 2 Enoch, **Adam** is referred to as the "second angel." See **Second Angel of the Trumpets.**

✤**SECOND ANGEL OF THE TRUMPETS**: In the book of Revelation, there are seven angels with **trumpets.** One at a time, each angel sounds his trumpet and an apocalyptic event takes place on the earth. Revelation 8:8–9 tells us that when the second angel sounded his trumpet, "something resembling a huge burning mountain was thrown into the sea. The third part of the sea became blood, the third part of the creatures of the sea died. And the third part of the ships were destroyed."

✤**SECOND CHOIR OF ANGELS**: See **Second Triad of Angels.**

✤**SECOND HEAVEN, ANGELS OF THE**: The angel **Barakiel** is the ruling prince of the Second Heaven, also called Raquia. The angels that stand guard over the great palace of the **Second Heaven** are Arfiel, Maspiel, Ragiel, Sahriel, Sakriel, Sehibiel, Shahariel, and **Tagriel.**

✤**SECOND ORDER**: The second order of angels in the angelic hierarchy is the **Cherubim.**

✤**SECOND TRIAD OF ANGELS**: The classes of angels found in the second triad of the angelic hierarchy include the **Dominations, Virtues,** and **Powers.**

✤**SECRET REGIONS, ANGEL OF THE**: **Raziel.**

✤**SECRETS OF GOD, ANGEL OF THE**: **Raziel.**

✤**SEED OF THE WATERS**: In Persian mythology Tishtrya was called seed of the waters. Tishtrya brought rain to the earth.

✤**SEERS, ANGEL OF**: Phaldor.

✤**SEFER HASIDIM**: A document written during the Jewish Middle Ages. Demons (fallen angels) are found throughout the text as well as ways to exorcise them.

✤**SEFIRA**: A variation of **Sefiroth.**

✤**SEFIROT**: A variation of **Sefiroth.**

✤**SEFIROTH:** The name of a superior group of angels found in the **Cabala.** See **Holy Sefiroth, Unholy Sefiroth.**

✤**SEFRIAL:** An angel who stands guard over the palace of Maon, the **Fifth Heaven.**

✤**SEHAQIM, ANGEL OF:** Sehaqim is the name of the **Third Heaven.** The ruling prince is **Baradi'el.**

✤**SEHIBIEL:** An angel who stands guard over the palace of Raquia, the **Second Heaven.**

✤**SEKINAH:** A high order of angels. It is also the name of a luminous substance in Heaven. Its brilliance is said to keep the demons out of Heaven.

✤**SELF-DISCIPLINE, ANGEL OF: Camael.**

✤**SEMANGELOF:** One of three angels (Sansenoy and Senoy were the other two) sent to bring Lilith (Adam's first wife) back to Adam. The name Semangelof appears on amulets made to protect pregnant women and infants from the revenge of Lilith. Lilith, who rebelled against Adam's authority, resents all of the daughters of **Eve** because of their submitting themselves to their husbands.

✤**SEMEILA:** A variation of the name **Samoila.**

✤**SEMIAZA:** A variation of the name **Shemyaza,** leader of the order of angels called **Watchers.**

✤**SEMIBEL:** One of the angels that the Church of Rome reprobated in 745 C.E. Semibel is also a variation of the name **Chamuel.**

✤**SEMITES:** Descendants of Shem. The Semites worshiped **Rimmon,** the angel of storms.

✤**SEMJAZA:** A variation of the name **Shemyaza.**

✤**SEMYAZA:** A variation of the name **Shemyaza.**

✤**SENIGRON:** One of the seventy-eight names of **Metatron.**

✤**SENNACHERIB:** In the Book of 2 Kings (19:35), Assyrian king Sennacherib's army is slain by an angel after Hezekiah prays to God to save them from Sennacherib's threats. The account states, "That night an angel of the Lord went to the Assyrian camp and killed 185,000 soldiers. At dawn the next day there they lay, all dead!" According to lore, the angel who slew Sennacherib's army was the angel of death.

✤**SENOY:** One of the three angels sent to bring **Lilith** back to **Adam** (Sansenoy and Semangelof are the other two). The name Senoy appears on amulets made to protect pregnant women and infants from the revenge of Lilith, who hates all mortal women and their children.

✤**SENSENYA:** See **Childbirth.**

✤**SENSINER:** A fallen angel who was once a devoted servant of God. He was a companion to the archangel **Michael.** He later became a high-ranking demon of Hell. In magic he is called upon to help men procure the love of a desired woman.

✤SEPHIROTH: A variation of **Sefiroth.**

✤SEPTEMBER, ANGEL OF: The archangel **Uriel.**

✤SERAPH: Short for **Seraphim.**

✤SERAPHIC DOCTOR: A title given to **Saint Bonaventure** because of his interest in angels. He spent much of his life studying the angels and wrote several discourses about them.

✤SERAPHIEL: A variation of the name **Serapiel.**

✤SERAPHIM: The highest order of angels in Heaven. They have been described as incorruptible, brilliant, and powerful. They are the closest angels to God and are in direct communication with Him. It is said that they are so radiant that not even the **Cherubim** and the **Ophanim** can look upon them. If humans stood in their presence, they would be incinerated. They control the motion of the Heavens as it flows out from God. Their essence is love, and they are called Angels of Love. Through their purifying powers, they move humans to a love of God. They surround God's throne continuously singing the **Trisagion,** a song of celebration. The Book of 3 Enoch (26:9–12) says that there are four Seraphim corresponding to the four **winds** of the world. They each have six wings corresponding to the six days of creation. Each wing is the size of Heaven. The name Seraphim is a combination of the Hebrew word *Rapha*, which means "healer," and *ser*, which means "higher being." They are represented by the serpent, which is a symbol of healing. The leader of the Seraphim is **Serapiel.** The ruling princes are **Michael,** Serapiel, Jahoel, **Uriel, Camael, Metatron,** and Nathanael. They are also called Seraphs.

✤SERAPIEL: Prince of the **Seraphim.** In 3 Enoch he is described as a great and respected leader of the Seraphim who is glorified, honored, and beloved. His majestic beauty overshadows many in Heaven. The crown on his head is the height of a journey of 502 years. The crown is called Prince of Peace. He stands over the Seraphim day and night and teaches them songs to glorify God. A variation of the name Serapiel is Seraphiel.

✤SERAQAEL: An angel who stands in God's **Divine Presence.**

✤SEREFS: The name of a group of angels who carry the souls of the Egyptian kings to Heaven.

✤SERPENT(S), ANGELS OF THE: In scripture and literature, certain angels are often identified with the serpent: Satan, because he used the guise of a serpent to trick **Eve** in the **Garden of Eden; Raphael** because he is the angel of healing, and the serpent represents healing; and the

Seraphim because their name means "healer." In the *Midrash Aggada Exodus*, the archangel **Uriel** is a fiery serpent who punishes **Moses** for not holding a rite of circumcision for his son.

✦**SERVANTS:** One of the many titles angels are sometimes called by.

✦**SETHLANS:** One of the **Novensiles.** In Etruscan beliefs the Novensiles were the rulers of the thunderbolts.

✦**SEVEN ARCHANGELS:** See **Archangels.**

✦**SEVEN DAYS OF THE WEEK, ANGELS OF THE:** During the Middle Ages, angels were assigned to each day of the week: **Sunday–Raphael; Monday–Gabriel; Tuesday–Camael; Wednesday–Michael; Thursday–Zidkiel; Friday–Haniel; Saturday–Casziel.**

✦**SEVEN DEADLY SINS, ANGELS OF THE: Pride,** envy, wrath, lust, **sloth, greed,** and **falsehood** are the seven deadly sins. These are also the names of the demon **Archons** in **gnosticism.**

✦**SEVEN HEAVENS:** See **Heaven, Heavenly Palaces.**

✦**SEVEN PLAGUES, ANGELS OF THE:** In the Book of Revelation 15:1, 6–8, seven angels carry seven plagues. The plagues are carried in seven vials that are opened at God's command and poured upon the earth. Revelation states, "And I saw another sign in heaven, great and marvelous, seven angels having the seven last plagues; for in them is filled up the wrath of God" (15:1). "And the seven angels came out of the temple, having the seven plagues, clothed in pure and white linen, and having their breasts girded with golden girdles. And one of the four beasts gave unto the seven angels seven golden vials full of the wrath of God, who liveth forever and ever. And the temple was filled with smoke from the glory of God, and from his power; and no man was able to enter into the temple, till the seven plagues of the seven angels were fulfilled" (15:6–8). See **Vials of the Wrath of God.**

✦**SEVEN TRUMPETS, ANGELS OF THE:** In the Book of Revelation, seven angels carry **trumpets.** As each angel sounds his trumpet, an apocalyptic event takes place. Revelation 8:2 states, "Then I saw the seven angels who stand before God, and they were given seven trumpets." See **First Angel of the Trumpets, Second Angel of the Trumpets, Third Angel of the Trumpets, Fourth Angel of the Trumpets, Fifth Angel of the Trumpets, Sixth Angel of the Trumpets, Seventh Angel of the Trumpets.**

✦**SEVENTH ANGEL OF THE TRUMPETS:** In the Book of Revelation there are seven angels with **trumpets.** One at a time, each angel sounds his **trumpet.** Revelation 11:15 states that when the seventh angel sounded his trumpet, loud voices in Heaven said, "The power to rule over the world belongs now to our Lord and his Messiah, and he will rule forever and ever!"

✦**SEVENTH HEAVEN, ANGELS OF THE:** The name of the Seventh Heaven is **Arabot.** It is where God and all of the highest **orders of angels** (such as the **Seraphim** and **Cherubim**) dwell. The archangel **Michael** is the ruling prince of the Seventh Heaven. The angels who guard the magnificent palace of the Seventh Heaven are Alat, Tutrbebial, and Zeburial.

✦**SEVENTH ORDER OF ANGELS:** The seventh **order of angels** in the angelic hierarchy are the **Principalities.**

✦**SEWIRYAH:** One of the seventy-eight names of **Metatron.**

✦**SEX, ANGELS AND:** See **Sexual Temptation.**

✦**SEXUAL TEMPTATION:** The angels are generally thought to be genderless, sexless beings. The Bible supports this idea with Jesus' comment regarding the resurrected ones: "For in the resurrection they neither marry, nor are given in marriage, but are as the angels of God in Heaven" (Matthew 22:30). However, both the Book of Genesis and 1 Enoch speak of angels who became attracted to women on earth. These angels descended to earth, took on fleshly bodies, and had sexual relations with women (Genesis 6:2). In the Koran, **Maroth** and **Haroth** are two angels who gave in to sexual temptation. In gnostic beliefs, the superior group of angels called the **Aeons** turned away from God when they became fascinated with human sexuality. See **Watchers.**

✦**SHADOW OF DEATH, ANGEL OF THE:** See **Shaftiel.**

✦**SHADRACH:** One of three Hebrew men in the book of Daniel (3:1–30) who were rescued from a fiery **furnace** by an angel.

✦**SHADRACH, MESHACH, AND ABEDNEGO:** See **Furnace.**

✦**SHAFTIEL:** A fallen angel. He is one of the principal rulers of Hell. He is called Lord of the Shadow of Death.

✦**SHAHARIEL:** An angel who stands guard over the palace of Raquia, the **Second Heaven.**

✦**SHAHREVAR:** Another name for Khshathra. Khshathra is one of the **Amesha Spentas** (archangels) in Zoroastrianism.

✦**SHAITANS: Demons** in Islam.

✦**SHAKESPEARE, WILLIAM:** English dramatist and poet (1564–1616), considered the greatest of all playwrights. In his play *Hamlet*, Shakespeare wrote the now famous line, "Angels and ministers of grace defend us."

✦**SHAKTI:** In Hinduism the Shakti are manifestations of God's energy in female form. Durga and **Kali** are considered the greatest of the Shakti.

✦**SHAKZIEL:** The angel who watches over water insects.

✦**SHALGIEL:** The angel of snow and blizzards. A variation of the name Shalgiel is Salgiel.

✦SHALMIAL: The ruling prince of the **Third Heaven,** also known as Sehaqim.

✦SHAMANISM: A religion of the **Native Americans, Eskimos,** and the people of northeast Asia. It is based on the belief in good and evil spirits, who are influenced by the shamans (medicine men). Some of the spirits are winged beings who could be considered angels. Shamanistic angels are iconified in the forms of eagles, ravens, and other spirits that are identified only in Shamanism.

✦SHAMAZYA: A variation of the name **Shemyaza.**

✦SHAMS-ED-DIN: An archangel of the **Yezidics.**

✦SHAMSHIEL: The angel of the day and daylight. A variation of Shamshiel is Shamsiel.

✦SHAMSIEL: A variation of **Shamshiel.**

✦SHATEIEL: An angel of **silence.**

✦SHCHINIAL: An angel who stands guard over the palace of Zebul, the **Fourth Heaven.**

✦SHE-ANGELS: See **Female Angels.**

✦SHE-DEMON(s): See **Female Demons.**

✦SHE-DRAGON(s): The she-demon named **Leviathan** is the female equivalent of the dragon of the **bottomless pit** (Satan). According to legend, her fins are so large that she is able to block out the sun. According to Babylonian lore, the she-dragon **Tiamat** existed before the creation of the world. It was believed that through Tiamat the world came into being.

✦SHEBNIEL: See **Childbirth.**

✦SHEBURIEL: An angel who stands guard over the palace of Sehaqim, the **Third Heaven.**

✦SHEIKH BAKRA: An archangel of the **Yezidics.**

✦SHEIKH ISM: An archangel of the **Yezidics.**

✦SHEKINAH: A variation of the word **Schechinah.** The Schechinah is the female manifestation of God.

✦SHELMAI: One of the **Uthri** who preserves the Jordan River.

✦SHEMHAZAI: A variation of the name **Shemyaza.**

✦SHEMIEL: The angel of **music** in Judaism.

✦SHEMJAZA: A variation of the name **Shemyaza.**

✦SHEMUEL: One of the ruling princes of the **Seraphim.**

✦SHEMUIL: One of the **chief angels** of Heaven.

✦SHEMYAZA: A fallen angel from the **Seraphim** class. He was also the leader of the **Watchers.** He was ousted from Heaven because of having sexual relations with a mortal woman named Ishtarah. Legend has it that he was so caught up in his passion that he revealed the secret name of

God to her. With Ishtarah he fathered two sons, Hiwa and Hiya. His sons became fierce giants. They along with other giant children of angels were called the **Nephillim.** When the angels of **destruction** were sent from Heaven to slay the Nephillim, Shemyaza is said to have become so distraught that he threw himself into the stars and into the constellation of Orion. He can still be seen to this day hanging upside down. Before his fall, he was ruler of the angels of **justice.** Variations of the name Shemyaza are Semiaza, Semjaza, Semyaza, Shemhazai, Shamazya, Shemjaza, and Azza.

✤**SHEN:** Angelic beings of Chinese lore. They are referred to by the Chinese as gods. Once human, they have attained salvation and immortality. They perform all of the duties of the angels of Judaism, Christianity, and Islam, including miraculous works, traveling between the spiritual and physical worlds, curing the sick, exorcising demons, instructing, and giving strength and protection. When delivering messages from God, they manifest as humans and animals.

✤**SHEOL, ANGELS OF:** According to ancient lore, Sheol is the abode of the dead. The souls of the wicked are taken to Sheol by two angels of **destruction** named **Za'apie'el** and Samki'el. The ruler of Sheol is **Beliar.** The archangel **Raphael** acts as a guide of Sheol.

✤**SHEPHERDS, ANGELS OF THE:** In the Bible's New Testament, an angel appeared to shepherds tending sheep in a field near Bethlehem. The angel spoke to them saying, "Don't be afraid! I am here with good news for you which will bring great joy to all the people. This very day in David's town your Savior was born—Christ the Lord! And this is what will prove it to you: you will find a baby wrapped in cloths and lying in a manger." Afterward, a multitude of angels appeared before the shepherds, praising God saying, "Glory to God in the highest heaven, and peace on earth to those with whom he is pleased." (Luke 2:9–15).

✤**SHETEL:** An angel who served as a ministering angel to Adam and Eve before they were cast out of Paradise.

✤**SHEVIEL:** An angel who stands guard over the palace of Wilon, the **First Heaven.**

✤**SHIN'AN:** A high order of angels. Their rulers are Sidquiel and **Zadkiel.** A variation of Shin'an is Shinanin.

✤**SHINANIN:** A variation of Shin'an.

✤**SHINING BEINGS:** A term sometimes used when referring to the angels. It is also another name for the **Elohim.**

✤**SHINING ONE WHO HEALS:** The meaning of the name **Raphael.**

✤**SHINING ONES:** Another name for the order of angels called **Virtues.**

It is also a term that is sometimes used in literature when referring to the angels.

✤SHOEL: An angel who stands guard over the palace of Wilon, the **First Heaven.**

✤SHOKAD: An angel who stands guard over the palace of Wilon, the **First Heaven.**

✤SHOQED CHOZI: A great prince of the class of angels called **Thrones.** Variations of the name Shoqed Chozi are Soqed Hozi and Skd Huzi.

✤SHTUKIAL: An angel who stands guard over the palace of Zebul, the **Fourth Heaven.**

✤SICKLE, ANGEL OF THE: In the Book of Revelation 14:14–15, **John** sees in a vision an angel seated on a cloud, holding a sickle, ready to reap a **harvest.** The angel is interpreted as being Jesus Christ ready to separate the good people from the bad.

✤SIDQUIEL: One of the ruling angels of the **Shin'an.**

✤SIDRI'EL: A ruling prince of Wilon, the **First Heaven.**

✤SIGRON: One of the seventy-eight names of **Metatron.**

✤SIJ-ED-DIN: An archangel of the **Yezidics.**

✤SILENCE, ANGEL OF: Shateiel and **Dumah** are both angels of silence.

✤SILVER, ANGEL OF: The **color** silver represents the archangel **Gabriel.**

✤SIMAEL: An angel who is thought to be one of the three unnamed **archangels** of Judeo-Christian lore.

✤SIMBIEL: An angel of **destruction.**

✤SIMIEL: A variation of the name **Chamuel,** one of the **archangels.**

✤SIN AND THE ANGELS: Angels are considered perfect, sinless beings (unlike humans, who are born into sin). They are referred to as holy because of this sinless state of existence. However, the angels are capable of sin. Because they have free will, they can "choose" to sin. When this occurs, they are no longer angels but become fallen angels (also called demons). The angels who sin lose their positions in heaven and fall out of God's favor. The scriptures show also that the angels are subject to punishment for their sins. In the New Testament, 2 Peter 2:4 states, "God did not spare the angels who sinned, but threw them into hell, where they are kept chained in darkness, waiting for the Day of Judgment." The choice to sin by an angel is different from the sin of mankind. Man is born into sin and has to struggle against it. Unlike mankind, for the angels there is no savior, and there is no repentance. Among the most famous tales of angels sinning is that of **Satan** and his rebellion against God, and the **Watchers** coming to earth to pursue women.

✤**SIN'ANIM:** A high order of angels. In 3 Enoch they are referred to as the "fiery Sin'anim."

✤**SINUI:** An angel called upon in Mosaic ceremonies to aid pregnant women.

✤**SIPWESE'EL:** One of the angels who brought the secret knowledge of Heaven to earth.

✤**SIREN(S):** Winged, birdlike female figures who give sensual pleasure to the gods. They are sometimes referred to as the **Birds of Paradise.**

✤**SIRUSHI:** A variation of the name **Surush.** Surush is the angel of **announcements** in Persian mythology.

✤**SISTINE CHAPEL, ANGELS OF THE:** The Sistine Chapel is the private chapel of the popes in the Vatican. It is world famous for its paintings and decorations, many of which feature angels. One of the most popular is that of the *Last Judgment*, painted by **Michelangelo,** in which he portrayed angels without wings. Other paintings in the chapel include works by **Perugino, Botticelli,** and **Ghirlandaio.**

✤**SIXTH ANGEL OF THE TRUMPETS:** In the Book of Revelation, there are seven angels with **trumpets.** One at a time, each angel sounds his trumpet and an apocalyptic event takes place. When the sixth angel sounded his trumpet, a voice said to the angel, "Loose the four angels which are bound in the great river Euphrates. And the four angels were loosed, which were prepared for an hour, and a day, and a month, and a year, to slay the third part of men" (Revelation 9:14–15).

✤**SIXTH HEAVEN, ANGELS OF THE:** The ruler of the Sixth Heaven (Makon) is the archangel **Gabriel.** It is also the residence of seven **Cherubim** and seven **Phoenixes** who sing praises to God. In his writings **Enoch** mentioned seeing archangels teaching and angels studying in the Sixth Heaven. In addition, angels also document the seasons, years, and mankind's history. Conduct and deeds are also recorded there. The angels who stand guard over the grand palace of the **Sixth Heaven** are Arsabrsbial, Egrumial, Gehegial, Katmial, Machkial, Parzial, Rumial, and Tufrial. See **Angelic School.**

✤**SIXTH ORDER OF ANGELS:** The sixth order of angels are called **Powers.**

✤**SIZAJASEL:** An angel of **Sagittarius.**

✤**SIZOUZE:** The angel of **prayers** in Persian lore.

✤**SKD HUZI:** A variation of the name **Shoqed Chozi.**

✤**SKY, ANGEL OF THE:** In Judaism the angel of the sky is Sahaquiel. In Zoroastrianism, **Khshathra Vairya** is the protector of the sky. In ancient Egypt the winged goddess Nut presided over the sky.

✤**SLEEPLESSNESS, ANGEL OF:** The archangel **Michael.**

✤**SLOTH:** In gnosticism, **sloth** is one of the seven deadly sins. Sloth is also a demon **Archon.** He is associated with the planet Saturn. His antithesis is **Kafziel.**

✤**SMITH, JONATHAN:** The name of the angel from the hit television series *Highway to Heaven.* Michael Landon starred as Jonathan Smith, an angel sent to earth to teach humans love and compassion, and to aid those in trouble.

✤**SMITH, JOSEPH:** In 1823 the angel Moroni appeared to Joseph Smith (founder of the Church of Jesus Christ of the Latter-Day Saints). He led Smith to a place where golden tablets were buried. Smith, with the help of Moroni, translated the text of the tablets. This text later became the Book of Mormon.

✤**SNIEL:** See **Childbirth.**

✤**SNOW, ANGEL OF:** Shalgiel.

✤**SOCRATES:** Greek philosopher of Athens, often regarded as one of the wisest men of all time. In his writings, Socrates spoke of an inner voice that he believed to be his guardian angel. He referred to it as his **daimonion.** He stated that throughout his life his daimonion guided him and was always with him.

✤**SODOM:** See **Sodom and Gomorrah.**

✤**SODOM AND GOMORRAH:** In the Bible they were two cities of the plain that were destroyed because of corruption. Before they were destroyed, **Abraham** was visited by angels who informed him of their impending destruction. The angels later rescued Abraham's nephew Lot and his family from Sodom before it was destroyed by fire and brimstone. (Note: The destruction of Sodom and Gomorrah would have been carried out by angels of destruction.)

✤**SOFIEL:** The angel who presides over the nurturing of fruit and vegetables.

✤**SOFRIEL:** A variation of the name **Sopheriel.**

✤**SOLITUDES, ANGEL OF:** Casziel.

✤**SOLOMON:** King of the ancient Hebrews. The son of and also successor of King **David.** In the Testament of Solomon (a book of the **Pseudepigrapha**), King Solomon prays to God for help against demons who are interfering with the building of his temple. God answers Solomon's prayer by giving him power over the demons. This power comes through a magical ring (according to some sources, it was called the Seal Ring) that was delivered to Solomon by the archangel **Michael.** Solomon uses the ring to overpower the demons and interrogates them. He learns the names of the demons, their evil activities, and the names of the angels who can overpower them. Afterward, while still under the power of the magic ring, the demons are made to help in the building of the Temple. In the Testament of Solomon many of the most powerful demons are made known. They include **Asmodeus, Beelzebub, Deception, Distress, Error, Fate, Kunopegos, Lion-Shaped Demon, Lix Tetrax, Modebel, Murder, Obyzouth, Ornias,** Physikoreth, **Power, Scepter, Strife, Winged Dragon,** and a group of demons referred to as the **Thirty-six Heavenly Bodies.** In addition, never-before-heard-of angels are given. The seven **archangels** are listed as **Michael, Gabriel, Uriel,** Sabrael, **Arael, Iaoth,** and **Adonael.** Other angels include **Karael, Uriel, Raphael, Gabriel, Lamechiel, Balthioul, Iameth, Azael, Asteraoth, Baruchiel, Bazazath, Briathos, Rathanael,** Rizoel, **Sabael,** Phounebiel, Rarideris, Raiouoth, Marmaraoth, Arara, Kalazael, Leikourgos, Iouda Zizabou, Kok, Phedismos.

✤**SOMCHAM:** An angel who safeguards the west **wind.**

✤**SON OF THE MORNING:** A title held by **Lucifer.**

✤**SONG, ANGEL OF:** In Judaism and Christianity, the angel of song is **Uriel.** In Islam it is **Israfel.** In Greek mythology **Euterpe** inspired men to compose song verses.

✤**SONGS, ANGELS IN:** The word *angel* can be found in much of today's popular music. In recent decades one in ten song titles held the word *angel.*

✤**SONNILLON:** A **fallen angel.**

✤**SONS OF DARKNESS:** In the **Dead Sea scrolls,** fallen angels are referred to as the sons of darkness.

✤**SONS OF GOD:** A term used when referring to the angels. It is also refers to the **Bene ha-Elohim.**

✤**SONS OF LIGHT:** In the **Dead Sea scrolls,** angels are referred to as the sons of light.

✤**SOOTHSAYERS, ANGEL OF:** Phaldor.

✤**SOPERI'EL YHWH:** A great angelic prince in Heaven. He is in charge of the books of the dead. He writes down the date of death for every human on earth.

✤**SOPERI'EL YWHW:** A great angelic prince in Heaven. He is in charge of the books of the living. He records the name of every human who lives on earth.

✤**SOPHER:** A variation of the name **Sopheriel.**

✤**SOPHERIEL:** The keeper of the records of both the living and the dead. Variations of the name Sopheriel are Sopher and Sofriel.

✤**SOPHIA:** See **Pistis-Sophia.**

✤**SOPRI'EL:** One of the seventy-eight names of **Metatron.**

✤**SOQED HOZI:** A variation of the name **Shoqed Chozi.**

✦**SOQEDHOZI YHWH:** A great angelic prince in Heaven. He weighs the good and evil deeds of men on scales in the **presence** of God.

✦**SORCERY, ANGELS OF:** In 3 Enoch, three angels named **Azzah, Uzzah,** and **Azael** are listed as having taught sorcery to mankind.

✦**SORE THROAT, DEMON OF:** According to the Testament of **Solomon,** Oropel is the name of the demon that causes sore throat. He can be thwarted by calling on the archangel **Raphael,** the angel of healing.

✦**SOTERASI'EL YHWH:** A great angelic prince in Heaven. He keeps records of the activities of all of the humans of earth. He presents these records to the **court of Heaven.** Anyone to go in before the **Sekinah** must first obtain his permission.

✦**SOUBELTI:** A demon who causes numbness and shivering. He can be thwarted by the angel Rizoel.

✦**SOUBIROUS, BERNADETTE:** In 1858, fourteen-year-old Bernadette Soubirous of Lourdes (a town in the southwest of France) received a visit from the **Virgin Mary.** The Virgin Mary instructed her to dig for a spring. Obediently, Bernadette did so, and the spring later became known for its miraculous healing. By 1959, there had been five thousand healings reported at Lourdes. Cancer, TB, and various other diseases and disabilities have been cured there. Today, millions of people travel to Lourdes to visit the Roman Catholic shrine where the Virgin Mary first appeared.

✦**SOUL, ANGEL OF THE:** Jeremiel.

✦**SOUL(S), ANGELS OF THE:** There are five angels who lead the souls of man to the **judgment** of God. They include **Araqiel, Aziel, Rumael, Samiel,** and **Uriel.** The **Powers** are the angels who guide the soul through the transition of death. The angel of the souls awaiting the **resurrection** is **Raziel.** During the Middle Ages, the archangel **Michael** was considered a conductor of souls to the spiritual realm. In Mandaean beliefs, Sanasel stood at the entrance to Heaven and prayed for souls. The **Lord of Souls** is **Beelzebub.**

✦**SOUL ANGELS:** Angels who once lived on the earth as humans.

✦**SOUTH, ANGEL OF THE:** The archangel **Uriel.**

✦**SOUTH WIND, ANGEL OF THE:** See **Wind.**

✦**SOVEREIGNS, ANGELS OF:** The angels in charge of protecting the sovereigns of the world and inspiring them to make the right decisions are the **Principalities.**

✦**SOVEREIGNTIES:** The name of a high order of angels.

✦**SPEED OF THE ANGELS:** According to the Book of Ezekiel, angels travel at the speed of lightning. Ezekiel 1:14 says, "The creatures [angels] themselves darted back and forth with the speed of lightning."

❖**SPELLS, ANGEL OF: Amasras,** who taught mankind how to use incantations and spells for magical purposes. His teachings have been with mankind for thousands of years and are still in practice in many parts of the world today.

❖**SPENAG MENOG:** Another name for **Ahura Mazda,** the Supreme Being in Zoroastrianism.

❖**SPENDARMAD:** Another name for **Armaiti,** one of the **Amesha Spentas** (angels) in Zoroastrianism.

❖**SPENTA ARMAITI:** Another name for **Armaiti,** an archangel of Zoroastrianism.

❖**SPENTA MAINYU:** Another name for **Ahura Mazda,** God's name in Zoroastrianism.

❖**SPHANDOR:** A demon listed in the Testament of **Solomon.** He takes pleasure in paralyzing the limbs of humans. He can be thwarted by the angel **Arael.**

❖**SPHENDONAEL:** A demon listed in the Testament of **Solomon.** He causes tetanic recurvation (a disease that causes the body to draw back and stiffen). He is thwarted by the angel Sabael.

❖**SPHERES:** A high order of angels. They are also called **Galgallin.**

❖**SPHINXES:** See **Winged Sphinxes.**

❖**SPIRIT GUIDES:** Spirits who act as personal instructors to humans on earth. They come and go according to an individual's needs, and the lessons that person is to learn while on earth. In her book *Messengers of Light*, **Terry Lynn Taylor** says, "Spiritual guides come in and out of our lives according to need. They usually represent the essence of a particular culture, race, or religion, or they can represent a career or avenue of life. They are teachers." It is believed that an individual can have many spirit guides during his or her lifetime.

❖**SPIRIT OF APOSTASY:** In Zoroastrianism, Indra is the spirit of apostasy. His opponent is **Asha** the angel of truth.

❖**SPIRIT OF DARKNESS: Satan.** In Islam it is **Iblis.** In Zoroastrianism it is **Angra Mainyu. Beelzebub** and **Sammael** are also referred to as the spirit of darkness.

❖**SPIRIT OF LIGHT:** Another name for the angel of **light.**

❖**SPIRIT OF PERVERSITY:** Another name for the angel of **darkness** (Satan).

❖**SPIRIT OF TRUTH:** Another name for the angel of light in the **Dead Sea scroll** *The Manual of Discipline.*

❖**SPIRITS:** The word *spirits* is sometimes used when referring to angels.

❖**SPIRITS OF NATURE:** See **Nature Spirits.**

✦SPIRITUAL COUNSELORS: In Persian mythology the **Fereshteh** are sometimes referred to as spiritual counselors.

✦SPLENDOR: An angel of the **Holy Sefiroth**.

✦SPLENDORS: Another name for the **Virtues**.

✦SPOKESMAN FOR GOD: See **God's Spokesman**.

✦SPRING, ANGEL OF: Talvi.

✦SPRING OF LOURDES, ANGEL OF THE: The **Virgin Mary**. See **Soubirous, Bernadette**.

✦SRAOSHA: The angel of discipline (also called **Obedience**) in Zoroastrianism. Sraosha is a warrior of God who battles with **Angra Mainyu** and his demons. His chief opponent is **Aeshma,** a demon of wrath. He protects the righteous people of the world at night when the demons are in search of victims to torment. He was the first angel to chant the Gathas (the seventeen hymns of Zoroaster), and to offer prayer to **Ahura Mazda.** According to Zoroastrian lore, Sraosha's house has a thousand pillars and sits on top of Mount Haraiti. The house is lit from within by the illumination of Sraosha himself. Outside, the house is lit from the brilliance of the stars. He drives a chariot of four swift, white horses.

✦SSAKMAKIEL: A variation of the name Tzakmaqiel, an angel of **Aquarius.**

✦STAR(S): In scripture, angels are sometimes referred to as stars. In the Book of Job, angels are referred to as "stars" who joyfully cry out while witnessing the **creation.** Job 38:6–7 says, "Who laid the cornerstone of the world? In the dawn of that day the stars sang together." In the Book of Judges, the stars fought from Heaven. Judges 5:20 says, "The stars fought from the sky; as they moved across the sky, they fought against Sisera." Revelation 9:1 says, "I saw a star which had fallen down to the earth, and it was given the key to the abyss. The star opened the abyss, and smoke poured out of it."

✦STAR WHICH HERALDS THE RISING SUN: A title held by **Lucifer.**

✦STARS, ANGELS OF THE: The angel **Kokabi'el** brought the knowledge of the stars and the **constellations** to earth. **Tam'el** is also an angel who taught mankind about the stars.

✦*STARSEED TRANSMISSIONS:* A book of spiritual information communicated by the archangel **Raphael** to **Kenneth X. Carey.**

✦STEINER, RUDOLPH: German philosophic genius and clairvoyant (1861–1925). From a very young age Steiner could see, hear, and communicate with angels. At the age of forty he began teaching about what had been communicated to him by the angels regarding the spiritual world. Steiner believed that every person has a companion angel that stays with him through each of his incarnations. He held that this same angel would reveal an individual's former lives to him at a certain point in his spiritual development. He held that during childhood, each individual has an angel who guides him. During the middle years, the angel leaves the person temporarily as he develops himself. Later in life, the angel returns, helping that person to develop his spirituality. Steiner wrote extensively about the **orders of angels** and their functions. He ranked the angels as follows: (1) **Seraphim**, (2) **Cherubim**, (3) **Thrones**, (4) **Dominions**, (5) **Mights**, (6) **Powers**, (7) **Archai**, (8) **Archangels** and (9) **Angels.** He believed that mankind and the angels were constantly evolving to a higher state of being, until they reached the pinnacle in evolution.

✦**STERILITY, ANGEL OF:** The angels **Akriel** and **Zidkiel** are both angels of sterility.

✦**STILLNESS OF DEATH, ANGEL OF THE: Dumah.**

✦**STOCK, ANGEL OF:** See **Livestock.**

✦**STOMACH AILMENTS, ANGEL OF:** God gave the angel **Adnachiel** a cure for colic and other stomach ailments through an Ethiopian talisman.

✦**STORM(S), ANGELS OF: Zaamael** and **Rimmon** are both angels of storms.

✦**STRENGTH:** One of the angels of the **Holy Sefiroth** found in the **Cabala.**

✦**STRENGTH, ANGEL OF:** Zeruel and **Cervihel** both hold the title of the angel of strength.

✦**STRIFE:** In the Testament of Solomon, Strife is a demon that King **Solomon** summoned and interrogated. Strife revealed to Solomon that he was a ruler in the world of darkness. His demonic activities include making weapons of war available to men. He can be thwarted by the angel **Baruchiel.**

✦**STUPIDITY, ANGELS OF:** The angels Anabiel and Hodniel can be called upon for curing stupidity. **Scepter** is the demon who causes stupidity.

✦**STURIEL:** See **Childbirth.**

✦**SUBSTITUTES, THE:** See **Abdals.**

✦**SUCCUBI:** A variation of **Succubus.**

✦**SUCCUBUS:** A demon who has intercourse with sleeping men. In medieval times they were believed to take on the form of beautiful women who would then seduce men. They later became thought of as invisible spirits who would climb into bed with men to have sexual intercourse. They especially enjoy (but are not limited to) pursuing those who are dedicated to a life of celibacy such as priests and monks. A variation of the word Succubus is Succubi. See **Lilim, Incubus.**

✦**SUFISM, ANGELS OF:** Sufism is a Muslim philosophical and literary movement. Winged beings mediating between Heaven and earth are found in mystical texts of the Sufi.

✢SUKALLI: A variation of the name **Sukallin.**

✢SUKALLIN: The **Sukallin** are Babylonian-Sumerian angels.

✢SUMMANUS: An Etruscan angel who belonged to the group of angels called the **Novensiles.** The Novensiles ruled over thunderbolts.

✢SUMMER, ANGEL OF: Both **Uriel** and Casmaran are called the angel of summer.

✢SUMMER EQUINOX, ANGEL OF THE: **Abrid.**

✢SUN, ANGELS OF THE: The archangel **Raphael** is the angel of the sun. He is responsible for the sun's heat. Aftiel is the angel of the evening sun. Each day the **Phoenix** (a great bird in Heaven) spreads his wings to cover the flaming rays of the sun. If he did not do so, all living creatures on earth would be incinerated.

✢SUNDAY, ANGEL OF: In **Essene** beliefs the archangel **Michael** is the angel of Sunday. In Judaism it is the archangel **Raphael.** The angels who preside over the hours of the day on Sunday are: 1:00-Michael, 2:00-**Haniel,** 3:00-Raphael, 4:00-**Gabriel,** 5:00-**Casziel,** 6:00-**Sachiel,** 7:00-**Sammael,** 8:00-Michael, 9:00-Haniel, 10:00-Raphael, 11:00-Gabriel, 12:00-Casziel. The angels who preside over the hours of the night are: 1:00-Sachiel, 2:00-Sammael, 3:00-Michael, 4:00-Haniel, 5:00-Raphael, 6:00-Gabriel, 7:00-Casziel, 8:00-Sachiel, 9:00-Sammael, 10:00-Michael, 11:00-Haniel, 12:00-Raphael.

✢SUN'S DISK, ANGEL OF THE: In Persian mythology, Chur is the angel of the sun's disk.

✢SUPREME MYSTERIES, ANGEL OF THE: **Raziel.**

✢SURAFEL: An angel found in the Book of 1 Enoch 9:1.

✢SURASUTI: One of the **Shakti** of Hinduism. Surasuti is a peaceful spirit. She represents tranquillity and light.

✢SURIA: An angel who stands guard over the palace of Wilon, the **First Heaven.**

✢SURIEL: A great angelic prince in Heaven, and one of the angels of the **presence.** Suriel is also a variation of the name **Sariel.**

✢SURIYEL: A variation of the name **Sariel,** the angel of death.

✢SURUSH: The angel of **announcements** and also the angel of paradise in Persian mythology. A variation of the name Surush is Sirushi.

✢SURYA: One of the **Adityas** (angels) of Vedic beliefs.

✢SUSTENANCE, ANGEL OF: In Islam the angel of sustenance is **Mikhail.** Mikhail is the Islamic name for the archangel **Michael.**

✢SWEDENBORG, EMANUEL: Swedish scientist, religious teacher, and mystic (1688–1772). His religious system is often referred to as Swedenborgianism.

He published many works on religion and philosophy. In his later years he gave himself fully to the contemplation of spiritual matters. He believed that God had revealed the true inner doctrines of the divine word to him alone. Throughout his life he regularly communicated with angels. He held that angels, like humans, have bodies, but are in the spiritual form. He believed that humans cannot see angels through their physical eyes but only through the spiritual eyes. About angels Swedenborg once wrote, "I am well aware that many will say that no one can possibly speak with spirits and angels so long as he is living in the body. Many say it is all fancy, others that I recount such things to win credence, while others will make other kinds of objection. But I am deterred by none of these: for I have seen, I have heard, I have felt." Swedenborg incorporated the information revealed to him from the angels in his many writings. His book that speaks most about the angels is *Heaven and Hell.* It is recognized as his greatest work.

✣**Sydik:** The name of the great angel **Melchizedek** in Phoenician mythology.

✣**Sylphs: Elemental** spirits who rule the air. They are ruled by **Raphael.**

✣**Symbol(s):** During medieval times it became popular to portray angels in art with symbols. These symbols continue to be portrayed in art today. Popular symbols include the lyre, a symbol of the angels' praise to God; the **trumpet,** a symbol of God's voice; **wings,** which symbolize the angels' role as messengers; the **halo,** which symbolizes virtue and innocence; **aureoles,** which symbolize the holiness of the angels; **diadems,** symbolizing the angels' heavenly sovereignty; the Lily, symbolizing their purity; **palms,** symbolizing victory; the **thurible,** symbolizing worship; the **pilgrim's staff,** symbolizing the readiness of angels to do God's bidding; the **codex,** symbolizing the scriptures; and the **sceptor,** symbolizing the archangels' authority.

✣**Syria:** A region of the ancient world located at the eastern end of the Mediterranean. In Syria, the angel **Rimmon** was worshipped as a deity. Rimmon was the angel of storms.

Then he will send out the angels, and gather his elect from the four winds, from the ends of the earth to the ends of heaven.

—MARK 13:27

✤**TABAET:** A fallen angel.

✤**TABRIS:** The angel of free will.

✤**TABTABI'EL:** One of the seventy-eight names of **Metatron.**

✤**TACOUIN:** Angels of Islamic lore. The Tacouin were beautiful angels who protected men from devils.

✤**TAFTHI:** An angel who worked closely with the angel **Alimon** to prevent individuals from being harmed by weapons of war.

✤**TAG'AS:** A great lord in Heaven. He is in charge of the heavenly choirs.

✤**TAGAS:** Ruler of the **Sarim,** a high order of angels in Hebrew lore.

✤**TAGORE, SIR RABINDRANATH:** Indian writer and philosopher (1861–1941). About angels, Tagore once wrote, "I believe we are free, within limits, and yet there is an unseen hand, a guiding angel that drives us on."

✤**TAGRIEL:** An angel who stands guard over the palace of Raquia, the **Second Heaven.** In the **Book of Raziel,** he is an amulet angel summoned during childbirth. He is also one of twenty-eight angels who preside over the **lunar mansions.**

✤**TAHARIEL:** See **Childbirth.**

✤**TAHSANYAH:** One of the seventy-eight names of **Metatron.**

✤**TALISMANIC MAGIC, ANGELS OF:** The seven **archangels** found in talismanic magic are **Zaphkiel, Zadkiel, Camael, Raphael, Haniel, Michael,** and **Gabriel.**

❖**TALLEST ANGEL: Metatron** is said to be the tallest angel in Heaven.

❖**TALMUD, ANGELS OF THE:** The Talmud is the collection of writings constituting the Jewish civil and religious law. It consists of two parts, the Mishnah and the Gemara. The Talmud tells us that for every Jew that is born God assigns eleven thousand guardian angels.

❖**TALTO:** One of many aliases used by the she-demon **Lilith** when she works evil against mortals.

❖**TALVI:** The angel of spring.

❖**TAM'EL (GOD'S PERFECTION):** A fallen angel from the **Grigori** class. In 1 Enoch he is listed as the angel who brought the knowledge of the stars to mankind. He was also one of the leaders of the angels who came to earth to have sexual relations with women. He is also called the angel of the deep. Variations of the name Tam'el are Tamiel, Tamel, Tamuel, and Temel.

❖**TAMEL:** A variation of the name **Tam'el.**

❖**TAMIEL:** A variation of the name **Tam'el.**

❖**TAMTAMYAH:** One of the seventy-eight names of **Metatron.**

❖**TAMUEL:** A variation of the name **Tam'el.**

❖**TANDAL:** An angel who stands guard over the palace of Wilon, the **First Heaven.**

❖**TANDU'EL:** One of the seventy-eight names of **Metatron.**

❖**TANKFIL:** An angel summoned in Arabic exorcism ceremonies.

❖**TAOISM, ANGELS OF:** Taoism is a Chinese religion and philosophy based on the principles of Lao-tzu. Taoists believe in ministering spirits. They are classified as gods **(shen),** but perform all of the functions of the angels in some of the main religions. These functions include traveling between the spiritual and physical realms, performing miracles, curing the sick, exorcising demons, and instructing humans.

❖**TAP:** A fallen angel.

❖**TAPESTRY:** See **Angel Organizations.**

❖**TAPSARIM:** The name of a high order of angels.

❖**TAPTAPYAH:** One of the seventy-eight names of **Metatron.**

❖**TARA:** A great celestial spirit. She is considered in many cultures to be the Earth Mother. In Hebrew she is called Terah, in Ireland she is Tara, in Latin she is Terra Mater, the Etruscans called her Turan. In Hinduism she is a star spirit. In Buddhism, she is the mother of all celestial spirits and is called upon to relieve pain and heartache. She is said to manifest as a young girl.

❖**TARFANIEL:** An angel who oversees the west **wind.**

✤TAROMAITI: The angel of presumption in Zoroastrianism. Her opponent is Pairimaiti, the angel of crooked mindedness.

✤TAROT (CARDS), ANGELS OF THE: The tarot is a set of seventy-eight cards with pictures and symbols used for divination. The Tarot has two angelic figures in the deck: Temperance (XIIII) and the angel of **Judgment** (XX). Temperance represents moderation, compromise, patience, and self-control. **Judgment** represents atonement, forgiveness, rebirth, and apology. The angel of the tarot is **Eistibus.**

✤TARQUAM: An angel who rules over autumn.

✤TARSHISH: A prince of the order of **Virtues.**

✤TARSHISHIM: Another name for the class of angels called **Virtues.**

✤TARTARUCHUS (HE WHO KEEPS HELL): An angel who is in charge of the torments and punishments given in Hell.

✤TARTARUS, ANGEL OF: Tartarus is another name for the underworld. In the Testament of **Solomon,** Abezethibou is the ruler of Tartarus.

✤TASBAS: One of the seventy-eight names of **Metatron.**

✤TASGAS: One of the seventy-eight names of **Metatron.**

✤TASHRIEL: An angel who stands guard over the palace of Wilon, the **First Heaven.**

✤TATNADI'EL: One of the seventy-eight names of **Metatron.**

✤TATRASI'EL YHWH: A great angelic prince in Heaven.

✤TATRI'EL: One of the seventy-eight names of **Metatron.**

✤TATRUSIA: See **Childbirth.**

✤TAURUS, ANGEL OF: **Asmodel.**

✤TAYLOR, TERRY LYNN: Author of several popular angel books including *Messengers of Light: The Angels' Guide to Spiritual Growth, Guardians of Hope: The Angels' Guide to Personal Growth, Answers from the Angels: A Book of Angel Letters,* and *Creating With the Angels: An Angel-Guided Journey Into Creativity.* Taylor also publishes an angel newsletter and conducts workshops and seminars on angels. For information, send a self-addressed, stamped envelope to Angels Can Fly, 2275 Huntington Drive #326, San Marino, CA 91108.

✤TEA LEAVES, ANGEL OF: **Eistibus.**

✤TEACHERS, ANGEL OF: The archangel **Uriel** inspires and imparts ideas to teachers.

✤TEARS, ANGEL OF: The angels **Casziel** and **Sandolphon** both hold the title of the angel of tears. The Islamic angel of tears resides in the **Fourth Heaven.** The name of this angel is unknown. According to Islamic lore, the **Cherubim** were created from the tears of **Mikhail** when he cried over the sins of the faithful.

✤Techial: An angel who stands guard over the palace of Maon, the **Fifth Heaven.**

✤Tehoriel: An angel who safeguards the south **wind.**

✤Teiaiel: A variation of the name Isiaiel, the angel of the future.

✤Teleleyakos: A variation of the name **Temeluchus,** a guardian angel of babies and children.

✤Television, Angels on: Television Shows. American television shows featuring angels include *Good Heavens,* starring Carl Reiner; *I Dream of Jeannie,* starring Barbara Eden; *Highway to Heaven,* starring **Michael Landon;** and *Touched by an Angel,* starring Roma Downey. Television Movies. American television movies that featured angels include *The Kid with the Broken Halo,* starring Gary Coleman and Robert Guillaume; *The Littlest Angel,* starring Johnny Whitaker; *It Happened One Christmas,* starring Marlo Thomas and Cloris Leachman; and *Human Feelings,* starring Billy Crystal and Nancy Walker.

✤Temel: A variation of the name **Tam'el.**

✤Temeluch: A variation of the name **Temeluchus.**

✤Temeluchus: A guardian angel of babies and children. Variations of the name Temeluchus are Temeluch and Teleleyakos.

✤Temperance: An angel found in **tarot** cards. Temperance (XIIII) represents moderation, compromise, patience, and self-control.

✤Temperance, Angel of: **Casziel.**

✤*Tempest, The:* A play by **William Shakespeare** which featured the angel **Ariel.**

✤Temptation, Angel of: **Satan.**

✤Tempters, Angel of: **Mammon.**

✤Tenth Order of Angels: The **Watchers** were once a part of the celestial hierarchy, the tenth order of angels. They are no longer considered an order of angels because of their sin.

✤Terah: The Hebrew name for **Tara,** a great celestial spirit.

✤Terebinth Tree, Angel of: **Zidkiel.**

✤Teresa Neumann: See **Neumann, Teresa.**

✤Teresa Palminota: See **Palminota, Teresa.**

✤Terpsichore: In Greek mythology Terpsichore inspired choirs to sing, men to write lyric poetry, and people in the art of dancing.

✤Terra Mater: The Latin name for **Tara,** a great celestial spirit.

✤Terror and Trembling, Angel of: The fallen angel **Dommiel.**

✤Tessub: The god of storms, worshiped by the Kassites. Tessub was also known as **Rimmon.** Rimmon was the angel of storms.

✤Testament of Solomon: See **Solomon.**

✤Thaleia: One of the Greek muses. Thaleia inspired men in the arts and sciences, intelligence and creativity. She also inspired them comedy.

✦**THANATOS:** The angel of death and rebirth. In Greek mythc Thanatos was the personification of the god of death. He came humans when their life was completed. Spreading his wings over th newly departed, he would cut off a lock of their hair and dedicate them to the underworld. He would then carry them away. In Roman mythology he was called **Mors.**

✦**THAUMIEL:** One of the **Unholy Sefiroth** of the **Cabala.**

✦**THELIEL:** An angel of love.

✦**THIEF OF PARADISE:** In John Milton's *Paradise Lost,* **Satan** is referred to as the thief of paradise.

✦**THIRD ANGEL OF THE TRUMPETS:** In the Book of Revelation, there are seven angels with **trumpets.** One at a time, each angel sounds his trumpet and an apocalyptic event takes place. When the third angel sounds his trumpet, a great star falls from Heaven. It lands upon a third of the rivers and fountains of water. The star's name is **Wormwood.** The third part of the waters become wormwood. Many die from drinking the water.

✦**THIRD CHOIR OF ANGELS:** See **Third Triad of Angels.**

✦**THIRD HEAVEN, ANGELS OF THE:** The name of the Third Heaven is Sehaqim. Baradi'el is the ruling prince. Three hundred angels of light also reside there. The angels of light continuously sing praises to God as they guard the **Garden of Eden** and the **Tree of Life,** also located in the Third Heaven. The angels who stand guard over the great palace of the Third Heaven are Amamael, Bezrial, Hadrial, Harhazial, Retsutsiel, Savlial, Sheburiel, and **Shalmial.**

✦**THIRD ORDER OF ANGELS:** The third order in the angelic hierarchy is the **Thrones.**

✦**THIRD TRIAD OF ANGELS:** The groups of angels that make up the third triad of angels in the angelic hierarchy are the **Principalities, Archangels,** and **Angels.**

✦**THIRTY-SIX HEAVENLY BODIES:** The Thirty-six Heavenly Bodies are thirty-six demons found in the Testament of **Solomon.** Their names are **Ruax, Barsafael, Artosael, Oropel, Kairoxanondalon, Sphendonael, Sphandor, Belbel, Kourtael, Metathiax, Katanikotael, Saphthorael, Phobothel, Leroel, Soubelti, Katrax, Ieropa, Modebel, Mardero,** Rhyx Achoneoth, **Rhyx Aktonme, Rhyx Alath,** Rhyx Aleureth, **Rhyx Anatreth, Rhyx Anoster, Rhyx Audameoth, Rhyx Autoth, Rhyx Axesbuth, Rhyx the Enautha, Rhyx Hapax, Rhyx Ichthuon,** Rhyx

✤**THURIBLE:** Angels are sometimes portrayed in art carrying a thu̶ (censer). The thurible symbolizes prayer. In ancient times it was belie̶ that incense carried prayers to the gods.

✤**THURIEL:** An angel who presides over **wild animals.**

✤**THURSDAY, ANGEL OF: Zidkiel.** In **Essene** beliefs it was **Sachiel.** Castiel is also an angel of Thursday. The angels who preside over the hours of the day of Thursday are: 1:00-**Sachiel,** 2:00-**Sammael,** 3:00-**Michael,** 4:00-**Haniel,** 5:00-**Raphael,** 6:00-**Gabriel,** 7:00-**Casziel,** 8:00-Sachiel, 9:00-Sammael, 10:00-Michael, 11:00-Haniel, 12:00-Raphael. The angels who preside over the hours of the night are: 1:00-Gabriel, 2:00-Casziel, 3:00-Sachiel, 4:00-Sammael, 5:00-Michael, 6:00-Haniel, 7:00-Raphael, 8:00-Gabriel, 9:00-Casziel, 10:00-Sachiel, 11:00-Sammael, 12:00-Michael.

✤**TIAMAT:** A female **dragon** spirit of ancient Babylonian lore. According to legend, Tiamat existed before the creation of the world. It was believed that through her the world came into being. She is believed to have given birth to the light. At the creation she divided her body and became Heaven and Earth.

✤**TIARA:** Angels are sometimes depicted in art wearing a tiara (a jeweled crown) to symbolize their heavenly sovereignty.

✤**TIEL:** An angel who oversees the north **wind.**

✤**TIME (ANGELS AND):** Says Swedish mystic **Emanuel Swedenborg,** the "angels have no idea or concept of time." In his book *Heaven and Hell,* Swedenborg states, "The reason for the existence of time in the world is the sun's sequential progression from one degree to another, producing the times called 'seasons of the year.' Heaven's sun is different. It does not produce days and years by sequential progression or orbital motion, but causes changes of state. This does not happen at fixed intervals. This is why angels are incapable of any concept of time, thinking instead in terms of state." According to occultists, an angel year is 365 earth years. Others believe that it is 145 earth years. Angels are believed to be immortal.

✤**TIME SPIRITS:** The **Archai** are a class of angels also known as Time Spirits. They can be found in the angelic hierarchy conceived by **Rudolph Steiner.**

✤**TINA:** An Etruscan angel who belonged to the group of angels called the **Novensiles.** The Novensiles ruled over the thunderbolts.

✤**TINKER BELL:** A character in J. M. Barrie's play *Peter Pan* (1904), a fantasy about a boy who refused to grow up. Tinker Bell was a **fairy** who befriended Peter Pan.

…HERETH: One of the ten **Holy Sefiroth** (angels) in the **Cabala.** He …so called Beauty.

TIRTAEL: An angel who oversees the east **wind.**

✤**TISHTRYA:** The angel of rain in Persian mythology. He is called the bright star and seed of the waters. He brings the rain and quenches the drought. His antithesis is Apaosha, the demon of drought.

✤**TITLES:** Throughout history angels have been called by many titles. Some of these titles include Good Spirits, Spirits, Gods, **Sons of God,** Ministers, **Sons of Light,** Servants, Celestial Choir, **Watchers, Holy Ones, Heavenly Army, Hosts, Living Creatures,** Morning Stars, **Stars,** and **Chariots of God.**

✤**TITRISYAH:** One of the seventy-eight names of **Metatron.**

✤**TITUS FLAVIUS CLEMENS:** See **Clemens, Titus Flavius.**

✤**TOBIAS:** "For a good angel will go with him, his journey will be successful, and he will come home safe and sound" (Tobit 5:21). The tale of Tobit and his son Tobias can be found in the Book of Tobit, one of the Apocryphal books to the Bible's Old Testament. Tobit is an elderly blind man who sends his young son Tobias to collect a debt for him. As Tobias is leaving the house, he finds the archangel **Raphael** waiting for him. He does not know that he is an angel. Raphael informs Tobias that he will guide him during his trip and uses the alias Azarias. While traveling, they come across a huge fish. Tobias kills the fish. Raphael then teaches Tobias the various uses of the different parts of the fish. After the journey, they return to the home of Tobit. Raphael instructs Tobias to put the gallbladder of the fish on Tobit's eyes. Tobias obeys and Tobit immediately regains his sight. Raphael then informs them that he is one of the seven angels who stand in the **presence** of God.

✤**TOBIT:** See **Tobias.**

✤**TOGARINI:** One of the **unholy Sefiroth** of the **Cabala.**

✤**TOMB OF JESUS:** Three days after the crucifixion of **Jesus, Mary Magdalene** and another woman also named Mary went to visit his tomb. Suddenly there was a fierce earthquake. The women watched as an angel of God descended from Heaven. He rolled away the stone of the tomb and then sat down upon it. His appearance was like lightning. His clothing was as white as snow. At the sight of him the guards fainted. The angel told the two women not to be afraid. He told them that Jesus had been resurrected and to go and tell his disciples (Matthew 28:1–7; Mark 16:1–7). In the account of Luke, Mary Magdalene, Joanna, and Mary the Mother of James went to the tomb of Jesus and found it empty. There two angels appeared to them. They were wearing "bright

shining clothes." The angels reminded them of Jesus' words, that h
would be resurrected in three days (Luke 24:1–10).

✦**TOMBS, ANGELS OF THE: Munkir and Nakir.**

✦**TOOTH FAIRY:** A **fairy** from folklore. When a child loses his tooth, he
is instructed to place it under his pillow when he goes to sleep at night. It
is believed that the tooth fairy will come and carry the tooth away,
leaving in its place a gift, usually money.

✦**TORAH, ANGEL OF THE: Metatron** is the Prince of the Torah. **Iophiel**
and **Zagzagel** are also angels of the Torah. Zagzagel is credited with
teaching **Moses** all of his knowledge and wisdom (Moses wrote the
Torah).

✦**TORCH:** A symbol of the archangel **Gabriel,** who brings the "light" of
God to mankind through his revelations.

✦**TORNADOES, ANGEL OF:** Za'amiel.

✦*TOUCHED BY AN ANGEL:* A 1995 television show in which an angel
comes to earth to help humans learn important lessons in courage, compassion, and love. The show stars Roma Downey as the angel and Della
Reese in the role of a heavenly messenger.

✦**TRADITIONAL ANGELS:** The angels of Judaism, Christianity, and Islam
are considered traditional angels. These angels are usually portrayed in
art with a halo, large wings, and wearing a long, light-colored robe. See
Nontraditional Angels.

✦**TRAFFIC, ANGELS OF:** Angels who protect people from the harm of a
traffic accident. In many books relaying true angel stories, people have
told of almost dying in a traffic accident but being miraculously saved by
angels. At times the angels are seen; other times a nudging hand is felt
when a driver has fallen asleep, or a warning is given before a crash.
Angels have also rescued those stranded in cars during adverse weather.
One such account was reported to author **Joan Wester Anderson** by her
son, who was stranded in a severe snowstorm while traveling home one
Christmas. That story inspired Anderson to write her first angel book,
Where Angels Walk, True Stories of Heavenly Visitors, in which she related
the experience.

✦**TRAGEDY, MUSE OF:** In Greek mythology the muse Melpomene
inspired men to write great tragedies.

✦**TRANSFORMATION ANGEL(S):** Angels found in the book *Ask Your
Angels* by authors Alma Daniel, Timothy Wyllie, and Andrew Ramer.
These angels transform spirit and thought into the physical realm.
Another name for the transformation angels are manifestation angels.

✦**TRANSPORT, ANGEL OF:** Ampharool.

✦**TRAVEL, ANGEL OF:** Ampharool is the angel of flying and instant travel.

✦**TREASURE, ANGEL OF:** Parasiel.

✦**TREE(S), ANGELS OF:** **Michael** is the angel of the **olive tree** and the **almond tree; Gabriel** is the angel of the **apple tree; Uriel** is the angel of **nut trees; Raphael** is the angel of the **broom tree; Kepharel** is the angel of the pomegranate tree; **Sammael** is the angel of the kermes oak; and **Zidkiel** is the angel of the terebinth tree.

✦**TREE OF LIFE, ANGELS OF THE:** The Tree of Life is the tree that bore the forbidden fruit in the **Garden of Eden.** God instructed **Adam** and **Eve** not to eat from the Tree of Life. **Satan** later deceived Eve into tasting the fruit. Eve convinced Adam to partake of it also. After Adam and Eve ate from the tree, God banished the couple from the garden. He placed two **Cherubim** at the entrance of the garden along with a turning, flaming sword to prevent them from reentering **Paradise.** The archangel **Raphael** is the guardian angel of the Tree of Life. **Baruch** is also considered a guardian of the Tree of Life. It is also called the Tree of Immortal Life and the Tree of Good and Bad.

✦**TREMORS, ANGEL OF:** Zi'iel.

✦**TRIGIAOB:** The angel of fowl.

✦**TRIPLE MOTHER GODDESS:** During ancient times, **Lilith,** a high-ranking female demon, was recognized as the Triple Mother Goddess by the early agrarian tribes of the Canaanites.

✦**TRISAGION:** A song of celebration that is sung continuously day and night to God by the **Seraphim.** As they encircle God's throne, they sing, "Holy, holy, holy, the Lord God the Almighty, who was and is and is to come" (Revelation 4:8).

✦**TRUMPET(S):** Angels are often depicted in art holding trumpets. The trumpet symbolizes the voice of God. The archangel **Gabriel** is associated with the trumpet because he is the personification of the voice of God. In the Book of **Revelation,** there are seven angels holding trumpets. As each angel sounds his trumpet, an apocalyptic event takes place.

✦**TRUMPETER OF THE LAST JUDGMENT:** A title held by the archangel **Gabriel.**

✦**TRUTH:** The name of one of the **Amesha Spentas** (archangels) in Zoroastrianism. He is also called **Asha.**

✦**TRUTH, ANGELS OF:** An angel whose purpose is to help individuals to discern spiritual truths. In Judeo-Christian lore, the angel of truth is **Gabriel.** In *The Manual of Discipline* of the **Dead Sea scrolls,** the angel of light is also referred to as the spirit of truth. According to one Talmud legend, God consulted the angel of truth in his decision to create humankind.

✤TSADKIEL: A variation of the name **Tzadkiel.**

✤TSAPHIEL: An angel of the moon in occult lore.

✤TSIRYA: See **Childbirth.**

✤TSURIA: See **Childbirth.**

✤TUBAL-CAIN: According to legend, Tubal-Cain is the father of **Asmodeus,** who is a great and powerful demon.

✤TUBUAS: One of the angels that the Church of Rome reprobated in 745 C.E.

✤TUBUEL: One of the angels that the church of Rome reprobated in 745 C.E.

✤TUESDAY, ANGEL OF: **Sammael.** In **Essene** beliefs it was **Camael.** The angels who preside over the hours of the day of Tuesday are: 1:00-Sammael, 2:00-**Michael,** 3:00-**Haniel,** 4:00-**Raphael,** 5:00-**Gabriel,** 6:00-**Casziel,** 7:00-**Sachiel,** 8:00-Sammael, 9:00-Michael, 10:00-Haniel, 11:00-Raphael, 12:00-Gabriel. The angels who preside over the hours of the night are: 1:00-Casziel, 2:00-Sachiel, 3:00-Sammael, 4:00-Michael, 5:00-Haniel, 6:00-Raphael, 7:00-Gabriel, 8:00-Casziel, 9:00-Sachiel, 10:00-Sammael, 11:00-Michael, 12:00-Haniel.

✤TUFIEL: An angel who stands guard over the palace of Wilon, the **First Heaven.**

✤TUFRIAL: An angel who stands guard over the palace of Makon, the **Sixth Heaven.**

✤TUMA'EL: A fallen angel. One of the angels who brought the secret knowledge of Heaven to earth.

✤TURAEL: A variation of the name **Turiel.**

✤TURAN: The Etruscan name for **Tara,** a great celestial spirit.

✤TUR'EL: A fallen angel. He was one of the leaders of the angels who came to the earth to have sexual relations with women. He is also one of the angels who brought the secret knowledge of Heaven to earth.

✤TUREL: A variation of the name **Turiel.**

✤TURIEL (ROCK OF GOD): A fallen angel from the class of angels called **Watchers.** Variations of the name Turiel are Turel and Turael.

✤TURMIEL: An angel who safeguards the west **wind.**

✤TUTELARY ANGELS: Guardian angels of **nations.**

✤TUTRBEBIAL: An angel who stands guard over the palace of **Arabot,** the Seventh Heaven.

✤TUTRECHIAL: An angel who stands guard over the palace of Wilon, the **First Heaven.**

✦**Tutrusiai:** An angel who stands guard over the palace of Wilon, the **First Heaven.**

✦**Twelve Aeons:** The name of a high-ranking group of angels found in **Manichaeism.**

✦**Twelve Archangels:** According to New Age angelologists, there are twelve archangels as opposed to the traditional seven. The twelve are Anthriel, Aquariel, **Chamuel, Gabriel, Jophiel, Michael,** Omniel, Perpetiel, **Raphael, Uriel,** Valeoel, and **Zadkiel.**

✦**Twelve Light Diadems:** A high order of angels found in **Manichaeism.**

✦**Twelve Months of the Year, Angels of the:** See **Months of the Year.**

✦**Twelve Tribes of Israel:** See **Israel.**

✦**Twentieth Century, Angels of the:** In the twentieth century, more than ever before, people are reporting direct communication with angels. According to a 1991 Gallup Poll, sixty-nine percent of Americans believe in angels. Thirty-two percent of Americans believe that they have had contact with an angel. There have also been books written containing information communicated from the angels about the future of humankind. In these publications new information on angels has been brought to light regarding their role in mankind's history and future. Some of these books include the *Starseed Transmissions* by **Kenneth X. Carey,** with information from **Raphael;** the *Crystal Stair* by Eric Klein, which features **Saint Michael;** and *Ask Your Angels* by Alma Daniel, Timothy Wyllie, and Andrew Ramer. The information in *Ask Your Angels* was communicated to the authors by several angels. In addition, there have been many UFO sightings during the twentieth century. Some believe these sightings may be angels. There is the story of **Orfeo Angelucci,** a businessman who claims to have been visited by higher beings from another world. Some believe these beings may have been angels. The stories of angels helping and aiding people on earth continue to be told. Several books have been written on modern encounters with angels, such as **Sophy Burnham's** *Angel Letters;* **Eileen Freeman's** *Touched by Angels;* and **Joan Wester Anderson's** *Where Angels Walk, True Stories of Heavenly Visitors.* These books relate tales of angels appearing to humans during times of need. There are also stories of near-death experiences where angels appeared to comfort people. In addition, there has been a resurgence in the interest in angels in the late twentieth century. Popular writers who have propelled the topic into the mainstream include Sophy Burnham, **Terry Lynn Taylor, Mortimer J. Adler,** Malcom Godwin, Joan Wester Anderson, and Eileen Freeman. All have written sensational books that have captivated angel lovers of all ages and that have kept angels in the spotlight for years. From reading these books many have come to believe that the angels are working closely with mankind in the twentieth century and will continue to do so in the future.

✤**Twilight, Angel of:** Aftiel.

✤**Twin Angels:** According to legend, when the prophet **Enoch** was transformed into the mighty angel **Metatron,** he was divided into two angels. The second angel is named **Sandolphon.** For this reason Metatron and Sandolphon are known as the twin angels. In other lore, the prophet **Elijah** is Sandolphon, twin to Metatron.

✤**"Two Angels":** The name of a poem written by **Longfellow** in which he writes about the angel of death and the angel of life.

✤**Two Camps, Angels of: Mahanaim.**

✤**Tzadkiel:** A great angelic prince in Heaven who is one of the angels of **justice.** His name can also be found on amulets worn by pregnant women for success in delivering a healthy baby. Variations of the name Tzadkiel are Tsadkiel, Tzadquiel, and Tzadqiel.

✤**Tzadqiel:** A variation of the name **Tzadkiel.**

✤**Tzadquiel:** A variation of the name **Tzadkiel.**

✤**Tzakmaqiel:** An angel of **Aquarius.**

✤**Tzaphqiel (God's Contemplation):** An angel who rules over the planet **Saturn.**

✤**Tzartak:** See **Childbirth.**

U

Let brotherly love continue. Be not forgetful to entertain strangers for thereby some have entertained angels unawares.

—HEBREWS 13:1–2

❧**UDRGAZYI:** See **Childbirth.**

❧**UDRIEL:** See **Childbirth.**

❧**ULYSSES:** The hero of the *Odyssey* (a Greek epic poem attributed to Homer). In the *Odyssey*, Ulysses is rescued several times by the goddess **Athena** and the winged god **Hermes,** who act as his guardian spirits.

❧**UNBORN, ANGEL OF THE: Armisael** is the guardian angel of the unborn.

❧**UNCLEAN SPIRITS:** A phrase sometimes used in scripture when referring to **demons.** In Acts 5:16 of the *New World Translation of the Holy Scriptures*, it states, "The multitude from the cities around Jerusalem kept coming together, bearing sick people and those troubled with unclean spirits."

❧**UNDERSTANDING:** The name of one of the angels of the **Holy Sefiroth.** He is also called Binah.

❧**UNDERWORLD, ANGELS OF THE:** In the Testament of **Solomon,** Abezethibou is ruler of the underworld. In other sources Abbaton is a guardian angel of the underworld, and the archangel **Raphael** is the guide of the underworld. To the Greeks, **Proserpina** was the Queen of the Underworld. Other names for the underworld include Tartarus, **Hades,** and **Hell.**

✤**UNDINES:** Female water spirits (also called **Elementals**) that dwell in the oceans and seas. They manifest as part fish and part woman. According to lore, the undines could acquire a soul by marrying and having a child by a mortal. They are ruled by the archangel **Gabriel.**

✤**UNGODLY MEN, ANGELS OF:** The angels of ungodly men can be found in the Apocalypse of Sephaniah. These angels have the faces of leopards, tusks like wild boars, and eyes mixed with blood. Their hair is long, and in their hands are fiery whips. These are the angels who carry men to the underworld for eternal punishment. The lion-headed angel Nagazdiel sees to it that Hell is filled with the souls of ungodly men.

✤**UNHOLY SEFIROTH:** The ten angels of the Unholy Sefiroth (angels of the **Cabala**) are named Chaigidiel, Gamaliel, Gamchicoth, Golab, Harab Serap, **Lilith, Sammael,** Sathariel, Thaumiel, and Togarini.

✤**UNITED STATES:** See **America; Washington, George.**

✤**UNITY, ANGEL OF:** The archangel **Michael.**

✤**UNIVERSE, ANGEL OF THE:** In gnostic beliefs the **Demiurge** is the creator of the universe. German astronomer **Johannes Kepler** believed that the angels are responsible for the movement, balance, and order of the universe. During medieval times the angels were considered administrators of the universe.

✤**UR, ANGEL OF:** Ur is a city in the Euphrates Valley. It was settled, near Babylon, in 4000 B.C. In Ur, archaeologists have discovered a stela that shows an angel descending from Heaven, pouring the water of life into the cup of a king. Scholars believe that it is the earliest known depiction of an angel.

✤**URA'EL:** One of the angels who escorted **Enoch** on his tour of earth and **Sheol.**

✤**URAKABARAMEEL:** A **fallen angel.**

✤**URANIA:** One of the nine muses in Greek mythology. Urania inspired men to study **astronomy.**

✤**URIEL (FIRE OF GOD):** One of the seven **archangels.** According to Judaic lore, **Uriel** holds the keys to Hell and will do away with the gates of Hell on **Judgment Day.** According to Judaic lore, he is the angel that **Jacob** wrestled with at Peniel. Legend has it that as they wrestled, Jacob and Uriel merged and became one. In one tale, Uriel is a serpent who reprimands the prophet **Moses** for not holding a rite of circumcision for his son. Uriel is symbolized by the **scroll** and an open hand holding a flame. The flame represents the meaning of his name, which is "fire of God." In John Milton's *Paradise Lost,* he is called Regent of the Sun. Uriel holds many titles including Prince of the **Seraphim,** Angel of the **Presence,** Angel of **Poetry,** Angel of Prophecy, Angel of Repentance,

Angel of Thunder and Terror, Angel of Music, Angel of **Summer,** Light of God, Angel of **Retribution,** Angel of September, Angel of Hunger, Angel of the South, Angel of Political Reform, Angel of the **Nut Tree,** and Ruler of Hades. Variations of the name Uriel are Auriel, Oriel, Ouriel, and Pheniel.

✦**URPANIEL:** An angel who protects individuals from demons.

✦**USIEL (GOD'S STRENGTH):** A fallen angel from the order of angels called the **Watchers.** He was one of the angels who came to the earth to have sexual relations with women and produce children. Variations of the name Usiel are Uziel and **Uzziel.**

✦**UTHRA:** A guardian angel in Mandaean beliefs.

✦**UTHRI:** The plural of **uthra.**

✦**UZIAL:** An angel who stands guard over the palace of Maon, the **Fifth Heaven.**

✦**UZIEL:** A variation of the name **Usiel.**

✦**UZZAH:** A **ministering angel.** In 3 Enoch 4:6–10, he questions God about his making **Enoch** a lofty angel and giving him a position in Heaven. He is later named as a fallen angel who teaches the knowledge of **sorcery** to mankind.

✦**UZZIEL:** A prince of the order of **Virtues.** In some sources the name Uzziel is a variation of **Usiel.**

V

His angel guards those who honor the Lord and rescues them from danger.

—PSALMS 34:7

✤**VAHMAN:** Another name for **Vohu Manah,** one of the **Amesha Spentas** (archangels) in Zoroastrianism.

✤**VALEOEL:** One of twelve **archangels** listed by New Age angelologists.

✤**VALHALLA, ANGELS OF:** Valhalla is the hall to which the **Valkyries** (female angels of death in German mythology) carry the souls of heroes.

✤**VALKYRIES:** Female angels of death in German mythology. In Germanic lore, the Valkyries, under **Brunnhilde**'s direction, oversaw wars and chose which warriors would live and which would die. They would carry the souls of the heroes to the hall of heroes called Valhalla.

✤**VALOR, ANGELS OF:** Angels who inspire courage and heroism in humans. The angels of valor come from the class of angels called **Virtues.**

✤**VAMANA:** One of the **avatars** of Hindu lore.

✤**VARAHA:** One of the **avatars** of Hindu lore.

✤**VARIEL:** See **Childbirth.**

✤**VARMA:** Chief of the **Adityas** (Vedic angels).

✤**VARUNA:** The leader of the **Adityas** (Vedic angels).

✤**VATA:** A variation of the name **Vayu.**

✤**VAYU:** One of the **Yazatas** in Persian mythology. In Zoroastrianism he was the angel of the air and winds. Vayu brings life in the rain, and death in the storm. He produces the lightning and makes the dawn appear. He is hailed as a fearsome warrior who seeks to destroy the spirit of darkness and protect the good creation of God. He is said to carry a golden spear and rides in a chariot drawn by a thousand horses. Men pray to Vayu in difficult times. A variation of the name Vayu is Vata.

✦**Vegetables, Angel of: Sofiel.**

✦**Vegetation, Angel of:** In Zoroastrianism, **Ameretat** is the angel who watches over the earth's vegetation.

✦**Vejovis:** An Etruscan angel who belonged to the group of angels called the **Novensiles.** The Novensiles ruled over the thunderbolts.

✦**Vengeance, Angels of:** Angels who execute **punishment** on God's behalf. **Gabriel, Michael, Nathanel, Raphael, Uriel,** and **Satan** are all angels of vengeance.

✦**Venus, Angel of: Zidkiel.** To the Cabalists, Rome's goddess Venus was the angel of love.

✦**Venus in the Morning:** A name given to **Astarte** (a she-demon) by the Egyptians.

✦**Verchiel:** The angel of July, the angel of Leo, and a prince of the **Virtues.**

✦**Verethraghna:** The angel of **victory** in Persian mythology. He is a powerful force who can take on many forms. These forms include a mighty wind; a bull with sharp, golden horns; a strong white horse; a sharp-toothed camel; a wrathful boar; a strong, brawny youth; a large, speedy bird; a bucking ram; a wild buck; and a man carrying a sword. He fights the maliciousness of men and demons. He punishes the unjust and the wicked.

✦**Vereviel:** A variation of the name **Vrevoil.**

✦**Verrier:** A **fallen angel.**

✦**Vial of Balm, Angel of the:** As the angel of **healing,** the archangel **Raphael** is said to carry a golden vial of balm to cure ailments.

✦**Vials of the Wrath of God, Angels of the:** The Book of Revelation 16:1 makes reference to seven angels who carry vials of the wrath of God. At God's command, these angels pour out the contents of these vials upon the earth. The account tells us, "The first angel went and poured his vial on the earth, and a foul and painful sore came on those who had the mark of the beast. The second angel poured out his vial upon the sea and every living soul died in the sea. The third angel poured out his vial upon the fountains of waters; and they became blood. The fourth angel poured out his vial upon the sun; and power was given unto him to scorch men with fire. The fifth angel poured out his vial upon the seat of the beast; and his kingdom was full of darkness; and they gnawed their tongues for pain. The sixth angel poured out his vial upon the great river Euphrates; and the water thereof was dried up, that the way of the kings of the east might be prepared. The seventh angel poured out his vial into the air; and there came a great voice out of the temple of Heaven, from the throne, saying, It is done."

✤**VICEROY OF HEAVEN:** A title held by the archangel **Michael.**

✤**VICTORIA:** Roman winged goddess of **victory.** She is the equivalent of the Greek goddess **Nike.**

✤**VICTORIUS:** An angel who regularly visited **Saint Patrick.** He appeared once a week to Saint Patrick to converse. Victorius asked Saint Patrick to go to Ireland and teach the pagans about Christianity.

✤**VICTORY, ANGELS OF:** In Persian mythology the angel of victory was **Verethraghna.** Victory is also the name of one of the angels of the **Holy Sefiroth** as listed in the **Cabala.** In Rome the winged goddess **Victoria** was the goddess of victory.

✤**VIKING(S), ANGELS OF THE:** Angels in **Viking** beliefs included the **Valkyries.** The **Valkyries** were **female angels** of **death.**

✤**VILA:** Eastern European **fairies.** They dwell in the forest and work closely with nature. According to legend, the Vila are born in the spring during the period of misty rains and fresh morning dew. It is said that when a rainbow appears, a Vila is born. The Vila also preside over rain, making sure that there is enough for the plants to grow.

✤**VINCI, LEONARDO DA:** Noted Italian Renaissance painter (1452–1519) who specialized in religious paintings. He often featured angels in his work. Three of his most famous paintings featuring angels are *Madonna of the Rocks*, the *Last Supper*, and the *Annunciation*.

✤**VINE, ANGEL OF:** In 3 Baruch it states that the vine was planted in the **Garden of Eden** by the angel **Satanael.** In relaying the story of the vine to Baruch, an angel reveals that it was the vine through which the serpent deceived **Eve,** and that the knowledge of good and bad is the "sinful desire" that Satanael spread over **Adam** and Eve. The angels said that because of this, God cursed the vine because Satanael had planted it. (Note: The vine is thought by some to be a grape vine.)

✤**VIOLENT-THRUSTERS:** Also called the Al-Zabaniya, they are the nineteen angels in the Koran who stand as guards of Hell.

✤**VIRGIN MARY:** The mother of **Jesus.** In the Book of Luke, the archangel **Gabriel** appears to the Virgin Mary and announces that she will give birth to the Messiah. After her death she became known as the Virgin Mary, the Madonna, the Blessed Virgin, Mother Mary, and Mother of God by the Catholics. Upon reaching Heaven the Virgin Mary is said to have become an angel of the class of **Virtues.** The Virtues bestow miracles from on high and are called angels of grace. According to lore, the Virgin Mary is one of the highest-ranking angels of Heaven, holding such titles as **Queen of Angels,** Queen of Heaven, Queen of Peace, Queen of Prophets, and **Mother of All People.** Throughout history the Virgin Mary has appeared to a number of people, bringing messages of love, repentance, and faith. She is said to be beautiful, having long, curly black hair and large blue eyes. When she appears, she is surrounded by **Cherubs** and comes floating on a cloud. Among the most famous sightings of the Virgin Mary is that at Lourdes in 1858, where she appeared to a young girl named Bernadette Soubirous. She told the girl to dig a well. The well later became famous for its healing powers. In 1917 she appeared in Fatima, to three shepherd children. Through these children she warned the world of coming punishments if people did not change their sinful lives. In 1981 she began appearing to six young people in **Medjugorje,** a small town in Yugoslavia. Through these young people she communicates with the world, bringing revelations about the future, and messages of hope and encouragement. She appears to these young people daily to this day. See **Annunciation.**

✤**VIRGO, ANGEL OF: Hamaliel.**

✤**VIRTUE, ANGEL OF:** In Zoroastrianism the angel of virtue was **Asha.**

✤**VIRTUES:** An order of angels ranking fifth in the angelic hierarchy. The Virtues are responsible for working miracles in God's name on earth. They also look after the heroes of the world and those who champion for the good. They also impart strength and courage to individuals when needed. Two angels from the Virtues class escorted Christ to Heaven in the **Ascension.** The Virtues are also referred to as the Angels of Grace, Angels of Valor, the **Brilliant Ones,** Splendors, Malakim, Mights and Tarshishim. Ruling princes of the order include **Haniel, Michael, Raphael, Barbiel, Usiel,** Tarshish, and Peliel.

✤**VISHNU:** One of the great gods of Hinduism. He is associated with the **avatars,** which are ten semi-angelic beings of Hindu lore.

✤**VISIONARIES:** In 1981 the **Virgin Mary** began appearing to six young people in Medjugorje (a small town in Yugoslavia). These six young people have become known around the world as the visionaries. Through them the Virgin Mary brings messages of hope and encouragement to mankind. She also reveals extraordinary secrets about mankind's future. She appears to these young people every day at 6:40 P.M. According to the Virgin Mary, these young people were selected to receive the visions because they are "ordinary."

✤**VISIONS, ANGEL OF: Remiel.**

✤*VISIONS OF THE DAUGHTERS OF ALBION:* A work by **William Blake.** In his *Visions of the Daughters of Albion*, Blake creates a fictitious angel called the "angel of Albion."

✤**VOHU MANAH:** One of the **Amesha Spentas** (archangels) in Zoroastrianism. He is also called Wisdom (in some writings Wisdom is substituted with Good Mind or Good Thought). He is the guardian angel of cattle. In rituals he is represented by milk.

✤**VOICE OF GOD, ANGEL OF THE:** The archangel **Gabriel** is known God's "personal spokesman." Because of this, he is sometimes referred to as the voice of God.

✤**VOICES:** An order of angels found in **gnosticism**.

✤**VRETIL:** A variation of the name **Vrevoil**.

✤**VREVOIL:** Another name for **Radweri'el YHWH**.

✤**VRIHASPATI:** In Vedic beliefs Vrihaspati was the guardian angel of hymns.

✤**VUAL:** A **fallen angel**.

The delight of the wisdom of the angels is to communicate to others what they know.

—Emanuel Swedenborg

✣**Wajima:** Angels of the Australian Aboriginals.

✣**War, Angel of:** The archangel **Michael.**

✣**War in Heaven:** The war in Heaven began when **Satan** became an opposer to God. God enlisted the archangel **Michael** to lead the battle on Satan and the other angels who rebelled against God's laws. Michael and the **Heavenly Army** threw Satan and his demons out of Heaven, hurling them downward to the earth. The Bible states, "Then war broke out in heaven. Michael and his angels fought against the dragon, who fought back with his angels; but the dragon was defeated, and he and his angels were not allowed to stay in heaven any longer. The huge dragon was thrown out—that ancient serpent, named the Devil, or Satan, that deceived the whole world. He was thrown down to earth, and all his angels with him." (Revelation 12:7–9)

✣**Warring Angels:** In her book *Embraced by the Light*, Betty J. Eadie relates her experience of seeing "warring angels" while visiting Heaven. According to Eadie, the warring angels do battle against Satan and his angels on behalf of people on earth. Eadie explains that even though we have guardian angels, the warring angels are sometimes necessary. Of their appearance, Eadie says, "They are giant men, very muscularly built, with a wonderful countenance about them. They are magnificent spirits." The warring angels are strong and confident spirits that cannot be thwarted by evil forces. As they go out on their missions, they are suited in armor. They also move with great speed, faster than the other angels.

✦WARRIORS: The name of an order of angels found in John Milton's epic poem *Paradise Lost.*

✦WARWAHYAH: One of the seventy-eight names of **Metatron.**

✦WASHINGTON, GEORGE: Angels were a part of Washington's faith and beliefs. According to legend, he was once visited by a female angel who showed him the history of the United States. Washington also attributed his success at Valley Forge to his guardian angel.

✦WATCHERS: An order of angels also called the Grigori. The Watchers were given the responsibility by God to be teachers to humankind. They are also said to have worked with the **archangels** in creating Paradise. The Watchers fell from grace when they became attracted to the women of earth. Twelve thousand years ago, two hundred of these Watchers left their positions in Heaven to come to the earth to have sexual relations with women. Out of fear of God they made a pact amongst themselves that each would go forward with the act. The Book of 1 Enoch 6:3–4 states, "And **Semyaza,** being their leader, said unto them, 'I fear that perhaps you will not consent that this deed should be done, and I alone will become [responsible] for this great sin.' But they all responded to him, 'Let us all swear an oath and bind everyone among us by a curse not to abandon this suggestion but to do the deed.' Then they all swore together and bound one another by [the curse.]" They descended upon **Mount Sinai,** taking on fleshly bodies. The Bible account at Genesis 6:2 says, "When people began to multiply on the face of the ground, and daughters were born to them, the sons of God saw that they were fair; and they took wives for themselves of all that they chose." The Book of 1 Enoch 6:1–2 states, "In those days, when the children of man had multiplied, it happened that there were born unto them beautiful daughters. And the angels, the children of Heaven, saw them and desired them; and they said to one another, 'Come, let us choose wives for ourselves from among the daughters of man and beget us children.' " From their union with women they produced children called the **Nephillim,** who turned out to be evil giants. In the Book of Genesis 6:4 it states, "The Nephillim were on the earth in those days—and also afterward—when the sons of God went in to the daughters of humans, who bore children to them." The Nephillim were part of the reason that God sent the deluge. According to one account, the Watchers shed their bodies and returned to the spiritual realm once the great **flood** came. **Azaz'el** was the chief of the Watchers. The leaders of the Watchers who came to the earth were named Azaz'el, Arakeb, Rame'el, **Tam'el,** Ram'el, Dan'el, **Ezeqel,** Baraqiyal, Asel, Armaros, Batar'el, Anan'el, Zaqe'el, Sasomaspe'el, Kestar'el, Tur'el, Yamayol, and Arazyal. The leader of the leaders was named **Shemyaza.** While on earth the Watchers taught their wives many things. Much of it was knowledge forbidden to humans. The Book of 1 Enoch talks extensively about this, saying, "And they took wives unto themselves, and everyone chose one woman for himself, and they began to go unto them. And they taught them magical medicine, incantations, the cutting of roots, and taught them about plants" (1 Enoch 7:1–2). After their descent to earth the Watchers were never allowed to enter Heaven again.

✤**WATER, ANGEL OF:** In **Essene** beliefs the angel of water was Sachiel. In Zoroastrianism, the guardian angel of water was **Haurvatat.** Haurvatat was represented in rituals by consecrated water. In Judaism, the Princes of Water are **Ariael** and **Anapiel YHWH.** In Persian mythology Harooda presided over the element of water.

✤**WATER BEARER, ANGEL OF THE: Tzakmaqiel.**

✤**WATER INSECTS, ANGEL OF:** Shakziel.

✤**WATER SPIRITS:** The **undines** are water spirits. They are also called angels of the water.

✤**WAY, THE:** Another name for **Asha Vahishta,** the angel of truth in Zoroastrianism.

✤**WEAKNESS, ANGEL OF: Amaliel.**

✤**WEAPONS, ANGELS OF:** The angel **Goden'el** taught mankind how to build weapons of war. The angel Alimon is a guardian angel who is prayed to for protection against weapons. Tafthi and Reivtip are also angels who aided in protecting individuals against harm by weapons.

✤**WEDNESDAY, ANGEL OF:** The archangel **Michael.** To the Essenes it was **Raphael.** The angels that preside over the hours of the day on Wednesday are: 1:00-Raphael, 2:00-**Gabriel,** 3:00-**Casziel,** 4:00-**Sachiel,** 5:00-**Sammael,** 6:00-Michael, 7:00-**Haniel,** 8:00-Raphael, 9:00-Gabriel, 10:00-Casziel, 11:00-Sachael, 12:00-Sammael. The angels that preside over the hours of the night are: 1:00-Michael, 2:00-Haniel, 3:00-Raphael, 4:00-Gabriel, 5:00-Casziel, 6:00-Sachiel, 7:00-Sammael, 8:00-Michael, 9:00-Haniel, 10:00-Raphael, 11:00-Gabriel, 12:00-Casziel.

✤**WEIGHER OF SOULS:** The archangel **Michael** is sometimes referred to as the Weigher of Souls. In Heaven, Michael weighs the deeds of the souls of men.

✤WEST, ANGEL OF THE: The archangel **Raphael.**

✤WEST WIND, ANGEL OF THE: See **Wind.**

✤WHEELS: Another name for the order of angels called **Thrones.** The Wheels symbolize the mobility of the angels. **Rikbiel YHWH** is the angel in charge of the order of Wheels.

✤WHIRLWINDS, ANGEL OF: Za'amiel.

✤WHITAKER, JOHNNY: Star of the made-for-television movie *The Littlest Angel* (1969). In the film Whitaker plays a shepherd boy who dies and then fights to become an angel. Eventually, he becomes an angel, but not before learning a few pointed lessons.

✤WHITE, ANGELS OF: In the Bible angels are often described as wearing white. The color white represents purity and holiness. It is also the **color** that symbolizes the archangel **Gabriel.**

✤WHO IS AS GOD: The meaning of the name **Michael.** (In some writings it is "looks like God").

✤WHOLENESS: The name of one of the **Amesha Spentas** (archangels) of Zoroastrianism. He is also called **Haurvatat.** He is the protector of **water.** In rituals he is represented by holy water.

✤WHOM GOD STRENGTHENS: The meaning of the name **Azael.** Once a **ministering angel** in Heaven, Azael became a fallen angel when he taught **sorcery** to humans and had sexual relations with a mortal woman.

✤WILD ANIMALS, ANGELS OF: Hayyal, Jehiel, Mtniel, and Thuriel are all angels who preside over wild animals.

✤WILLOW TREE, ANGEL OF THE: The archangel **Gabriel.**

✤WILON, ANGELS OF: Wilon is the name of the **First Heaven.** The ruling prince is the archangel Sidri'el. Angels who dwell in Wilon include the angels of astronomy, the angels of ice, the angels of snow, and the angels of morning dew. At the border dwells the order of angels called the **Powers.**

✤WIND(S), ANGELS OF THE: The angel who presides over all of the four winds is named Ruhiel. **Lix Tetrax** is the demon of the wind. According to the chronicles of **Enoch,** the winds at the four corners of the world correspond to each of the four **Seraphim.** ANGELS OF THE WINDS OF DESTRUCTION. In the Book of Revelation 7:1, the apostle **John** wrote of seeing four angels holding back the four winds: "I saw four angels standing at the four corners of the earth, holding back the four winds, so that no wind should blow on the earth." These winds are known as the winds of destruction. GUARDIANS OF THE FOUR WINDS. There are guardian angels of the four winds. Angels who stand guard over the north wind are Beliael, Bezaliel, El El, Gonael, Halqim, In Hii, Madgabiel, Mahananel, Tiel, and Yonel. South wind: Bachliel,

Chushiel, Darkiel, Donel, Jachniel, Kadashiel, Klaha, Korniel, Loel, Nachmiel, Nafriel, Nakriel, Nichbadiel, Qalbam, Qamiel, Qaniel, and Tehoriel. East wind: Arson, Bahaliel, Dormiel, Karmiel, Masim, Modiel, Nohariel, Ramamiel, Tirtael, Yahanaq Rabba, Yarashiel. West wind: Karniel, Kashiel, Lobkir, Pilalael, Raquiel, Sakniel, Somcham, Tarfaniel, Turmiel, and Yahala.

✦WIND, DEMON OF: Lix Tetrax.

✦WINDS OF DESTRUCTION, ANGELS OF THE: See Wind.

✦WINDSTORMS, ANGELS OF: Ruhiel.

✦WINGED BABIES: The winged baby angels seen in art are called Cherubs.

✦WINGED CREATURES: The Seraphim are sometimes referred to as "winged creatures." This is because each of them has six wings. This is supported in the Bible at Revelation 4:8 where it says, "And the four living creatures [Seraphim], each of them with six wings, are full of eyes all around and inside." In some translations of the Book of Exodus, the Cherubim are referred to as "winged creatures." When building the Ark of the Covenant, the Hebrews made two golden Cherubim, one to sit at each end. In some translations of the Bible, these Cherubim are referred to as "winged creatures." The *Good News Bible* states, "Make two winged creatures of hammered gold, one for each end of the lid" (Exodus 25:18).

✦WINGED DRAGON: A demon found in the Testament of Solomon. He is described as having the face and feet of a man, with limbs of a dragon, and wings. He copulates with women while in the form of a winged spirit. He can be thwarted by the angel Bazazath.

✦WINGED MERMAIDS: In art, Balinese angels are depicted as winged mermaids.

✦WINGED SPHINXES: In Assyrian art, the Cherubim were portrayed as creatures with human faces and the bodies of winged sphinxes.

✦WING(s): The Koran states, "God sends forth the angels as His messengers, with two, three, or four pairs of wings." The first depiction of a winged being was discovered in the city of Ur. It was found on a stela that shows an angel descending from Heaven, pouring the water of life into the cup of a king. Mesopotamians believed that their gods dwelled in the sky. In art they portrayed their gods as winged men, using the wings of birds as an example. The Greeks and Romans later incorporated this idea into their beliefs, depicting their heavenly messengers as winged beings. The angels of Judeo-Christian beliefs were later patterned after the winged gods of the Greeks and Romans. Wings showed up in Christian art during the reign of the Roman emperor

Constantine (A.D. 312), after he converted to Christianity. During the Middle Ages artists painted angels with wings to distinguish them from human beings. The wings suggest the angels' ability to fly and to travel between Heaven and earth. They also symbolize the angels' role as God's divine messengers. **Plato** wrote, "The function of the wing is to take what is heavy and raise it up into the region above, where the gods dwell; of all things connected with the body, it has the greatest affinity with the divine."

✤*WINGS OF DESIRE:* A 1988 film, set in Berlin. It is the story of two angels named Dommartin and Ganz who travel about the city listening to people's thoughts. Ganz becomes tired of observing the pain of others, consoling them, but never being seen or having his love returned. Eventually, he decides to reenter the world as a mortal.

✤**WINTER, ANGEL OF:** Farlas. Other angels of winter include Attaris, Cetarari, and Amabael.

✤**WIRTH, OSWALD:** A designer of a deck of **tarot** cards in which angels appear in a variety of situations.

✤**WISDOM:** The name of one of the **Amesha Spentas** (archangels) in Zoroastrianism. He is also called Vohu Manah.

✤**WISDOM, ANGELS OF:** In Judaism, Zagzagel is credited for giving **Moses** his wisdom that was later recorded in the **Torah.** In the **Cabala** the angel of wisdom is named **Chokmah.** The **Cherubim** are also angels of wisdom. They are said to emanate a subtle vibration of knowledge and wisdom that they receive from God.

✤**WISE LORD:** In Zoroastrianism, **Ahura Mazda** (God) is referred to as Wise Lord.

✤**WITCHES, ANGELS OF: Familiars** are the guardian spirits of Witches.

✤**WIZARDS OF EGYPT:** See **Jannes and Jambres.**

✤**WOMAN DRESSED WITH THE SUN:** See **Pregnant Angel.**

✤**WOMB(S), ANGEL OF THE: Armisael.**

✤**WOOD SPRITES: Fairy**like spirits of nature.

✤**WOODS, ANGEL OF: Zulphas.**

✤**WORLD, ANGELS OF THE:** The angel **Metatron** is known as the **Demiurge,** the creator of the world. The guardian of the world is a celestial bird of Heaven. Each day he goes before the sun and stretches out his wings to block the burning rays of the sun. If he did not do so, all living creatures would be incinerated. The name of this bird is Phoenix.

✤**WORLD LEADERS, ANGEL OF: Haniel** is the angel who controls the government leaders of earth. The angels in charge of protecting the world's leaders and inspiring them to make the right decisions are the **Principalities.** In addition, **Satan** is credited with controlling the world leaders.

Evidence of this is given in the Bible when Satan offers Jesus all of the kingdoms of the world in an effort to tempt him. According to the Testament of **Solomon,** the demon named **Power** puts tyrants in power and deposes righteous kings.

✦**WORLD WAR I:** According to eyewitness accounts, during World War I angels appeared at the scene of battle. In late August of 1914, British soldiers fighting at Mons in Belgium saw troops of angels appear in the sky. The angels defended them against the Germans. Reports received from the Germans said that spectral riders and shining beings with swords, bows, and arrows were fighting in the sky over the British soldiers, impeding the German attack while protecting the British.

✦**WORLDWIDE COOPERATION, ANGEL OF:** The archangel **Michael.**

✦**WORMS, ELEAZER OF:** Medieval writer credited with writing the **Book of Raziel.**

✦**WORMWOOD, ANGEL OF:** In the Book of Revelation, Wormwood is a great star that falls from Heaven when the **third angel** sounds his **trumpet.** Revelation 8:10–11 says, "The third angel blew his trumpet, and a great star fell from Heaven, blazing like a torch, and it fell on a third of the rivers and on the springs of water. The name of the star is Wormwood. A third of the waters became wormwood, and many died from the water, because it was made bitter."

✦**WORSHIP OF ANGELS:** See **Angelolatry.**

✦**WRATH, ANGEL OF:** **Aeshma** is the demon of wrath in Zoroastrianism. His opponent is **Sraosha,** the angel of discipline. Wrath is also the name of a demon **Archon** in gnosticism.

✦**WRATH, ANGELS OF:** **Af.** He represents God's wrath toward the sinful state of the world. His antithesis is **Sammael.** In the underworld there are angels of wrath who apply everlasting torments to sinners. The angels of wraths dwell in **Arabot,** the Seventh Heaven. They are made of fire.

✦**WRITING, ANGELS OF:** The angel **Penemuel** taught men how to communicate through the written word. Even though mankind has made much progress out of this knowledge, it was considered a grave sin in Heaven for Penemuel to teach humans to write. According to lore, God had forbidden it because he believed that mankind would use the written word to spread evil. ANGEL OF WRITERS. The archangel **Uriel** is called the angel of writers. He inspires and imparts ideas to writers of all genres.

✦**WRITING CASE, ANGEL WITH THE:** The Book of Ezekiel mentions an angel dressed in linen carrying a writing case. The angel was to use the writing case to mark the righteous people in the city of Jerusalem.

Ezekiel 9:4 states, "The Lord called to the man clothed in linen, who had the writing case at his side, and said to him, 'Go through Jerusalem, and put a mark on the forehead of those who sigh and groan over all the abominations that are committed in it.' "

XY

Angels are bright still, though the brightest fell.
—SHAKESPEARE, *Macbeth*

We trust, in plumed procession, For such the angels go, Rank after rank, with even feet and uniforms of snow.

—EMILY DICKINSON

✣**XAPHAN:** A fallen angel.

✣**YABBASHAEL:** An angel of the **earth.**
✣**YAHALA:** An angel who oversees the west **wind.**
✣**YAHANAQ RABBA:** An angel who watches over the east **wind.**
✣**YAHO'EL YAH:** One of the seventy-eight names of **Metatron.**
✣**YAHRIEL:** A ruling Prince of the **Dominations,** also referred to as the **Hashmallim.**
✣**YAHWEH, ANGEL OF: Metatron,** who is also referred to as the Lesser Yahweh. See **YHWH.**
✣**YAMAYOL:** One of the leaders of the group of **Watchers** who descended to earth to pursue women.
✣**YARASHIEL:** An angel who watches over the east **wind.**
✣**YAZATAS:** Angels in Zoroastrianism. The Yazatas guard the interests of humankind.
✣**YEFEHFIAH:** A variation of the name **Jefefiyah.**
✣**YEHEMIEL:** An angel who wards off evil.
✣**YEHUDIAM:** An angel of death in rabbinical lore. He carries the souls of the dead (and the dying) to Heaven.

✦**YELLOW, ANGEL OF:** The color yellow represents the archangel **Michael.**

✦**YEMAYA:** A guardian female spirit of ancient African beliefs. She presides over the **moon** and childbirth. She is also the guardian spirit of the sea and the protector of the womb of creation. She is known as the Queen of the Sea.

✦**YEPHIEL:** An angel who chases away evil spirits.

✦**YEQON:** A **fallen angel.** He was one of the angels who encouraged the **Watchers** to come to earth and have sexual relations with women.

✦**YERUEL:** An angel whose name can be found on charms worn by pregnant women. It is believed that the charm will aid them in having a safe and successful delivery.

✦**YETER'EL:** One of the angels who brought the secret knowledge of Heaven to earth.

✦**YETZER-HARA:** One of the angels of death in rabbinical lore.

✦**YEZIDIC(S):** In Yezidic beliefs, there are six archangels. They include Shams-ed-din, Fakr-ed-din, Nasr-ed-Din, Sij-ed-din, Sheikh Ism, and Sheikh Bakra.

✦**YEZRIEL:** An angel whose name can be found on charms worn by pregnant women. It is believed that the charm will aid them in having a safe and successful delivery.

✦**YGAL:** An angel whose name can be found on charms worn by pregnant women. It is believed that the charm will aid them in having a safe and successful delivery.

✦**YHWH:** The tetragrammaton (four consonants of the ancient Hebrew name for God). In ancient times, the name of God was considered too sacred to be spoken. The word Adonai (Lord) was substituted in its place. Reconstructions of the name are Yahweh and **Jehovah.** Many of the angels' names include YHWH. (YHWH has been variously transliterated as JHVH, IHVH, JHWH, and YHVH.) The angel **Metatron** is called the Lesser YHWH.

✦**YOFIEL:** An angel whose name can be found on charms worn by pregnant women. It is believed that the charm will aid them in having a safe and successful delivery.

✦**YONEL:** An angel who oversees the north **wind.**

✦**YOPPIE'EL:** One of the seventy-eight names of **Metatron.**

✦**YOUTH:** The name in Heaven by which the mighty angel **Metatron** is called. He is called Youth because he was placed above angels who were much older and who had existed in Heaven much longer than he.

✦**YROUEL:** The angel of fear. His name can be found on amulets worn to remove fear from an individual. A variation of the name Yrouel is Yroul.

♣YROUL: A variation of **Yrouel.**

Z

The chariots of God are twenty thousand, even thousands of angels: the Lord is among them, as in Sinai, in the holy place.

—Psalms 68:17

✤**Za'afiel:** A variation of the name **Za'aphiel.**

✤**Zaamael:** The angel of storms.

✤**Za'amiel:** The angel of whirlwinds.

✤**Za'aphiel:** One of the leaders of the angels of **destruction.** A variation of the name Za'aphiel is Za'afiel.

✤**Za'apie'el:** An angel of **destruction.** Za'apie'el is in charge of taking the souls of the wicked from Heaven to **Sheol.**

✤**Za'apiel:** The angel of hurricanes.

✤**Zabkiel:** A prince of the order of **Thrones.**

✤**Zachariel:** An angel listed by **Saint Gregory the Great** as one of the seven **archangels.** He is also called the angel of the **Apocalypse.**

✤**Zadkiel:** A ruling prince of the class of angels called **Dominations** (also called **Hashmallim**), a ruler of the **Shin'an,** and one of the angels of **charity.** He is also thought to be one of the three unnamed **archangels.**

✤**Zafrire:** The Zafrire are angels of the morning.

✤**Zagzagel:** A great angelic prince in Heaven. He holds the title Angel of the Torah. Zagzagel is credited with teaching **Moses** all of his knowledge and wisdom.

✤**Zagzagyah:** One of the seventy-eight names of **Metatron.**

✤**Zahabriel:** An angel who stands guard over the palace of Wilon, the **First Heaven.**

✤**Zahzahyah:** One of the seventy-eight names of **Metatron.**

✤**Zakzaki'el YHWH:** A great angelic prince in Heaven. He was appointed by God to record the deeds of Israel.

✤**Zakzakyah:** One of the seventy-eight names of **Metatron.**

✤**Zamarchad:** An angel who protects individuals from evil spirits.

✤**Zaphiel:** A fallen angel known as God's Spy. According to legend, Zaphiel was a Cherub who became a double agent between Heaven and Hell. Eventually, his loyalties went exclusively to Hell. He later became known as the **Herald of Hell.** He is thought to be one of the three unnamed **archangels.**

✤**Zaphkiel:** The angel of contemplation. He is also a prince of the order of angels called **Thrones.**

✤**Zaqe'el:** One of the leaders of the angels who came to earth to have sexual relations with women.

✤**Zaquiel:** One of the **Watchers** who became attracted to the women of earth.

✤**Zarall:** According to Judaic lore, Zarall was the name of one of the angels depicted on the **Ark of the Covenant.**

✤**Zarobi:** The angel of precipices.

✤**Zavebe:** A **fallen angel.**

✤**Za'za'yah:** One of the seventy-eight names of **Metatron.**

✤**Zazri'el YHWH:** A great angelic prince in Heaven.

✤**Zazruyah:** One of the seventy-eight names of **Metatron.**

✤**Zebul, Angels of:** Zebul is the name of the **Fourth Heaven.** The angel Sahaqi'el is the ruling prince of Zebul.

✤**Zebuli'el:** One of the seventy-eight names of **Metatron.**

✤**Zeburial:** An angel who stands guard over the palace of **Arabot,** the Seventh Heaven.

✤**Zechariah:** See **John the Baptist.**

✤**Zechriel:** An angel whose name can be found on charms worn by pregnant women. It is believed that the charm will aid them in having a safe and successful delivery.

✤**Zehanpuryu YHWH:** A great angelic prince in Heaven. He has a strong dislike for the river of fire and continuously seeks out ways to extinguish it. He is also one of the angels of **judgment.**

✤**Zehapnuryah:** One of the seventy-eight names of **Metatron.**

✤**Zephaniah:** In the Apocalypse of Zephaniah, Zephaniah is escorted through Heaven by an angel of the Lord. While visiting Heaven, he observes the angels of **ungodly men.** These are the angels who carry men to the underworld for eternal punishment.

✤**ZEPHON:** An apostate angel. According to legend, after Zephon joined the ranks of the fallen angels, he planned to set fire to Heaven. However, before he could do so, he along with the other fallen angels were ousted from Heaven by the archangel **Michael** during the great **war in Heaven.** Zephon later became a demon in Hell. He now fans the embers to the fires of Hell.

✤**ZERACHIEL:** A variation of the name **Sariel,** who is one of the seven **archangels.**

✤**ZERAH ZERAHYAH:** One of the seventy-eight names of **Metatron.**

✤**ZERUEL:** A variation of the name **Cervihel.** Cervihel is the angel of strength, and a ruler of the **Principalities.**

✤**ZETHAR:** The angel of immortality. He is also one of the angels of **confusion.**

✤**ZEUS:** The Supreme Being in Greek mythology. The name Zeus means "good angel."

✤**ZIDKIEL:** The angel Zidkiel holds several titles including the Angel of Venus, Angel of the Terebinth Tree, Angel of **Thursday,** Angel of Fruitfulness, and the **Angel of Barrenness.**

✤**ZI'IEL:** The angel of tremors.

✤**ZIKIEL:** A variation of the name **Ziquiel.**

✤**ZIQUIEL:** The angel of comets and meteors.

✤**ZKZOROMTIEL:** The angel of irateness.

✤**ZODIAC, ANGELS OF THE:** The angels who govern the twelve signs of the Zodiac are: Aquarius-**Gabriel,** Pisces-**Barakiel,** Aries-**Machidiel,** Taurus-**Asmodel,** Gemini-**Ambriel,** Cancer-**Muriel,** Leo-**Verchiel,** Virgo-**Hamaliel,** Libra-**Uriel,** Scorpio-**Barbiel,** Sagittarius-**Adnachiel,** Capricorn-**Hanael.**

✤**ZOHAR (BOOK OF SPLENDOR):** A primary Cabalistic text. It is a mystical commentary on the Pentateuch written by Moses de Leon (thirteenth century) but attributed to Simon ben Yohai, a great scholar of the second century. In the Zohar the **orders of angels** are ranked as follows: (1) **Malachim,** (2) **Erelim,** (3) **Seraphim,** (4) **Hayyoth,** (5) **Opha-nim,** (6) **Hashmallim,** (7) Elim, (8) **Elohim,** (9) **Bene ha-Elohim,** (10) **Izachim.** The Zohar also gives methods of how to alter one's consciousness in order to talk with angels. The Zohar states, "Angels, who are God's messengers, turn themselves into different shapes."

✤**ZOPHIEL:** A prince of the **Cherubim.**

✤**ZOROASTRIANISM, ANGELS OF:** Zoroastrianism is an ancient religion of Persia founded by Zoroaster. In the **Avesta,** Zoroaster wrote down his experiences with angels. He believed that the angels emanated from **Ahura Mazda** (God) and were a part of him. Zoroaster wrote that there are both male and female angels. He portrayed them as large and humanlike. According to Zoroaster, six **archangels** called the **Amesha Spentas** assist Ahura Mazda. Together with Ahura Mazda, they represent seven fundamental moral ideas: Ahura Mazda (Holy Spirit); **Vohu Manah** (wisdom); **Asha** (truth); **Armaiti** (devotion); **Khshathra Vairya** (desirable dominion); **Haurvatat** (wholeness); and **Ameretat** (immortality). Each Amesha Spenta is a protector of an aspect of creation: Ahura Mazda—mankind; Vohu Manah—cattle; Asha—fire; Armaiti—earth; Khshathra Vairya—sky; Haurvatat—water; Ameretat—plants. Other angels in Zoroastrianism include **Ardvi Sura Anahita,** the angel of fertility and fruitfulness; Atar, the angel of fire; **Ashi,** the angel of **blessings** (Asha is the male form of Ashi, and is the angel of truth, justice, holiness, and virtue); **Sraosha,** the angel of divine intuition; **Rashnu,** the angel of justice; and **Meher,** the angel of light and mercy. In addition, there are the Yazatas, angels who guard the interests of humankind. There is also the spirit of darkness, **Angra Mainyu,** who is Ahura Mazda's adversary.

✦**ZORTEK:** An angel who stands guard over the palace of Wilon, the **First Heaven.**

✦**ZULPHAS:** The angel of **forests.**

✦**ZUMIEL:** An amulet angel listed in the **Book of Raziel** and summoned at the time of **childbirth.**

✦**ZURIEL:** An amulet angel listed in the **Book of Raziel** and summoned at the time of **childbirth.**

✦**ZUTU'EL:** An angel found in the chronicles of **Enoch.**

APPENDIXES

Appendix 1: Biblical References to Angels

(Each reference includes the word *angel* or *angels*)

Genesis 16:7, 9, 10, 11, Genesis 19:1, 15, Genesis 21:17, Genesis 22:11, 15, Genesis 24:7, 40, Genesis 28:12, Genesis 31:11, Genesis 32:1, Genesis 48:16, Exodus 3:2, Exodus 14:19, Exodus 23:20, 23, Exodus 33: 2, Numbers 20:16, Numbers 22:22, 23, 24, 25, 26, 27, 31, 32, 34, 35, Judges 2:1,4, Judges 5:23, Judges 6:11, 12, 20, 21, 22; Judges 13:3, 6, 9, 13, 15, 16, 17, 18, 19, 20, 21, I Samuel 29:9, II Samuel 14:17, 20, II Samuel 19:27, II Samuel 24:16, 17, I Kings 13:18, I Kings 19:5, 7, II Kings 1:3, 15, I Chronicles 21:12, 15, 16, 18, 20, 27, 30, II Chronicles 32:21, Job 4:18, Psalms 8:5, Psalms 34:7, Psalms 35:5, 6, Psalms 68: 17, Psalms 78:25, 49, Psalms 91:11, Psalms 103:20, Psalms 104:4, Psalms 148:2, Ecclesiastes 5:6, Isaiah 63:9, Daniel 6:22, Hosea 12:4, Zechariah 1:9, 11, 12, 13, 14, 19, Zechariah 2:3, Zechariah 3:1, 3, 5, 6, Zechariah 4:1, 4, 5, Zechariah 5:5, 10, Zechariah 6:4, 5, Zechariah 12:8, Matthew 1:20, 24, Matthew 2:13, 19, Matthew 4:6, 11, Matthew 16: 27, Matthew 18:10, Matthew 22:30, Matthew 24:31, 36, Matthew 25: 31, 41, Matthew 28:2, 5, Mark 1:13, Mark 8:38, Mark 12:25, Mark 13: 27, 32, Luke 1:11, 13, 18, 19, 26, 28, 30, 34, 35, 38, Luke 2:9, 10, 13, 15, 21, Luke 4:10, Luke 9:26, Luke 12:8, 9, Luke 15:10, Luke 16:22, Luke 20:36, Luke 22:43, Luke 24:23, John 5:4, John 12:29, John 20: 12, Acts 5:19, Acts 6:15, Acts 7:30, 35, 38, 53, Acts 8:26, Acts 10:3, 7, 22, Acts 11:13, Acts 12:7, 8, 9, 10, 11, 15, 23, Acts 23:8, 9, Acts 27:23, I Corinthians 4:9, I Corinthians 6:3, I Corinthians 11:10, I Corinthians 13:1, II Corinthians 11:14, Galations 1:8, Galations 3:19, Galations 4:14, Colossians 2:18, II Thessalonians 1:7, I Timothy 3:16, I Timothy 5:21, Hebrews 2:2, 5, 7, 9, 16, 22, Hebrews 13:2, I Peter 1: 12, I Peter 3:22, Jude 1:6, 9, Revelation 1:1, 20, Revelation 3:1, 5, 7, 14, Revelation 5:2, 11, Revelation 7:1, 2, 11, Revelation 8:2, 3, 4, 5, 6, 7, 8, 10, 12, 13, Revelation 9:1, 11, 13, 14, 15, Revelation 10:1, 5, 7, 8, 9, 10, Revelation 11:1, 15, Revelation 12:7, 9, Revelation 14:6, 8, 9, 10, 15, 17, 18, 19, Revelation 15:1, 6, 7, 8, Revelation 16:1, 2, 3, 4, 5, 8, 10, 12, 17, Revelation 17:1, 7, Revelation 18:1, 21, Revelation 19:17, Revelation 20:1, Revelation 21:9, 12, 17, Revelation 22:6, 8, 16.

Appendix 2: Recommended Books on Angels for Further Reading

Adler, Mortimer J. *The Angels and Us*. New York: Macmillan, 1982.

Anderson, Joan Wester. *An Angel to Watch over Me: True Stories of Children's Encounters with Angels*. New York: Ballantine, 1994.

————. *Where Miracles Happen: True Stories of Heavenly Encounters*. Brooklyn, N.Y.: Breet, 1994.

Bittleston, Adam. *Our Spiritual Companions: From Angels and Archangels to Cherubim and Seraphim*. Edinburgh, Scotland: Floris, 1980.

Burnham, Sophy. *Angel Letters*. New York: Ballantine, 1991.

————. *A Book of Angels*. New York: Ballantine, 1989.

Cameron, Ann. *The Angel Book*. New York: Ballantine, 1977.

Church, F. Forrester. *Entertaining Angels: A Guide to Heaven for Atheists and True Believers*. San Francisco: Harper and Row, 1987.

Clement, Clara Erskine. *Angels in Art*. Boston: L. C. Page, 1898.

Connolly, David. *In Search of Angels: A Celestial Sourcebook for Beginning Your Journey*. New York: Perigee, 1993.

Corbin, Henry. *Spiritual Body and Celestial Earth*. Princeton, N.J.: Princeton University Press, 1977.

D'Angelo, Dorie. *Living with Angels*. Carmel, Calif.: First Church of Angels, 1980.

Daniel, Alma, Timothy Wyllie, and Andrew Ramer. *Ask Your Angels*. New York: Ballantine, 1992.

Fearheiley, Don. *Angels Among Us*. New York: Avon, 1993.

Freeman, Eileen Elias. *Touched by Angels: True Cases of Close Encounters of the Celestial Kind*. New York: Warner, 1993.

Gilmore, G. Don. *Angels, Angels, Everywhere*. New York: Pilgrim Press, 1981.

Goldman, Karen. *Angel Encounters: Real Stories of Angelic Intervention*. New York: Simon & Schuster, 1995.

Graham, Billy. *Angels, God's Secret Agents*. Waco, Tex.: Word Books, 1986.

Guiley, Rosemary. *Angels of Mercy*. New York: Pocket, 1994.

Hodson, Geoffrey. *The Brotherhood of Angels and Men*. Wheaton, Ill.: Quest Books, 1927.

Howard, Jane M. *Commune with the Angels: A Heavenly Handbook*. Virginia Beach, Va.: A.R.E. Press, 1992.

Humann, Harvey. *The Many Faces of Angels*. Marina del Rey, Calif.: DeVorss, 1986.

Leadbetter, C. W. *Invisible Helpers*. Wheaton, Ill.: Theosophical Publishing House, 1896.

MacGregor, Geddes. *Angels: Ministers of Grace*. New York: Paragon House, 1988.

Mallasz, Gitta. *Talking with Angels*. Einsiedeln, Switzerland: Daimon Verlag, 1989.

Moolenburgh, H. C. *A Handbook of Angels*. Essex, England: C. D. Daniel, 1984.

———. *Meetings with Angels: A Hundred & One Real-Life Encounters*. Middlebury, Vt.: Atrium, 1993.

Parente, Fr. Pascal P. *Beyond Space: A Book About the Angels*. Rockford, Ill.: Tan, 1973.

Price, John Randolph. *The Angels Within Us: A Spiritual Guide to the Twenty-two Angels That Govern Our Lives*. New York: Fawcett Columbine, 1993.

Pruitt, James. *Angels Beside You*. New York: Avon, 1994.

Ronner, John. *Do You Have a Guardian Angel?* Indialantic, Fla.: Mamre, 1985.

Smith, Robert C. *In the Presence of Angels*. Virginia Beach, Va.: A.R.E. Press, 1993.

Solara. *Invoking Your Celestial Guardians*. Portal, Ariz.: Star-Borne Unlimited, 1986.

———. *The Star-Borne: A Remembrance for the Awakened Ones*. Charlottesville, Va.: Star-Borne Unlimited, 1989.

Steiner, Rudolph. *The Influence of Spiritual Beings upon Man*. Hudson, N.Y.: Anthroposophical Press, 1982.

———. *Spiritual Beings in the Heavenly Bodies and in the Kingdoms of Nature*. Hudson, N.Y.: Anthroposophical Press, 1992.

———. *The Spiritual Hierarchies and Their Reflections in the Physical World: Zodiac, Planets, Cosmos*. Hudson, N.Y.: Anthroposophical Press, 1983.

Swedenborg, Emanuel. *Angelic Wisdom Concerning the Divine Love and Wisdom*. London: Swedenborg Society, 1969.

———. *Heaven and Hell*. New York: Swedenborg Foundation, 1979.

Tyler, Kelsey. *There's an Angel on Your Shoulder: Angel Encounters in Everyday Life*. New York: Berkley, 1994.

Ward, Theodora. *Men and Angels*. New York: Viking, 1969.

Webber, Marylinn Carlson, and William D. Webber. *A Rustle of Angels: The Truth About Angels in Real-Life Stories and Scripture*. Grand Rapids, Mich.: Zondervan, 1994.

Wilson, Peter Lamborn. *Angels*. New York: Pantheon, 1980.

Wulfing, Sulamith. *Angels Great and Small*. Amsterdam, Holland: V.O.C., Angel Books, 1981.

Wyllie, Timothy. *Dolphins, Extraterrestrials, Angels: Adventures Among Spiritual Intelligences*. Fort Wayne, Ind.: Knoll, 1984.

Books on the Devic Kingdom

Andrews, Ted. *Enchantment of the Faerie Realm: Communicate with Nature Spirits & Elementals*. St. Paul, Minn.: Llewellyn, 1993.

Bloom, William. *Devas, Fairies and Angels (A Modern Approach)*. Somerset, England: Gothic Image, 1986.

Maclean, Dorothy. *To Hear the Angels Sing*. Issaquah, Wash.: Lorian, 1987.

Newhouse, Flower A. *Rediscovering the Angels and Natives of Eternity*. Escondido, Calif.: Christwatch Ministry, 1937; reprint, 1976.

Recommended Books for Children

Barwick, Mary. *The Alabama Angels*. New York: Ballantine, 1993.

Boone, Debby. *The Snow Angel*. Oregon: Harvest House, 1991.

Dellinger, Annetta E. *Angels Are My Friends*. St. Louis: Concordia, 1985.

Rylant, Cynthia. *An Angel for Solomen Singer*. New York: Orchard, 1992.

Sinetar, Marsha. *Why Can't Grownups Believe in Angels?* Liguori, Mo.: Triumph, 1993.

Appendix 3: References to Angels in the Koran

Sura Name	Sura No.	Verse No.
Fatehah	2	31
Fatehah	2	35
Fatehah	2	99
Fatehah	2	103
Fatehah	2	162
Fatehah	2	178
Fatehah	2	211
Fatehah	2	249
Fatehah	2	286
Al-Baqarah	3	19
Al-Baqarah	3	40
Al-Baqarah	3	43
Al-Baqarah	3	46
Al-Baqarah	3	81
Al-Baqarah	3	88
Al-Baqarah	3	125
Al-Baqarah	3	126
Al-Imran	4	98
Al-Imran	4	137
Al-Imran	4	167
Al-Imran	4	173
Al-Maidah	6	9
Al-Maidah	6	10
Al-Maidah	6	51
Al-Maidah	6	94
Al-Maidah	6	112
Al-Maidah	6	159
Al-Anam	7	12
Al-Anam	7	21
Al-A'Raf	8	10
Al-A'Raf	8	13
Al-A'Raf	8	51
Yunus	11	13
Yunus	11	32
Hud	12	32
Yousuf	13	12
Yousuf	13	14
Yousuf	13	24

Ibhrahim	15	8
Ibhrahim	15	9
Ibhrahim	15	29
Ibhrahim	15	31
Al-Hijr	16	3
Al-Hijr	16	29
Al-Hijr	16	33
Al-Hijr	16	34
Al-Hijr	16	50
Al-Nahl	17	41
Al-Nahl	17	62
Al-Nahl	17	93
Al-Nahl	17	96
Banilsrail	18	51
Al-Kahf	19	10
Al-Kahf	19	18
Al-Kahf	19	20
Al-Kahf	19	22
Al-Kahf	19	25
Al-Kahf	19	65
Maryam	20	117
TaHa	21	104
Al-Anbiya	22	76
Al-Ḥajj	23	25
Al-Nur	25	8
Al-Nur	25	22
Al-Nur	25	23
Al-Nur	25	26
Luqman	32	12
As-Sajdah	33	44
As-Sajdah	33	57
Al-Ahzab	34	41
Al-Saba	35	2
Ya'sin	37	9
Ya'sin	37	23
Ya'sin	37	151
As-Saffat	38	72
As-Saffat	38	74
Sad	39	76
Az-Zamar	40	47
Al-Mumin	41	15
Al-Mumin	41	31

HamimSajdah	42	6
Ash-Shura	43	20
Ash-Shura	43	54
Ash-Shura	43	61
Al-Aukhruf	44	48
Al-Ahqaf	47	28
Al-Hujurat	50	18
Al-Hujurat	50	19
Al-Hujurat	50	22
Al-Tur	53	27
Al-Tur	53	28
Al-Waqiah	57	13
Al-Talaq	66	5
Al-Talaq	66	7
Al-Qalam	69	18
Al-Qalam	69	31
Al-Haqqah	70	5
Noah	72	28
Al-Muzammil	74	31
Al-Muzammil	74	32
Al-Mursalat	78	39
Al-Ghashiya	89	23
Al-T'in	96	19
Al-Alaq	97	5

Appendix 4: Famous Paintings of Angels (in Chronological Order)

Artist	Painting	Date Created	Place
Guariento	*Archangel*	1350	Museo Civico, Padua
French School	*Wilton Diptych*	ca. 1395	National Gallery, London
School of Avignon	*Jacob's Ladder*	ca. 1400	Musée de Petit Palais, Avignon
Fra Angelico	*The Coronation of the Virgin*	ca. 1430	Louvre, Paris
Jan van Eyck	*Adoration of the Lamb* (detail)	1432	St. Bavo, Ghent
Stefan Lochner	*Mary in a Rose Garden*	ca. 1440	Rhenisches Bildarchiv, Wallraf Richartz Museum, Cologne
Petrus Christus	*Annunciation*	1452	Gemäldegalerie, Berlin
Petrus Christus	*The Last Judgment* (detail)	ca. 1452	Gemäldegalerie, Berlin
Simon Marmion	*Choir of Angels* (detail)	ca. 1459	National Gallery, London
Antonio Pollaiuolo	*Tobias and the Angel*	ca. 1460	Galleria Sabauda, Turin

Piero della Francesca	*St. Michael*	ca. 1469	National Gallery, London
Leonardo da Vinci	*Annunciation*	ca. 1472	Uffizi Gallery, Florence
Andrea del Verrocchio	*Baptism of Christ*	1472–75	Uffizi Gallery, Florence
Melozzo da Forli	*Angel Musicians*	1480	Vatican
Kartner Meister	*St. Michael Weighing Souls*	ca. 1480	Gemäldegalerie, Berlin
Hans Memling	*The Archangel Michael*	ca. 1480	Wallace Collection, London
Leonardo da Vinci	*Madonna of the Rocks*	ca. 1483–95	Louvre, Paris
Hieronymus Bosch	*St. John on Patmos*	ca. 1485	Gemäldegalerie, Berlin
Hans Memling	*Musician Angels*	ca. 1485	Koninklijk Museum, Antwerp
Carlo Crivelli	*Annunciation with Saint Emidius*	1486	National Gallery, London
Sandro Botticelli	*Mystic Nativity*	1500	National Gallery, London
Giovanni Bellini	*Virgin with Saints Mark, Benedict, Nicholas, and Peter* (detail)	ca. 1500	Santa Maria Gloriosa die Frari, Venice
Giovanni Bellini	*The Doge Barbarigo, St. John, and Musician Angels* (detail)	ca. 1500	S. Pietro di Murano, Venice

Raphael	*Angel Holding an Inscription*, fragment from the altarpiece of St. Nicholas of Tolentino	1501	Louvre, Paris
Raphael	*Christ on the Cross with the Virgin, St. Jerome, Mary Magdalene, and John the Baptist*	1502	National Gallery, London
Matthias Grünewald	*The Isenheimer Altarpiece* (detail)	1510–15	Musée d'Unterlinden, Colmar
Raphael	*Deliverance of St. Peter*	ca. 1512	Vatican, Stanza d'Eliodoro
Raphael	*The Sistine Madonna* (detail)	ca. 1512	Gemäldegalerie Alte Meister, Dresden
Gaudenzio Ferrari	*Annunciation*	ca. 1512–13	Gemäldegalerie, Berlin
Gerard Hornebout	*Nativity* from the *Breviary of Bona Sforza*	ca. 1517	British Library, London
Raphael	*St. Michael Trampling the Dragon*	ca. 1518	Louvre, Paris
Rosso Fiorentino	*Angel Musician*	ca. 1520	Uffizi Gallery, Florence
Michelangelo	*The Last Judgment*	1536–41	Sistine Chapel, Vatican
Hendrick Von Balen	*The Judgment of Paris*	ca. 1599	Gemäldegalerie, Berlin
Francesco Albani	*Adonis Led by Cupids to Venus*	ca. 1600	Louvre, Paris

Giovanni Baglione	*Heavenly Love Conquering Earthly Love*	ca. 1602	Gemäldegalerie, Berlin
Giovanni Battistello	*The Agony of Christ*	ca. 1615	Kunsthistorisches Museum, Vienna
Peter Paul Rubens	*Madonna in a Garland of Flowers*	ca. 1616	Alte Pinakothek, Munich
Peter Paul Rubens	*The Apotheosis of Henri IV and the Proclamation of the Regency of Marie de Medicis on May 14, 1610*	ca. 1622	Louvre, Paris
Orazio Gentileschi	*Annunciation*	ca. 1623	Galleria Sabauda, Turin
Rembrandt van Rijn	*Balaam's Ass*	1626	Musée Cognacq-Jay, Paris
Anthony Van Dyck	*Virgin with Donors* (detail)	ca. 1627	Louvre, Paris
Rembrandt van Rinj	*Sacrifice of Isaac*	1635	Hermitage Museum, St. Petersburg
Alonso Cano	*Vision of St. John*	ca. 1635	Wallace Collection, London
Gianlorenzo Bernini	*The Ecstasy of St. Teresa*	1645–52	Santa Maria della Vittoria, Rome
Laurent De La Hyre	*Astronomy*	ca. 1650	Musée des Beaux-Arts, Orléans
Willem Drost	*The Vision of Daniel*	ca. 1650	Gemäldegalerie, Berlin

Sassoferrato	*The Mystic Marriage of St. Catherine*	ca. 1650	Wallace Collection, London
Il Guercino	*Virgin and Child and the Patron Saints of Modena*	ca. 1651	Louvre, Paris
Luca Giordano	*The Archangel Michael Flinging the Rebel Angels into the Abyss*	ca. 1655	Kunsthistorisches Museum, Vienna
Carlo Saraceni	*St. Cecilia with an Angel*	ca. 1660	Galleria Nazionale di Arte Antica, Rome
Juan Antonia Escalante	*An Angel Awakens the Prophet Elijah*	ca. 1667	Gemäldegalerie, Berlin
Carlo Maratta	*Cupids with a Garland of Flowers*	1670	Louvre, Paris
Charles Le Brun	*Adoration of the Shepherds*	ca. 1690	Louvre, Paris
François Boucher	*Autumn*	1745	Wallace Collection, London
François Boucher	*The Visit of Venus to Vulcan*	1754	Wallace Collection, London
Joshua Reynolds	*Heads of Angels*	1787	Tate Gallery, London
Marie Louise-Elisabeth Vigée-Lebrun	*Portrait of Prince Henry Lubomirski*	ca. 1789	Gemäldegalerie, Berlin
J. H. S. Mann	*Guardian Angels*	ca. 1860	Haynes Fine Art at the Bindery Galleries

Alexandre Cabanel	*The Birth of Venus*	1863	Musée d'Orsay, Paris
Gustave Doré	*Jacob Wrestling with the Angel*	1866	[unknown]
William Adolphe Bouguereau	*Cupidon*	ca. 1875	Bridgeman Art Library, London
Elihu Vedder	*The Cup of Death*	ca. 1885	Fine Arts Museum, Richmond, Virginia
John Meluish Strudwick	*An Angel*	ca. 1900	Roy Miles Gallery, London
Marc Chagall	*The Parting of the Red Sea*	1966	Private collection, New York

Appendix 5: The Angelus

The Angel of the Lord declared unto Mary. And she conceived by the power of the Holy Spirit (Hail Mary). Behold the handmaid of the Lord. Let it be done to me according to your word (Hail Mary). And the word was made flesh. And dwelled among us (Hail Mary). Pray for us, O Holy Mother of God. That we may be made ready of the promises of Christ. Let us pray. Pour forth, we beseech you, O Lord, your grace into our hearts; that we, to whom the Incarnation of Christ your son was made known by the message of an angel, may by His passion and cross, be brought to the glory of His Resurrection; through the same Christ Our Lord. Amen.

Appendix 6: *Israfel*

by Edgar Allan Poe

In Heaven a spirit doth dwell
"Whose heart-strings are a lute;"
None sing so wildly well
As the angel Israfel,
And the giddy stars (so legends tell)
Ceasing their hymns, attend the spell
Of his voice, all mute.

Tottering above
In her highest noon,
The enamoured moon
Blushes with love,
While, to listen, the red levin
(With the rapid Pleiads, even,
Which were seven,)
Pauses in Heaven.

And they say (the starry choir
And the other listening things)
That Israfeli's fire
Is owing to that lyre
By which he sits and sings—
The trembling living wire
Of those unusual strings.

But the skies that angel trod,
Where deep thoughts are a duty—
Where Love's a grown-up God—
Where the Houri glances are
Imbued with all the beauty
Which we worship in a star.

Therefore, thou art not wrong,
Israfeli, who despisest
An unimpassioned song;
To thee the laurels belong,

Best bard, because the wisest!
Merrily live, and long!

The ecstasies above
With thy burning measures suit—
Thy grief, thy joy, thy hate, thy love,
With the fervour of thy lute—
Well may the stars be mute!

Yes, Heaven is thine; but this
Is a world of sweets and sours;
Our flowers are merely—flowers,
And the shadow of thy perfect bliss
Is the sunshine of ours.

If I could dwell
Where Israfel
Hath dwelt, and he where I,
He might not sing so wildly well
A mortal melody,
While a bolder note than this might swell
From my lyre within the sky.

Sources

The American Heritage Dictionary. Second College Edition. Boston: Houghton Mifflin, 1982.

The Ancient & Shining Ones: World Myth, Magic & Religion. D. J. Conway. St. Paul, Minn.: Llewellyn, 1993.

An Angel to Watch over Me. Joan Wester Anderson. New York: Ballantine, 1994.

Angelic Healing: Working with Your Angels to Heal Your Life. Eileen Elias Freeman. New York: Warner, 1994.

Angels. James Underhill. Rockport, Mass.: Element, 1995.

"Angels." Kenneth L. Woodward. *Newsweek*, December 27, 1993.

Angels A to Z. James R. Lewis and Evelyn Dorothy Oliver. Detroit, Mich.: Visible Ink, 1996.

Angels A to Z: A Who's Who of the Heavenly Host. Matthew Bunson. New York: Crown, 1996.

Angels, an Endangered Species. Malcolm Godwin. New York: Simon and Schuster, 1990.

The Angels and Us. Mortimer J. Adler. New York: Collier Books, Macmillan, 1982.

Angels the Mysterious Messengers. Alexandria, Va.: Greystone Communications/American Artists Film Corp., Time Life Video, c. 1994.

Angels: The Role of Celestial Guardians and Beings of Light. Paola Giovetti. York Beach, Me.: Samuel Weiser, 1993.

The Angels Within Us. John Randolph Price. New York: Ballantine, 1993.

Anthology of American Literature. Vol. 1, Colonial Through Romantic. General ed.: George McMichael, Advisory eds.: Frederick Crews, J. C. Levenson, Leo Marx, David E. Smith. New York: Macmillan, 1993.

Apocalypse of Abraham. The Old Testament Pseudepigrapha, Apocalyptic Literature & Testaments. James H. Charlesworth, ed. Garden City, N.Y.: Doubleday, 1983.

Apocalypse of Zephaniah. The Old Testament Pseudepigrapha, Apocalyptic Literature & Testaments. James H. Charlesworth, ed. Garden City, N.Y.: Doubleday, 1983.

Asimov's Annotated Paradise Lost: An original interpretation of Milton's epic poem. Garden City, N.Y.: Doubleday, 1974.

Ask Your Angels. Alma Daniel, Timothy Wyllie, and Andrew Ramer. New York: Ballantine, 1992.

3 Baruch. The Old Testament Pseudepigrapha, Apocalyptic Literature & Testaments. James H. Charlesworth, ed. Garden City, N.Y.: Doubleday, 1983.

A Book of Angels. Sophy Burnham. New York: Ballantine, 1990.

The Book of Mormon: Another Testament of Jesus Christ. Salt Lake City, Utah: Church of Jesus Christ of Latter-day Saints, 1986.

Buckland's Complete Book of Witchcraft. Raymond Buckland. St. Paul, Minn.: Llewellyn, 1993.

Concise Columbia Encyclopedia. 2d ed. New York: Columbia University Press, 1983.

The Crystal Stair: A Guide to the Ascension. Eric Klein. Livermore, Calif.: Oughten House, 1992.

A Dictionary of Angels: Including the Fallen Angels. Gustav Davidson. New York: Free Press, 1967.

Dictionary of Saints. John J. Delaney. Garden City, N.Y.: Doubleday, 1980.

Eerdmans Bible Dictionary. Revision edited by Allen C. Myers. Grand Rapids, Mich.: Eerdmans, 1987.

Embraced by the Light. Betty J. Eadie. Placerville, Calif.: Gold Leaf, 1992.

The Enchanted Tarot. Amy Zerner and Monte Farber. New York: St. Martin's, 1990.

Enchantment of the Faerie Realm: Communicate with Nature Spirits & Elementals. Ted Andrews. St. Paul, Minn.: Llewellyn, 1993.

Encyclopedia Americana. Vol. 6. NY: Americana, 1962.

Encyclopedia of Religion. Vol. 1. New York: Macmillan, 1987.

1 Enoch. The Old Testament Pseudepigrapha, Apocalyptic Literature & Testaments. James H. Charlesworth, ed. Garden City, N.Y.: Doubleday, 1983.

2 Enoch. The Old Testament Pseudepigrapha, Apocalyptic Literature & Testaments. James H. Charlesworth, ed. Garden City, N.Y.: Doubleday, 1983.

3 Enoch. The Old Testament Pseudepigrapha, Apocalyptic Literature & Testaments. James H. Charlesworth, ed. Garden City, N.Y.: Doubleday, 1983.

A Gathering of Angels. Rabbi Morris B. Margolies. New York: Ballantine, 1994.

Goddesses for Every Season. Nancy Blair. Rockport, Me.: Element, 1995.

Goddesses in World Mythology: A Biographical Dictionary. Martha Ann and Dorothy Myers Imel. New York: Oxford University Press, 1993.

Good News Bible. Today's English Version. New York: American Bible Society, 1976.

Great Ages of Man, a History of the World's Cultures, Early Islam. Desmond Stewart and the editors of Time-Life Books. New York: Time-Life Books, 1967.

HALOS (flyer). Denny Dahlmann. Farmington Hills, Mich.: Angel Treasures Inc., 1994.

Heaven and Hell. Emanuel Swedenborg. New York: Swedenborg Foundation, 1990.

Historic India, Great Ages of Man. Lucille Schulberg and the editors of Time-Life Books. Alexandria, Va.: Time-Life Books, 1979.

The Holy Bible. New Revised Standard Version. Nashville: Tenn.: Thomas Nelson, 1989.

In Search of Angels: A Celestial Sourcebook for Beginning Your Journey. David Connolly. New York: Perigee Books, 1993.

The Influence of Spiritual Beings Upon Man. Rudolph Steiner. Spring Valley, N.Y.: Anthroposophic Press, 1982.

Letters to the editor. R. J. Alcala. Washington Post, February 13, 1995.

Messengers of Light: The Angel's Guide to Spiritual Growth. Terry Lynn Taylor. Tiburon, Calif.: H. J. Kramer, 1990.

New World Translation of the Holy Scriptures. Brooklyn, N.Y.: Watch-Tower Bible and Tract Society of New York, Inc., International Bible Students Association, 1984.

The New York Public Library Desk Reference. New York: Webster's New World, 1989.

One Hundred Saints. New York: Little, Brown, 1993.

Persian Mythology. John R. Hinnells. London: Newnes, 1985.

The Quotable Angel. Lee Ann Chearney, ed. Albany, John Wiley and Sons, N.Y.: 1995.

Religion and Man, Indian and Far Eastern Religious Traditions. Robert D. Baird and Alfred Bloom. New York: Harper & Row, 1971.

Rudolph Steiner: A Sketch of His Life and Work. John Davy. Hudson, N.Y.: Anthroposophic Press, n.d.

Saints, Signs, and Symbols. W. Ellwood Post. Wilton, Conn.: Morehouse-Barlow, 1980.

Sibylline Oracles. The Old Testament Pseudepigrapha, Apocalyptic Literature & Testaments. James H. Charlesworth, ed. Garden City, N.Y.: Doubleday, 1983.

Spiritual Cleansing: A Handbook of Psychic Protection. Draja Mickaharic. York Beach, Me.: Samuel Weiser, 1991.

The Starseed Transmissions: An Extraterrestrial Report. Kenneth X. Carey. Kansas City, Mo.: UniSun, 1982.

Stories From Iran: A Chicago Anthology 1921–1991. Heshmat Moayyad, ed. Washington, D.C.: Mage, 1994.

The Tarot of the Witches Book. Stuart R. Kaplan. Stamford, Conn.: US Games Systems, 1982.

Teach Yourself Fortune-Telling: Palmistry, the Crystal Ball, Runes, Tea Leaves, the Tarot. Rachel Pollack. NY: Henry Holt, 1986.

Testament of Solomon. The Old Testament Pseudepigrapha, Apocalyptic Literature & Testaments. James H. Charlesworth, ed. Garden City, N.Y.: Doubleday, 1983.

To Hear the Angels Sing: An Odyssey of Co-Creation with the Devic Kingdom. Dorothy Maclean. Hudson, N.Y.: Lindisfarne Press, 1990.

To Ride a Silver Broomstick: New Generation Witchcraft. Silver Raven Wolf. St. Paul, Minn.: Llewellyn, 1993.

Video Movie Guide. Mick Martin and Marsha Porter. New York: Ballantine, 1988.

The Visions of the Children: The Apparitions of the Blessed Mother at Medjugorje. Janice T. Connell. New York: St. Martin's, 1992.

Webster's New World Dictionary. Second College Edition. New York: Simon & Schuster, 1986.

Where Angels Walk, True Stories of Heavenly Visitors. Joan Wester Anderson. New York: Ballantine, 1992.

Who's Who Classical Mythology. Michael Grant and John Hazel. New York: Oxford University Press, 1993.

You Can Live Forever in Paradise on Earth. Brooklyn, N.Y.: WatchTower Bible and Tract Society of New York, Inc., International Bible Students Association, 1982.